D1552739

Computational Complexity
and Natural Language

Computational Models of Cognition and Perception

Editors

Jerome A. Feldman
Patrick J. Hayes
David E. Rumelhart

Computational Complexity
and Natural Language

G. Edward Barton, Jr.
Robert C. Berwick
Eric Sven Ristad

A Bradford Book
The MIT Press
Cambridge, Massachusetts
London, England

QA
267
.B36
1987

Publisher's Note: This format is intended to reduce the cost of publishing certain works in book form and to shorten the gap between editorial preparation and final publication. The time and expense of detailed editing and composition in print have been avoided by photographing the text of this book directly from the authors' typeset copy.

Second printing, 1988

This book was typeset with Donald E. Knuth's TEX and Leslie Lamport's LATEX.

Printed and bound in the United States of America.

Library of Congress Cataloging-in-Publication Data

Barton, G. Edward.
  Computational complexity and natural language.

  (Computational models of cognition and perception)
  "A Bradford book."
  Bibliography: p.
  Includes index.
  1. Computational complexity.   2. Linguistics—Data processing.   I. Berwick, Robert C.   II. Ristad, Eric Sven.   III. Title.   IV. Series.
  QA267.B36 1987   415   86-27204
  ISBN 0-262-02266-4

CONTENTS

PREFACE

Generative grammar holds that a grammar or language is natural just in case it is learnable under a constellation of auxiliary assumptions about the input evidence available to children. Yet another, more formal approach seeks some central mathematical property that distinguishes the natural grammars from the set of all possible symbol systems. For the most part, formalists have stuck to one technical attack, classifying grammatical systems according to the string sets (*languages*) they can generate. The results of this *weak generative capacity* analysis have been few and far between. One can count on one hand the familiar examples: for example, Chomsky's demonstration that a full characterization of our grammatical knowledge lies outside the power of finite-state grammars. And language classification has its limits, sometimes unrecognized: As we shall see later on in this book, just because a grammatical framework uses finite-state or context-free machinery *doesn't* guarantee that it will be "easy to process," yet that sentiment remains very much in the air.

Why stick to the old formal language theory classifications—grounded in the Chomsky hierarchy of finite-state, context-free, and context-sensitive languages? Computer science has come a long way in the past thirty years; it has greatly enriched its armamentarium for classifying formal systems. Yet few researchers seemed to be probing the complexity of grammatical theories with modern tools.

About three years ago I started trying. The first results—concerning lexical-functional grammar—were obtained by 1981. Graduate students were enlisted along the way, to explore other grammatical theories. This book is a progress report on our efforts.

Our findings underscore the power of a newer, central tool of modern computer science—computational complexity theory. Complexity theory gives us an algorithm-neutral way to classify the intrinsic difficulty of solving problems. From a cognitive science point of view, algorithm-neutrality is desirable, because we don't know what algorithms the brain uses, while from an engineering point of view, it's desirable because it can tell us when a problem is too hard to solve in general no matter how clever we could be at programming. We apply complexity theory to grammatical frameworks by casting a familiar problem—such as "how hard is it, in general, to look up a word in a dictionary?"—in formal terms, and then proving how hard it might be, in the worst case. Oftentimes, much to our surprise, seemingly simple problems are inherently intractable; they don't have efficient solution algorithms.

In the rest of the book we'll look at several systems: simple grammars that can express agreement (as between the subject and verb of a sentence) and lexical ambiguity (the brute fact that a single word like *kiss* can be a noun or a verb), and so model almost any grammatical system that contains these very basic processes; lexical-functional grammar; dictionary and morphological analysis; a generalization of context-free grammars for free-word order languages; and generalized phrase structure grammar. Regrettably absent from this list is any analysis of modern transformational grammar, government-binding theory (GB theory). The reason for this is simple: we lack a complete, faithful formalization of GB theory, and it is unclear what our complexity analysis would tell us if we had one. Even so, we do agree that this would be a worthwhile goal.

As to the grammatical frameworks we do cover, for the most part we show that they allow one to pose problems that are probably "too hard" to solve by any efficient algorithm. We do not see this as a bad thing. Our complexity diagnosis often gives us important clues as to *why* that's so and how to alter a grammatical framework to bring the framework more in line with linguistic reality. Complexity diagnosis, then, ought not to be thought of as necessarily negative, but rather as the first step to insight and repair. Chapter 1 lays out our basic philosophy on this matter; it also gives a thumbnail sketch of modern complexity theory, to put things in perspective for those who have no familiarity with the subject, as well as to show how our methods work so that other researchers may apply them. Chapter 2 continues with a more formal treatment, while the remaining chapters present our results.

As we've said, in a way this book is just a progress report. We have not yet begun to tap the enormous wealth of material on parallel processing, probabilistic algorithms, and the like, that continues to flow from the work of complexity theorists. On the other hand, we do hope that this book sets the stage for a new approach to studying the complexity of natural language so that we and others can begin to use these newest techniques.

Acknowledgements

The MIT Artificial Intelligence Laboratory has provided a very special working environment that has made this research possible. And without the leadership and support of the Laboratory's director, Patrick H. Winston, the Laboratory would not be the special place that it is. Thanks are also due to the Defense Advanced Research Projects Agency of the Department of Defense for its generous support, provided in part by the Advanced Research Projects Agency of the Department of Defense under Office of Naval Research contract N00014-80-C-0505.

The Fannie and John Hertz Foundation has provided partial support for G. Edward Barton's graduate studies, while Thinking Machines Corporation and IBM Corporation have supported Eric Ristad's research.

As one might expect from research that draws on linguistics and computer science, we have had help from both quarters in our research and writing. Scott Weinstein, Jim Higginbotham, Richard Larson, Aravind Joshi, and Joyce Friedman enlarged and enlivened our perspectives. Noam Chomsky, Richard Larson, and Scott Weinstein deserve special mention for providing detailed and careful commentary.

Discussion with complexity theorists has aided our work considerably. We would like to thank Christos Papadimitriou, Michael Sipser and Albert Meyer for their classroom instruction and comments. Our discussion of parallel computation benefited from comments by Philip Klein.

We also benefited from discussions with a number of colleagues, including Guy Blelloch, Michael Brent, Gene Charniak, Bonnie Dorr, Sandiway Fong, W. Eric Grimson, Norbert Hornstein, Ron Kaplan, Michael Kashket, Ray Perrault, Geoff Pullum, Robert Thau, David Waltz, and Ken Wexler.

Some of this material was presented at conferences of the Association for Computational Linguistics, a summer workshop on morphology at Stanford University sponsored by the Center for the Study of Language and Information, and talks at Brown University, the University of Maryland, and the University of Pennsylvania. We would like to thank Lauri Karttunen, Gene Charniak, Amy Weinberg, Ben Schneiderman, Aravind Joshi, and Scott Weinstein for making those things happen and providing stimulating discussion.

A much different version of chapter 3 first appeared in *The American Journal of Computational Linguistics* and benefited from comments of anonymous referees. Chapter 6, on ID/LP parsing, appeared earlier under that journal's new banner, *Computational Linguistics*, and was improved in response to remarks from the anonymous referees for that journal.

Robert Cregar Berwick
Cambridge, Massachusetts
October, 1986

Computational Complexity
and Natural Language

Chapter 1

Introduction

What makes a language a *natural* language? One long-standing and fruitful approach holds that a language is natural just in case it is learnable. Antedating this focus on learnability, though, was a mathematically grounded taxonomy that sought to classify the power of grammatical theories via the string sets (*languages*) the theories could generate—their *weak generative capacity*. Weak generative capacity analysis can sometimes identify inadequate grammatical theories: for example, since most linguists would say that any natural grammar must be able to generate sentences of unbounded length, we can disqualify any grammatical system that generates only finite languages. For the most part, formal grammatical analysis has remained firmly wedded to weak generative capacity and the Chomsky hierarchy of finite-state, context-free, context-sensitive, and type-0 languages. Linguists still quarrel about whether the set of English sentences (regarded just as a set of strings) is context-free or not, or whether one or another formalism can generate the strictly context-sensitive string pattern xx.

This book aims to update that analytic tradition by using a more recent, powerful, and refined classification tool of modern computer science: computational complexity theory. It explains what complexity theory is and how to use it to analyze several current grammatical formalisms, ranging from lexical-functional grammar, to morphological analysis systems, to generalized phrase structure grammar; and it outlines its strengths and limits.[1]

---

[1] Other recent formal approaches also seek alternatives to weak generative capacity analysis. For example, Rounds, Manaster-Ramer, and Friedman (1986) propose that natural language grammars cannot be "too large" in the sense that the number of sentences they can generate must be substantially larger than the number of nonterminals they contain. This formal constraint, plainly intertwined with the issues of succinctness and learnability

Complexity theory studies the computational resources—usually time and memory space—needed to solve particular problems, abstracting away from the details of the algorithm and machine used to solve them. It gives us robust classification schemes—*complexity classes*—telling us that certain problems are likely or certain to be computationally tractable or intractable—where, roughly speaking, "tractable" means always solvable in a reasonable amount of time and/or space on an ordinary computer. It works by comparing new problems to problems already known to be tractable or intractable. (Section 1.2 below says more, still informally, about what we mean by a tractable or intractable problem and how we show a new problem to be tractable or intractable. Chapter 2 gives a more formal account.)

Importantly, this classification holds regardless of what algorithm we use or how many top-notch programmers we hire—in other words, a hard problem can't be switched into an easier complexity class by using a clever algorithm—and it holds regardless of whether we use a modest PC or a much faster mainframe computer. Abstracting away from computer and algorithm details seems especially apt for consideration of linguistic processing, since for the most part we don't know what algorithm or computing machinery the brain uses, but we *do* know—with the linguist's help—something about the abstract natural language problems that language processing mechanisms must grapple with.[2]

1.1 Complexity Theory as a Theoretical Probe

If we're investigating the processing difficulty of grammatical problems, complexity theory offers four main advantages over weak generative capacity analysis:

- It is *more direct* and *more refined.* If we want to know something about how long it takes to process a grammatical problem on a computer, then that's what complexity theory tells us, without going through any intermediate steps linking weak generative capacity to time or space use.

so dear to the linguist's heart, may also yield interesting results, yet is quite distinct from the results of conventional complexity theory.

[2]Given complexity theory's focus on "ordinary" computers, those interested in the impact of parallel computation on our results should consult section 1.4.5 at the end of this chapter and section 2.4 in the next.

Further, we can set up many more than just the four rough categories of the Chomsky hierarchy—and that's useful for probing the complexity of systems that don't fit neatly into the finite-state–context-free–context-sensitive picture. (See section 1.2 and chapters 2 and 8 for examples.)

- It is *more accurate*. Weak generative capacity results can give a misleading picture of processing difficulty. For example, just because a grammatical system uses finite-state machinery does *not* guarantee that it can be efficiently processed; chapter 5 shows why. Similarly, strictly context-free generative power does *not* guarantee efficient parsability (see chapters 7 and 8).

- It is *more robust*. We have already mentioned the theory's independence from details of computer model and algorithm. But it can also tell us something about the beneficial effects of parallel computation, if any, without having to wait to buy a parallel computer (see sections 1.4 and 2.4).

- It is *more helpful*. Since complexity analysis can tell us *why* a grammatical formalism is too complex, it can also sometimes tell us *how* to make it less complex. Chapters 8 and 9 show how to use complexity theory to revise generalized phrase structure grammar so as to make it much more tractable (though still potentially difficult).

But some might question why we need this computational armament at all. Isn't it enough just to pick grammatical machinery that has more than enough power to describe natural languages, and and then go out and use it? One reason we need help from complexity theory and other tools is that using a powerful metalanguage to express grammars—whether it's drawn from mathematics or plain English—doesn't give us much guidance toward writing down only *natural* grammars instead of unwittingly composing unnatural ones.

To take a standard linguistic example, suppose we use the language of context-free grammars as our descriptive machinery. Then we can write down natural grammar rules for English like these:

$$VP \rightarrow Verb\ NP \quad PP \rightarrow Prep\ NP$$

but we can also write down the unnatural rules,

$$VP \rightarrow Noun\ NP \quad PP \rightarrow VP\ Noun\ PP$$

In this case, the generality of the machinery blinds us to some of the natural structure of the problem—we miss the fact that every phrase of type X has a distinguished head of the same type, with verb phrases headed by verbs, prepositional phrases by prepositions, and so forth (as expressed in many modern frameworks by $\overline{\text{X}}$ theory). For linguistic purposes, a better framework would yield only the natural grammars, steering us clear of such errors.

We should like to enlist complexity theory in this same cause. Implicitly, our faith in complexity analysis boils down to this: complexity analysis tells us *why* problems are easy or hard to solve, hence giving us insight into the *information processing structure* of grammatical systems. It can help pinpoint the exact way in which our formalized systems seem to allow too much latitude—for instance, identifying the parts of our apparatus that let us describe languages that seem more difficult to process than natural languages. Especially deserving of closer scrutiny are formal devices that can express problems requiring blind, exhaustive, and computationally intractable search for their solution. Informally, such computationally difficult problems don't have any special structure that would support an efficient solution algorithm, so there's little choice but brute force, trying every possible answer combination until we find one that works. Thus, it's particularly important to examine features of a framework that allow such problems to be encoded— making sure there's not some special structure to the natural problem that's been missed in the formalism.

In fact, problems that require combinatorial search might well be characterized as *unnaturally hard problems*.[3] While there is no *a priori* reason why a theory of grammatical competence must guarantee efficient processing, there is every reason to believe that natural language has an intricate computational structure that is not reflected in combinatorial search methods. Thus, a formalized problem that requires such search probably leaves unmentioned some constraints of the natural problem. We'll argue in chapter 6 that the best grammatical framework will sometimes leave a residue of worst-case computational difficulty, so hard problems don't automatically indicate an overly general formalism; like other tools, complexity results should be interpreted intelligently, in the light of other evidence. But even when the framework must allow hard problems, we believe the intractability still warns that we may have missed some of the particular structure of natural language—and it can guide us toward what and where. *Performance methods* may well assume special properties of natural language beyond those that are guaranteed by the grammatical formalism, hence succeeding when the special

---

[3]Such problems are difficult even if one allows a physically realistic amount of parallel computation; see section 1.4.5.

properties hold, but failing in harder situations where they do not. In chapters 5 and 6 we explore such a possibility (among other topics), sketching a processing method that assumes natural problems typically have a more modular and local structure than computationally difficult problems.

To consider a simple example here, chapter 5 studies the dictionary-retrieval component of a natural language processing system: for instance, a surface form like `tries` may be recovered as the underlying form `try+s`. We can solve this abstract problem by modeling possible spelling changes with a set of finite-state transducers that map between surface and underlying forms. However, this *two-level model* can demand exhaustive search. For example, when processing the character sequence "s p i..." left-to-right, the two-level system must decide whether or not to change the surface "i" to an underlying "y", guessing that underlying word is something like `spy+s`. But this guess could go awry because the underlying word could be `spiel`, and when we look closely at the range of problems allowed by the two-level model, full combinatorial search—guessing and backtracking—seems to be required. In fact, chapter 5 shows that the backtracking isn't just symptomatic of a bad algorithm for implementing this model; in the general case, the two-level model is computationally intractable, independent of algorithm and computer design.

In practice, two-level processing for natural languages does involve search, but less search than we find when we run the reduction that demonstrates possible intractability. We should therefore ask whether there is something special about the structure of the natural problems that makes them more manageable than the formal model would suggest—something that the model fails to capture, hence allowing unnaturally difficult situations to arise. Chapter 6 suggests that this might be so, for preliminary results indicate that a weaker but noncombinatorial processing method—constraint propagation—may suffice for natural spelling-change systems. The constraint-propagation method assumes natural spelling changes have a local and separable character that is not implied in the two-level model.

If our approach is on the right track, then a grammatical formalism that in effect poses brute-force problems should make us suspicious; complexity analysis gives us reason to suspect that the special structure of the human linguistic system is not being exploited. Then complexity analysis may help pinpoint the computational sore spots that deserve special attention, suggesting additional restrictions for the grammatical systems or alternative, approximate solution methods. Chapter 4 applies complexity-theory diagnostic aids to help repair lexical-functional grammar; as we mentioned earlier, chapters 8 and 9 do the same for generalized phrase structure grammar.

But when linguistic scrutiny bears out the basic validity of the formal system—when the grammatically defined natural problems are just plain hard—then the complexity diagnosis suggests where to seek performance constraints. Chapter 3 gives an example based on a simple grammatical system that contains just the machinery of *agreement* (like the agreement between a noun phrase subject and a verb in English) and *lexical ambiguity* (in English, a word such as *kiss* can be either a noun or a verb). This system is computationally intractable, but in a way that's roughly reflected in human performance: sentences that lack surface information of categorial features are hard to process, as we see from the sentence BUFFALO BUFFALO BUFFALO. We mention this example again in chapters 3 and 6.

Finally, if a grammatical problem is easy, then complexity analysis again can tell us why that's so, based on the structure of the problem rather than the particular algorithms we've picked for solving the problem; it can help tell us why our fast algorithms work fast. In a similar way, it can help us recognize systems in which fast processing is founded on unrealistic restrictions (for instance, perhaps a prohibition against lexical ambiguity).

To give the reader a further glimpse of our methods and results, the rest of this chapter quickly and informally surveys what complexity theory is about, how we apply it to actual grammatical systems, and what its limits are. The next chapter takes a more detailed and thorough look at the connection between complexity theory and natural language.

Section 1.2 introduces a few core concepts from complexity theory: it identifies the class P as the class of tractable problems, includes the hardest problems of the class NP in the class of intractable problems, and briefly discusses how we can use representative problems in each class to tell us something about the complexity of new problems. Section 1.3 illustrates how we apply complexity theory techniques to grammatical systems by analyzing an artificially simplified grammatical formalism. Section 1.4 briefly reviews the virtues and limits of complexity analysis for cognitive science, addressing questions about idealization, compilation effects, and parallel computation. Section 1.5 concludes the chapter with an outline of the rest of the book, highlighting our main results.

1.2   What Complexity Theory is About

We know that some problems can be solved quickly on ordinary computers, while others cannot be. Complexity theory captures our intuitions by defining classes that lump together entire sets of problems that are easy to solve or not.

1.2.1   Problem vs. algorithm complexity

We have said several times that we aim to study problem complexity, not algorithm complexity, because it's possible—even easy—to write a slow algorithm for an easy problem, and this could be seriously misleading. So let us drive home this distinction early on, before moving on to problem complexity analysis itself.

Consider the problem of searching a list of alphabetically sorted names to retrieve a particular one. Many algorithms solve this problem, but some of them are more efficient than others. For example, if we're looking for "Bloomfield," we could simply scan through our list starting with the "A" words, comparing the name we want against the names we see until we hit the right name. In the worst case we might have to search all the way through to the end to find the one we're looking for—for a list of n names, this would be at worst proportional to n basic comparisons.

This smacks of brute-force search, though it's certainly not the exponential search we're usually referring to when we mention brute-force methods. Another algorithm does much better by exploiting the structure of the problem. If we look at the middle name in our list—say, "Jespersen"—we can compare it to our target name. If that name ranks alphabetically below our target, then we repeat our procedure by taking just the top half of our list of names, finding the middle in that new halved list, and comparing it against our target. (If the name ranks alphabetically above our target, then we repeat our search in the bottom half of the list.) It's easy to see that in the worst case this *binary search* algorithm makes fewer comparisons—we can keep halving things only so far before we get a lone name in each half, and the number of splits is roughly proportional to $\log_2 n$. This second algorithm exploits the special structure of our alphabetically sorted list to work better than blind search. In this case then, complexity lies in the algorithm, not in the problem.

1.2.2   Easy and hard problems; $\mathcal{P}$ and $\mathcal{NP}$

With the algorithm–problem distinction behind us, we can move on to look at problem complexity. Easy-to-solve problems include alphabetical sorting, finite-state parsing, and context-free language recognition, among others. For example, context-free language recognition takes at worst time proportional to $|x|^3$, where $|x|$ is the number of words in the sentence, if we use a standard context-free recognition algorithm like CKY (Hopcroft and Ullman 1979). Indeed, all of the above-mentioned problems take time proportional to n, or $\log n$, $n \log n$, or n^3, where n measures the "size" of the problem to solve. More generally, all such problems take at most some *polynomial* amount of time to solve on a computer—at most time proportional to n^j, for some integer j. Complexity theory dubs this the class $\mathcal{P}$: the class of problems solvable (by some algorithm or other) in polynomial time on an ordinary computer. (Recall that an *algorithm's* complexity is to be distinguished from a *problem's* complexity: it's possible to write a bad alphabetic sorting algorithm that takes more than polynomial time, yet the sorting problem is in $\mathcal{P}$. Significantly, it's not possible to write a preternaturally good algorithm that takes *less* time in the worst case than the complexity of the problem would indicate.)

Still other problems seem to take longer to solve no matter what algorithm one tries. Consider the following example, known as Satisfiability or SAT: Given an arbitrary Boolean formula like the following:

$$(x \lor \overline{y} \lor \overline{z}) \land (y \lor z \lor u) \land (x \lor z \lor \overline{u}) \land (\overline{x} \lor y \lor u)$$

is there an assignment of **true** and **false** to the variables such that the whole expression is true? In this case we say that the formula is *satisfiable*, otherwise, *unsatisfiable*. Note that $\land$ is logical *and* while $\lor$ is logical *or*, so every clause in parentheses has to have at least one literal that is true, where $\overline{x}$ is true if x is false, and vice-versa.[4]

---

[4]We assume that satisfiability formulas are in *conjunctive normal form*, stated as a collection of clauses each of which contains any number of negated or unnegated variables (so-called *literals*) in the form x or $\overline{x}$. Each clause must contain at least one literal that is true. A slightly more general version of Boolean expressions is sometimes used, for example, in Hopcroft and Ullman (1979:325). It is easy to show that the more restricted version entails no loss of generality; again see Hopcroft and Ullman (1979:328–330). Our example illustrates a particularly restricted version of satisfiability where there are exactly three so-called literals per clause, dubbed *3SAT*. As we shall see in chapter 2, this restricted problem is just as hard as the unrestricted version of satisfiability, where there are any number of literals per clause.

	Problem size, n		
Time complexity	10	50	100
n^3	.001 second	.125 second	1.0 second
2^n	.001 second	35.7 years	10^{15} centuries

Figure 1.1: Exponential growth limits solvable problem sizes. A cubic-time algorithm (second line in the table) can solve problems of size 100 in a second, while a corresponding exponential time algorithm (last line) would take far too long. The entries in the table, modeled after Garey and Johnson (1979), assume that each algorithm instruction takes 1 microsecond, but the shape of the curve relating problem size to processing time is more important than the exact time values.

There's good reason to identify SAT as a prototypical computationally *intractable* problem. Let us see why. If you try to solve this example in your head, you'll quickly note that you mentally run through *every* possible combination of assignments, testing each in turn. With n binary-valued variables in an arbitrary formula, there are 2^n possible truth-value assignments to test. In fact, every known algorithm for solving this problem takes at least time proportional to 2^n, or *exponential time*, where the number of variables n can obviously rise proportionally with length of the tested input formula.

Figure 1.1, adapted from Garey and Johnson (1979), shows why we say that $\mathcal{P}$ corresponds to the class of computationally tractable problems, while problems for which only exponential solution algorithms are known— including SAT—are intractable. Assuming that a solution algorithm's running time is proportional to the problem size to be solved, the first line in the table shows that if an algorithm takes time proportional to n^3, then even large-sized problems can be done in a second or less. But we can't wait around for an exponential-time algorithm working on a problem of the same size.

Of course, there are familiar pitfalls in comparing exponential time and polynomial time algorithms—n^{10000} can be quite slow, particularly for smaller values of n, when compared to 2^n or $2^{0.01n}$. But in fact it turns out that this bifurcation fares quite well in classifying naturally occurring computer science problems; if a problem is efficiently solvable at all, it will in general be solvable by a polynomial algorithm of low degree, and this seems to hold for linguistically relevant problems as well.[5]

What class of problems does SAT fall into, then? The difficult part about SAT seems to be guessing all the possible truth assignments—2^n of them, for n distinct variables. Suppose we had a computer that could try out all these possible combinations, in parallel, without getting "charged" for this extra ability. We might imagine such a computer to have a "guessing" component (a factory-added option) that writes down a guess—just a list— of the *true* and *false* assignments. Given any SAT formula, we could verify quite quickly whether any guess works: just scan the formula, checking the tentative assignment along the way. It should be clear that checking a guess will not take very long, proportional to the length of the tested formula (we will have to scan down our guess list a few times, but nothing worse than that; since the list is proportional to n in length, to be conservative we could say that we will have to scan it n times, for a total time proportional to n^2). In short, *checking* or *verifying* one guess will take no more than polynomial time and so is in P, and tractable.

Therefore, our hypothetical computer that can try out *all* guesses in parallel, without being charged for guessing wrong, would be able to solve SAT in polynomial time. Such a computer is called *nondeterministic* (for a more precise definition, see chapter 2, section 2.1), and the class of problems solvable by a Nondeterministic computer in Polynomial time is dubbed NP.

1.2.3   Problems with no efficient solution algorithms

Plainly, all the problems in P are also in NP, because a problem solvable in deterministic polynomial time can be solved by our guessing computer simply by "switching off" the guessing feature. But SAT is in NP and not known to be in P. For the practically minded, this poses a problem, because our hypothetical guessing computer doesn't really exist; all we have are deterministic computers, fast or slow, and with the best algorithms we know these all take exponential time to solve general SAT instances. (See section 1.4 for a discussion of the potentials for parallel computation.) In fact, complexity

---

[5]However, there are some linguistic formalisms whose language recognition problems take time proportional to n^6, such as Head Grammars (Pollard 1984), and some linguistic problems such as morphological analysis tend to have short inputs. We take up these matters again in chapter 2 and elsewhere.

theorists have discovered many hundreds of problems like SAT, for which only exponential-time deterministic algorithms are known, but which have efficient nondeterministic solutions. For this reason, among others, computer scientists strongly suspect that $P \neq NP$.

Complexity theory says more than this, however: it tells us that problems like SAT serve to "summarize" the complexity of an entire class like NP, in the sense that *if* we had an algorithm for solving SAT in deterministic polynomial time then we would have an algorithm for solving *all* the problems in NP in deterministic polynomial time, and we would have $P = NP$. (We'll see why that's so just below and in the next section.) Such problems are dubbed *NP-hard*, since they are "as hard as" any problem in NP. If an NP-hard problem is also known to be *in* NP—solvable by our hypothetical guessing computer, as we showed SAT to be—then we say that it is *NP-complete*.

Roughly speaking then, all NP-complete problems like SAT are in the same computational boat: solvable, so far as we know, only by exponential-time algorithms. Because there are many hundreds of such problems, because none seems to be tractable, and because the tractability of any one of them would imply the tractability of all, the $P \neq NP$ hypothesis is correspondingly strengthened. In short, showing that a problem is NP-hard or NP-complete is enough to show that it's unlikely to be efficiently solvable by computer. We stress once more that such a result about a *problem's* complexity holds independently of any algorithm's complexity and independently of any ordinary computer model.[6]

We pause here to clear up one technical point. Frequently we will contrast polynomial-time algorithms with combinatorial search and other exponential-time algorithms. However, even if $P \neq NP$—as seems overwhelmingly likely—it might turn out that the true complexity of hard problems in NP lies somewhere between polynomial time and exponential time. For instance, the function $n^{\log n}$ outstrips any polynomial because (informally) its degree keeps slowly increasing, but the function grows less rapidly than an exponential function (Hopcroft and Ullman 1979:341). However, because only exponential-time algorithms are currently known for NP-complete problems, we will continue to say informally that problems in NP seem to require combinatorial search.

---

[6]We discuss familiar caveats to this claim in chapter 2; these include the possibility of heuristics that work for problems encountered in practice, the effect of preprocessing, and the possibility of parallel speedup.

1.2.4   The method of reduction

Because demonstrating that a problem is NP-hard or NP-complete forms the linchpin for the results described in the rest of the book, we will briefly describe the key idea behind this method and, in the next section, illustrate how to apply it to a very simple, artificial grammatical system; for a more formal, systematic discussion, see chapter 2.

Showing that one problem is computationally as difficult as another relies on the technique of *problem transformation* or *reduction*, illustrated in figure 1.2. Given a new problem T, there are three steps to demonstrating that T is NP-hard, and there's a fourth to show T is NP-complete:

1. Start with some known NP-hard (or NP-complete) problem S. Selection of S is usually based on some plain correspondence between S and T (see the example just below and chapter 2 for further examples).

2. Construct a mapping Π (called a *reduction*) from instances of the known problem S to instances of the new problem T, and show that the mapping takes polynomial time or less to compute. In this book, problems will always be posed as *decision problems* that have either Yes or No answers, *e.g.*, is a particular Boolean formula satisfiable or not?[7]

3. Show that Π preserves Yes and No answers to problems. That is, if S has a Yes answer on some instance x, then T must have a Yes answer on its instance $\Pi(x)$, and similarly for No answers.

4. If an NP-completeness proof is desired, show in addition that T is in $\mathcal{NP}$, that is, can be solved by a "guessing" computer in polynomial time. Note that this step isn't required to demonstrate computational intractability, because an NP-hard problem is at least as hard as any problem in $\mathcal{NP}$.

If one likes to think in terms of subroutines, then such a *polynomial-time reduction* shows that the new problem T must be at least as hard to solve as the problem S of known complexity, for the following reason. If we had a polynomial-time subroutine for solving T, then S could also be solved in polynomial time. We could use the mapping Π to convert instances of S into instances of T, and then use the polynomial-time subroutine for solving

---

[7]Well-defined problems that don't have simple Yes/No answers—such as "what's the shortest cycle in this graph?"—can always be reformulated as decision problems; see Garey and Johnson 1979:19–21.

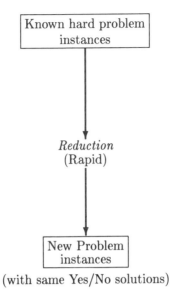

Figure 1.2: Reduction shows that a new problem is complex by rapidly transforming instances of a known difficult problem to a new problem, with the same Yes/No answers.

T on this converted problem. The answer returned for T always coincides with the original answer for S, because Π is known to preserve answers. Because we also know that Π can be computed in polynomial time, and since the composition of two polynomial-time subroutines is also polynomial-time, this procedure would solve S in polynomial time. But the problem S, such as SAT, is NP-hard and not thought to be solvable in polynomial time. Therefore either S and all other problems in $\mathcal{NP}$ are efficiently solvable, a tremendous surprise, or else no polynomial-time subroutine for T exists.

In short, our reduction proves that the new problem T is at least as hard the old one S *with respect to polynomial time reductions*. Either T is even harder than S, or else the two are in the same computational boat. (One can now see why the problem transformation itself must be "fast"—polynomial time or better—for otherwise we would introduce spurious complexity and could not make this argument.)

Before proceeding with a more linguistically oriented example in the next section, we'll consider the obvious question of how all this can ever get started. Step 1 of the reduction technique demands that we start with a known NP-hard or NP-complete problem, and we've said several times that SAT fits the bill. But how does one get things off the ground to show that SAT is NP-complete? There is no choice but to confront the definition of NP-hardness directly: we must show that, given any algorithm that runs on our hypothetical "guessing" computer in polynomial time, we can (in polynomial time) build a corresponding SAT problem that gives the same answers as that algorithm. Such a construction shows that SAT instances can "simulate" any polynomial-time nondeterministic algorithm on any ordinary computer, and so SAT is NP-hard. In fact, SAT must also be NP-complete, as it's clearly solvable by our guessing computer.[8] Starting with SAT as a base, we can begin to use reduction to show that other problems are NP-hard or NP-complete. Section 2.2 in the next chapter shows how this is done, including how to transform SAT to 3SAT.

1.3   A Simple Grammatical Reduction

To give an introduction to how we use reduction to analyze grammatical formalisms, in this section we consider a very simple and artificial grammatical example. Readers familiar with how reductions work may skip this discussion; chapter 3 contains a more formal treatment of a similar problem.

Our grammatical system expresses two basic linguistic processes: lexical ambiguity (words can be either nouns or verbs) and agreement (as in subject-verb agreement in English). These processes surface in many natural languages in other guises, for example, languages with case agreement between nouns and verbs.

In particular, our artificial grammatical system exhibits a special kind of global agreement: once a particular word is picked as a noun or a verb in a sentence, any later use of that word in the same sentence must agree with the previous one—and so its syntactic category must also be the same. (One might like to think of this as a sort of syntactic analog of the vowel harmony that appears within words in languages like Turkish: all the vowels of a series of Turkish suffixes may have to agree in certain features with a preceding root vowel.)

---

[8] Chapter 2 gives more detail on this. Garey and Johnson (1979:38–44) give a full proof, originally by Cook (1971).

The one exception to this agreement is when a word ends in a suffix *s*. Then, it must *disagree* with the same preceding or following word without the suffix. Finally, this language's sentences contain any number of clauses, with three words per clause, and each clause must contain at least one verb.

For example, if we temporarily ignored (for brevity) the requirement that a clause must contain three words, then

apple bananas, apples banana, AND apples bananas

could be a sentence. It's hard to tell what's a noun and what's a verb, given the lexical ambiguity that holds; if *apple* is a verb, then *apples* must not be, so *banana* is the only possible verb in the second clause—so far, so good. But then *apples* and *bananas* must both be nouns, and the last clause has no verb. Consequently, *apple* has to be a noun instead, and *bananas* must be the verb of the first clause. *Banana* is then a noun, but we already know *apples* is a verb, so the second clause is okay. Finally, the last clause now has two verbs, so the whole thing is a sentence (except for the three-word requirement).

How hard will it be to recognize sentences generated by a grammatical system like this? One might try many different algorithms, and never be sure of having found the best one. But it is precisely here that complexity theory's power comes to the fore. A simple reduction can tell us that this general problem is computationally intractable—NP-hard—and almost certainly, there's no easy way to recognize the sentences of languages like this.

It should be clear that this artificial grammatical system is but a thinly disguised version of the restricted SAT problem—known as 3SAT—where there are exactly three literals (negated or unnegated variables) per clause. Some proofs are simplified if 3SAT is defined to require exactly three *distinct* literals per clause, though we will not always impose this requirement.[9]

Given any 3SAT instance, it is easy to quickly transform it into a language recognition problem in our grammatical framework, with corresponding Yes/No answers. The verb-noun ambiguity stands for whether a literal gets assigned **true** or **false**; agreement together with disagreement via the *s* marker replaces truth assignment consistency, so that if an x is assigned **true** (that is, is a verb) in one place, it has the same value everywhere, and if it is $\bar{x}$ (has the *s* marker) it gets the opposite value; finally, demanding one verb per

---

[9]It is easy to show that 3SAT—like SAT—is NP-complete; see section 2.2. Also, it is easy to show that the restriction to distinct literals is inessential.

clause is just like requiring one true literal per satisfiability clause. The actual transformation simply replaces variable names with words, adds s markers to words corresponding to negated literals, tidies things up by setting off each clause with a comma, and deletes the extraneous logical notation. The result is a sentence to test for membership in the language generated by our artificial grammar. Plainly, this conversion can be done in polynomial time, so we've satisfied steps 1 and 2 of our reduction technique.[10]

Figure 1.3 shows the reduction procedure in action on one example problem instance. The figure shows what happens to the Boolean formula given earlier:

$$(x \vee \overline{y} \vee \overline{z}) \wedge (y \vee z \vee u) \wedge (x \vee z \vee \overline{u}) \wedge (\overline{x} \vee y \vee u)$$

We can convert this satisfiability formula to a possible sentence in our hypothetical language by turning u, x, y, and z into words (*e.g., apple, banana, carrot, ...*), adding the disagreement marker s when required, putting a comma after each clause (as you might do in English), and sticking an *and* before the last clause. Running this through our reduction processor yields a sentence with four clauses of three words each:

apple bananas carrots, banana carrot dandelion, apple carrot dandelions, AND
apples banana dandelion

We now check step 3 of the reduction technique: answer preservation. The output sentence is grammatical in our artificial system if and only if each clause contains at least one verb. But this is so if and only if the original formula was satisfiable. Since this holds no matter what formula we started with, the transformation preserves problem solutions, as desired. We conclude that the new grammatical formalism can pose problems that are NP-hard. Remember how potent this result is: we now know that *no matter what* algorithm or ordinary computer we pick, this grammatical *problem* is computationally intractable.

Our example also illustrates a few subtle points about problem reductions to keep in mind throughout the remainder of the book. When a reduction involves constructing some grammar G, the language $L(G)$ that the grammar generates will often be a particularly simple language; for instance,

---

[10]We can just sweep through the original formula left-to-right; the only thing to keep track of is which variables (words) we've already seen, and this we can do by writing these down in a list we (at worst) have to rescan n times.

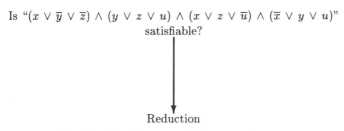

Figure 1.3: A reduction from 3SAT shows ambiguity-plus-agreement to be hard. This example shows how just one 3SAT problem instance may be rapidly transformed to a corresponding sentence to test for membership in an artificial grammar. In this case, the original formula is satisfiable with x, y, and z set to **true**, and the corresponding sentence is grammatical, so Yes answers to the original and new problems coincide as desired.

$L(G)$ might contain only the single string "#", or $L(G)$ might be the empty set. (Section 5.7.2 uses an example of this sort.) It's important to distinguish between the complexity of the set $L(G)$ (certainly trivial, if $L(G) = \{\#\}$) and the difficulty of figuring out *from the grammar G* whether $L(G)$ contains some string. For example, we might know that no matter what happens, the reduction *always* constructs a grammar that generates either the empty set or the set $\{\#\}$—either way, a language of trivial complexity—yet it might still be very hard to figure out *which one* of those two possible languages a given G would generate. In technical terms, this means we must distinguish the complexity of the *recognition problem for some class of grammars* from the complexity of *an individual language that some grammar from the class generates.*

A second, related point is the distinction between the *input* to the problem transformation algorithm (an instance of a problem of known complexity) and the *string inputs* to the problems of known and unknown complexity; these problem inputs are typically simple strings. In all, then, there are three distinct "inputs" to keep track of, and these can be easily confused when all three are string languages that look alike.

To summarize, while our example is artificial, our method and moral are not. Chapters 3–9 use exactly the same technique. The only difference is that later on we'll work with real grammatical formalisms, use fancier reductions, and sometimes use other hard problems besides SAT. (Section 2.2 outlines these alternative problems.)

1.4   The Idealizations of Complexity Theory

Having seen a bit of what complexity theory is about, and how we can use it to show that a grammatical formalism can pose intractable (NP-hard) problems, we now step back a bit and question whether this technique—like all mathematical tools—commits us to idealizations that lead us in the right direction. We believe the answer is Yes, and in this section we'll briefly survey why we think so. In the next chapter, sections 2.3 and 2.4 delve more deeply into each of these issues (and consider some others besides).

To evaluate the idealizations of complexity theory, we must reconsider our goals in using it. Complexity theory can tell us *why* the processing problems for a formalized grammatical system have the complexity they do, whether the problems are easy or difficult. By probing sources of processing difficulty, it can suggest ways in which the formalism and processing methods may fail to reflect the special structure of a problem. Thus, complexity theory can tell us where to look for new constraints on an overly powerful system, whether they are imposed as constraints on the grammatical formalism or as performance constraints. It can also help isolate unnatural restrictions on suspiciously simple systems. In a nutshell, these goals require that our idealizations must be *natural* ones—in the sense that they don't run roughshod over the grammatical systems themselves, contorting them so that we lose touch with what we want to discover.

We feel that the potential "unnaturalness" surrounding mathematical results in general must be addressed: are the grammatical problems posed in such a way that they lead to the insights we desire? Although a discussion of those insights must wait for later chapters, here we can at least show that the idealizations we've adopted are designed to be as natural and nonartificial as possible. Some of our basic idealizations seem essential: given current ignorance about human brainpower, we want to adopt an approach as independent of algorithm and machines as possible, and that's exactly what the theory buys us. Other idealizations need more careful support because they seem more artificial. The following sections will address several issues. First, there are questions about complexity theory's measures of problem complexity; we'll consider the assumption that problems can grow without bound, the relevance to grammatical investigations of linguistically bizarre NP-complete problems such as SAT, and the status of the more traditional "complexity" yardstick of weak generative capacity. Next, we'll discuss our assumption that we should study the complexity of grammatical *systems*, which corresponds to posing certain kinds of problems (universal problems) rather than others; and finally, we'll turn to our reliance on invariance with respect to *serial* computer models.

1.4.1 The role of arbitrarily large problems

Complexity theory assumes that problems can grow arbitrarily in size; for instance, the length of Boolean formulas in the SAT problem can grow arbitrarily, and algorithms for solving SAT must work on an infinity of SAT instances. We adopt this idealization wholeheartedly simply because we have to in order to use complexity theory at all. That's because the complexity of a problem that's bounded in size is actually *zero*, according to the way complexity theory works—so the theory would tell us nothing at all if we assumed that grammatical problems couldn't grow without bound.[11]

Some might question this infinity-based assumption for natural language. After all, the sentences we encounter are all of bounded length—

---

[11]That result is not as strange as it first appears. It's simply because one can solve, in advance, *all* the problems less than a certain size, and store the results in a giant table. Then the small problems may be rapidly retrieved, in bounded time, and large problems can be rejected out of hand as soon as we've seen enough symbols to realize they're too big. In this case, then, complexity doesn't depend on the problem size at all. For instance, we can certainly number and then solve all the satisfiability problems less than 8 clauses long with 3 literals per clause.

certainly less than 100 words long. The number of distinct words in a natural language, though very large, is also bounded. Therefore, natural language problems are always bounded in size; they can't grow as complexity theory assumes. Aren't then the complexity results irrelevant because they apply only to problems with arbitrarily long sentences or arbitrarily large dictionaries, while natural languages all deal with finite-sized problems?

It is comforting to see that this argument explodes on complexity theoretic grounds just as it does in introductory linguistics classes. The familiar linguistic refrain against finiteness runs like this: Classifying a language as finite or not isn't our *raison d'être*. The question appears in a different light if our goal is to determine the form and content of linguistic knowledge. When we say that languages are infinite, we don't really intend a simple classification. Instead, what we mean is that once we have identified the principles that seem to govern the construction of sentences of reasonable length, there doesn't seem to be any natural bound on the operation of those principles. The principles—that is, the principles of grammar—characterize indefinitely long sentences, but very long sentences aren't used in practice because of other factors that don't seem to have anything to do with how sentences are put together. If humans had more memory, greater lung capacity, and longer lifespan—so the standard response goes—then the apparent bound on the length of sentences would be removed.

In just the same way, complexity theorists standardly generalize problems along natural dimensions: for instance, they study the playing of checkers on an arbitrary $n \times n$ board, rather than "real" checkers, because then they can use complexity theory to study the structure and difficulty of the problem. The problem with looking at problems of bounded size is that results are distorted by the boring possibility of just writing down all the answers beforehand. If we study checkers as a bounded game, it comes out (counterintuitively!) as having no appreciable complexity—just calculate all the moves in advance—but if we study arbitrary $n \times n$ boards, we learn that checkers is computationally intractable (as we suspected).[12] Thus, the idealization of unboundedness is necessary for the same reason in both linguistics and complexity theory: by studying problems of arbitrary size we remove factors that would obscure the structure of the domain we're studying.

---

[12] In fact, this checkers generalization is probably harder than problems in $\mathcal{NP}$; it is PSPACE-hard. See Garey and Johnson (1979:173) for this result and chapter 2 for a definition of *PSPACE*, consisting of the problems that can be solved by an ordinary computer in polynomial *space*.

Related is the question of whether it's valid to place a bound on some particular parameter k of a problem—such as the length of a grammar rule or the number of variables in a SAT problem—in order to remove a factor from the complexity formula, while leaving other parameters of the problem unbounded. Here, the answer depends on the details of the problem. As a general rule, we obscure complexity instead of improving it if we simply impose a bound. For instance, if the complexity of our algorithm is $2^k \cdot n^3$, we haven't helped anything if we set a bound of $k = 50$ and then bound our computational effort by $K \cdot n^3$ where $K = 2^{50}$. But this kind of truncation can be genuinely valid if a linguistically justified bound produces a small constant in the complexity formula, or (more interestingly) if the bound can actually be exploited in an algorithm—for instance by using resolution on 2SAT (see section 1.4.2) or by building some small and clever table into the program.[13] (Sections 7.10 and 9.1.2 discuss computational and linguistic considerations that bear on the possibility of limiting the length of one computationally troublesome kind of grammar rule.)

Except in these special situations, truncation buys nothing but obfuscation, for the algorithm will behave just the same on the truncated problem as it does on the full problem—except that its complexity curve will artificially level out when the bound is reached. For instance, if we use a standard exponential algorithm to process SAT formulas, but limit the formulas to at most 10 distinct variables, we can expect the complexity curve to resemble the one shown in figure 1.4. Before the bound on variables is reached, longer formulas can get exponentially harder because they can contain more and more variables whose truth-values must be guessed; but after the bound is reached, runtime will increase at a much slower rate.

Since complexity theory deals in asymptotes, the complexity formula will be derived from the flattened-out portion of the curve, and the problem will look easy. But the initial, exponentially growing portion of the curve tells a different tale—naturally so, since by hypothesis we're using the same exponential algorithm as always. Nothing about any special structure of the

---

[13]In addition, more sophisticated "truncation" moves are possible. S. Weinstein has suggested that one option for a theory of performance involves quickly transforming a competence grammar G into a performance grammar $f(G)$ that can be rapidly processed. The function f "truncates" the full grammar in such a way that the symmetric difference between the languages $L(G)$ and $L(f(G))$ is negligible, in some natural sense that remains to be clarified; for instance, the truncated grammar might reject center-embedding or flatten deeply right-branching constructions. Many questions arise, among them the status of G and the relationship between the formalism(s) in which G and $f(G)$ are expressed.

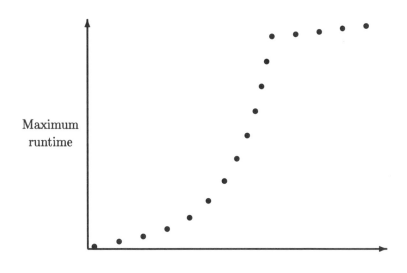

Figure 1.4: If a bounded problem is derived by pure truncation of a difficult parameter, with no change in an underlying exponential algorithm, we can expect runtime to grow exponentially at first and then level off when the artificial bound is reached.

truncated problem has been exploited; there's only the happy circumstance of a finite search space, and lurking below a patina of efficiency, brute-force search still reigns. Clearly, the initial region of the curve tells us more about the structure of the algorithm than the artificially flattened part. In a case like this, truncation is not an appropriate move because it only muddies the water. Just as in the linguistic case—when the structure of grammatical constraints could be better understood by considering unbounded problems— the structure of the algorithm is better revealed by considering how it operates on unlimited cases, without the truncation bound.

We conclude that if we want to use computational complexity theory then it makes sense to think of natural language processing problems *as if* they are of arbitrary size, even if they are not. To do otherwise is to risk masking the symptoms of exponential-time search through artificial means.

1.4.2   Why hard problems needn't be artificial

A second basic assumption of our approach is that the $P-\mathcal{N}P$ distinction isn't just an artificial one for natural languages: that hard problems like SAT do turn up in natural grammatical systems, and what's more, such problems do highlight the information processing structure of natural grammars.

The worry about artificiality seems to boil down to this: problems like SAT don't seem to be much like anything that any natural language processor would ever compute. Indeed, if by hypothesis natural problems are easier than SAT, then we might automatically avoid computational difficulty by using the frameworks only for real linguistic tasks instead of mathematical troublemaking.

Again, both our natural language analyses and complexity theory itself dismiss such worries as groundless. First, natural grammars *do* contain hard problems: as chapter 3 shows, the difficulty of processing sentences like BUFFALO BUFFALO BUFFALO seems to arise precisely because grammars can pose difficult problems. Similarly, chapter 5's spelling-change and dictionary system is computationally intractable as shown by a reduction that at least superficially mirrors ordinary language processes like vowel harmony. Finally, chapter 8 and appendix B show that generalized phrase structure grammar parsing can be difficult in practice.

Restrictions to "natural" cases, then, won't automatically save us from intractability. But this is no surprise to the complexity theorist. Here too, examples demonstrate that unless one exploits the special information structure of a problem, "natural" restrictions may not suffice to win processing efficiency.

A good example is a restricted version of SAT where there are two literals per clause, known as 2SAT. 2SAT is easier than 3SAT—it's in P—and so doesn't require exponential time for solution; yet if you take the usual exponential algorithm for SAT and expect it to run faster on 2SAT problems because they're easier, you will be sorely disappointed. The SAT algorithm will simply do the same kind of combinatorial search as before and will take exponential time. One must use a specialized algorithm such as resolution theorem proving to get any mileage out of the special structure of this restricted problem.[14] There's no reason why the same thing shouldn't happen

---

[14]In particular, the "special" structure is that there are two literals per clause. When resolution combines two such clauses together, the resolvent, by definition, is no longer

with grammatical machinery—a problem that's not intrinsically hard can be made difficult through failings of the grammatical framework, perhaps not obvious ones. In fact, section 7.8.1 gives an example of an easy problem that's made to look difficult when it's encoded in a context-free grammar.

1.4.3   Weak generative capacity can be misleading

Like our complexity tools, considerations of weak generative capacity can aid us in linguistic investigations; recall Chomsky's (1956) early demonstration of the inadequacy of finite-state descriptions of natural languages, which was based partially on grounds of weak generative capacity. Yet for many reasons, weak generative capacity alone may not give good clues about the appropriateness or processing difficulty of a grammatical formalism—one fundamental reason that we generally reject weak generative capacity analysis as too blunt and focus on complexity classifications instead.

A weak-generative-capacity restriction to strictly context-free languages is often thought to guarantee efficient parsability, but no such result holds. The reason, briefly, is that some context-free languages are generated only by very large context-free grammars—and grammar size *does* affect parsing time for all known general context-free parsing algorithms. We won't belabor this point here, as it is adequately discussed in chapters 7 and 8.

Similarly, models based on finite-state automata are often considered the hallmark of computational efficiency. Yet they, too, can lead one astray. While it is true that some finite-state problems are easy, other finite-state problems can be computationally costly. One must carefully examine *how* finite-state machinery is being used before pronouncing it safe from computational intractability; oversights have led to much confusion in the linguistics literature. Most researchers know casually that it's fast to figure out whether a sentence can be accepted or rejected by a finite-state automaton. No search is involved; the machine just processes the sentence one word at a time, and at the end, it just gives a Yes or No answer—the sentence either is or is not accepted. In short, the problem of *finite-state recognition* is easy.

But one cannot always rely on this approach to model all finite-state processes. For example, suppose we wanted to know the complexity of finite-

---

than the length of either of the original clauses. This monotonicity allows resolution to work in polynomial time. If one tries the same trick with 3SAT, then one quickly discovers that resolved clauses can grow in length, frustrating a polynomial time solution.

state *parsing*. That is, suppose we wanted not simply a Yes/No nod from our automaton, but a detailed description of the sentence's internal structure—perhaps a sequence of word category names. After all, this cuts closer to the heart of what we want from natural language analysis. But it looks like a harder problem, because it demands more information. Do our previous results about mere finite-state recognition apply? (In general, parsing is harder than recognition because a parsing algorithm must output a representation of how a sentence was derived with respect to a particular grammar, not merely a Yes/No recognition answer.)

Even if a problem is carefully posed, a solution in terms of finite-state machinery may be inappropriate if it does not accurately reflect the underlying constraints of a language. Rather, the finite-state character may be an accidental by-product, one that has little to do with the nature of the constraints that characterize the problem. In such a case, considerations of weak generative capacity are uninformative at best and misleading at worst. As was noted many years ago, weak generative capacity analysis serves as a kind of "stress test" that doesn't tell us much unless a grammar *fails* the test:

> The study of weak generative capacity is of rather marginal linguistic interest. It is important only in those cases where some proposed theory fails even in weak generative capacity—that is, where there is some natural language even the *sentences* of which cannot be enumerated by any grammar permitted by this theory .... It is important to note, however, that the fundamental defect of [many systems] is not their limitation in weak generative capacity but rather their many inadequacies in strong generative capacity .... Presumably, discussion of weak generative capacity marks only a very early and primitive stage of the study of generative grammar. (Chomsky 1965:60f)

Flaws in a formal system can easily go undetected by weak generative capacity analysis.

To see what goes wrong in a specific example, consider another simple artificial language, a *bounded palindrome language*—a set of sentences shorter than some fixed length k that can be read the same backwards or forwards. Over the alphabet a, b, c with a length restriction of 3, this gives us the language a, b, c, aa, bb, cc, aaa, aba, aca, bab, bbb, bcb, cac, cbc, ccc. Now, it is well known that an infinite palindrome language over the same alphabet cannot be generated by any finite-state grammar; the implicit mirror-image pairing between similar letters demands a context-free system. But our *k*-bounded palindrome language contains only a finite number of sentences, hence is technically and mechanically finite-state; therefore, the finite-state framework fails to break under the stress test of generative capacity.

But despite the fact that the language is finite-state, it is seriously misleading to stop and conclude that the finite-state framework accurately expresses the underlying constraints of this language. Just as with our earlier 2SAT vs. 3SAT example, it's instructive to consider the details of what's happening. *What kind* of finite-state machine generates our bounded palindrome language? Going through the tedious exercise of constructing the machine, say for $k = 6$, one finds that the underlying automaton, though indeed finite-state, represents a kind of huge brute-force encoding of *all* possible sentences—just a list, if you will. And just as with our exhaustive combinatorial algorithms, *nothing* about the special mirror-image structure of palindromes is exploited; such a machine could have just as easily encoded a random, finite list of sentences. It makes sense to remove this unilluminating accident by idealizing to an infinite palindrome language—which isn't finite-state—and then imposing boundedness as a separate condition.

Many examples of this kind also exist in natural languages. For example, many *reduplicative* processes—the kind that double constituents like syllables, roots, affixes, and so forth—in fact duplicate only a bounded amount of material. Technically, then, they can be encoded with context-free or even finite-state machinery, though the related language $\{ww\}$ where w ranges over unbounded strings is strictly not context-free. But clearly, the reduplicated material's boundedness may tell us nothing about the true nature of the constraints that are involved. In this case too, the machinery may pass the weak generative capacity test for accidental reasons. The point is that simple classification—the question of whether natural languages are context-free, for instance—doesn't have a privileged position in linguistic investigations. Unless very carefully used, the classification scheme of weak generative capacity may well be too blunt to tell us anything illuminating about natural languages.[15] We prefer complexity theory because it gives us more direct insight into the structure of grammatical problems.

---

[15]Rounds, Manaster-Ramer, and Friedman (1986) have more to say on related points.

1.4.4 Universal vs. fixed-language recognition problems

Beyond these basic idealizations, we have posed the grammatical problems described in the rest of this book in a particular way. Because our problem descriptions sometimes seem at odds with those familiar from the tradition of weak generative capacity analysis, we shall briefly review why we think our approach heads in the right direction; in the next chapter, section 2.3 provides a more complete discussion of the same issue.

We aim to study the complexity of entire *families* of grammars—namely, those specified by some linguistic formalism, like lexical-functional grammar or generalized phrase structure grammar. This leads most naturally to the following complexity problems, which are most often called *universal problems* because they deal with an entire grammatical class:

Given a grammar G (in some grammatical framework) and a string x, is x in the language generated by G?

We contrast this way of posing complexity problems with the way such problems are often stated in the weak generative capacity tradition, dubbed *fixed language recognition problems* (FLR problems):

Given a string x, is x in some independently specified set of strings L?

These two problems may look very much alike, but they are not. Universal grammar problems contain two variables: the grammar and an input sentence. Fixed language recognition problems contain one variable, just the sentence to recognize. No particular grammar is specified—just as no particular grammar is mentioned when we say that a certain string language is or isn't context-free, in the weak generative capacity approach. Generally speaking, universal problems are harder, because the grammar is variable: a potential solution algorithm must be braced for any possible grammar thrown at it. In contrast, FLR problems are easier: because one is permitted to vary the grammar at will to get the most efficient algorithm possible, and because no grammar is mentioned in the problem, there's no "grammar size" parameter to appear in complexity formulas.[16]

---

[16] For example, the FLR problem for context-free *languages* takes only time proportional to n^3, as is well known (Hopcroft and Ullman 1979). However, the corresponding universal problem, where the grammar must be taken directly into account, is much harder: it is

Even though FLR problems are usually easier in a formal sense, they are misleadingly so. In a nutshell, FLR problems ignore grammars, parsing, and complexity theory practice, while universal problems focus on all these things in the right way—they explicitly grapple with grammars instead of languages, take into account parsing difficulties, and accord with complexity theory practice:

- Universal problems study entire grammatical families by definition, while FLR problems consider only language complexity and so allow one to vary the grammar at will. Implicitly, an FLR problem can allow one to completely ignore the grammatical formalism under study just to get the simplest language complexity possible. But this cuts directly against our aim to study properties of the grammatical formalisms themselves, not just the languages they happen to generate. In addition, if one believes that grammars, not languages, are mentally represented, acquired, and used, then the universal problem is more appropriate.

- Universal problems consider all relevant inputs to parsing problems, while FLR problems do not. First of all, we're interested in parsing with respect to linguistically relevant grammars; we're not just interested in language recognition problems. Second, we know that grammar size frequently enters into the running time of parsing algorithms, usually multiplied by sentence length. For example, the maximum time to recognize a sentence of length n of a general context-free language using the Earley algorithm is proportional to $|G|^2 \cdot n^3$ where $|G|$ is the size of the grammar, measured as the total number of of symbols it takes to write the grammar down (Earley 1968). What's more, it's typically the grammar size that dominates: because a natural language grammar will have several hundred rules but a sentence will be just a dozen words long, it's often been noted that grammar size contributes more than the input sentence length to parsing time. (See Berwick and Weinberg (1984), as well as appendix B for some evidence of this effect in generalized phrase structure grammars.) Because this is a relevant input to the final complexity tally, we should explicitly consider it.

- A survey of the computational literature confirms that universal problems are widely adopted, for many of the reasons sketched above. For

---

P-complete (as difficult as any problem that takes deterministic time n^j) (Jones and Laaser 1976).

example, Hopcroft and Ullman (1979:139) define the context-free grammar recognition problem as follows: "Given a context-free grammar G and a string $x \ldots$ is x in [the language generated by G]?" Garey and Johnson (1979), in a standard reference work in the field of computational complexity, give all 10 automata and language recognition problems covered in the book (1979:265–271) in universal form: "Given an instance of a machine/grammar and an input, does the machine/grammar accept the input?"

All of these considerations favor the use of universal problems, but it is also fair to ask whether one could somehow preprocess a problem in some way—particularly a problem that includes a grammar—to bypass apparent computational intractability. After all, a child learning language may have a lot of time at its disposal to discover some compact, highly efficient grammatical form to use. Similarly, people are thought to use just *one* grammar to process sentences, not a family of grammars. So isn't the FLR model the right one after all?

The preprocessing issue—essentially, the issue of compilation—is a subtle one that we'll address in detail in the next chapter (section 2.3). However, we can summarize our main points here. Compilation suffers from a number of defects.

First of all, compilation is neither computationally free nor even always computationally possible. Compilation cannot be invoked simply as a promissory note; one must at least hint at an effective compilation step.

Second, if we permit just *any* sort of preprocessing changes to the grammar in order to get a language that is easy to process, then there is a tremendous temptation to ignore the grammatical formalism and allow clever programming (the unspecified preprocessing) to take over. If, on the other hand, we believe that grammars are incorporated rather directly into models of language use, then this independence seems too high a price to pay.

Finally, *known* compilation steps for spelling change and dictionary retrieval systems, lexical-functional grammar, generalized phrase structure grammars, and subsystems of GPSGs known as ID/LP grammars all fail: they cannot rescue us from computational intractability. Typically, what happens is that compilation expands the grammar size so much that parsing algorithms take exponential time.[17] See chapters 4, 5, 7, and 8 for the details, and chapter 2 (section 2.3) for a more thorough discussion of the compilation issue.

1.4.5   The effect of parallel computation

A final issue is that, for the most part, the complexity classes we use here remain firmly wedded to what we've been calling "ordinary" computers— serial computers that execute one instruction at a time. We have already stressed that complexity results are invariant with respect to a wide range of such sequential computer models.

This invariance is a plus—if the sequential computer model is the right kind of idealization. However, since many believe the brain uses some sort of parallel computation, it is important to ask whether a shift to parallel computers would make any difference for our complexity probes. Complexity researchers have developed a set of general models for describing parallel computation that subsume all parallel machines either proposed or actually being built today; here we can only briefly outline one way to think about parallel computation effects and their impact, reserving more detailed discussion for section 2.4 of chapter 2.[18]

Importantly, it doesn't appear that parallel computers will affect our complexity results. NP-hard problems are still intractable on any physically realizable parallel computer. Problems harder than that are harder still. In brief, we can still use our complexity classification to probe grammatical theories.

This invariance stems from a fundamental equation linking serial (ordinary) computation time to the maximum possible speedup won via parallel computation. We envision a computer where many thousands of processors

---

[17]Of course, this does not rule out the possibility of a much more clever kind of prepro-cessing. It's just that no such examples have been forthcoming, and they all run the risk of destroying any close connection between the grammatical theory and language processing (if that kind of transparency is desirable).

[18]Chapter 2 briefly mentions the related topics of approximate solution algorithms but does not address yet another area of modern complexity—probabilistic algorithms—that might also shed light on grammatical formalisms. The end of chapter 2 also discusses the relevance of fixed-network "relaxation" neural models for solving hard problems, such as the neural model recently described by Hopfield and Tank (1986).

work together (synchronously) to solve a single problem.

$$
\begin{array}{ccc}
\text{Serial time} & & \text{Parallel time} \\
\text{to solve} & \leq & \times \\
\text{a problem} & & \text{\# of parallel processors}
\end{array}
$$

This equation subsumes a wide range of examples. Suppose we have only a fixed number, k, of parallel processors. Our equation tells us that the best we could hope for would be a constant speedup. To do better than this requires a number of processors that varies with the input problem size.

Consider for example context-free language recognition; this takes time proportional to n^3, where n as usual is input sentence length. Suppose we had proportional to n^2 parallel processors; then our equation suggests that the maximum speedup would yield parallel processing time proportional to n. Kosaraju (1975) shows how this speedup can in fact be attained by simple *array automaton* parsers for context-free languages.

Using this equation, what would it take to solve an NP-hard problem in parallel polynomial time? It's easy to see that we would need more than a polynomial number of processors: because the left-hand side of the equation for serial time could be proportional to 2^n (recall that we assume that NP-hard problems cannot be solved in polynomial time and in fact all known solution algorithms take exponential time), and because the first factor on the right would be proportional to n^j (polynomial time), in order for the inequality to hold we could need an exponential number of parallel processors.

If we reconsider figure 1.1 in terms of processors instead of microseconds, we see that the required number of processors would quickly outstrip the number we can build, to say nothing of the difficulty of connecting them all together. Of course, we could build enough processors for small problems—but small problems are within the reach of serial machines as well. We conclude that if a grammatical problem is NP-hard or worse, parallel computation won't really rescue it.[19] We can rest secure that our complexity analyses stand—though we hope that the theory of parallel complexity can lead to even more fine-grained and illuminating results in the future.

---

[19]Section 2.4 of chapter 2 discusses certain problems that benefit from a superfast speedup using parallel processing; these include context-free language recognition, as mentioned (but probably *not* the corresponding universal context-free parsing problem); sorting; and the graph connectivity problem. This superfast parallel speedup may be closely related to the possibility of representing these problems as highly separable (modular) planar graphs.

1.5   An Outline of Things to Come

Having said something about what complexity analysis is and how it works, we conclude with a summary of what's to come: a more thorough look at complexity theory and its application to several grammatical systems.

Chapter 2: Before plunging into new and unfamiliar technical territory, any reader deserves an account of what to expect. Chapter 2 fills this need for readers unfamiliar with complexity theory. It sketches more formally the core concepts of complexity theory and the notation we'll use in the rest of the book. It also surveys the key problem transformations—like the one we used in our toy grammar example—that we'll use later on. Finally, it addresses in more depth the questions raised in chapter 1: whether our complexity theory idealizations are the right ones, including such topics as the effects of compilation and parallel computers.

Chapter 3: Agreement and lexical ambiguity are pervasive in natural languages: in English, subjects must agree with verbs in number and person, while many words like *kiss* can be either nouns or verbs. Chapter 3 defines a general class of agreement grammars (AGs) to formalize these notions, and shows that these two mechanisms alone suffice to make a grammatical formalism computationally intractable. Because of the simplicity of the result, *any* grammatical theory that incorporates agreement and lexical ambiguity—including most existing theories—will inherit the computational intractability of AGs. To resolve this dilemma, section 3.3 argues that this difficulty reflects a real possibility in natural language, and that performance theory truncations may be required to win efficient sentence processing.

Chapter 4: Lexical-functional grammar (LFG) has been proposed as a computationally more efficient grammatical formalism than transformational grammar (Kaplan and Bresnan 1982). Chapter 4 shows that LFGs contain enough agreement machinery and lexical ambiguity to inherit the intractability of AGs. Nothing in the LFG formalism, then, accounts for efficient human sentence processing; we need to supply an additional performance theory and/or new formal restrictions here. Chapter 4 proposes linguistic constraints—importing more $\overline{\text{X}}$ theory into the lexical-functional framework—as well as locality constraints to improve computational tractability.

Chapter 5: Most natural language processing systems have some way to decompose words into their parts so that they can be looked up in a dictionary and their constituent features returned; this precedes sentence analysis. Note that two factors are involved: dictionary lookup and spelling analysis are needed because a surface form like `tries` is retrieved from the dictionary as `try+s`. How hard is it to do this in general (and not just in English)? Chapter 5 probes this question by investigating one recently proposed model for dictionary analysis and retrieval—the *two-level* model of Koskenniemi (1983). Though the model is grounded on finite-state automata and gives an initial appearance of efficiency, two-level processing is in fact computationally intractable in the worst case; while some examples of spelling change–dictionary retrieval can be solved efficiently, not all of them can be. Chapter 5 shows why and underscores the point that simply relying on finite-state machinery need not save one from computational difficulties. It also shows that "compiling" a set of two-level automata into a single, larger one does not save us from computational trouble here.

Chapter 6: Chapter 5's analysis makes us suspect that there's something about the special properties of natural morphological systems that's not being exploited by the two-level model. Something less powerful than combinatorial search seems to be all that's required for analyzing words of English, Turkish, or other natural languages. To explore this possibility in a preliminary way, chapter 6 proposes to use constraint propagation for doing morphological analysis. Besides being demonstrably weaker than combinatorial search, constraint propagation seems to more accurately reflect the special features of local information flow and linear separability that seem characteristic of natural morphological analysis.

Chapter 7: Many modern linguistic theories cast surface sentence complexity as the result of several modular, interacting components. For example, the ID/LP formalism (Gazdar *et al.* 1985) separates out immediate dominance information (a sentence dominates an *NP* and a *VP*) from linear precedence (LP) information (a verb comes before an *NP* object). ID/LP systems have been proposed to partially describe so-called free-word-order languages, where noun phrases may appear in any order. Chapter 7 examines how hard it is to parse sentences generated by just the ID component of ID/LP grammars, dubbed *unordered context-free grammars* (UCFGs). While the literature suggests that straightforward extensions of known parsing algorithms will work efficiently with these grammars, chapter 7 proves that this is not so: though writing down a free-word-order language in ID/IP form can often be beneficial, in the worst case, the sentences of an arbitrary ID system cannot be efficiently parsed. Here again the proof gives us some clues as to why natural free-word-order languages don't generally run into this difficulty, and suggests some natural constraints that might salvage computational tractability. Appendix A gives formal proofs for this chapter's claims.

Chapter 8: *Generalized phrase structure grammar* (GPSG), a recent linguistic theory, also seems to promise efficient parsing algorithms for its grammars, but this chapter shows that nothing in the formal framework of GPSG guarantees this. Modern GPSGs include a complex system of features and rules. While feature systems—simply saying that a noun phrase like *dogs* is singular and animate—may seem innocuous, much to our surprise they are not. It is an error to sweep features under the rug: the feature system of GPSG is very powerful, and this chapter shows that even determining what the possible feature-based syntactic categories of a GPSG are can be computationally difficult. Taken together, the components of GPSG are extraordinarily complex. The problem of parsing a sentence using an arbitrary GPSG is very hard indeed—harder than parsing sentences of arbitrary LFGs, harder than context-sensitive language recognition, and harder even than playing checkers on an $n \times n$ board. (See appendix B for some actual calculations of English GPSG grammar sizes.) The analysis pinpoints unnatural sources of complexity in the GPSG system, paving the way for the following chapter's linguistic and computational constraints.

Chapter 9: Drawing on the computational insights of chapter 8, this chapter proposes several restrictions that rid GPSGs of some computational difficulties. For example, we strictly enforce $\overline{\text{X}}$ theory, constrain the distribution of gaps, and limit immediate dominance rules to binary branching (reducing the system's unnatural ability to count categories). These restrictions do help. However, because revised GPSGs retain machinery for feature agreement and lexical ambiguity, revised GPSGs, like AGs, can be computationally intractable. Chapter 9 suggests this as a good place to import independently motivated performance constraints—substantive constraints on human sentence processing that aren't a part of the grammatical formalism.

Chapter 2

Complexity Theory and Natural Language

Like much of mathematics, complexity theory boils down to a struggle for *invariance*—in the computational world, for results that remain valid across variation in computers, algorithms, and the precise way problems are formulated. Chapter 1 introduced the basic tools that complexity theorists use to handle such variation. This chapter elaborates that sketch with a more thorough and formal treatment of the abstractions and methods of complexity theory—once again giving particular attention to what complexity theory can tell us about formal grammatical systems for natural language.[1] We will explain how complexity theory abstracts away from the details of algorithms, problem formulations, problem inputs, and computer models:

- Invariance with respect to *algorithms* is won by focusing on *problem* complexity rather than particular *algorithm* complexity. A *problem* poses a general question—such as whether an arbitrary Boolean formula is satisfiable—while an *algorithm* is a particular procedure for solving a problem. A *problem instance* is a particular instantiation of a general question, such as whether the Boolean formula f is satisfiable.

- Invariance with respect to *problem formulations* is won (for our purposes) by posing all problems as *decision problems* with Yes/No answers and by requiring problem instances to be encoded in a "reasonable" fashion that includes all computationally relevant inputs.[2] A machine

---

[1] For a more detailed treatment of complexity theory, the reader should consult Garey and Johnson (1979) or Hopcroft and Ullman (1979), chapter 12.

[2] Well-defined problems that demand more than Yes/No answers, typically optimization problems in a variable z, can always be converted into decision problems by grafting a numerical bound k onto the problem itself and then posing the decision problem "Does

receives a problem instance encoded as a string x over some alphabet Σ and is required to accept or reject it. For example, in asking whether the lexical-functional grammar G can generate the sentence w, we would feed the machine an x formed by writing down both G and w and it would say Yes or No.[3] Both G and w would contribute to the size of the problem instance, measured as the number of symbols in x (written $|x|$). The convention of posing all problems in this standard way allows us to probe complexity with *reductions* that transform one problem into another while preserving Yes/No answers.[4] The complexity of a problem will not hinge on the details of an encoding scheme as long as the encoding is "reasonable." That is, the encoded problem instance must not be encoded in unary or otherwise padded out so as to give an algorithm too much rope to play with.[5]

- Invariance with respect to *different instances* of the same problem is gained in part by calculating complexity as a function of the encoded input length $n = |x|$. This means we'll generally have to consider the *maximum* time our best algorithm takes over all inputs of length n, as n grows without bound. (While this seems like an upper bound on problem complexity, many of our reductions in effect set a *lower bound* by showing that a new problem is at least as hard as a very difficult previously known one.[6])

---

there exist a solution where z is no greater than k?" Decision problems are at least as hard as their corresponding original optimization problems, provided the cost bound doesn't take much time to compute. We won't deal with this subtlety here because our grammatical problems will already be posed as decision problems.

[3] Any decision problem T may be interpreted as a language recognition problem by equating the language with the set of encoded instances to which T says Yes. However, we do not stress this possibility here because of its potential for confusion. For instance, the language of our LFG decision problem consists of every string that encodes a grammar-input pair $\langle G', w' \rangle$ such that $w' \in L(G')$—quite a different thing from the language accepted by the LFG G that we had in mind.

[4] For our purposes, reductions are required to be *polynomial-time* problem transformations so that our purported complexity probe does not introduce spurious complexity. This point will be explained in more detail later in the chapter.

[5] The amount of rope depends on what problems we want to lump together: if we use complexity classes based on polynomial time, then the encoding must not expand the size of a problem instance more than polynomially. Suppose, for example, that our best algorithm for SAT takes time proportional to $2^{|x|}$. If we were allowed to add $2^{|x|}$ dummy characters to the input string x as part of our encoding, the execution time of our algorithm would be *linear* in the length of the bloated input string. Clearly, such an encoding would only distort our understanding of the algorithm's complexity.

[6] For instance, if we show that a problem T is NP-hard, and if $P \neq \mathcal{NP}$, then T cannot have a polynomial-time algorithm. Generally, if we show that a problem T is C-hard for

Choices other than upper bounds are possible. If the distribution of input instances is known, the *average case* complexity can sometimes be calculated, and this might be more relevant.[7] Such bounds are usually difficult to come by, and for convenience we adopt worst-case cost measures, noting that for many problems these effectively give us lower bounds.

The requirement that an algorithm handle an unbounded range of inputs is harder to avoid because it serves to plug troublesome technical loopholes. For instance, there is a trivial program to answer the question of whether the fourteen-trillionth decimal digit of π is 7 or not: the program is either PRINT YES or PRINT NO, and either way it's trivial, though it may be harder to figure out which program is correct. Such unilluminating possibilities are ruled out by generalizing the problem to cover questions about about any decimal position instead of just one.

- Invariance with respect to *computer models* is won through two linked choices: the *deterministic Turing machine* (DTM) chosen as our basic reference machine can simulate all other reasonable serial machines in polynomial time (section 2.1.2), while the definitions of the major *complexity classes* abstract away from polynomial-time variation. (DTMs are generalized to *nondeterministic Turing machines* (NTMs) to provide a model for "guessing" computers; see section 2.1 for definitions.) Because all reasonable serial computer models are polynomial-time equivalent to one another, a problem shown to be intractable for a DTM will be intractable for any real serial computer. Similarly, any problem that can be solved in polynomial time on a DTM can be solved in polynomial time on any other serial computer. (Section 2.4 examines what happens if we use a parallel computer instead.)

- Invariance with respect to *resource measures* can be gained by defining general principles that govern all resources (*e.g.*, time, space, processors, electricity) and proving results that measure the rate at which an abstract resource is consumed as the computation procceds. The Blum axioms (Blum 1967) make up one set of such principles, resting on the insight that an exponentially growing need for *any* computational resource indicates intractability in a very real sense.

---

some computationally difficult problem class C, we have not set an upper bound on the difficulty of T; instead, the most we have shown about the upper bound is that whatever the bound is, it is at least as large as the upper bound for the difficult problems in C.

[7] Often it is not sufficient to know the distribution of input *lengths*, since the performance of an algorithm may vary widely on different instances of a given length.

Given this background, our discussion in this chapter falls naturally into two parts. The first part of the chapter describes the formal machinery of complexity theory in sufficient detail for the reductions of succeeding chapters. The second part continues from chapter 1 our discussion of whether the idealizations of complexity theory are appropriate for natural-language investigations.

We will begin (section 2.1) by describing how computer scientists measure algorithm and problem complexity with Turing machines, showing why the Turing machine model works well for complexity theory even though it seems to lack the power of a "real" computer. This section can be read independently as it does not address connections between complexity theory and grammatical analysis; it serves mainly as a reference for our technical assumptions and notation.

The remaining sections bear more directly on our approach. Section 2.2 gives several examples of polynomial-time problem transformations (reductions), to both illustrate this important technique and introduce other complexity classes that we'll use in later chapters for natural language analysis. Readers familiar with complexity theory may skip this section as well, though they should review figures 2.9–2.12 for a roadmap to the problem transformations we use later on.

Turning once again to issues that arise in the application of complexity theory to grammatical systems, section 2.3 probes more deeply into the issue of grammar preprocessing or compilation that we outlined in chapter 1. Section 2.4 concludes with more thorough consideration of what happens if we use a parallel computer model instead of a serial one, along with some speculation about possible computational effects of modular information structure in linguistics.

2.1   Computer Models for Measuring Complexity

This section defines and justifies the main abstractions and notations that we adopt: problems, problem instances, and problem encodings; our reference computer models, deterministic and nondeterministic Turing machines; and complexity classes. The next section continues with more formal definitions of the complexity classes $\mathcal{P}$ and $\mathcal{NP}$, hard problems, reductions, and completeness.

First we define DTMs and NTMs, time and space complexity, upper-bound and lower-bound complexity costs, and the classes $\mathcal{P}$ and $\mathcal{NP}$. After we discuss the polynomial invariance of serial machine models, section 2.2 describes how polynomial machine invariance works hand in hand with complexity classes to capture the notion of a *hard problem* and *complete for a (complexity) class*.

A Turing machine is a simple mathematical model of a computer—that is, it formalizes the notion of an *effective procedure*. An effective procedure is finitely describable and consists of discrete steps, each of which can be carried out mechanically. We use a 1-tape deterministic Turing machine (DTM) as defined in Hopcroft and Ullman (1979) as our basic serial machine model. As we shall see, for complexity purposes we could just as well use a multitape DTM or any one of a number of alternative serial machines.

A Turing machine consists of three components. There is a *finite-state control* that defines the operation of the machine. There is an *input tape* that is bounded on the left but extends indefinitely far to the right; the tape is divided into an infinite number of discrete cells, and each cell can hold one of a finite number of tape symbols. There is a *tape head* that looks at one cell of the tape at a time. The machine starts with its tape head looking at the leftmost tape cell; the tape symbols in the leftmost n cells spell out the *input* to the TM, while the remaining cells hold special blank symbols. (We will often choose to mark the ends of the input by placing a special endmarker "$" at each end.)

According to its finite-state control, in a single move a DTM (1) changes state; (2) prints a symbol on the tape cell it is scanning, overwriting what was there before; and (3) moves its scanning head left or right. The machine is *deterministic* because its finite-state control specifies exactly one possible next move, given some combination of current state and scanned tape symbol.

We measure the resources used by a DTM M by counting each *move* as one time unit and each *tape cell* scanned as one space unit:

- If, for every input of length n, M makes at most $T(n)$ moves before halting, then M is of *time bound* $T(n)$. Plainly, if the entire input must be read, then a DTM takes at least linear time, because this model takes $n + 1$ moves just to scan past the input.[8]

- If, for every input of length n, M scans at most $S(n)$ tape cells, then M is of *space bound* $S(n)$. Because every tape scan implies a move, the time M uses to process an input must be at least as great as the space it uses. But because tape space can be reused, time usage may be much greater than space usage.

Turing machines are most often described as *accepting* or *recognizing* certain languages or sets of strings. A TM accepts an input string x if and only if it halts and accepts on that input. A TM rejects an input string if it fails to halt or halts in a nonaccepting state on that input.[9]

We can now formally define the "guessing" computer that was described in chapter 1 as a *nondeterministic Turing machine* (NTM). The changes from the DTM definition are simple: Alter the DTM so that instead of giving just one possible tape head movement and new state, its finite-state control may specify any finite number of alternative movements and new states.[10]

The vital difference between a DTM and a NTM surfaces when we talk about how such machines successfully accept (recognize) strings. While a DTM computation accepts if and only if there is a straight-line sequence of configurations leading from the starting configuration to a final state, an NTM computation looks like an *OR*-tree: it succeeds if there exists *any* computation sequence that leads to a final state. With other sets of choices, the machine may not reach an accepting state or may not even halt. See figures 2.1 and 2.2. An NTM rejects (fails to recognize) its input only if *no* sequence of choices leads to acceptance.[11]

---

[8]For making finer distinctions among problems that take linear time in this sense, complexity theorists use slightly different TM formulations that do not count the time required to read the input.

[9]Recall that our language recognition problems will involve an x that encodes both a grammar G and an input w for the grammar. Thus, the language accepted by the TM (*i.e.*, the set of acceptable x-strings) generally will *not* be the language $L(G)$ accepted by the grammar.

[10]The transition function (conventionally δ) for a deterministic TM maps a state and a currently scanned tape symbol to a tuple ⟨new state, newly written symbol, movement direction⟩. When we alter the DTM definition to define NTMs, δ becomes a mapping from a state and currently scanned tape symbol to a *set* of such tuples. Formally, the revised δ maps Q (states) $\times$ Γ (input symbols) to $2^{(Q \times \Gamma \times \{Left, Right\})}$. Equivalently, δ can be regarded as a nonfunctional relation.

[11]Thus, the definition of an NTM includes a single tacit existential quantifier. This approach may be generalized in a straightforward way to define *alternating* Turing ma-

The time complexity of an NTM computation is the *smallest* number of moves required for an accepting computation (as there may be more than one accepting sequence); it is undefined otherwise. Nonaccepting dead-ends just do not count. Note how this formalization effectively captures the notion of a "guessing" computer where only *verifying* or *checking* guesses costs time.

2.1.1 Nondeterminism and SAT revisited

We can now see in detail how guessing power makes it easy to solve SAT problems. SAT is difficult because it may not be possible to figure out locally whether any particular Boolean variable should be assigned the value **true** or **false**. NTMs, on the other hand, can avoid this difficulty because for every variable in the formula, one move of the NTM can guess **true** while another move simultaneously guesses **false**.

As we suggested informally in the previous chapter, nondeterminism makes SAT instances solvable in polynomial time on our special guessing computer. Figure 2.3 shows part of the tree of guesses that is explored while trying to discover whether the formula

$$(\overline{x} \vee y) \wedge (\overline{y} \vee z) \wedge (y \vee \overline{z}) \wedge (x \vee y \vee z)$$

is satisfiable. There are dead-ends that do not work out, as indicated by the XXX-entries; however, there *is* an accepting computation sequence—terminated by *Success*—and thus the machine accepts. (Not all computation sequences are shown.) Clearly, the length of the accepting sequence is polynomial in the length of the input formula (for details, see Garey and Johnson 1979). This is why we said that SAT instances are easy to *verify* in polynomial time.

To summarize then, arbitrary SAT problems can be solved in polynomial time on our hypothetical NTM model; if a DTM is used, only exponential time algorithms are known.

2.1.2 Polynomial invariance of machine models

Our choice of DTMs to measure computational complexity does not affect what problems count as NP-hard (intractable) or polynomially solvable

---

chines, which may use any number of alternating existential and universal quantifiers; see section 2.2.4 and chapter 8.

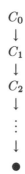

Figure 2.1: The computation sequence of a deterministic TM is a straight line: at each step, there is only one possible next move. The accepting state is indicated by a large dot.

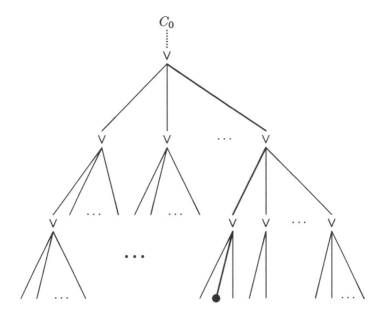

Figure 2.2: A nondeterministic Turing machine computation corresponds to an OR-tree. The computation succeeds if *any* accepting state can be reached, as indicated by the OR-symbols ($\vee$) in the tree nodes. Here, the accepting state is symbolized by a large dot and the accepting path is marked with dark lines. There could be more than one accepting state; some computation sequences might not accept at all. The *shortest* accepting computation sequence is used in measuring the complexity of the NTM computation.

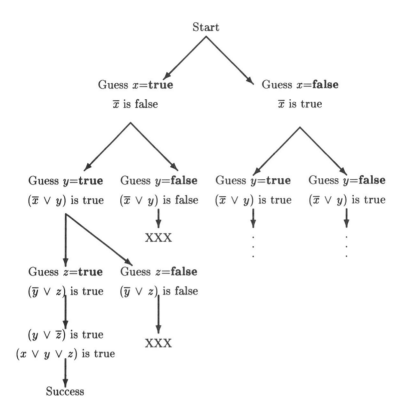

Figure 2.3: A nondeterministic TM makes solving SAT problems easy because failed guesses do not cost time. XXX-entries stand for computation sequences that do not succeed; these do not count in the final complexity tally. Not all computational sequences are displayed here.

(tractable); any other sequential machine model would have given the same results. This section shows why.

Turing machines come in many different shapes and sizes: one can vary the number of tapes, make the tape infinite in both directions, add multiple tape-scanning heads, and so forth. Further, there are other abstract machine models that seem much closer to "real" computers. While a Turing machine must lumber sequentially along its tape to read a single number from memory, a random access machine (RAM) is allowed access in constant time to any of a finite number of registers that can hold arbitrarily large numbers;

more familiar still, a random access stored program machine (RASP) can also store its program in memory. Both machines can solve problems much more efficiently than DTMs.

But these variations do not affect the classes P and NP—which is just what we want. Two facts secure this result: the use of complexity measures that abstract away from polynomially bounded variation, and the polynomial-time interchangeability of serial computer models.

Standard complexity measures abstract away from limited variation in two ways. To begin with, the use of "big-O" notation for upper bounds wipes out detailed constants from complexity formulas. This allows us to see the general shape of a complexity curve while ignore timing details that we wish to avoid (for example, whether the computer's clock runs at 6 or 8 megahertz). Technically, we write $f(n) = O(g(n))$ (f is "of order g" or "big-O of g") if and only if there exist positive constants c and k such that for all $n \geq k$, $|f(n)| \leq c \cdot |g(n)|$; for example, $8n^3 + n^2 + 76$ is $O(n^3)$ because $8n^3 + n^2 + 76 \leq 85n^3$ for all $n \geq 1$.[12] O-notation lets us ignore multiplicative constants as well as lower-order terms and any other peculiarities that are confined to small n. The relation "$\leq$" in the definition is appropriate for upper bounds, but similar definitions exist for talking about when a $f(n)$ is bounded from below or from both above and below (*exactly bounded*) by another function.[13] O-notation wipes out overly fine distinctions between algorithm running times in an obvious way: if an algorithm runs in time exactly $4n^2 + 105$ on some American-made PC, but in time $3n^2 + 62$ on a foreign import, then this difference is washed out when we say that both machines run the algorithm in time $O(n^2)$.

Standard complexity measures also abstract away from polynomially bounded variation in a more direct way: major complexity classes are defined in terms of gross distinctions that do not distinguish among different polynomials. For example, we'll see below that the class P is defined to include all problems that can be solved in time $p(n)$ for *any polynomial p*. This definition produces a robust complexity classification that won't be affected by polynomially bounded variation in our reference standards. For instance, we'd get the same classification if we switched from a DTM to a more efficient

---

[12]Note that the function is also $O(1000^{3n})$.

[13]$f(n)$ is bounded from below by $g(n)$, written $f(n) = \Omega(g(n))$, iff there exist positive constants c and k such that $\forall n > k, |f(n)| \geq c|g(n)|$. $f(n)$ is exactly bounded by $g(n)$, written $f(n) = \theta(g(n))$, if and only if $f(n) = O(g(n))$ and $f(n) = \Omega(g(n))$.

machine that the DTM requires $O(n^3)$ overhead to simulate. (O-notation lets us use an even simpler definition for P, given below).

This invariance extends over a wide range of machine models because any DTM, RAM, or RASP machine can simulate any of the others with at worst a deterministic polynomial time loss. For instance, Lewis and Papadimitriou (1981:325) show how a language that can be recognized in time $T(n)$ on a k-tape TM can be recognized in time $O(T(n^2))$ on a 1-tape TM. To take another example, the computation of a random access machine that runs in time T can be simulated by a 1-tape Turing machine in time $O(T^3)$ (Garcy and Johnson 1979:11).

For fine-grained distinctions, the machine model we select can make more of a difference. For instance, if we were interested in what problems we could solve in linear time $O(n)$, then changing gears from two tapes to one tape would matter; the one-tape machine would take more time. But in this chapter we're interested in defining the classes P and NP using our DTM reference model:[14]

- P is the class of problems that can be solved by a deterministic Turing machine in Polynomial time (time $O(n^j)$ for any integer j).

- NP is the class of problems that can be solved by a Nondeterministic TM in Polynomial time.

The polynomial interchangeability of machine models implies that if a problem can be solved in deterministic polynomial time by, say, a RASP algorithm, then it is in P, because a DTM can simulate the RASP algorithm by using only a small amount of additional polynomial time. Thus, our complexity class is invariant with respect to serial machine models.

Plainly, the same polynomial interchangeability holds for NP as well, because any machine that adds a nondeterministic "guessing component" such as that in a NTM will still be able to have a guess verified by a polynomial-time TM simulation. So, no matter what serial computer model we use, P and NP look the same.

We showed in chapter 1 that one can identify P with the class of computationally tractable problems; we also identified the hardest problems in NP as computationally intractable problems (which have no known solution in

---

[14]Recall that decision problems are equivalent to language recognition problems, so P is also a class of *languages*. But once again, we don't stress this because of the potential for confusion.

deterministic polynomial time). The next section shows more formally how
problem transformations and the key concept of a *hard problem* for a complexity class may be used to justify this distinction. It also outlines the problem
transformations we'll use in the rest of the book.

2.2   Hard Problems, Complexity Classes, and Reduction

The polynomial invariance of serial computer models provides one half of the
power of the P vs. NP distinction. The second half comes from the polynomial equivalence of NP-complete problems, which establishes that certain
problems in NP are the hardest problems in that class. We define problems
that are *complete for a complexity class* in a general way as follows:

- For the complexity class NP, a problem T is *NP-hard* if every problem
  in NP can be reduced to T. That is, for any $T' \in NP$, there must exist an answer-preserving polynomial-time problem transformation that
  maps instances of T' to instances of T. If, in addition, T itself is in NP,
  then T is said to be *NP-complete*.

- Similarly, we can replace NP with any complexity class C that subsumes
  NP to get definitions for the terms *C-hard* and *C-complete*.

Recall from chapter 1 that there exists a polynomial-time transformation
or reduction from one problem to another if (i) the transformation runs in
polynomial time on a DTM, and (ii) the transformation ensures that the
answers for the two problems coincide.[15]

Defined this way, reductions possess two key properties that tie into
complexity-class invariance. First, the polynomial-time speed of a reduction preserves membership in the complexity classes we've defined. If T_1 is
polynomial-time reducible to T_2, and if T_2 is in P, then so is T_1; but if T_2 is
not in P, then neither is T_1. (This result follows directly from composing the
DTM program that reduces T_1 to T_2 with the TM program that solves T_2.)

---

[15]If our complexity class is P or smaller, then reductions must be done more carefully
to guarantee that the transformation function does not introduce spurious complexity.
For instance, to show that a problem is P-complete, we must rely on *logarithmic space*
reductions, for otherwise the reduction function itself could be big enough to encompass
any polynomial-time computation. In this book, polynomial-time reductions suffice because
the classes we use are all supersets of NP.

Second, reductions are transitive: if T_1 is polynomially reducible to T_2, and if T_2 is polynomially reducible to T_3, then T_1 must also be polynomially reducible to T_3. This again follows directly, because the composition of two polynomial-time DTM programs will itself be only polynomial-time.

These two key properties allow us to use any one NP-complete problem as a "signature" for the hardest problems in $\mathcal{NP}$. Let us now see why.

The transitivity of reductions guarantees that if we start with a known NP-complete problem T_1, and we show that T_1 reduces to T_{new}, a new problem whose complexity we wish to probe, then *all* problems in $\mathcal{NP}$ are polynomially reducible to T_{new} (as T_1 was NP-complete, by assumption). Then by definition, T_{new} must be NP-hard, though it could still be *harder* than problems in $\mathcal{NP}$. If, in addition, we can show that T_{new} is in $\mathcal{NP}$, we know it is NP-complete.

These results justify the claim that any single NP-complete problem "summarizes" the entire class $\mathcal{NP}$: if any one such problem T_1 could be solved in deterministic polynomial time, then all could be, because we could compose two polynomial-time problem transformations to map any problem T_2 in $\mathcal{NP}$ to T_1 (by the definition of NP-completeness) and then solve T_1 in polynomial time, returning a Yes answer that corresponds to a Yes answer for T_2. The nonexistence of known fast solution algorithms for many hundreds of NP-complete problems fortifies the hypothesis that $\mathcal{P} \neq \mathcal{NP}$ and our belief that $\mathcal{NP}$ characterizes the computationally intractable problems.

We point out once again that for our purpose of spotting computational difficulty in grammatical systems, it suffices to prove a problem NP-hard rather than NP-complete. Such a result shows that a grammatical problem is as least as difficult as any problem in $\mathcal{NP}$.

2.2.1   The difficulty of SAT

The reduction and computer simulation results show that SAT and the other problems we have classed as NP-complete are all in the same complexity class, but we still need to carry out one more step: to show that this class actually comprises all NTM computations. As we mentioned in chapter 1, we can do this with a general reduction from *any* polynomial-time NTM computation to some SAT problem instance, as first proved by Cook (1971). This shows that SAT is NP-hard. Because SAT is also in $\mathcal{NP}$, as follows informally from our description of NTMs and figure 2.3, SAT is NP-complete.

From this launching point, SAT may be used to show that several other basic problems, such as 3SAT, are NP-complete (see below, section 2.2); one can build outward from there. The following section shows exactly how this is done, with an eye toward the results in the rest of the book.

But before proceeding with these example reductions, we will briefly sketch how the NTM–SAT reduction works. Our aim is not to reproduce the proof in detail (that is left for the references), but rather to demonstrate how intricate SAT problems may become and give a deeper account of just why SAT and other NP-complete problems are so computationally difficult. This will set the stage for our discussion in section 2.4 of restricted subclasses of SAT problems that are more efficiently solvable, especially on a parallel computer, and may be of more linguistic relevance.[16] The reader familiar with Cook's result or not interested in its details may skip this discussion and turn immediately to section 2.2.2, which describes the problem transformations we use in the rest of the book. For a more complete recounting of Cook's theorem, consult Garey and Johnson (1979:39–44).

Cook (1971) begins by observing that by definition every problem in $\mathcal{N}\mathcal{P}$ can be solved by some NTM program in polynomial time. His proof then starts with a generic problem $T \in \mathcal{N}\mathcal{P}$. By the definition of $\mathcal{N}\mathcal{P}$, some NTM program M can solve T within some polynomial time bound $p(n)$. Cast in language terms, if $L(M)$ is the set of encoded problem instances x for which problem T has a Yes answer, then M must accept all such $x \in L(M)$ within $p(|x|)$ steps. Given any such M and p for the problem T, Cook describes a polynomial-time problem transformation $\Pi_{M,p}$ that maps instances of T to instances of SAT. Each transformation $\Pi_{M,p}$ takes any string x as input and outputs a Boolean formula that simulates the computation of M on x. The simulation must be faithful, so that $x \in L(M)$ iff $\Pi_{M,p}(x)$ is satisfiable. Each transformation must also run in polynomial time based on the length of x.

Formally, the machine M and its polynomial time bound p are not inputs to Cook's problem transformation; instead, Cook describes a different problem transformation for each M, taking only x as input. In Garey and John-

---

[16]To summarize that discussion here, 3SAT problems that can be drawn in a plane (so that no lines connecting identical variables cross) can be solved in time $O(2^{c\sqrt{x}})$ by a divide-and-conquer algorithm (Kasif, Reif, and Sherlekar 1986); this is substantially less time than that required for fully backtracking, exponential-time search. Thus it seems that modular information structure—the separability of variables—makes SAT more efficiently solvable.

son's (1979:39) words, the construction involves "a simultaneous proof for all $T \in \mathcal{NP}$ that T is reducible to SAT."[17]

Because of the time bound, an accepting computation sequence involves only $p(|x|)$ different machine configurations. Cook's proof uses a large number of logical variables to encode the various parts of these configurations. Many conjoined clauses constrain these variables so that the encoded configurations for step i and step $i+1$ must always be related by a legal move of M. Because the machine is nondeterministic, there will in general be many possible (but finite) successor configurations at step $i+1$ for a given configuration at step i, and this is where the "guessing power" of satisfiability comes in. A formula is satisfiable if there is *any* way of assigning truth-values to its variables so that it comes out true. Similarly, a nondeterministic machine accepts if there is *any* legal sequence of configurations that starts with the initial configuration and ends with an accepting configuration.

For each step i there is a separate set of variables to encode the configuration of M at that step; again, the time bound means we only need to consider $0 \le i \le p(|x|)$. A configuration consists of machine state, read-head position, and tape-cell contents; because the machine only makes $p(|x|)$ moves, the number of tape cells it uses is also bounded by $p(|x|)$. The index j that we use for possible tape positions will therefore range over $1 \le j \le p(|x|)$. We need the following Boolean variables:

- For every step i and for every possible state q of M, we need the variable $Q[i, q]$ that will be true iff M is in state q at step i.

- For every step i, for every possible tape index j, and for every possible tape symbol a (including blank), we need the variable $S[i, j, a]$ (S standing for "symbol") that will be true iff tape square j contains the symbol a after step i.

- For every step i and for every possible tape index j, we need the variable $H[i, j]$ that is true iff the tape head of M is scanning tape square j after step i.

Although we need a large set of variables, the size of the set is still polynomial in $|x|$.

In order to use these variables to actually simulate an accepting computation of M, we conjoin six sets of clauses. We must ensure (1) that M starts

---

[17]We have made minor notational changes in this quotation for consistency with our discussion.

correctly; (2) that computation step $i + 1$ follows from step i (as defined by the next-move relation for M); and (3) that M is in an accepting state after a polynomial amount of time at the end of the computation. Besides these obvious requirements, we must also ensure the integrity of the encoding. At each step, our variables must indicate that (4) M is in exactly one state, (5) M is scanning exactly one tape cell, and (6) each tape square contains exactly one symbol. Because these clauses are all conjoined, each one must be satisfied, and this ensures that the satisfying truth assignments are exactly those that mimic accepting computations of M on x.

To give just two examples of what these clauses look like, we will consider the simplest cases: making sure M ends up in an accepting configuration, and making sure M starts correctly. The other cases are more complicated. For instance, to make sure M is in exactly one state, scanning one cell, with one symbol per cell, we need negated variables (to ensure that M is in one state and *not* in any other state, and so forth). The clause that enforces a correct transition from step i to step $i + 1$ is the most complicated of all because it must ensure that certain malfunctions do not take place, while allowing only the moves licensed by M's finite-state control. See Garey and Johnson (1979:43) for an accessible presentation of the details.

Many small variations are possible in the definition of an accepting configuration; we might require the machine to end up in an *accepting state* or to have halted and printed Y on the first tape square. To ensure that at time $N = p(|x|)$, M has halted in a distinguished state **halt** and accepted by printing Y on the first tape square, the reduction's output must include the two-literal conjunction $Q[N, \textbf{halt}] \wedge S[N, 0, \text{Y}]$. (If M accepts before this time, we set things up so that M loops until we reach step N.) Note that if the constraints of the machine are enforced properly, these literals will be true if and only if M accepts.

M begins its computation (i) in state 0, scanning the input endmarker $\$$ in cell 0, (ii) with $x = x_1 \ldots x_n$ in tape cells 1 through $n = |x|$, (iii) with the other endmarker $\$$ in the next tape cell, and (iv) with the distinguished blank symbol B in the remaining tape cells. The corresponding enforcing clauses are

(i) $Q[0, 0] \wedge H[0, 0] \wedge S[0, 0, \$]$

(ii) $S[0, 1, x_1] \wedge \ldots \wedge S[0, n, x_n]$

(iii) $S[0, n + 1, \$]$

(iv) $S[0, n + 2, B] \wedge \ldots \wedge S[0, p(n), B]$

only one instance

Clearly, these clauses will be satisfied if and only if the encoded machine starts properly.

Assuming the other four clause sets are built properly, we have what we were after: a SAT instance, the conjunction of six sets of clauses, that is satisfiable if and only if M accepts x in $p(|x|)$ or fewer steps. We must also demonstrate that our clause-producing program $\Pi_{M,p}$ works in deterministic polynomial time relative to the size n of x, and this detail we leave for the reader to consult in Garey and Johnson (1979:39–44) or in Cook (1971). Since the polynomial-time NTM problem T that we chose was arbitrary, we conclude that any NTM polynomial-time problem—any problem in $\mathcal{NP}$— may be reduced to SAT.

Now that we've gotten off the ground with SAT as one example of an NP-complete problem, we will continue in the next section with two examples illustrating how the reduction technique works in practice. At the same time, we'll introduce the NP-complete problems we will use in later chapters.

2.2.2 Examples of the reduction technique

Constructing reductions is the real art of complexity analysis; we must "match" the problem to be studied with a known problem that's close enough for building a polynomial-time reduction from one problem to the other. For this reason, a particular NP-complete problem is often chosen as a reduction source because of its close structural similarity to the target problem.

To gain some familiarity with this art, this section gives two examples that are instructive in their own right. The first is a polynomial-time transformation of SAT to 3SAT. This easy-to-understand reduction is instructive because it shows that a transformation need not output a problem that is *completely equivalent* to the original problem, but merely one whose Yes/No answers correspond to those of the original problem. The formula f' that we construct will not be logically equivalent to the original formula f, but the important thing is that f' will be satisfiable if and only if f is. Further, the restricted form of 3SAT formulas makes them especially useful for proving that grammatical problems are NP-complete; the grammar that the reduction builds needs only to mirror this tightly constrained structure.

The second reduction will be from 3SAT to a graph problem known as VERTEX COVER. This example shows how one can build up a stock of NP-complete graph problems. More importantly, though, it illuminates the *topological* relationship between the difficulty of simultaneously determining truth-assignments for SAT and the intertwined structure of a graph. This structural relationship bears close scrutiny, for it provides valuable insight into the essential computational intractability of NP-complete problems. We also use VERTEX COVER as the source for a reduction in chapter 7.

In this section we will assume the restrictive version of 3SAT in which a clause cannot contain duplicate literals. Many of our grammatical reductions will not make this assumption.

Reducing SAT to 3SAT

First, let us transform SAT to 3SAT, a restricted version of satisfiability where there are exactly three literals per conjoined clause (3-conjunctive normal form, or 3CNF). For example, the formula

$$(x \vee \overline{y} \vee \overline{w}) \wedge (y \vee z \vee \overline{w})$$

is in 3CNF, but the formula

$$(x \vee y \vee \overline{z}) \wedge (u \vee \overline{x} \vee y \vee z)$$

is not (because the second clause has four literals). If we were allowing 3SAT clauses to contain duplicate literals, the problem transformation would be simpler because clauses that contain only one or two literals could be padded out with copies of literals already present.

Our reduction follows that in Hopcroft and Ullman (1979:328–330), but we make the additional assumption that our SAT problem is already in conjunctive normal form (as in the example above). The proof consists of two steps: showing that the transformed problem is in $\mathcal{NP}$, and exhibiting a polynomial-time transformation from SAT to 3SAT instances. We take up each step in turn.

The first step is easy. Given a 3SAT instance, we can use the guessing power of a nondeterministic TM to test truth assignments just as in the general SAT problem. It should be clear that it takes no more than polynomial time to verify any satisfying assignment as all 3SAT instances are also instances of SAT.

In the second step, we show how to convert any arbitrary SAT instance into a 3SAT instance while preserving satisfiability. Suppose we are given an arbitrary SAT instance. Our aim is to transform it to a 3SAT instance that is satisfiable if and only if the original instance is.

The basic idea is to process each clause of the SAT formula in turn. If it already has just three literals, we do nothing; if it has fewer than three, we pad it out in such a way that satisfying assignments are not altered; if it has more than three, we break it up into groups of three-literal clauses, again preserving satisfiability. Our new clauses need *not* be logically equivalent to the old ones, but our new clauses will be satisfiable if and only if the old ones were. There are four cases:

Case 1. There is exactly one literal α in the clause. Then we add two new literals and produce four new conjoined clauses that combine the original literal with all possible negated and unnegated combinations of the two new literals:

$$(\alpha \vee y_1 \vee y_2) \wedge (\alpha \vee y_1 \vee \overline{y}_2) \wedge (\alpha \vee \overline{y}_1 \vee y_2) \wedge (\alpha \vee \overline{y}_1 \vee \overline{y}_2)$$

Any assignment that satisfies α will satisfy our new clauses. Conversely, our new variables can't introduce any new satisfying assignments because of the way we have placed all of their possible combinations into the clauses.

Case 2. There are two literals α_1 and α_2 in the clause. Then we add one new literal w and form two new conjoined clauses:

$$(\alpha_1 \vee \alpha_2 \vee w) \wedge (\alpha_1 \vee \alpha_2 \vee \overline{w})$$

Again, if some assignment satisfies the original clause then it will satisfy the new ones as well, because in each new clause either α_1 or α_2 can make the clause true. Conversely, our new variables can't introduce any new satisfying assignments; if some assignment causes the new variables to satisfy one of the new clauses, they can't satisfy all of the others because of the way negated and unnegated occurrences have been combined. The new formula is satisfiable if and only if the original formula was.

Case 3. There are three literals in the clause. We do nothing, because the clause is already in the correct form.

Case 4. There are more than three literals in the clause. This is the most complicated situation. The idea is to break up the original clause and add new literals as we did with cases 1 and 2, carefully introducing negated and unnegated variables to ensure that the added literals can't add any new satisfying assignments. Specifically, if we are given the clause

$$(\alpha_1 \vee \alpha_2 \vee \alpha_3 \ldots \vee \alpha_l), \; l > 3$$

then we add new variables $z_1, z_2, \ldots, z_{l-3}$ and we create new clauses,

$$(\alpha_1 \vee \alpha_2 \vee z_1) \wedge (\alpha_3 \vee \overline{z}_1 \vee z_2) \wedge (\alpha_4 \vee \overline{z}_2 \vee z_3) \wedge \ldots$$
$$\wedge (\alpha_{l-2} \vee \overline{z}_{l-4} \vee z_{l-3}) \wedge (\alpha_{l-1} \vee \alpha_l \vee \overline{z}_{l-3})$$

Note carefully the structure of these new clauses. Aside from the first and the last, each clause has only one of the original literals in it. Further, each successive pair of clauses contains one of the new unnegated variables and then the same variable negated. Finally, each old literal α_j is grouped with z_{j-1} and $\overline{z}_{j-2}$.

As we'll see, this structure preserves satisfiability. No matter which α_j in the old clause was true in the satisfying assignment, we can choose truth-values for the new variables so that the new clauses also come out true. Conversely, if any set of truth-values for the new variables can satisfy the new clauses, there must have been a satisfying assignment for the old clause as well.

Suppose that the original clause was satisfiable because of some α_j being true. If $j = 1$ or 2, then we can just set all the z_i to **false**, and because they appear negated in all the other clauses, the new conjunction will be satisfiable. If α_j satisfies the original formula with $j > 2$, then we set z_i to **true** for all z_i up to and including $j - 2$, and we set all other values of z_i to **false**. Then the clauses before the clause containing α_j will be satisfied, because each contains a z_i set to **true**, while the clauses after the one containing α_j will be satisfied, because each contains a $\overline{z}_i$ set to **false**. Thus the new set of conjoined clauses is satisfiable if the old one was.

Now suppose some truth-assignment satisfies the new conjoined set; we must show that it also satisfies one of the old clauses α_j. Imagine to the contrary that no α_j is true. Then for the new conjoined clause to be satisfiable, z_1 must be true; since the next clause down the line contains $\overline{z}_1$, α_3, and z_2, the only free choice left in order to make this clause satisfied sets z_2 to **true**. Continuing this reasoning, we have that z_{l-3} must be set to **true**. But then $\overline{z}_{l-3}$ is false and the last clause contains all false values; the conjoined clauses are not satisfiable, a contradiction. Therefore, our initial assumption must be false: some α_j must be true, and the original formula satisfiable.

Cases 1–4 cover all the possibilities. The full transformation, then, consists in grinding through the original clauses of the SAT instance, one by one, and spitting out the transformed 3SAT clauses according to the case analysis. It remains to show that the transformation can be carried out in polynomial time. Let n be the original number of SAT clauses and m the original number of SAT literals. The set of new clauses cannot be larger than some polynomial in $m \cdot n$: by our construction, each clause we process takes at most some polynomial amount of time in m, and there are n such clauses. Therefore, 3SAT is NP-hard; because it is also in $\mathcal{N}\mathcal{P}$, it is NP-complete. $\square$

We'll use 3SAT in reductions involving generalized phrase structure grammar, morphological analysis, lexical-functional grammar, and agreement grammars.

Reducing 3SAT to VERTEX COVER

As a final example of an NP-complete problem that we shall use later on, and one that illustrates how we exploit structural problem similarity, consider the *vertex cover problem* (Garey and Johnson 1979:46). This involves finding a small set of vertices in a graph such that every edge of the graph has an endpoint in the set. We shall discuss this problem in some detail because it shows how a logical problem (3SAT) may be transformed into an essentially topological problem (a graph problem).

More precisely, define a graph (V, E) as a collection of vertices V joined by edges E. A *vertex cover* for (V, E) is a set $V' \subseteq V$ such that for every edge in E, at least one endpoint of the edge is included in V'. The vertex cover problem (VERTEX COVER) is to decide whether (V, E) has a vertex cover of size $\leq k$. Figure 2.4 gives a trivial example that does have a solution.[18]

VERTEX COVER is easily shown to be NP-complete by a polynomial transformation from 3SAT. The construction is instructive because it shows how the global interactions in 3SAT (and SAT generally) may be mirrored structurally by a graph, and so in turn by linguistic formalisms that use graph structures. We shall exploit this global structural interaction in many linguistic problems, for we believe it is precisely the kind of structural interaction that generally is *not* found in natural languages (see chapter 6).

First of all, it is easy to see that the vertex cover problem is in $\mathcal{N}\mathcal{P}$; a nondeterministic TM can guess a subset of vertices as a potential cover and then check in polynomial time whether all edges of the full graph are covered. It remains to show that this problem is NP-hard. To do this,

---

[18]Encoding VERTEX COVER instances as strings is easy; see Hopcroft and Ullman (1979:331).

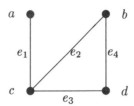

Figure 2.4: This graph illustrates a trivial instance of the vertex cover problem. The set $\{c, d\}$ is a vertex cover of size 2.

we must exhibit the usual answer-preserving polynomial-time transformation from 3SAT instances to VERTEX COVER instances. We shall omit any formal demonstration that the transformation is polynomial time and that the resulting output VERTEX COVER instance has a solution iff the input 3SAT instance is satisfiable; see Garey and Johnson (1979:53–56) for details.

Given a 3SAT problem, the key idea behind the transformation is to build a graph that consists of two parts: (1) a truth-setting component that will allow each encoded literal to get the value **true** or **false**, and (2) a satisfaction component that will require at least one literal in each 3-literal clause to get the value **true**. Finally, we must tie these two graph substructures together to ensure that literals are assigned consistent truth-values.

To see how this works, it is easiest to refer to an example. Suppose we are given the 3SAT formula

$$(u_1 \lor \overline{u}_2 \lor u_4) \land (\overline{u}_1 \lor u_2 \lor \overline{u}_4).$$

Then figures 2.5 through 2.8 show the details of the construction.

Figure 2.5 shows how the corresponding satisfaction component involves a triangular graph for each clause in the original 3SAT problem. There is one vertex for each literal in the clause, and there are three edges joining them.

Next, above these triangles we draw a list of the negated and unnegated variables. They are connected by lines to ensure that if any u_i is given the value **true**, then $\overline{u}_i$ must be given the value **false**. The lines will ultimately produce this constraint because of the scarcity of vertices in a small vertex cover; a line with both endpoints covered uses a larger vertex cover than necessary. In addition, any vertex cover will have to hit either u_i or $\overline{u}_i$ in order to include all edges in the graph; thus these lines ensure that all literals are given truth assignments. Figure 2.6 illustrates.

Finally, we hook up the nodes representing the literals in each clause to their appropriate u_i or $\overline{u}_i$ nodes on the top level. This gives us the final graph G, shown in figure 2.7.

We claim that the original set of clauses is satisfiable if and only if G has a vertex cover of size k or less, where k is the number of variables plus twice the number of clauses. That is, we must select at least one vertex from every coupled pair in the top row—corresponding to setting either u_i or $\overline{u}_i$ **true**. Otherwise, we cannot possibly cover all the graph's edges. Also, we must select at least two vertices from every clause-triple graph, or otherwise we cannot cover the edges in the triangle. Figure 2.8 gives the final construction.

Note that in our example, $k = 3 + 2 \cdot 2 = 7$. The original formula is satisfiable with (for instance) $u_1 = $ **true** and $u_2 = $ **true**, and this corresponds to a vertex cover that includes the vertices u_1 and u_2. We must also freely select either u_4 or $\overline{u}_4$ as true; if so, we make the corresponding vertex part of the cover. In our example, we select $\overline{u}_4$ as true, so it is circled.

Because the original formula was satisfiable, by setting at least one literal in each clause to **true**, we have automatically included at least one of the edges connecting the top row vertices to the two clause triangles. We must now pick at least two more vertices in each clause triangle to cover the remaining edges in each triangle, for a total of seven vertices in all. This we can do by picking the topmost and rightmost vertices of the first clause triangle, and the topmost and leftmost vertices of the second clause triangle. Figure 2.8 shows the covering.

Suppose in contrast that we have a vertex cover V' for G with $|V'| \leq k$. We must show this implies a satisfying assignment for the original 3SAT problem. By the way things are wired up, V' must include least one vertex from each line in the top row of literals in addition to at least two vertices from each clause triangle. Since this gives at least $n + 2m = k$ vertices, which is the maximum we are allowed, V' includes precisely one vertex from each of the literal pairs on the top row and two vertices from each clause graph triple. We can now read off a satisfying assignment by setting the truth assignments to literals according to the vertices in $|V'|$ that are in the top row. That is, we set u_i to **true** if $u_i \in V'$ and u_i to **false** if $\overline{u}_i \in V'$. But this is indeed a satisfying assignment, because each clause gets at least one

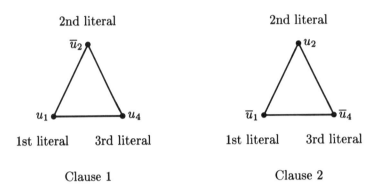

Figure 2.5: Step 1 in the VERTEX COVER reduction from a 3SAT instance represents each 3-literal clause as three vertices connected as a triangle. Each vertex stands for a single literal (unnegated or negated variable) that appears in a clause. The 3SAT formula $(u_1 \vee \overline{u}_2 \vee u_4) \wedge (\overline{u}_1 \vee u_2 \vee \overline{u}_4)$ has two clauses, so there are two triangles.

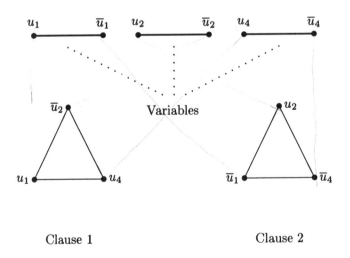

Figure 2.6: Step 2 in the VERTEX COVER reduction from a 3SAT instance adds a row showing all possible literals, linking corresponding unnegated and negated variables. This will eventually ensure that variables are assigned consistent truth-values.

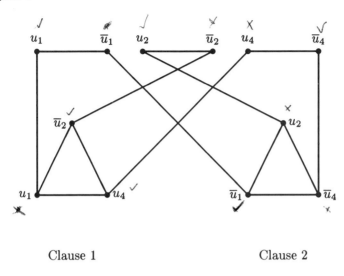

Clause 1   Clause 2

Figure 2.7: Step 3 in the reduction of 3SAT to VERTEX COVER connects each triangle vertex—representing a single literal in a 3SAT clause—to its corresponding mate above. For example, the top vertex in the first triangle corresponds to literal $\overline{u}_2$ in the 3SAT formula, so it is connected to this literal in the top row. This will ultimately guarantee that variable truth assignment consistency is "transmitted" to the literals in each clause. A vertex cover will now automatically correspond to a satisfying truth assignment, as the next figure illustrates.

---

true literal, as the figure shows; it is easy to prove that this must be so (see Garey and Johnson 1979:56).

Plainly the transformation itself takes only polynomial time: to build the graph we can process each clause in turn, merely keeping track of the literals seen so far. (We can do this by running down a list of the distinct variables we have seen.) The size of the graph is polynomially proportional to the input formula size, for the number of edges cannot be greater than the number of distinct variables times the length of the input formula. (Note that this product must be less than the square of the length of the input formula.) Therefore, VERTEX COVER is NP-hard; because it is also in $\mathcal{NP}$, it is NP-complete. $\Box$

VERTEX COVER illustrates the globally interactive character of $\mathcal{NP}$ problems. The connecting lines of the graph may cross over long distances; the graph may not be planar or separable into subparts. This highly inter-twined topology is what we believe to be uncharacteristic of natural language

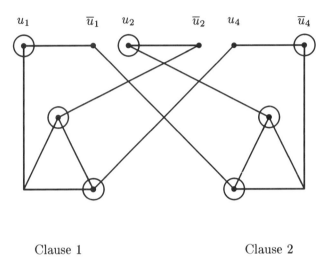

$$u_1 \quad \overline{u}_1 \quad u_2 \quad \overline{u}_2 \quad u_4 \quad \overline{u}_4$$

Clause 1   Clause 2

Figure 2.8: The circled vertices make up a vertex cover for the transformed SAT problem of the example, with $k = 7$. A circled vertex in the top row assigns the value **true** to a literal.

structures, or at the very least, those natural language structures that people process easily.[19] (See chapter 6 for discussion.)

To turn VERTEX COVER into a recognition problem, we can encode the connections of the graph in a restricted sort of grammar. In chapter 7 we exploit this structural similarity to construct a special kind of context-free grammar whose parsing solutions match vertex cover solutions.

2.2.3   A guide to our reductions

By building up our stock of NP-complete problems, we have amassed a toolbox of ready-made problems to use for reductions later on in this book. Figure 2.9 summarizes the complete set of $\mathcal{NP}$ reductions we use in the rest of the book.

In this figure, the arrows indicate polynomial-time problem transformations. We've already shown how SAT may be reduced to 3SAT, and

---

[19] As chapter 3 shows, *general* lexical ambiguity plus agreement can easily give rise to problem structures that are NP-hard.

3SAT to VERTEX COVER. In subsequent chapters, we will reduce SAT or
3SAT to agreement grammar recognition, lexical-functional grammar recognition, two-level morphological generation and recognition, generalized phrase
structure grammar finite closure, and revised GPSG recognition. VERTEX
COVER will be reduced to ID/LP grammar recognition. *All* of these problems are NP-hard and thus computationally intractable.

2.2.4   Beyond $\mathcal{NP}$: other complexity classes

A demonstration that a grammatical problem is NP-hard suffices to show
it is computationally intractable; in some cases we will show that problems
are probably—or even provably—harder still. These results are obtained by
reducing problems that are likely to be even harder than SAT. This section
gives a guide to those reductions, as summarized in figures 2.10 and 2.11.
We briefly review these here; for more complete descriptions, see chapters 5
and 8.

We will use two more complexity classes: first, *PSPACE*, the class of
problems solvable in polynomial *space* on a deterministic TM, and second,
EXP-POLY, the class of problems solvable in deterministic time $O(c^{f(n)})$
for any constant c and polynomial $f(n)$. Note that this last class includes all
exponential time problems, and so includes problems that are *provably* rather
than just *probably* intractable.   Figure 2.10 shows relationships among the
PSPACE-hard problems used in the remainder of the book; figure 2.11 depicts
the *EXP-POLY* reduction.

All problems solvable in polynomial time can be solved in polynomial
space, because a DTM that moves at most a polynomial number of times can
move across at most a polynomial number of tape cells. However, complexity
theorists hypothesize that some problems can be solved in polynomial space
but cannot be solved in polynomial time. Intuitively, polynomial-space computations seem potentially very powerful because space—unlike time—can
be reused. While we've already seen that problems in $\mathcal{NP}$ can be *verified*
in polynomial time, problems in *PSPACE* probably cannot be. (Chapter 8's
more detailed description of the QBF problem, informally presented just below, says more about why *PSPACE* problems seem to be harder than $\mathcal{NP}$
problems.) *EXP-POLY* subsumes both these classes,because it covers all exponential time problems where the exponent is a polynomial. (See Hopcroft
and Ullman (1979) for additional information on complexity hierarchies.)

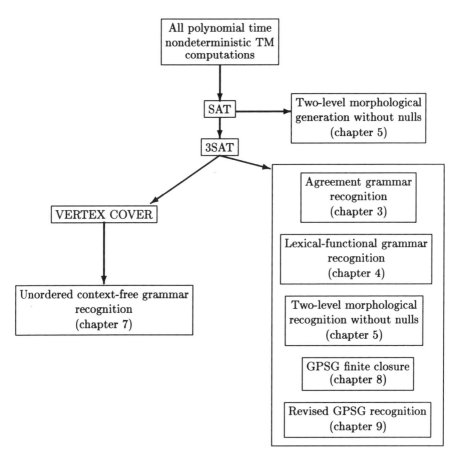

Figure 2.9: Starting from the class of polynomial-time nondeterministic TM computations, the transitivity of polynomial reductions can be used to show that many natural language problems are intractable. The arrows indicate polynomial-time problem transformations, with one right-hand arrow showing that 3SAT can be reduced to five different grammatical problems.

To convey an intuition about the difference between $\mathcal{N}P$ and *PSPACE*, we will briefly describe a key PSPACE-complete problem that we use in chapter 8, known as the quantified Boolean formula (QBF) problem. As its name implies, QBF combines the quantifiers $\exists$ and $\forall$ with Boolean expressions. While the SAT problem asks whether there are any choices for variable truth-values that would make a formula come out true, the QBF problem focuses on formulas in which all the variables are explicitly bound by $\forall$ or $\exists$. There are no free variables to guess values for; instead, the question is whether the formula *is* true when the quantifiers range over the set {**true**, **false**}. $\forall x \exists y (x \vee \overline{y})$ is a true QBF, while $\exists x (x \wedge \overline{x})$ is a false QBF.

QUANTIFIED BOOLEAN FORMULAS (QBF). An instance of QBF is a quantified Boolean formula with no free variables,

$$Q_1 y_1 Q_2 y_2 \ldots Q_m y_m F(y_1, y_2, \ldots, y_m) : Q_i \in \{\forall, \exists\}$$

where we may assume without loss of generality that F is in 3CNF. The question to answer is whether the quantified formula is true.

Note that a QBF instance might allow an arbitrary number of alternating existential and universal quantifiers; intuitively, this is what makes satisfying assignments for QBF so hard even to verify.

Besides QBF, we shall make use of the following PSPACE-complete problem, as stated in Garey and Johnson (1979:266) and originally proven complete by Kozen (1977). We describe it here because it shows how seemingly innocent problems (from the generative capacity viewpoint) can be intractable.

FINITE STATE AUTOMATA INTERSECTION. An instance of the problem is a sequence $A_1, A_2, \ldots, A_n$ of deterministic finite-state automata having the same input alphabet Σ. The question to answer is whether there exists any string $x \in \Sigma^*$ that is accepted by all of the automata.

Many other familiar problems, including games generalized to $n \times n$ boards (checkers, chess) are PSPACE-complete; the reductions exploit the correspondence between game decision trees and QBF quantifier alternations. Alternations between $\exists$ and $\forall$ correspond to alternations between players' moves in the playing of a two-person game.

As one final example of a *PSPACE* problem with some linguistic relevance, we note that context-sensitive language (CSL) membership is also PSPACE-complete:

> Given a context-sensitive grammar $G = \langle N, \Sigma, P, Start \rangle$ and a string $w \in \Sigma^*$, is w in the language generated by G?

This is a somewhat surprising result as it is well known that CSLs take only linear space on a nondeterministic TM. In fact, the membership problem for *deterministic* CSLs is also PSPACE-complete (Garey and Johnson 1979:271).

Figure 2.10, like figure 2.9 above, shows how we exploit these reductions in later chapters.

Figure 2.11 shows the remaining reduction transformation we will use: a mapping from alternating Turing machine computations using polynomial space to generalized phrase structure grammar recognition.

Chapter 8 describes what an alternating Turing machine is. Alternating Turing machines using polynomial space define a complexity class far larger than exponential time: they characterize exactly the exponential-polynomial time problems—that is, problems that take deterministic time $O(c^{f(n)})$ for some constant c and polynomial $f(n)$.

Figure 2.12 summarizes the complexity classes we'll draw on in the rest of the book, along with example problems in each class, and Turing machine resource-bounded definitions for each. One gap in the table remains: so far we know only that GPSG recognition is exponential-polynomial time-hard; we do not know whether it is in this class.

2.3   Compilation and Complexity

We have now covered the formal machinery that succeeding chapters will use to analyze the complexity of grammatical formalisms. However, we have repeatedly stressed that the yardstick provided by complexity theory is only as trustworthy as its fundamental idealizations. Chapter 1 partially justified some of these idealizations: arbitrary problem sizes, universal problem formulations, and serial computer models. With the framework of complexity theory firmly in place, we now return to two important questions about the validity of our analyses. The issue of *grammar preprocessing* that we will discuss in this section is closely linked to our practice of posing grammatical

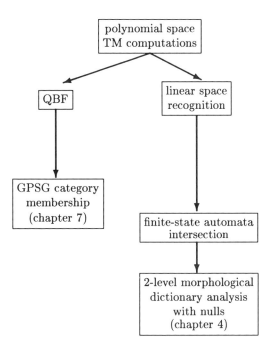

Figure 2.10: This diagram outlines the *PSPACE* reductions used in the rest of the book. The quantified Boolean formula (QBF) and finite-state automata intersection (FSAI) problems are the key problems used. Arrows denote polynomial-time reductions.

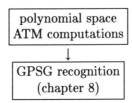

Figure 2.11: The remaining reduction used in the book maps alternating Turing machine (ATM) computations to GPSG recognition problems.

Class	Example problem	Resource bound
$\mathcal{P}$	SORT, context-free language recognition	polynomial time on a deterministic TM
$\mathcal{NP}$	SAT; 3SAT; VERTEX COVER	polynomial time on a nondeterministic TM
PSPACE	Context-sensitive language recognition; finite-state automata intersection; QBF; $n \times n$-board chess (endgame restricted)	polynomial space on a deterministic TM
EXP	Certain transformational language recognition problems	exponential time on a deterministic TM
EXP-POLY	GPSG Recognition?	deterministic time $O(c^{f(n)})$ for some constant c and polynomial $f(n)$

Figure 2.12: This table summarizes major complexity classes and their associated computational problems. The left column names a complexity class used in this book, the middle column gives example problems known to have that complexity, and the right column defines that complexity class as a Turing machine resource bound.

problems as universal rather than fixed-language recognition problems. The issue of *parallel computation* is relevant because of our use of serial computer models, and we will take it up in section 2.4. Both issues raise the same general question: is it possible that either grammar preprocessing or parallel computation will vitiate our complexity results, clouding the promise of insights into natural grammars? Or do our complexity probes give us results that aren't really affected by these possibilities?

At first glance, preprocessing seems to be just the right remedy for our grammatical difficulties. Weak generative capacity results for some computationally troublesome frameworks seem to guarantee that we can convert grammars to a tractable context-free form. It's no surprise that doing the expansion can be a computationally intensive step; thus preprocessing appears to account for the difficulty that the reductions show, while presumably allowing runtime processing to be much easier.

For language acquisition, too, the compilation idea seems promising. A child generally acquires just one adult grammar G and has years to internalize it. Why not reanalyze the computational difficulty of the recognition problem for $\langle G, x \rangle$ so that the difficulty is charged to the compilation of an internal form of G? More specifically, it could be that children apply a computationally intensive compilation function f to produce a revised grammar $G' = f(G)$ such that processing x according to G' is fast both in the length of x and in the size of the original target grammar G. Here, f is a "smart" function that carries out some sort of clever compaction.[20] Plainly, one must exclude obviously degenerate cases: for instance, an adult target grammar that is "padded out" with so many extra symbols as to allow a trivial compaction that would result in fast recognition problems based on the size of the original grammar.

The possibility of grammar preprocessing or compilation might also be linked to the linguistically familiar notion of grammatical succinctness. The very heart and soul of linguistic generalization is the ability to succinctly describe infinite sets of sentence/meaning pairs. On this account, we should *expect* successful grammatical theories to be computationally complex; the whole point of their rule schemas and axiom systems is to compactly express large numbers of "expanded" rules.

We believe that many of these arguments are misleading and none of them affect the validity of our results. In the following sections we discuss

---

[20] We owe this example to S. Weinstein.

fixed vs. universal problems, the feasibility of compilation, the implications of compilation for language acquisition, and the relationship between computational complexity and representational succinctness.

2.3.1   Universal and fixed-language recognition revisited

Grammar preprocessing, often called "compilation" or "preprocessing," lies close to the universal vs. fixed language recognition issue that we discussed in chapter 1. To say that we can preprocess a grammar before we do complexity analysis is to say that we can carry out some computation whose effect might eliminate potential complexity difficulties. After all, that is what a compiler does: it can produce a more efficient program by removing redundant computations, optimizing the use of memory, and so forth. In grammatical terms, we might find some way to expand out grammatical complexities ahead of time so that they are not computed every time a sentence is processed.[21] This possibility relates to the distinction between universal and fixed-language recognition problems as well as to the difference in viewpoint between the study of natural-language grammars and the tradition of weak generative capacity analysis.

First, we observe that a reduction uncovering computational difficulty in the universal formulation does not immediately establish difficulty in the fixed-language formulation. Indeed, this possibility is why compilation suggests itself in response to complexity results. An effective preprocessing procedure might blunt the force of the reduction by concentrating grammar-induced difficulty into the compilation step. However, such benefits follow only if a suitable compilation step is actually available; as we've noted, it's not enough to issue a promissory note. Clever compilation methods are not automatically available, and frequently a compilation step would have to be so powerful that its existence is doubtful (see below).

Second, we argued in chapter 1 that the fixed-language formulation of recognition problems hails from the same tradition as weak generative capacity analysis. Both grant the freedom to choose any grammar or representation that will generate the proper string set. A compilation approach—particularly one that assumes compilation of an unspecified nature—may

---

[21]For example, the construction of an $LR(k)$ parsing table is such a step, though it cannot be applied to all grammars. See Aho and Ullman (1972).

have much the same character; an arbitrary compilation step is free to virtually ignore the input grammar, replacing it with any other representation that will produce the same string language or the same grammatical analyses. Thus a compilation approach may inherit many of the same weaknesses as weak generative capacity analysis: it focuses on languages rather than on the grammars linguistics is interested in, it may fail to study grammatical families as a whole, and so forth (see chapter 1).

But putting aside these possible defects, weak generative capacity analysis may seem to guarantee the freedom to assume that compilation is possible. For instance, if we know that the language generated by a certain formalism is guaranteed to be finite-state, that might seem to guarantee a compilation step that can select an appropriate finite-state machine to use in processing. However, a nonlinguistic example shows one reason that the appeal to arbitrary preprocessing can be too hasty. Consider the question for arbitrary k of whether the infinite decimal expansion of some transcendental number includes at least k instances of the numeral 5. We may have no idea whether the number of fives in the expansion is unlimited or whether only a few or a few thousand exist. But no matter how many fives there are in the expansion, either the answer to our question is always Yes or else it is Yes up to some maximum k followed by No. Either way, the answers are easy to encode in an efficient finite-state machine. Thus, in theory, we know that our question can be compiled into an efficient form—but in practice, we have no idea how the compilation step should work.[22]

This somewhat frivolous example was invented to trip up beginning students of complexity and computability, but it should be remembered whenever an appeal to preprocessing or an "expanded grammar" is justified only on the basis of weak generative capacity. By themselves, weak generative capacity results allow too much cleverness in the compilation step: for instance, a set of strings is context-free if there *exists* a context-free grammar that generates it, regardless of how much cleverness it would take to find such a grammar. Just as in our mathematical example, we might have no idea how the necessary compilation step should work. It is an equally serious problem in practical terms if the compilation step is possible, but produces an expanded grammar of wildly unmanageable size (see chapter 8). As we'll see below, huge grammars are generally not tractable even if context-free.

---

[22] The requirement of *uniformity* helps rule out a generalization of this kind of pathology in parallel computer circuitry; see section 2.4.

2.3.2   Is compilation possible?

The problem with the preprocessing assumption comes down to this: preprocessing may be impossible, may sometimes be unprofitable, and—worse still—for the grammatical systems we study in this book, it has never been demonstrated. It remains a promissory note—perhaps possible, but unrealized.

Perhaps by their very nature, preprocessing proposals almost always suggest some way of "expanding out" rule schemas or grammatical constraints in advance of sentence processing. This does not seem to work very well in practice, and we should see why.

Compilation can slow down parsing

First of all, the process of expanding out rule schemas does not always produce a compiled grammar that supports rapid parsing. To take a simple example from chapter 7, consider a set-based rule scheme that might be advanced as a model for a free-word-order language of five-word sentences, where any permutation of the words a, b, c, d, and e is a possible sentence. This hypothetical language is finite.

One classic model for this kind of language looks like this. Replace the usual ordered context-free rule with a rule that has a multiset on its right-hand side:[23]

$$S \rightarrow \{a, b, c, d, e\}$$

This means that any possible permutation of elements is permitted in a derivation from S. An obvious compilation step for these grammars just writes out an expanded, equivalent context-free grammar rule set: $S \rightarrow abcde$, S→ *bacde*, and so forth. It uses the Earley algorithm—an ordinary context-free parsing algorithm—on the expanded grammar. Unfortunately, as chapter 7 shows, the expanded grammar has many more rules and parsing actually *slows down*, precisely because grammar size enters as a multiplicative factor into parsing algorithms.[24]

---

[23]See Chomsky (1965:124) discussing such a system proposed in the early 1960s; this approach is further described in chapter 7.

[24]Some classes of grammars allow parsing methods that are little affected by grammar size. The $LR(k)$ grammars are one example; see Aho and Ullman (1972). However, these restricted classes of grammars are generally incapable of dealing with lexical ambiguity and other features of natural languages.

For this very reason, straightforward compilation by rule expansion falls short in other cases as well. Chapter 8 shows how this happens with generalized phrase structure grammars (GPSGs). GPSG theory specifies grammars whose languages are only context-free. Since context-free grammars of reasonable size are computationally tractable, this weak generative capacity argument has been invoked as part of an explanation of efficient human sentence processing (see section 7.9).

But a closer look shows that this explanation rings hollow. *Nothing in the formal framework of GPSG guarantees that the standard context-free parsing algorithms will work efficiently with a GPSG grammar.* To use a standard algorithm, we must first convert our GPSG grammar G into an equivalent context-free grammar G'; this is our compilation step. As chapter 8 shows, in the worst case, this compilation step creates a grammar much, much larger than the original.[25]

In fact, if we use the Earley algorithm once more, in terms of our *original* grammar G our supposedly swift parsing algorithm may now run in time

$$O(3^{m^m} \cdot n^3)$$

where n is the number of words in the input sentence and m is the size of the original grammar. For grammars of linguistically relevant size—where, say, $|G|$ is 50—this will be very slow indeed. If our goal was a guarantee of speedy execution time, an algorithm that can take as long as $3^{50^{50}} \cdot n^3$ steps falls short. Appendix B argues that this is not just idle mathematical speculation, but describes what would happen if "real" GPSG grammars were expanded into true context-free form.

Compilation is sometimes impossible

More generally, in some cases compilation may be unable *in principle* to win efficiency. For example, suppose we have a parsing problem that provably requires $2^{|G|} \cdot n^3$ steps for solution (where n is the input sentence length and $|G|$ is the grammar size, as usual). If we are willing to spend, say, $10 \cdot 2^{|G|}$ steps to compile the grammar in some clever way, can we reduce parsing-phase complexity to something less than exponential, such as $|G|^8 \cdot n^3$ steps? The answer is No. Because by hypothesis it takes at least $2^{|G|} \cdot n^3$ steps to

---

[25]For details of the particular version of GPSG assumed in this result, see chapter 8, though in fact similar blowup occurs for all versions of GPSG that we know of.

solve the problem, there must be at least $(2^{|G|} \cdot n^3 - 10 \cdot 2^{|G|})$ steps left to perform after compilation. Since compilation processes just the grammar, the sentence length parameter n is necessarily absent from the compilation complexity, hence the term $2^{|G|} \cdot n^3$ will eventually dominate.

In other cases, the details of a reduction may show that a compilation step would have to be extremely powerful—so powerful as to argue against the possibility of compilation. A reduction in chapter 8 shows how to construct a GPSG that simulates alternating Turing machine computations that proceed within a polynomial space bound. The construction can be varied in ways that make an effective compilation step quite difficult. The constructed GPSG accepts all machine inputs up to a fixed size, and each can take an exponential-polynomial amount of time to process. The inputs and the grammar could be intertwined within the construction to further complicate grammar-preprocessing methods; $L(G)$ could also be enlarged to "hide" the space bound from the compilation function, thus preventing simple compilation steps based on boundedness. (See page 253 for more discussion.)

A formal model of compilation

Compilation has a broader interest in complexity theory, and hence we will briefly pursue a more formal approach to the possibility of compilation. Let T be a problem with instances of the form $\langle a_1, \ldots, a_n \rangle$. We want a compilation of T to preprocess some of the arguments of the original problem into constants of some kind that can be wired into the runtime problem defined by the remaining arguments. In the linguistic case, compilation would process our grammar G into some more efficient G'. Formally, a k-compilation of T, written $T^k(a_1, \ldots, a_k)$, is a new and algorithmically constructible problem whose instances are $(n-k)$-tuples $\langle a_{k+1}, \ldots, a_n \rangle$, such that

$$\langle a_{k+1}, \ldots, a_n \rangle \in T^k(a_1, \ldots, a_k)$$
$$\text{iff} \quad \langle a_1, \ldots, a_k, a_{k+1}, \ldots, a_n \rangle \in T$$

In effect, this requirement on the output of the compilation says that T^k must be faithful in the process of wiring a_1 through a_k into the new problem.

So far, we haven't said anything that requires the "compiled" problem $T^k(a_1, \ldots, a_k)$ to do anything more than save away a_1 through a_k and supply them to the original problem T whenever a runtime problem $\langle a_{k+1}, \ldots, a_n \rangle$ comes along. Naturally, we want compilation to do better than that. Let's say the runtime argument size is $z = |\langle a_{k+1}, \ldots, a_n \rangle|$ and the compiled-in argument size is $y = |\langle a_1, \ldots, a_k \rangle|$. Our original problem is solvable in some time (space, *etc.*) $F_1(|\langle a_1, \ldots, a_n \rangle|) = F_1(y + z)$. Similarly, the compiled problem can be solved with some resource bound F_2. We might write this as $F_2(|\langle a_{k+1}, \ldots, a_n \rangle|) = F_2(z)$, but F_2 will actually depend on the "wired-in" arguments as well, so we write it as $F_2(y, z)$. Now that we have the necessary notation, we can say that our k-compilation is *efficient* iff $F_2(y, z) \ll F_1(y + z)$.[26] In other words, the compilation is efficient if we are much better off using the compiled problem (regardless of how long the compilation process itself takes).

To sharpen these computational issues, we will consider the following two 1-compilations, one efficient and the other inefficient.

A *clique* C in a graph G is a complete subgraph of G. That is, each vertex in C must be directly connected to every other vertex in C. CLIQUE, the clique problem, is: Given a problem instance $\langle G, k \rangle$, does the graph G contain a clique of size k? A 1-compilation of CLIQUE, written $\text{CLIQUE}^1(G)$, is: Given an integer k, is k in the finite set of all integers j such that G has a clique of size j? While CLIQUE is NP-complete, $\text{CLIQUE}^1(G)$ may be solved in linear time (*i.e.*, the time needed to read k). The compilation step consists of simply computing and storing away all possible clique sizes j for $1 \leq j \leq |G|$. $\text{CLIQUE}^1(G)$ is fast because the size of G does not affect the problem's running time. Many other similar NP-complete problems have efficient 1-compilations; see for example the vertex cover problem that was described in section 2.2.

Compilation can be inefficient, however. In chapter 7 we analyze a generalization of context-free grammars, called unordered context-free grammars (UCFGs), to formalize the permutation-type rules we described earlier. For example, the UCFG rule $S \rightarrow \{NP, VP\}$ corresponds to the two ordinary context-free productions $S \rightarrow NP \; VP$ and $S \rightarrow VP \; NP$. As we mentioned at the end of chapter 1, a UCFG specifies merely the *immediate dominance* relationships that hold between the elements on the left-hand and right-hand sides. Our example rule says only that S dominates NP and VP; it does not

---

[26]If linguistic theory is concerned with the form of linguistic knowledge, the grammar G' that is produced during compilation is as interesting as the original G; presumably the only legal grammars in either case are those licensed by linguistic theory. Note that it is quite proper to measure the cost of compiled grammar-recognition in terms of $|G|$ rather than $|G'|$. If the cost were measured using $|G'|$ (in addition to $|x|$, of course) then any compilation step that simply appends a large number of useless symbols to G would seem to speed up the recognition problem.

order *NP* and *VP* with respect to each other, as the ordinary context-free rule $S \rightarrow NP\ VP$ would.

Chapter 7 defines the UCFG recognition problem as follows: Given a string x and a UCFG G, is $x \in L(G)$? This problem is *NP*-complete. Now let us recast the process of expanding G into context-free form as a 1-compilation. Then our compiled problem $T^1(G)$ is to determine if $x \in L(G')$ where G' is the strongly equivalent context-free grammar that is constructed from G by expanding out all admissible linear sequences. Because G could admit approximately $|G|!$ such sequences, G' may be more than exponentially larger than G. If we use the Earley algorithm, we can solve $T^1(G)$ in time $F_2(|G|, |x|) = O((|G|!)^2 \cdot |x|^3) = O(|G|^{2 \cdot |G|} \cdot |x|^3)$; some other general CFG parsing algorithms would do slightly better. While $T \in \mathcal{NP}$, T^1 can take more than exponential time. As we saw earlier in an informal way, the proposed 1-compilation is inefficient (even if $\mathcal{P} = \mathcal{NP}$).

In general, a similar situation holds for the grammatical systems we study later on in this book: there are no preprocessing or compilation steps that are known to be effective, and preprocessing may sometimes be ineffective in principle.

2.3.3   Preprocessing and language acquisition

We now turn to the language acquisition side of the preprocessing account. It makes some sense to say a person uses a fixed grammar to process sentences, and hence that this grammar might in principle be "compiled" into an efficient form. However, subtleties remain.

First, one must acquire the target grammar somehow. Most language acquisition algorithms presume that the child fixes an adult target grammar by encountering sentences from that target, one by one, and then altering its internalized grammar to match. For the learner the grammar is not fixed but changing.

In the simplest acquisition model, this means the learner may conjecture a grammar at one point, only to throw it away and use another when some sentence comes along that cannot be handled. If this is so, then it makes little sense to go through the possibly expensive process of grammar compilation at each point; it's worth spending time compiling the final grammar, but not discarded conjectures. Practically, this is often so; for example, one kind of grammar compilation that builds so-called deterministic *LR* parsers constructs efficient parsing tables in a time-consuming preprocessing stage. But if one adds a single rule to the original grammar, the entire preprocessing step must be repeated.

Still, the learner must be able to process input sentences quickly, if only to discover where a current conjecture fails. Therefore, the learner's fast processing must apply to sentences of any grammar in the class of accessible grammars—a universal problem that tacitly assumes no time-consuming preprocessing.

Even so, such a model could still allow incremental compilation if the acquisition hypotheses themselves formed a class amenable to preprocessing; we might also assume that the learner has plenty of time to acquire language, relative to the number of hypotheses to entertain. For example, this is true for the acquisition model proposed by Berwick (1985): at each acquisition step one new rule may be acquired, and this is placed into the rule database after merger with any existing rules of the same type. At each stage the system maintains a highly efficient, deterministic parser. However, in this approach, each member of the target family is itself computationally tractable. It is not clear whether the same approach would work for computationally intractable grammatical families. The only other well-worked-out acquisition example we know of, for lexical-functional grammar, contains no such preprocessing or incremental compilation steps (Pinker 1984); though it does merge common lexical entries, it does nothing to eliminate the NP-hardness of the lexical-function system itself.[27]

Even if there is preprocessing during language acquisition, our complexity analysis is still useful. In this case, complexity analysis can still pinpoint what *kind* of preprocessing would have to be carried out during language acquisition. Thus, it could tell us something about the performance aspects of language acquisition that rounds out our understanding of what it means to be a natural grammar.

---

[27]Note that we are not talking about whether acquisition itself is difficult or easy; a finite family of languages may be easy to learn even if the languages are not even recursively enumerable. Rather, we want to know whether incremental compilation or preprocessing is possible in such cases.

2.3.4   Complexity theory and representational succinctness

The final preprocessing issue that we take up here concerns the relationship between computational difficulty and representational succinctness. Succinctness affects the possibility of preprocessing because expressive economy can make one particular preprocessing approach impractical: specifically, the preprocessing step of producing an "expanded grammar" in some less compact but easier-to-process form. Though succinctness and complexity are often related in practice, they do not always go hand in hand—simply because the two notions are mathematically distinct.[28]

Informally, succinctness of some kind tends to be a necessary condition for computational difficulty. For example, the NP-completeness proof for UCFG recognition (chapter 7) relies on the fact that a single UCFG rule of the form $X \rightarrow A_1 \ldots A_n$ can match $n!$ different orderings of the A_i, corresponding to $n!$ different rules in the standard CFG framework. In the proof, this provides a crucial part of the "guessing ability" that is needed to solve the vertex cover problem. A reduction using standard CFGs instead of UCFGs would fail because the constructed CFG would be more than polynomially larger than the vertex cover instance. In fact, the "suspiciously powerful" representational economy of ID/LP grammars was our original reason for suspecting that UCFG recognition might be difficult.

Misled by this apparent connection between succinctness and computational difficulty, some have concluded that our complexity results for GPSG are no more than trivial consequences of GPSG's well-known ability to encode vast numbers of rules in compact form. In this view, we have created the apparent complexity of UCFG recognition and other problems through inappropriate definitions—in particular, by measuring complexity in terms of GPSG size rather "expanded object grammar" size. Far from discovering significant results, we have simply portrayed GPSG's advantages as difficulties—deviously miscasting "expressive economy as procedural profligacy," in Pullum's (1985) words.

It is certainly possible to introduce spurious complexity through bad definitions. For instance, CFG parsing becomes exponential in sentence length if we are required to print all parses rather than only one, just because a

---

[28]There is a complexity theory based on succinctness, namely Kolmogorov (1965) complexity, but its results do not connect directly to those computational complexity classifications we use here.

sentence may have exponentially many parses. Nonetheless, our definitions are not at fault. As we noted in chapter 1, our formulation of recognition problems is quite standard in the complexity literature—and for good reason. But beyond the question of what is standard practice, we can easily explain why our complexity results are more than the simple consequences of bad definitions.

The key observation is that—had matters been somewhat different—the succinctness of the GPSG framework would *not* have resulted in computational difficulty. For instance, suppose UCFGs are restricted to have *terminal symbols only* on the right-hand sides of unordered rules (ordered rules might be permitted as well). Under the restriction to terminal-symbol UCFGs, representational succinctness remains; a UCFG rule with k elements on its right-hand side will still correspond to $k!$ standard CFG rules. Computational difficulty, however, vanishes—which would obviously be an impossible situation, if the difficulty of unrestricted UCFG recognition resulted solely from succinctness or from our formulation of the recognition problem.

Putting the same point another way, there exist problems for which a change in representation really does help—for which succinctness carries over into a processing advantage. Chapter 7 contains some concrete examples, continually stressing the point that direct parsing of an ID/LP grammar often wins out over parsing the corresponding expanded CFG. Therefore, computational difficulty can't be automatically built into the problem through our definitions. Instead, whatever difficulty is uncovered represents a true property of the problem.

Closely related to this issue is the distinction between *problem complexity* and *algorithm complexity*, which we have been at pains to stress. The complexity of a *problem* is its *inherent complexity*, measuring how much of a computational resource is required to solve it with the best possible algorithm—regardless of whether anyone has discovered that algorithm. We can easily be misled by confusing this with the complexity of a *particular algorithm* for solving a problem. For instance, if we process terminal-symbol UCFGs (defined above) by the particular method of converting them to CFGs and using the Earley parser, this confusion would lead us to believe that terminal-symbol UCFG recognition is exponential in grammar size. Yet the actual problem is much easier.

Similarly, in the case of GPSG, we must not draw conclusions about problem complexity *simply* by noticing that a small GPSG may correspond to a huge number of CFG rules. Given this succinctness advantage, we know immediately that one particular algorithm will be computationally intractable: namely, the algorithm that consists of producing an expanded CFG and parsing it with the Earley algorithm. However, we have no assurance that this is the *best* algorithm, and consequently we cannot know from this fact alone that the *problem* of GPSG recognition will be difficult.

Thus, we see that representational succinctness does not automatically result in computational difficulty. If it turns out that the processing problem for an expressively efficient formalism is NP-complete—thus suggesting that the formalism in effect forces expansion into a less compact form—then that tells us something significant about the formalism.

This discussion suffices to show that succinctness and computational complexity do not always coincide; we have mentioned the possibilities [+succinct, +difficult] and [+succinct, −difficult]. The conceptual separation of the two notions is reinforced by the fact that the other two possibilities are also instantiated. A list of random numbers is neither succinctly encoded nor difficult to process ([−succinct, −difficult]). A very large Turing machine designed to solve a difficult number-theoretic question with at most one answer can serve as an example of a representation that is [−succinct, +difficult].

It is also interesting to consider what happens when we convert CFL recognition problems (known to be polynomial-time) into context-sensitive language recognition problems (known to be PSPACE-complete in general and hence very likely intractable). Depending on circumstances, this can significantly *speed up* recognition if the conversion decreases the size of the context-free grammar sufficiently. For example, experience with the context-sensitive NYU grammar (Hobbs 1974) demonstrated that its equivalent context-free grammar would be several orders of magnitude larger, and hence run much more slowly. (Berwick and Weinberg (1984) discuss this matter as well.)

Finally, we note briefly that no formalism can represent every CFG compactly (by counting arguments). In general, this leaves open the possibility that the class of grammars that a formalism *can* represent succinctly will comprise only a family of uninteresting grammars that can't encode any difficult problems despite their size—thus driving a wedge between succinctness and complexity once again.

In fact, it is possible to set up an artificial formalism in such a way that its meaning depends on complexity properties: if the language defined would be hard to parse, invoke a clause in the definition of the formalism that switches the defined language to something easier. Given this way of defining things, exponential compression could still be possible in cases where the CFG representation is "unnecessarily stupid," as with our *abcde*-permutation language, but because of the representational escape clause it would be impossible to use the compression to drive a reduction.[29]

2.4 Parallel Computation and Complexity Theory

Our complexity analysis uses a serial computer to measure computational resources. We've seen that variation in serial computer models makes little difference, since NP-hard problems remain so on all reasonable serial computer models, as do problems in $\mathcal{P}$. This invariance holds even more strongly for *PSPACE*, *EXP*, and the problems and complexity classes beyond these.

But what happens if we use a parallel computer instead? Chapter 1 touched briefly on this important issue, and in this section we probe more deeply into its implications. To repeat chapter 1's bottom line, our intractability results still hold; grammatical problems that are NP-hard or worse remain intractable using parallel computer models.

Still, it's worthwhile investigating what problems would be solvable more quickly on parallel computers, if only to see what insight it gives us into computational intractability. We think there's much to be gained by this approach; near the end of this section we can even speculate a little about what grammatical theories would fit together well with parallel computation.

Cook (1980, 1981) surveys major complexity theory results for parallel computers, and we follow his taxonomy. There are two top level choices: In *synchronous* parallel computation, some global executive coordinates the moves of the various processors; in *asynchronous* parallel computation, independent processors compete for common resources. Among the synchronous parallel models, the most commonly studied type, we can assume either fixed

---

[29]As an example, take the ID/LP formalism as it stands but change the definition of the language generated: say that an input of length n is accepted by G just in case the Shieber parser (chapter 7) accepts n according to G within $|G|^2 \cdot n^3$ steps. Then exponential compression will still be possible in some easy cases, but a reduction will be impossible unless $\mathcal{P} = \mathcal{NP}$.

storage structure models (like Turing machines) or self-modifying models (like random access machines).

The fundamental and absolute limit on parallel speedup is governed by the following inequality, which we gave earlier in chapter 1:

Serial time $\leq$ parallel time $\times$ # of parallel processors

This equation holds because it is always possible for a serial computer to simulate a parallel one, one processor at a time. As we mentioned in chapter 1, this inequality also tells us that an NP-hard problem could require an exponential number of parallel processors for its solution—too many to actually build except for very small problems.

2.4.1   The circuit model of parallel computation

That settles one basic question, but to get more refined results, complexity theorists have developed a range of parallel computer models that let them study time and space resource tradeoffs, what counts as a "feasible" parallel computer model, and superfast parallel computations. We'll look at these topics by presenting just one type of parallel computer model here: the so-called circuit model. The circuit model seems to be a particularly apt choice because it's relatively straightforward to understand whether a circuit is physically realizable or not. Further, circuit models have an interesting, robust, mathematical foundation and have led to a variety of intriguing results relating serial and parallel computing resources—as well as a better understanding of problems that have superfast parallel solutions versus those that do not. Johnson (1986:290–291) gives a useful introduction to circuit complexity:

> When theoreticians speak of "circuit complexity" they normally refer to feedback-free ("combinational") circuits in which the circuit elements are 2-input "∧" gates, 2-input "∨" gates, and 1-input "¬" gates, and where arbitrary fan-out is allowed from each gate (as well as from each input). The *size* of such a circuit is the number of circuit elements it contains. The *circuit complexity* $c(f)$ of a Boolean function f is the size of the smallest circuit that computes f.

The idea is that the circuit looks like a directed, acyclic graph: we apply the inputs to one end, the circuit does its work, and the answer appears at certain other output nodes. Circuit size measures the amount of hardware needed to actually build a circuit—an appealing and natural measure. Circuit *size* represents the number of basic operations that must be performed in a computation, and therefore is closely linked to sequential time.

The other natural circuit complexity measure is the shortest distance from input to output—its *depth*. Depth is a proxy for parallel time, since it will tell us how long it takes for an answer to appear.

The same questions of invariance arise here as with sequential machines. The circuit model is a good one because *size* and *depth* seem to be relatively invariant for a wide range of parallel computer models (Cook 1983).

A second issue leads back to the question of input invariance. Because a circuit computes only a single-sized problem, we must actually use a *family* of circuits to compute a family of fixed-size problems T_n, where n denotes the length of the problem instance. Then we can define the circuit complexity of the general problem T by making it a function of n just as before; in this case the function $c(T_n)$ stands for the circuit complexity of the family. As Johnson observes, it is easy to show that membership in $\mathcal{P}$ implies polynomial circuit size, but the converse is false; even undecidable problems can have polynomial circuit complexity. This possibility arises because the program that builds the circuits may be arbitrarily powerful. (Consider an undecidable language L, where for each n either no strings of length n or all strings of length n are in L. The corresponding circuit T_n is trivial, since it is either a Boolean 0 or 1, but all the work must go into figuring out which circuit to construct at each step.)

To sidestep this apparent anomaly, we must ensure that circuit construction is not too powerful. One approach is to require circuits to be "uniformly constructible" in the sense that once we have built the circuit for a problem of size n, building the next size circuit $n+1$ does not entail much more work. Given this caveat,[30]

> [the class of] problems that have polynomial circuit complexity is immune to "reasonable" changes in the set of allowable circuits. For instance, we might limit fan-out to two outputs, or replace

---

[30]Ruzzo (1981) considers several definitions for uniformity and demonstrates that circuit complexity is relatively insensitive to most of them; however, in some cases the choice does matter.

the $\wedge$, $\vee$, and $\neg$ gates by some other finite complete basis for Boolean logic. (Johnson 1986:291)

Some of these modifications make physical and computational sense; see Johnson (1986) for a recent update.

With this background, we can summarize some relevant results for circuit models. We will first consider what happens if we look at parallel time and space independently; then we will consider what happens if time and space are varied jointly, trading off one for the other.

Pratt and Stockmeyer's (1976) parallel computation thesis, which was extensively studied by Goldschlager (1978) for a large class of parallel machines, links serial space to parallel time: a polynomial-space-bounded DTM using unlimited *time* can solve exactly the same problems as a polynomial-time-bounded parallel machine using an unlimited number of *processors*.

Using uniformly constructible circuits, we can also link serial time and parallel space, on the one hand, and serial space and parallel time, on the other (Ruzzo 1981):

$$DTIME(T) \subseteq \text{uniform size } (T \log T) \subseteq DTIME(T \log^3 T)$$
$$NSPACE(S) \subseteq \text{uniform depth } (S^2) \subseteq DSPACE(S^2).$$

What do these results imply for complexity theory? As Perrault (1984:166) observes following Cook's (1981) review, algorithms with sequential solutions that have small space demands—such as deterministic context-sensitive language recognition—will have polynomial parallel time solutions, although they may require an unbounded number of processors. Thus, these parallel implementations are probably *not* feasible. The resulting circuit size is presumably large (recall the parallel speedup inequality above); indeed, we'll see below that many problems are not likely to admit fast speedup with polynomially many parallel processors. The implications for natural language analysis remain murky.

To get a grip on more reasonably sized circuits, other theorists have defined classes that simultaneously bound circuit size and depth, and we'll examine one here. (There is still some debate even here as to how "feasible" these models are, as we shall see.)

2.4.2 The circuit-complexity class $\mathcal{NC}$

Ruzzo (1981) examines the class $\mathcal{NC}$ of functions computable by uniform circuits of polynomial size *and* $c \cdot \log^k n$ depth ("polynomial logarithmic," or poly-log circuits), first defined by Nick Pippenger (1979).[31] Because this depth is so shallow, it implies a superfast parallel computation; since it uses only a polynomial number of gates, it's supposed to be physically realizable.

$\mathcal{NC}$ has other attractive properties, as Ruzzo (1981:366-367) goes on to observe:[32]

> There are several reasons for interest in $\mathcal{NC}$. First, this class seems to encompass the functions for which dramatic speedups are possible on feasible constructible parallel machines. Second, poly-log time may not be achievable in some applications, say, due to machine architecture or I/O bottlenecks. However, the existence of such rapid parallel algorithms for these problems implies that they are somehow decomposable into a large number of nearly independent subproblems .... Third, some problems of great practical importance are known to be in $\mathcal{NC}$.

$\mathcal{NC}$ is known to be a subset of $\mathcal{P}$ (Pippenger 1979); informally, deterministic, serial polynomial time gives us enough time to simulate the polynomial-sized circuit, one gate at a time. Problems in $\mathcal{NC}$ include sorting, graph connectivity, 2SAT, computing matrix determinants, and context-free language recognition.[33]

However, it is unlikely that $\mathcal{NC} = \mathcal{P}$, because this would imply that all deterministic polynomial-time problems could be solved in poly-logarithmic space—a surprise that would be almost as great as if $\mathcal{P} = \mathcal{NP}$. Thus, if

---

[31] Hence the abbreviation, for "Nick's Class."

[32] On the other hand, there is some reason to doubt the significance of $\mathcal{NC}$ as an interesting class. One way to think of $\mathcal{NC}$ is as a resource tradeoff class: if time is very expensive, and processors cheap, then it makes sense to look at problems in $\mathcal{NC}$. But, as mentioned, the polynomial-size circuits for $\mathcal{NC}$ problems are typically so huge that they are perhaps not so physically realizable as the Ruzzo quote indicates. Taking a look at our limiting serial–parallel equation, we note that because $\mathcal{NC}$ uses many parallel processors and only logarithmic parallel time, it really doesn't squeeze out the maximum possible gain that could be wrung from a parallel machine. To say that $\mathcal{NC}$ defines the class of problems that can be sped up by parallelism may not be saying enough.

[33] Ruzzo (1981:380) indicates that a depth $O(\log^2 n)$ Boolean circuit of size $O(n^6)$ can recognize context-free languages and notes that the circuit is still too large to be of any practical significance.

we use logarithmic space reductions to show that a problem is complete for polynomial time (P-complete), then some theorists have suggested that we've essentially shown that it does not admit a superfast parallel solution (unless $\mathcal{N}C = P$, a highly unlikely result).

In particular, the universal context-free *parsing* problem is P-complete (Jones and Laaser 1976) and therefore is unlikely to have a superfast parallel solution. The crucial difference between context-free language recognition and the corresponding universal parsing problem hinges once again on grammar preprocessing: Jones and Laaser observe that in order to get fast recognition for any context-free language, we must pick a fast grammar. This can be difficult, because some grammars can be extremely slow.[34]

Thus, the hypothesis that $\mathcal{N}C \neq P$ can be used to show that some problems aren't likely to admit superfast speedup via polynomial parallel processors. Examples include universal context-free parsing and relaxed constraint labeling; for example, constraint propagation as described by Waltz (see chapter 6) probably won't admit this kind of parallel speedup in general (Kasif 1986).

Still, controversy remains. Even if a problem is not in $\mathcal{N}C$, it may still be amenable to parallel speedup. For example, the problem of finding the maximum flow through a network can be sped up by a linear amount with feasible parallel processing, even though it can't be done using the supershallow circuits $\mathcal{N}C$ demands (Leiserson, personal communication). Similarly, the parallel context-free recognizer of Kosaraju (1975) enjoys a significant time speedup over serial algorithms, with no "wasted" time or processor resources.

We will not attempt to resolve this ongoing controversy here. Instead, we'll simply start with the observation that problems in $\mathcal{N}C$ do in general lend themselves to fast parallel circuit solution. In the next section we speculate that this fact may have linguistic relevance.

---

[34]Converting a slow grammar into a fast, weakly equivalent one can take too long in some cases. For example, eliminating null transitions or converting to Chomsky normal form can significantly expand the grammar size. Whether this grammar expansion occurs in linguistically relevant cases is another story, of course; appendix B gives some indications of what can happen with generalized phrase structure grammars.

2.4.3 Modularity and parallelism

Many of the graph problems in $\mathcal{NC}$ share an important property: their graphs are highly modular or *separable*. Intuitively, the easier it is to divide a graph into distinct and roughly equal pieces, the easier it is to use more efficient divide-and-conquer algorithms instead of combinatorial backtracking (see Aho, Hopcroft, and Ullman 1974). Intuitively, a graph's *separability* tells us how many vertices we have to remove in order to obtain two roughly equal sets of nodes with no connections between them. For example, trees are highly separable; by removing a single vertex we can divide any n-vertex tree into two parts, each with no more than $2n/3$ vertices. Therefore, we would expect divide-and-conquer methods to be especially efficient on tree structures.[35] Divide-and-conquer algorithms divide the original problem into two or more smaller problems. The subproblems are then solved by applying the divide-and-conquer algorithm recursively; the solutions to the subproblems are then combined to form the solution to the original problem. Divide-and-conquer methods work best when the subproblems are significantly smaller than the original problem.

Similarly, certain separable 3SAT problems can be solved more quickly than general 3SAT problems, though the algorithms still take exponential time. In recent work, Kasif, Reif, and Sherlekar (1986) show that planar 3SAT problems—roughly, the class of 3SAT problems representable in a plane so that truth assignments don't cross—can be solved in serial time $O(2^{c\sqrt{n}})$ by a divide-and-conquer algorithm. This is still not polynomial time, but is much better than "brute force" backtracking with its $O(2^n)$ complexity. (On a parallel random access machine, they show this approach takes time $O(\log^3 n)$ using $O(n^2 \cdot 2^{O(\sqrt{n})})$ processors.)

---

[35]Lipton and Tarjan (1979) examine more general conditions under which divide-and-conquer methods are efficient for graph problems. They prove that any n-vertex *planar* graph can be divided into components of roughly equal size by removing only $O(\sqrt{n})$ vertices. Formally, let S be a class of graphs closed under the subgraph relation (that is, if $G_1 \in S$ and G_2 is a subgraph of G_1, then $G_2 \in S$). S has an *f(n)-separator theorem* if there exist constants $\alpha < 1$ and $\beta > 1$ such that for any n-vertex graph G in S, the vertices of G can be partitioned into three sets A, B, C with no edge joining a vertex in A with a vertex in B, with neither A nor B containing more than αn vertices, and with C containing no more than $\beta f(n)$ vertices. Lipton and Tarjan prove that planar graphs have an $2\sqrt{2}\sqrt{n}$-separator with $\alpha = 2/3$. They also provide an $O(n)$ time algorithm for obtaining the separator. Lipton and Tarjan (1980) go on to describe how this separator theorem for planar graphs leads to efficient algorithms for many planar graph problems.

When the modularity of a 3SAT problem is even stronger, so that we can split a graphical 3SAT representation into two roughly equal pieces by removing only a *constant* number of vertices, then we can do even better: these problems are in $\mathcal{NC}$ and so can be solved by superfast parallel algorithms (Kasif, Reif, and Sherlekar 1986).

These examples may be linguistically relevant. Chapter 6 develops an account of morphological analysis that relies on the algorithm known as constraint propagation. Constraint propagation is usually fast, but it can compute only local satisfiability constraints based on consistency between adjacent elements, not the global consistency and satisfaction properties reflected in SAT or VERTEX COVER.

What is more interesting, however, is that while constraint propagation cannot always give correct answers to NP-hard problems of the sort that certain morphological or agreement frameworks may provide (see chapter 6), it *does* appear to solve rapidly the modular problems that arise in natural morphological systems—at least for the examples described in chapter 6. In this respect, it corresponds more closely to natural grammatical systems than to morphological frameworks that are NP-hard or worse. We speculate that the separable character of natural morphological systems may yield this result. For example, one current line of phonological research known as *autosegmental theory* favors highly separable feature analyses; given our speculations, such grammatical systems may be more amenable to nonbacktracking and fast parallel algorithms than the two-level morphological system described in chapter 5.

To summarize, graph separability may provide a formalization for the notion of problem modularity that leads directly to efficient parallel algorithms. If this speculation is on the right track, then modular grammatical representations—whose components are separable in this way—may have precisely the right sort of structural characteristics for efficient parallel processing. If correct, such a view would direct us away from monostratal grammatical systems that attempt to characterize sentences at a single level of constraint and toward separable constraint systems such as ID/LP grammars (chapter 7), the constraint modules of government-binding theory, or autosegmental theory in phonology. However, as chapter 6 notes, not every kind of modularity supports modular processing; thus it is not an immediate result that separable constraint systems of this sort have significant advantages for parallel processing.

2.4.4 New areas of complexity theory

To close this chapter, we mention a few developing areas of complexity theory that may also prove relevant to linguistic analysis.

Approximate solutions to difficult problems represent one such area. For some problems it is possible to show that solutions obtained by heuristic methods will never differ from optimal results by more than a specified percentage. (See Garey and Johnson (1979;148–151), and chapter 6 of that book in general, for further discussion of such performance guarantees.) The bin packing problem is one example that Garey and Johnson use. Given a finite set of items $U = \{u_1, u_2, \ldots, u_n\}$ and a size $s(u) \in [0, 1]$ for each, the problem is to partition u into disjoint "bins" such that no bin is overfull (the sum of the sizes of the items is no more than 1) and the number of bins is as small as possible. This problem is NP-complete and hence—so far as is known—it has no efficient exact solution method. However, Garey and Johnson (1979:124–127) show that a fast heuristic algorithm can be developed that is never more than 22 percent worse than optimal. (On occasion it can be this bad.)

Recently, some connectionist researchers (Hopfield and Tank 1986) have proposed that other NP-complete problems such as the traveling salesman problem may be efficiently solved by parallel neural-type networks exploiting a constraint relaxation scheme. However, as it turns out, their approach works only for planar graphs. Moreover, it finds only approximate solutions that are worse than those found by other approximation algorithms, and it appears to run more slowly than those better approximation methods.

In addition to approximate solution algorithms and parallel complexity theory, several other new areas of complexity theory remain untapped for grammatical analysis. These include probabilistic algorithms (where information is gained by consulting the outcome of random events) and computational information theory (which measures the amount of information required to compute something and connects that to ordinary complexity theory). This last complexity theory research is so recent that it's not surprising natural language researchers have not yet turned to it. It has taken years to even move away from the weak generative capacity paradigm, even though complexity theory techniques have been available for over a decade. We cannot say as yet whether computational information theory will prove of value in analyzing natural grammars. As we said at the outset, however, the results set out in the remaining chapters serve only as a progress report on our attempt to apply the tools of modern computational complexity theory to grammatical analysis. We expect more recent complexity research to give us still further insight into the modularity of grammatical theories, parallel computation and grammars, and, above all, what counts as a natural grammatical system.

Chapter 3

Agreement and Ambiguity

In this chapter, we begin our series of case studies with a particularly straight-forward reduction. Analyzing a simple, theory-neutral model of *feature agreement* and *lexical ambiguity*, we show (section 3.2) that these two phenomena in combination can lead to computational intractability. Turning in section 3.3 to the implications of this result, we argue that the difficulty uncovered by the reduction reflects a real possibility of language and therefore should not be ruled out by the competence model. Instead, the constraints that make ordinary sentences relatively easy to parse should be embodied in a performance model. In section 3.4 we suggest that a deterministic performance model, when coupled with our linguistic model of agreement and ambiguity, can account for a subtle aspect of the processing difficulty of certain sentences.

3.1 Agreement and Ambiguity in Human Language

Feature agreement and related processes are widespread in human languages. Subject/verb agreement in English involves at least the features of person and number; in many languages, adjectives and determiners must agree with nouns in gender, number, and other features; in some languages a form of agreement descends to the intra-morpheme level, as with vowel harmony in Finnish, Turkish, or Warlpiri. Often morphologically marked, such processes can potentially hold across unbounded distances and among unlimited sets of elements. Verbs may in effect agree with their arguments in quantity, abstractness, [±human], [±animate], and other features. Case-marking is another form of agreement that manifests itself both morphologically and syntactically in human languages. Nominals such as epithets, pronouns, and anaphors may be required to agree (or disagree) with other nominals in reference, hence along other dimensions also. Agreement is ever-present in syntactic processes as well; a moved constituent must agree with its trace, conjuncts must exhibit agreement, and gaps in conjuncts exhibit complex forms of agreement among themselves.

Various forms of lexical and structural ambiguity are equally universal in natural language. Homonyms are commonplace; the English form *block* might have the categorial features of a noun or a verb. Transitivity alternations are common; the subject NP bears different roles in the sentences *John sank the boat* and *the boat sank*. Other syntactic and semantic selectional ambiguities abound, and ambiguity in reference and quantifier scope are also common.

Linguistic theory must accommodate both agreement and ambiguity. All major grammatical theories (Aspects- and EST-style transformational grammar, government-binding, lexical-functional grammar, and GPSG) and all post-Jakobson phonological theories use a combination of three devices to this end: (1) distinctive features to represent the dimensions of agreement; (2) a mechanism to enforce feature agreement; and (3) provision for lexical and structural ambiguity. We introduce agreement grammars as a simple model with exactly these three devices.

Agreement grammars (AGs) are context-free grammars whose nonterminals are sets of feature-value pairs; for example, [PERSON 3] is a possible feature-value pair. (For brevity, we will often write a singleton feature-value set $\{[f\ v]\}$ as simply $[f\ v]$.) The features represent dimensions of linguistic agreement; an agreement convention ensures consistency among the nonterminals in a production.[1]

The feature system of an agreement grammar is defined by a *specification* $\langle F, A, \rho \rangle$ in which F is a finite set of features and A is a finite set of feature-values. ρ is a function from features to permissible feature values; that is, $\rho : F \rightarrow 2^A$. F, A, and ρ *specify* a finite set K of categories, where a category is a partial function from features to feature-values (subject to the constraints

---

[1] Agreement grammars are loosely based on current GPSG theory, and compute agreement with a greatly simplified form of that theory's head feature convention. They may also be thought of as a restricted form of attribute grammars, which have been used to specify the syntax of programming languages. See the discussion of syntax-directed definitions in chapter 5 of Aho, Sethi, and Ullman (1986).

of ρ). Formally,

$$K = \{C \in A^{(F)} : \forall f \in \text{DOM}(C)[C(f) \in \rho(f)]\}$$

where $Y^{(X)}$ is the set of all partial functions from X to Y. $\text{DOM}(C)$ here is the domain of the function C, in other words the set $\{x : \exists y[\langle x, y \rangle \in C]\}$. A category C' is an *extension* of C (written $C' \sqsupseteq C$) if and only if $\forall f \in \text{DOM}(C)$, $[C'(f) = C(f)]$.

In addition to its feature system, an agreement grammar contains a finite set P of productions or rules, each taking one of the following two forms:

$$C \to a, \qquad \text{where } C \in K \text{ and } a \in V_T.$$
$$C_0 \to C_1 \ldots C_n, \quad \text{where each } C_i \in K.$$

Here V_T is the set of terminal elements. No null-transitions are permitted; any rule must have at least one element on its right-hand side. Crucially, a rule of an agreement grammar can apply in a derivation to categories that have additional features beyond those mentioned in the rule. We say that a production $C_0' \to C_1' \ldots C_n'$ is the extension of a production $C_0 \to C_1 \ldots C_n$ if and only if two conditions hold. First, for every i $(0 \le i \le n)$ we must have $C_i' \sqsupseteq C_i$. Second, the extension must satisfy an *agreement convention* that requires the daughters of the rule to bear all *agreement features* that the mother does. F_A is the set of agreement features, $F_A \subseteq F$:

$$\forall f \in (\text{DOM}(C_0') \cap F_A),$$
$$\forall i, \ 1 \le i \le n,$$
$$[(f \in \text{DOM}(C_i')) \wedge (C_i'(f) = C_0'(f))]$$

If P contains a production $A \to \gamma$ with an extension $A' \to \gamma'$, then for any $\alpha, \beta \in (K \cup V_T)^*$, we write $\alpha A' \beta \Longrightarrow \alpha \gamma' \beta$. Let $\stackrel{*}{\Longrightarrow}$ be the reflexive transitive closure of $\Longrightarrow$. The language $L(G)$ generated by G is then defined as follows:

$$L(G) = \{x \in V_T^* : \exists S'[S' \sqsupseteq S \wedge S' \stackrel{*}{\Longrightarrow} x]\}$$

In other words, the language is the set of terminal strings that can ultimately be derived from any extension of the start category.

Taken all together, an agreement grammar is a 5-tuple

$$\langle \langle F, A, \rho \rangle, V_T, F_A, P, S \rangle.$$

$\langle F, A, \rho \rangle$ specifies the set K of syntactic categories, V_T is a finite terminal vocabulary, F_A is the set of agreement features, P is the set of productions or rules, and $S \in K$ is the start category.

A Natural Language Example. The following toy agreement grammar G_1 models subject-verb agreement for person and number in English.

1. G_1 uses the set F of features $\{\texttt{CAT}, \texttt{PLU}, \texttt{PER}\}$ and the corresponding ρ is defined by these cases:

$$
\begin{aligned}
\rho(\texttt{CAT}) &= \{\texttt{S}, \texttt{VP}, \texttt{NP}, \texttt{V}, \texttt{N}\} \\
\rho(\texttt{PER}) &= \{1, 2, 3\} \\
\rho(\texttt{PLU}) &= \{\texttt{+}, \texttt{-}\}
\end{aligned}
$$

The start category S is $[\texttt{CAT S}]$, and the set of agreement features $F_A = \{\texttt{PER}, \texttt{PLU}\}$. The feature $\texttt{CAT}$ encodes the syntactic category of the nonterminal (sentence, noun phrase, and so forth). $\texttt{PER}$ encodes person (first, second, or third), and $\texttt{PLU}$ encodes number ($[\texttt{PLU +}]$ is plural, $[\texttt{PLU -}]$ is singular).

2. The terminal vocabulary of G_1 is

$$
V_T = \{I, men, John, sleep, sleeps\}.
$$

3. G_1 contains the following 7 productions:

$$
\begin{aligned}
[\texttt{CAT S}] &\rightarrow [\texttt{CAT NP}]\ [\texttt{CAT VP}] \\
[\texttt{CAT VP}] &\rightarrow [\texttt{CAT V}] \\
[\texttt{CAT NP}] &\rightarrow [\texttt{CAT N}] \\
\{[\texttt{CAT N}], [\texttt{PER 1}]\} &\rightarrow I \\
\{[\texttt{CAT N}], [\texttt{PLU +}]\} &\rightarrow men \\
\{[\texttt{CAT N}], [\texttt{PLU -}], [\texttt{PER 3}]\} &\rightarrow John \\
\{[\texttt{CAT V}], [\texttt{PLU +}]\} &\rightarrow sleep \\
\{[\texttt{CAT V}], [\texttt{PLU -}], [\texttt{PER 3}]\} &\rightarrow sleeps
\end{aligned}
$$

The sample grammar generates exactly the sentences in 3.1.[2]

$$
\begin{array}{lll}
\text{a.} & \text{I sleep} & (= [\texttt{CAT S}], [\texttt{PER 1}], [\texttt{PLU +}]) \\
\text{b.} & \text{men sleep} & (= [\texttt{CAT S}], [\texttt{PLU +}]) \\
\text{c.} & \text{John sleeps} & (= [\texttt{CAT S}], [\texttt{PER 3}], [\texttt{PLU -}])
\end{array} \tag{3.1}
$$

---

[2]The sentence 3.1a is assigned the linguistically suspect feature specification $[\texttt{PLU +}]$, but this is easily fixed by increasing the number of lexical entries in the grammar.

3.2 AG Recognition is NP-Complete

With agreement grammars as a simple model of agreement and ambiguity, we now show that these two features in combination can produce computational intractability: the universal recognition problem for agreement grammars is NP-complete. This problem is to determine for an arbitrary AG G and input string w whether $w \in L(G)$. We begin by observing that a bound can be placed on the length of an AG derivation.

Lemma 3.2.1: Let $(\varphi_0, \ldots, \varphi_k)$ be a shortest leftmost derivation of φ_k from φ_0 in an agreement grammar G. If $k > |P|$, where P is the set of productions in G, then $|\varphi_k| > |\varphi_0|$.[3]

Proof. In the step $\varphi_i \implies \varphi_{i+1}$, where $\varphi_i = \alpha A' \beta$ and $\varphi_{i+1} = \alpha \gamma' \beta$ for $\alpha \in V_T^*$, $\beta \in (V_T \cup K)^*$, one of the following cases must hold:

Case 1. The production $A \to \gamma$ with extension $A' \to \gamma'$ is nonbranching ($|\gamma| = 1$). In the worst case, we could cycle through every possible nonbranching production (without using a branching production), after which we would begin to reuse them. Any extension of a production that has already been used in this run of nonbranching productions could have been guessed previously, and the length of the shortest nonbranching run must be less than $|P|$.

Case 2. The production $A \to \gamma$ with extension $A' \to \gamma'$ is branching ($|\gamma| > 1$). Then $|\varphi_i| > |\varphi_{i+1}|$.

A total of at most $n - 1$ branching productions derives an utterance of length n, because there are no null-transitions in an agreement grammar. Each branching production can be separated from the closest other branching production in the derivation by a run of at most $|G|$ nonbranching productions, and the shortest derivation of x will be of length $\theta(|G| \cdot |x|)$.

Theorem 1: Agreement grammar recognition is in $\mathcal{NP}$.

Proof. On input agreement grammar G and input string $x \in V_T^*$, guess a derivation of x in nondeterministic polynomial time as follows.[4]

1. Guess an extension S' of S, and let S' be the derivation string.

---

[3] We assume the agreement grammar G contains at least one branching production. If not, then $L(G)$ contains only strings of length one and all shortest derivations are shorter than $|P|$: membership for such a grammar is clearly in $\mathcal{NP}$.

[4] Again, we assume G contains at least one branching production. If not, then we should only loop as many times as there are productions, and then halt.

2. For a derivation string $\alpha A' \beta$, where $\alpha \in V_T^*, \beta \in (V_T \cup K)^*$, guess a production $A \rightarrow \gamma$ and extension $A' \rightarrow \gamma'$ of it. Let $\alpha \gamma' \beta$ be the new derivation string.

3. If $\alpha \gamma' \beta = x$, accept.

4. If $|\alpha \gamma' \beta| > |x|$, reject.

5. Loop to step 2 (at most $|G| \cdot |x|$ times).

Every loop of the nondeterministic algorithm performs one step in the derivation. By lemma 3.2.1, the shortest derivation of x is at most of length $\theta(|G| \cdot |x|)$, so we need to loop through the algorithm at most that many times. Guessing an extension of a category may be performed in time $\theta(|F|)$, and an extension of a production may be guessed in time $\theta(|F| \cdot |P|)$. This nondeterministic algorithm runs in polynomial time and accepts exactly $L(G)$; hence AG Recognition is in $\mathcal{NP}$. $\square$

Theorem 2: AG Recognition is NP-hard.

Proof. We will reduce 3SAT to AG Recognition in polynomial time. Given a 3CNF formula f of length m using the n variables $q_1 \ldots q_n$, we construct an agreement grammar G_f such that the string w is an element of $L(G_f)$ iff f is satisfiable, where w is the string of formula literals in f. (In other words, w does not contain parentheses or the operators " $\wedge$ " and " $\vee$ ", which are redundant for 3CNF formulas.) G_f is constructed in the following way:

1. G_f uses the set F of features {STAGE, LITERAL, $q_1, \ldots, q_n$} with values defined by the function ρ, where

$$\begin{aligned}
\rho(\text{STAGE}) &= \{1, \ldots, n+3\} \\
\rho(\text{LITERAL}) &= \{+, -\} \\
\rho(q_i) &= \{0, 1\}
\end{aligned}$$

The grammar will assign truth-values and check satisfaction in $n + 3$ stages as synchronized by the feature STAGE. The start category is [STAGE 1].

2. At each of the first n stages, a value is chosen for one variable; because the q_i are declared as agreement features, the values that are chosen will be constant throughout the derivation tree. We need the following $2n$ rules, constructed for all i, $1 \le i \le n$.

$$\begin{aligned}
\{[\text{STAGE } i], [q_i \ 0]\} &\rightarrow \{[\text{STAGE } i+1], [q_i \ 0]\} \\
\{[\text{STAGE } i], [q_i \ 1]\} &\rightarrow \{[\text{STAGE } i+1], [q_i \ 1]\}
\end{aligned}$$

3. At stage $n+1$, enough right-branching tree structure will be constructed to cover all of the three-literal clauses that make up w. The following two rules suffice:

$$\begin{aligned} \texttt{[STAGE } n+1] &\rightarrow \texttt{[STAGE } n+2] \\ \texttt{[STAGE } n+1] &\rightarrow \texttt{[STAGE } n+1] \texttt{ [STAGE } n+2] \end{aligned}$$

4. At stage $n+2$, a pattern of true and false literals is selected for each clause. Let C_0 and C_1 be the following categories:

$$\begin{aligned} C_0 &= \{\texttt{[STAGE } n+3], \texttt{[LITERAL -]}\} \\ C_1 &= \{\texttt{[STAGE } n+3], \texttt{[LITERAL +]}\} \end{aligned}$$

Then the following 7 rules are needed; any pattern of true and false literals will do, except for all three being false:

$$\begin{aligned} \texttt{[STAGE } n+2] &\rightarrow C_0 \ C_0 \ C_1 \\ \texttt{[STAGE } n+2] &\rightarrow C_0 \ C_1 \ C_0 \\ \texttt{[STAGE } n+2] &\rightarrow C_1 \ C_0 \ C_0 \\ \texttt{[STAGE } n+2] &\rightarrow C_0 \ C_1 \ C_1 \\ \texttt{[STAGE } n+2] &\rightarrow C_1 \ C_0 \ C_1 \\ \texttt{[STAGE } n+2] &\rightarrow C_1 \ C_1 \ C_0 \\ \texttt{[STAGE } n+2] &\rightarrow C_1 \ C_1 \ C_1 \end{aligned}$$

5. Finally, lexical insertion at stage $n+3$ ties together the truth-values chosen for the variables and the literals. For every q_i, $1 \leq i \leq n$, we need the following four rules, bringing us to a total of $6n+9$ rules:

$$\begin{aligned} \{\texttt{[STAGE } n+3], \texttt{[LITERAL +]}, [q_i \ 1]\} &\rightarrow q_i \\ \{\texttt{[STAGE } n+3], \texttt{[LITERAL -]}, [q_i \ 0]\} &\rightarrow q_i \\ \{\texttt{[STAGE } n+3], \texttt{[LITERAL +]}, [q_i \ 0]\} &\rightarrow \bar{q}_i \\ \{\texttt{[STAGE } n+3], \texttt{[LITERAL -]}, [q_i \ 1]\} &\rightarrow \bar{q}_i \end{aligned}$$

If some extension of the start category $S = \texttt{[STAGE 1]}$ can be recognized, then the formula f is satisfiable; each recognized extension of the start category encodes a satisfying truth assignment. For example, if the category

$$\{\texttt{[STAGE 1]}, [q_1 \ 1], [q_2 \ 0], \ldots, [q_n \ 1]\}$$

is recognized, then the formula f has a satisfying assignment $q_1 = 1, q_2 = 0, \ldots, q_n = 1$. Note that the agreement grammar constructed in the reduction accepts *any* satisfiable 3CNF boolean formula, of any length, using n or fewer variables. □

The preceding proof demonstrates that intractability can arise from a particularly deadly combination of agreement and ambiguity. Informally, human languages and the NP-complete SAT problem share two costly computational mechanisms: both enforce agreement among terminal symbols across unbounded distances and both allow lexical ambiguity. In natural language, lexical elements may be required to agree (or disagree) on such features as person, number, gender, case, count, category, reference, thematic role, tense, and abstractness; in SAT, agreement ensures the consistency of truth-assignments to variables. Lexical ambiguity can appear freely in natural language utterances (is *can* a noun, verb, or modal?), while a variable in a SAT formula may be either true or false. Thus, the linguistic mechanisms for agreement and ambiguity are exactly those needed to solve satisfiability—any linguistic theory that uses them, as any descriptively adequate theory must, will probably be computationally intractable.

3.3   Competence and Performance

We now turn to the implications of our complexity result. Should grammatical theory be restricted in some way so that computationally difficult situations are ruled out in principle? We think not; the proper conclusion is more subtle.

Scientific explanation of any complex biological information-processing system occurs at three levels: (1) a *computational theory*, which explains what is computed and why; (2) a *representation* for the input and output of the process and the *algorithm* for the transformation; and (3) the hardware *implementation*, or the device in which the representation and algorithm are physically realized.[5] Accordingly, the study of linguistic knowledge divides into the traditional subtheories of *competence* and *performance*. The competence theories of linguistics correspond to Marr's (1980) topmost level of computational theory—explaining what structures are computed and why, ig-

---

[5]Marr (1980:25) elaborates: "These three levels are coupled, but only loosely. The choice of an algorithm is influenced for example, by what it has to do and by the hardware in which it must run. But there is a wide choice available at each level, and the explication of each level involves issues that are rather independent of the other two. Each of the three levels of description will have its place in the eventual understanding of perceptual information processing, and of course they are logically and causally related. But an important point to note is that since the three levels are only rather loosely related, some phenomena may be explained at only one or two of them. This means, for example, that a correct explanation of some psychophysical observation must be formulated at the appropriate level."

noring memory limitations, shifts of attention or interest, and errors. Marr's remaining levels belong to the theory of performance, which proposes a representation and algorithm to account for the actual concrete use of language.

Once we understand the topmost of Marr's levels—the computational theory of an information-processing problem—we understand more about the other levels as well:

> Although algorithms and mechanisms are empirically more accessible, it is the top level, the level of computational theory, which is critically important from an information-processing point of view. The reason for this is that the nature of the computations that underlie perception depends more upon the computational problems that have to be solved than upon the particular hardware in which their solutions are implemented. To phrase the matter another way, an algorithm is likely to be understood more readily by understanding the nature of the problem being solved than by examining the mechanism (and the hardware) in which it is embodied. (Marr 1980:27)

But where do complexity results fit into this picture?

Complexity analysis can aid the study of biological information processing systems—and linguistics in particular—in two ways. First, it can help identify computational properties of *linguistic theories* that don't match properties of natural language, thereby improving the theories. For example, it can both root out *spurious* sources of complexity in linguistic theories and identify *unnaturally simple* theories, showing how they don't accurately model the underlying linguistic phenomena. Second, because complexity theory measures the intrinsic difficulty of solving a problem no matter how the solution is obtained, it can illuminate the *structure of linguistic problems* in a way that is invariant across across a wide range of machine models, representational choices, algorithms, implementations, and even complexity measures. Marr (1980:347) identifies the structure of information-processing problems as crucial to our understanding of them, and this is no less true when the information-processing problems in question are two fundamental questions of linguistics: what is the knowledge that underlies linguistic ability and how is it put to use?

In some ways, complexity analysis can guide the construction of representations, algorithms, and implementations rather directly. Whenever the computational cost of a task accords with its observed cognitive cost, this suggests that scientific explanation of the task should occur primarily in a theory of competence; the performance theory is likely to be straightforward in this regard. But whenever the inherent computational cost differs from the cognitive cost, we get specific insight into the performance theory—what needs to be explained at that level and the form such explanation might take.

Suppose that complexity theory classifies a cognitive problem as intractable, yet humans appear to solve the problem with ease. By illuminating the nature of the possible difficulties, complexity analysis helps us understand the additional constraints that performance mechanisms may impose to attain speed. Processing methods might restrict the domain of the problem (as when deep center-embedding is rejected) or solve costly instances of the problem only approximately (as when deeply right-branching structures are "flattened"; see also chapter 6). Alternately, we might consider very powerful mental hardware—massively parallel, perhaps—and complexity theory would help us understand precisely how powerful it would have to be.

On the other hand, suppose that the cognitive problem is easy in principle but apparently difficult for humans to solve. In this case complexity analysis can pinpoint the properties of the problem that make it easy in principle, thus telling us specific ways in which the performance algorithm may be simple-minded, inefficient, or restricted (as with the "no reentrant procedures" constraint of one early performance model). Hardware limitations on memory use or processing time represent one special case.

We have shown that a simple computational model of agreement and ambiguity in natural language can lead to intractability. This result is, therefore, a preliminary indication that natural language may not be efficiently parsable. This result may seem surprising, given universally held expectations about the efficiency of natural language processing. Yet no serious scientific argument has ever been advanced in support of the necessity of accounting for "efficient processability" in one's *competence theory*. Here we argue that such expectations are unreasonable and can deter scientific progress. There is no principled reason why our theories of linguistic competence must only characterize grammars that support efficient processing. It would be an arbitrary limitation to say *a priori* that our theories of linguistic knowledge must obey principles that make them always efficient in the limit. Miller and Chomsky (1963:471) and Chomsky (1981:119–125) make similar arguments in a slightly different form.

Although there may be principled limits on agreement and related processes, the haphazard and accidental nature of lexical ambiguity makes it unlikely that the computational difficulties associated with ambiguity can be ruled out by grammatical theory in any principled way. Thus we believe that the apparent efficiency of linguistic processing is, in this case, best explained by a theory of language use. It is *not* best explained by arbitrarily bounding the grammatical theory for the purpose of ruling out the reduction. Agreement grammars better express the computational structure of natural language than does a model that bounds agreement or ambiguity in order to obtain efficiency; thus agreement grammars are the better scientific model. (See chapters 1, 2, and 6 for further discussion.) In the following section, we end this chapter by exploring the linguistic implications of a simple performance model of language users.

3.4   Modeling Performance Limitations

Let us imagine a performance model M that is fundamentally deterministic and assigns structural descriptions to utterances in real time. A consequence of these assumptions is that M will not be able to parse certain constructions involving both ambiguity and long-distance agreement—constructions involving significant "nonlocal information flow," to use a term we will discuss more fully in chapter 6.[6] M will, however, be able to "verify" (in a sense to be clarified below) many of the constructions it fails to parse. The choice of a deterministic performance model, when coupled with the AG model of competence, indicates that some performance limitations will arise out of the *deterministic* nature of processing (see Marcus 1980) rather than from a restriction to finite memory (see Miller and Chomsky 1963).

For instance, such a performance limitation will arise given excessive lexical and structural ambiguity; (see example 3.2, where *buffalo* can be one or many shaggy beasts, a city, or a transitive verb that means *fool*). It can also show up with the elaborate agreement processes found in consecutive constituent coordination, discontinuous constituent coordination, rightward

---

[6]The intractability of agreement grammar recognition implies that natural language may be intractable in the worst case and in the limit: any faithful natural language recognizer must be slow on some utterances, although it may be fast on others. The result does not dispute that short, unambiguous, or structurally simple utterances can be processed efficiently. More importantly, given the apparent speed of ordinary language use, the result suggests that actual biological recognizers may be both fast and occasionally inaccurate.

movement out of coordinate structures, and gapping (the examples of 3.3).[7]
Sentence 3.2 has an amusing array of possible interpretations, ranging from
the simple interpretation suggested by the parallel sentence "Boston buffalo
fool Boston buffalo" to more elaborate ones with relative clauses, *e.g.,* "[Buf-
falo that buffalo fool] can fool buffalo."[8]

$$\text{buffalo buffalo buffalo buffalo buffalo} \qquad (3.2)$$

a. John owned and then sold
   hundreds of late model cars to us that he waxed all the time.
b. John liked and wanted to tease Sue and Bill, Mary.
c. John owned and then sold   (3.3)
   hundreds of late model cars to us and Bill, trucks.
d. John owned and then sold
   hundreds of late model cars to us and to Bill, trucks.

Worst of all would be the (incomprehensible) examples combining the two
insidious phenomena, *e.g., Buffalo buffalo buffalo and buffalo buffalo buffalo
of buffalo buffalo to buffalo buffalo buffalo buffalo and buffalo, buffalo buffalo.*

Linguistic agreement and ambiguity may cause intractability in other
languages as well. Nonconfigurational languages such as Warlpiri, a central Australian aborigine language, have special morphology for verbs and
for nominal arguments that make sentences such as 3.2 easy to understand
when they are directly translated. But the morphological processes in these
languages typically allow other highly ambiguous constructions that are difficult to understand. Even worse, Warlpiri fails to distinguish adjectives and
nouns either morphologically or configurationally (as in English), making the
direct translation of such trivial English sentences as *John flushed the Air
Force space shuttle toilet* computationally analogous to the intractable "buffalo" sentences of English. Contrary to common belief, natural language may

---

[7]The acceptability gradation between example 3.3a and examples 3.3b,c,d is probably
due to the gapping structures found in the latter examples. From the fact that our linguistic
capabilities are deterministic we can conclude only that some ambiguous structures should
be difficult to understand. If our model M further assumes that linguistic perception
occurs in real time, it predicts difficulties even with slightly ambiguous constructions or
those with significant long-distance "information flow," such as gapping structures. Thus
the difficulty of accepting gapping structures is a rough corollary to the arguments of this
chapter; see Berwick and Weinberg (1984).

[8]Equivalent sentences can be constructed out of any word whose plural noun form is
morphologically identical to its plural verb form: *police police police police police . . .,* and *french
french french french french, etc.*

not be efficiently parsable. (Warlpiri also has a number of constraints that limit *embedding,* although not ambiguity, and thus make parsing easier than it might otherwise be.)

Significantly, the preceding natural language examples have exactly the same computational character as NP-complete problems: solutions may be hard to find, but they are easy to verify. The reader's first attempt to understand example 3.2 is likely to fail and label the sentence gibberish; however, it should be easy to check the paraphrased "solution." The curious nature of this phenomenon confirms the predictions of our rough model-sketch. It also strengthens our conclusion that the difficulty uncovered by our NP-completeness reduction represents a real grammatical possibility in natural language—though one that seldom turns up in practice, as we discuss below.

An explanation of the psycholinguistic dichotomy between solving and verifying relies critically on the competence/performance distinction. The *possibility* of understanding (verifying) the utterances at all is explained by our competence theory, which does not bound agreement or ambiguity. On the other hand, the *difficulty* of understanding (solving) the utterances is best explained by the deterministic nature of our performance model.

Agreement and ambiguity, if permitted to operate without bound in the speaker, will quickly generate utterances that exceed the (deterministic) perceptual capabilities of hearers. These sentences, being too difficult for the hearer to understand, will not be used due to the *fidelity criterion* of communication systems (see Shannon 1949 and Chomsky and Miller 1963:273). The fidelity criterion states that the receiver establishes the criterion of acceptability of a communication system: if the receiver cannot process a signal, then the fidelity of the communication channel is wasted. Simply put, unacceptably ambiguous sentences, being difficult for the hearer, are not used in practice, "just as many other proliferations of syntactic devices that produce well-formed sentences will never actually be found" (Miller and Chomsky 1963:471).

Nearly all utterances evince both agreement processes and ambiguity, to varying degrees. Therefore, there is no reason to expect that occasional unacceptability introduced by excessive agreement and ambiguity will cause those processes to disappear from language over the course of time. In fact, all known natural languages employ these mechanisms. It would be reasonable to expect, however, that a natural language might develop techniques to efficiently process the "easy" cases and approximately process the "hard" ones.

In this chapter, we argued that the insights of complexity theory can explain subtle psycholinguistic phenomena, in addition to guiding the construction of linguistic theories. Chapter 6 translates the arguments of this chapter into the morphological domain, where we argue that complexity theory can help identify special properties of linguistic systems that should be reflected in the processing machinery. In the next chapter and in chapters 5, 8, and 9 we use complexity theory to isolate spurious sources of intractability in existing linguistic theories and to motivate linguistic restrictions with computational consequences.

Chapter 4

The Complexity of LFG

The previous chapter showed that lexical ambiguity plus long-distance agreement machinery suffices to make a grammatical formalism NP-hard. Since lexical-functional grammar (LFG) contains both lexical ambiguity and agreement checking—as we shall see—it should come as no surprise that the following problem is NP-hard:

> Given an arbitrary lexical-functional grammar G and a sentence x, is $x \in L(G)$?

A straightforward reduction from Agreement Grammar recognition can establish this,[1] but it is perhaps more instructive to give an independent reduction from 3SAT and see just *why* LFG processing is NP-hard.[2]

This chapter has three sections. First, we sketch the major components of LFG, particularly those relevant to the reduction proof. We follow Kaplan and Bresnan's (1982) formal description of LFG. As it turns out, much LFG machinery is not needed for the reduction. In particular, so-called long distance binding—used for handling *wh* movement in examples such as *Who did John say Mary kissed*—is not needed. Next we present a reduction from 3SAT. A concluding section discusses possible revisions to the formalism that would avoid computational intractability.

---

[1] We can turn any agreement grammar into a lexical-functional grammar, as the reduction later in this chapter will make clear.

[2] Kaplan and Bresnan (1982) show that LFGs can generate some strictly context-sensitive languages, and refer to an unpublished proof sketch that LFGs can generate only context-sensitive languages. However, no one has demonstrated that LFGs can generate all context-sensitive languages and there is some suspicion that LFGs can generate only a proper subset of the CSLs.

4.1   Lexical-Functional Grammar: a Brief Introduction

A core idea of lexical-functional grammar is to associate with each sentence at least two distinct representations: the *constituent structure* or *c-structure* and the *functional structure* or *f-structure*. The c-structure of a sentence is roughly a surface parse tree that indicates phrasal structure; the f-structure is roughly a representation of the predicate-argument structure of a sentence that highlights the relationships between verb, subject, object, and other so-called grammatical relations (oblique object and the like). Crucially, f-structure can be hierarchical, just as c-structure is: for instance, one can have a sentence—such as *John persuaded Mary to leave*—whose top-level f-structure contains the predicate *persuade*, which in turn contains an f-structure representation of the embedded sentence *Mary to leave*. (One component of LFG that we shall not describe here or exploit in the reduction is the set of semantic interpretation rules that are attached to predicates; thus we analyze basically the syntactic machinery of LFG.)

C-structure and f-structure are built up jointly. C-structure is described by context-free rules of the usual sort augmented by abbreviatory devices of a familiar kind: Kleene-star repetition of right-hand-side constituents, optionality indicated by parentheses, and so forth. For instance, the following rules are valid LFG c-structure rules:

$$
\begin{aligned}
S &\rightarrow & NP\ VP \\
NP &\rightarrow & Determiner\ Noun\ PP^* \\
VP &\rightarrow & Verb\ (NP) \\
& & etc.
\end{aligned}
$$

Context-free rules such as $NP \rightarrow \lambda$ are used to generate sentences with "gaps," such as *Who did John see*, where there is a missing object after the verb *see*.

Note that the c-structure rules are assumed to include a lexicon with syntactic categorization, and this includes lexical ambiguity: *kiss* can be in either of the categories N and V. For our purposes, lexical insertion can be described by means of preterminal rules such as $N \rightarrow kiss$, and so forth. C-structure well-formedness is necessary but not sufficient for a sentence to be in the language generated by an LFG; it provides a basic parse tree on which to ground f-structure construction, described next.[3]

F-structure is specified by means of *f-structure equations* optionally associated with each element of a c-structure rule. Part of their role is to account for cooccurrence restrictions in natural language, such as subject-verb agreement in English. An example shows how. Here, a simple c-structure rule for expanding sentences has added two f-structure annotations, one below the *NP* and one below the *VP*.

$$S \rightarrow \quad\quad NP \quad\quad\quad\quad VP$$
$$(\uparrow \textit{ Subject Number } = \downarrow) \quad (\uparrow = \downarrow)$$

The f-structure annotations are interpreted as follows. The equation $(\uparrow = \downarrow)$ means that *all* the features associated with the f-structure built up at the *VP* c-structure node are to be *unified* with the features at the node above the *VP*, namely the *S*. We may imagine these features being "passed up" and written alongside the *S* node. What would these features include? That depends, in turn, on the features passed along by f-structure annotations on the c-structure nodes expanding *VP*, all the way until one reaches the lexical entries for terminal elements. For instance, if the *VP* were expanded as a *Verb* plus an *NP* object, then we might find the following annotation:

$$VP \rightarrow \quad\quad\quad Verb \quad\quad\quad NP$$
$$(\uparrow \textit{ Subject} = \downarrow)$$

(Lexical entry)
Verb: *kiss* $(\uparrow \textit{ Number} = \textit{singular})$

If we follow the "percolation" imagery, then we see that these rules specify the following f-structure construction steps: first, the lexical entry for *kisses* (or rather its morphological signature) gives the *Verb* node the feature **Number** with the *value* **singular**. We represent this conventionally by placing the feature-value combination in square brackets, as [*feature value*], *e.g.,*

---

[3]One constraint on c-structure rules is that no derivations of the form $A \rightarrow \ldots \rightarrow A$ are allowed; that is, there cannot be arbitrarily long nonbranching derivation chains. Kaplan and Bresnan (1982) take this as linguistically plausible.

[Number singular]. In this example, the f-structure associated with the *Verb* node contains just a single feature-value pair; in general, the collection of feature-value pairs may be more complicated, including other pairs, and may even be hierarchically structured (as mentioned).

The annotation on the *Verb* node dictates that this entire f-structure in turn be passed to the *VP* node as the *value* of the Subject feature. More precisely, it says to *merge* or *unify* the f-structure at the *Verb* node with that at the *VP* node. Thus, the f-structure for the *VP* node will contain, among other things, the structure [Subject [Number singular]]. Finally, the *VP* f-structure annotation says that all f-structures at the VP should also reside at the S node, so our final step is to in effect copy this entire structure to the S node.

Returning now to the subject *NP*, its associated f-structure annotation is a bit more complicated. It says that whatever the f-structure above the *NP*, its Subject Number feature should have the value singular. We would expect this value in turn to have been passed up from an annotation on the rule expanding *NP* as, say, a *Determiner* plus a *Noun*, with the lexical entry *guy* providing the desired singular value. Note that this value matches (more precisely, unifies with) the specification spelled out by the *VP* annotation, so the cooccurrence check is satisfied.

If the verb had been *kiss* or the noun had been plural (*guys*), then the match would have failed. A basic constraint on well-formedness for LFGs is that all f-structure equations must allow such feature unification. This requirement is called *functional coherence*. It should be clear that one can use this agreement machinery to force coherent variable truth assignments in a 3SAT reduction (see the next section).

A second constraint on f-structure well-formedness is *functional completeness*. Functional completeness has a linguistic motivation, and we provide a simple example. Consider verb subcategorization. A transitive verb like *kiss* can demand that the grammatical relations subject and object be filled in from *somewhere* in the sentence. We do this by attaching to the lexical entry for *kiss* a grammatical function template that serves as a constraint on a well-formed f-structure:

$$Kiss: \quad \uparrow \langle \text{Subject Object} \rangle$$

Once inserted as a terminal element, the lexical entry for *kiss* requires that there exist some subject or object f-structure feature associated with the root (S) node of the c-structure tree. If, for example, the subject feature were never filled in—because of some poor choice of f-structure annotations or c-structure rules—then the f-structure would be *functionally incomplete* and the corresponding sentence ill-formed. However, the reduction does not even need to use this part of the LFG machinery.

To summarize then, the only parts of the LFG system that we need for the reduction are basic c-structure rules, f-structure annotations, the principles of f-structure assembly, and the constraint of functional coherence.

4.2   LFG Recognition is NP-hard

Following our usual procedure, we define the LFG recognition problem with respect to an input sentence x and an LFG G as follows:

The *LFG Recognition Problem* is: given a sentence x and an LFG G, is $x \in L(G)$?

We then proceed with the reduction.

Theorem 3: LFG Recognition (LFGR) is NP-hard.

Proof. The reduction is from 3SAT. On input 3CNF formula F of length n using the m variables $x_1 \ldots x_m$, reduce 3SAT, a known NP-complete problem, to LFGR in polynomial time.

To construct the required LFG problem, we first output a sentence to be tested for LFG membership. This is simply $w = h(F)$, where h is a homomorphism that erases the parentheses, $\vee$, and $\wedge$ symbols in F; it returns just the string of literals.

Next, we build the lexical-functional grammar to use for the membership test. First we construct a context-free base that reproduces the clause structure of F and forces at least one true value per clause. Then we add f-structure equations that enforce coherent truth assignments. This grammar is fixed for all 3SAT problem instances. Finally, we need lexical entries, one pair for each literal x_i and $\overline{x}_i$. The lexicon varies with the particular 3SAT instance.

The output LFG consists of the following context-free c-structure rules, where S is the starting symbol of the CF rules.

The first rule is the only recursive one; along with the remaining rules, it lets us generate all possible clause sequences. The remaining seven rules generate all triples with at least one true literal in a clause; this will force any derivation to include at least one true assignment per clause.

$$
\begin{array}{ll}
1 & S \rightarrow SS \\
2 & S \rightarrow TTT \\
3 & S \rightarrow TTF \\
4 & S \rightarrow TFT \\
5 & S \rightarrow FTT \\
6 & S \rightarrow TFF \\
7 & S \rightarrow FFT \\
8 & S \rightarrow FTF
\end{array}
$$

Now we add lexical entries. Any nonterminal T can be expanded as either the terminal x_i or $\overline{x}_i$, $1 \leq i \leq m$, but with the additional constraint that the lexical entry for x_i must have a feature value annotation saying that the x_i feature has the value **true** (**T**). We can do this quite simply with the following lexical entries:

$$
\begin{array}{lll}
T: & x_i & 1 \leq i \leq m \\
   & (\uparrow x_i = \mathbf{T}) &
\end{array}
$$

The nonterminal T is should also permit $\overline{x}_i$, but in this case the feature x_i should have the value **F**. So we also add these entries:

$$
\begin{array}{lll}
T: & \overline{x}_i & 1 \leq i \leq m \\
   & (\uparrow x_i = \mathbf{F}) &
\end{array}
$$

The f-structure annotation will propagate the feature-value combination up the tree, to be checked against other variable truth assignments through the functional coherence principle.

So much for the expansions of T. The expansions of F are just the duals of those for T: if F expands to x_i, then the x_i value is **F**, and if F expands as $\overline{x}_i$, then the x_i value passed up is **T**:

$$F: \qquad x_i \qquad 1 \leq i \leq m:$$
$$(\uparrow x_i = \mathbf{F})$$

$$F: \qquad \overline{x}_i \qquad 1 \leq i \leq m:$$
$$(\uparrow x_i = \mathbf{T})$$

Note that we need $4 \cdot m$ lexical entries in all; their size, including f-structure annotations, is clearly polynomial in the length of F.

Finally, we add ($\uparrow = \downarrow$) f-structure annotations to all right-hand side constituents in rules (1)–(8), for instance these:

$$S \rightarrow \quad S \qquad S$$
$$(\uparrow = \downarrow) \quad (\uparrow = \downarrow)$$

$$S \rightarrow \quad T \qquad T \qquad T$$
$$(\uparrow = \downarrow) \quad (\uparrow = \downarrow) \quad (\uparrow = \downarrow)$$

$$S \rightarrow \quad T \qquad T \qquad F$$
$$(\uparrow = \downarrow) \quad (\uparrow = \downarrow) \quad (\uparrow = \downarrow)$$

(etc.)

Plainly, this construction takes time polynomial in the size of the formula F: The homomorphism h can be carried out in a linear left-to-right scan of the input formula. G also takes at most polynomial time to build; the c-structure and f-structure annotations are fixed. The lexicon can clearly be constructed in time polynomial in the length of F, because it is only of size $4m$; we can keep track of what variables we have already seen in a list that we rescan at most a polynomial number of times. Thus the total time to output the corresponding LFG is polynomial in $|F|$.

It remains to show that F is satisfiable iff $w \in L(G)$. Suppose that $w \in L(G)$. We must show that F is satisfiable. If $w \in L(G)$, then by the c-structure rules for G, there must be a derivation line of T and F preterminals that directly derives w. But this means that each preterminal triple contains at least one T, and assigning **true** to the literal corresponding to this lexical item yields a satisfying assignment (each clause contains at least one true literal). Functional coherence guarantees consistent assignments.

Now suppose that F is satisfiable. Then at least one literal in each clause triple must be true; we must exhibit a valid LFG derivation corresponding to this satisfying assignment. We simply choose the context-free expansion that expands out to the appropriate pattern of Ts and Fs; this can clearly be done. Then we select lexical entries that correspond to $h(F)$, from left to right, ensuring that we pick the proper entry according to whether a lexical item is dominated by T or F. This is clearly a valid sentence in G, because it satisfies the c-structure derivation and because consistency of variable feature values guarantees functional coherence. $\square$

To see the reduction in action, consider the 3SAT problem instance: is $(x_1 \vee \overline{x}_3 \vee x_4) \wedge (x_3 \vee x_4 \vee x_5)$ satisfiable? Figure 4.1 shows the LFG and associated derivation tree showing how setting $x_4 = \textbf{true}$ (and $x_1, x_3, x_5 = \textbf{false}$) satisfies the formula and corresponds to the sentence $x_1\overline{x}_3x_4x_3x_4x_5$ being in $L(G)$. The figure shows the f-structures built up at each c-structure node. Note how these check feature compatibility at the topmost S node; if, for example, we had set x_4 to be **false** in the first clause and **true** in the second, then this clash would be detected at the root of the tree.

4.3 Implications of the Complexity Result

What are the implications of this reduction? A complexity result like this one tells us that while *verifying* the correctness of an LFG parse might be easy (on the presumption that LFGR is indeed in $\mathcal{NP}$), *finding* that solution in the first place might be an intractable problem. In short, *nothing in the formal framework of LFG guarantees efficient parsability.* If there is an explanation of efficient sentence processing, then it is to be had by *adding* restrictions to the LFG framework—presumably, restrictions motivated by other things we know about natural languages, human performance, and the like. LFG does not, in and of itself, explain efficient human parsing.

How could one restrict the LFG theory formally so as to avoid NP-hardness? Two constraints spring immediately to mind.

- Add locality principles for parsing. One could simply stipulate a performance constraint (see chapter 1) to guarantee efficient parsability, like the LR-type constraints advanced by Knuth (1965) and typified in

3SAT problem instance:
Is $(x_1 \lor \overline{x}_3 \lor x_4) \land (x_3 \lor x_4 \lor x_5)$ satisfiable?

Answer: Yes, with $x_4 = $ **true**

LFG problem instance:
Is $x_1\overline{x}_3x_4x_3x_4x_5 \in L(G)$?

Answer: Yes, with following derivation:

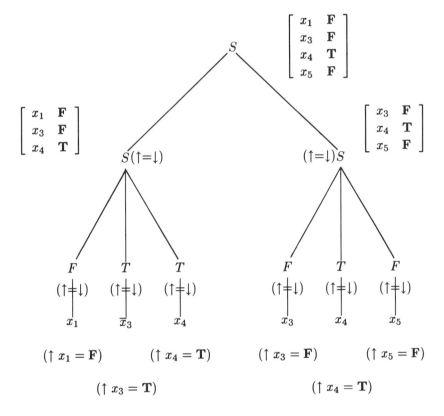

Figure 4.1: The reduction described in the text produces this LFG and derivation tree on a sample 3SAT instance.

Marcus's work (1980). In this case we would say that people construct only one derivation at a time and somehow ignore global lexical ambiguity; if such global interactions do arise, the resulting sentences are difficult or impossible to process. In some ways, this constraint seems like the most natural one; certainly $LR(k)$ restrictions suffice, and we need a theory of linguistic performance in any case.

- Rule out the "worst case" languages as linguistically irrelevant—either unlearnable or, from an empirical standpoint, nonoccurring. The LFG complexity result, like the agreement grammar result, arises because arbitrary lexical ambiguity coupled with arbitrary feature cooccurrence restrictions is a computationally deadly combination. If this can somehow be ruled out in natural languages, then we would escape from this possibility. This remains an open empirical issue, but as far as LFG goes, it could solve other problems as well, so we shall address this point in more detail.

One direct way to enforce this restriction would be simply to say that unification cannot act over, say, more than one bounding domain. Then unbounded hierarchical functional structure unification would be disbarred and the offending reduction rendered impotent.

But why make such a restriction? Is there any other way to motivate it? Here one answer would be simply to import the machinery of $\overline{X}$ theory into the functional structure language itself. Williams (1984) has made exactly this point. As he observes, many of the troubles of the LFG f-structure language stem from its failure to observe $\overline{X}$ restrictions. (LFG has $\overline{X}$ theory in its constituent structure but not its f-structure.) The result is that f-structure winds up trying to express generalizations over the vocabulary *head* and *projection* without having these notions at its disposal. As we have seen, in the LFG theory, any part of a phrase is accessible through hierarchical composition. But only features on the head of a phrase ought to be accessible to subcategorization. (As Williams notes, we don't have rules that force *e.g.,* the object of an embedded verb to be plural.) If f-structures obeyed $\overline{X}$ theory, then one might expect maximal projections—*NP, PP, VP*—to block further hierarchical unification, since the only thing "visible" beyond the head of a phrase would be that head's features (now identifying the head of a phrase and its lexical head as a single kind of unit). There would be no possibility of "percolating" any more information than this, and this would salvage LFG's complexity.

Such a finding would increase the similarity between LFG and government-binding theory. It would also be a positive result, since it would further characterize all and only the natural languages as those abiding by $\overline{\text{X}}$ restrictions at the level of f-structure. It remains to pursue the full computational and linguistic implications of this restriction.

Chapter 5

The Complexity of Two-Level Morphology

The "dictionary lookup" stage in a sophisticated natural-language system can involve much more than simple retrieval. In text, the words that the system knows may show up in heavily disguised form. Inflectional endings such as tense and plural markings may be present; the addition of prefixes and suffixes may change part-of-speech and meaning in systematic ways; in many languages words may have unrelated clitics attached. The addition of prefixes, suffixes, and endings is often accompanied by spelling changes as well; in English, `try+s` becomes `tries` and `dig+er` becomes `digger`. The rules of spelling change can be rather complex, and in some languages they act over long distances in surface forms.

Perhaps all these factors combined are sufficient to make morphological analysis complicated and difficult. In this chapter we approach the question more formally by investigating the computational characteristics of Koskenniemi's (1983) "two-level" model of morphological processing, considering the model as concretely embodied in the KIMMO system of Karttunen (1983). Given the kinds of constraints that can be encoded in the model, how difficult can it be to translate between lexical and surface forms?

Although the use of finite-state machinery in the two-level model gives it the appearance of computational efficiency, the model itself does not guarantee efficient processing. Traces of system operation show that the KIMMO machinery faces several kinds of choices in the course of analyzing familiar languages such as English. With the our standard technique of reduction we can probe the potential difficulty of such decisions. Taking the SAT problem (section 2.1.1) as an abstract model of a difficult choice system, sections 5.5 and 5.7 will show that two-level model allows language-descriptions that are computationally troublesome. Hence, the two-level framework can't guarantee ease of processing; if natural languages are easy to process, the reason must lie elsewhere.

The general problem of mapping between lexical and surface forms in two-level systems thus turns out to be computationally difficult in the worst case. If null characters are excluded, the problem is NP-complete. If null characters are completely unrestricted, the problem is PSPACE-complete and thus probably even harder in the worst case. Moreover, the fundamental difficulty of the problems does not seem to be just a precompilation effect (section 5.6).

The satisfiability reductions show that it can be hard to find the proper lexical/surface correspondence in a two-level generation or recognition problem. On a more positive note, however, another source of difficulty in the existing algorithms can be sharply reduced by changing the implementation of the dictionary component (section 5.8). A merged dictionary with bit vectors reduces the number of choices among alternative dictionary subdivisions by allowing several subdivisions to be searched at once.

5.1   Morphological Analysis

The word-level processing carried out by a natural-language system is formally a type of *morphological analysis,* concerned with recovering the internal structures of input words. For example, **singing** can be recognized as an inflected form of the verb **sing**, while **unhappy** can be analyzed as **un+happy**. However, the morphological component cannot break words up blindly; despite appearances, **duckling** is not the **-ing** form of a verb. The morphological analyzer must know the basic words of the language in addition to the prefixes and suffixes. In fact, analysis must be guided by more specific constraints as well. Not every word can combine with every affix; it would be an error to analyze **unit** as **un+it** or **beer** as **be+er** (compare **doer**).

The number of inflected forms of a given word is smaller in English than in many other languages. As a result, for a system with small scope it often suffices to trivialize morphological analysis by listing all inflected forms in the dictionary directly. The trivial approach is not feasible for heavily inflected languages such as Finnish, in which a word can have thousands of possible forms. In such cases, both practicality and elegance require a more systematic treatment in terms of inflectional endings, mood and tense markers, clitics, and so forth.

The problem of recovering the internal structures of words can take an extreme form in languages that allow productive compounding. Kay and Kaplan (1982) illustrate such a situation with the German word

`Lebensversicherungsgesellschaftsangestellter`,

which means *life insurance company employee*. An exhaustive dictionary is impractical when such free compounding is possible.

5.2   Spelling Changes

Besides knowing the stems, affixes, and co-occurrence restrictions of a language, a successful morphological analyzer must take into account the *spelling changes* that often accompany the addition of suffixes and similar elements. The program must expect `love+ing` to appear as `loving`, `fly+s` as `flies`, `lie+ing` as `lying`, and `big+er` as `bigger`. Its knowledge must be sufficiently sophisticated to distinguish such surface forms as `hopped` (= `hop+ed`) and `hoped` (= `hope+ed`). Cross-linguistically, spelling-change processes may span either a limited or a more extended range of characters, and the material that triggers a change may occur either before or after the character that is affected. Complex copying processes may be found in addition to simpler, more specific changes.

Spelling-change processes actually represent a superficial amalgam of phonological changes and orthographic conventions. Here, these two aspects of spelling changes will not be distinguished. The phonology and the orthography of a language do not have the same status for linguistics, but the differences are not relevant for the present purpose of analyzing the two-level framework. In any case, it is surface spelling that is input to program that analyzes text.

5.1   Local and long-distance processes

The spelling changes associated with the addition of English suffixes are *local* in the sense that they do not affect letters far away from the word–suffix boundary. However, there are processes in other languages that operate over longer distances. The spelling of Turkish suffixes is systematically affected by *vowel harmony* processes, which require the vowels in a word to agree in certain respects.[1] The vowels that appear in a typical suffix are not completely determined by the suffix, but are determined in part by the rules of vowel harmony. The suffix that Underhill (1976) writes as -sInIz may appear in an actual word as -siniz, -sunuz, -sünüz, or -sınız depending on the preceding vowel. Turkish words may contain large numbers of suffixes, and the effects of vowel harmony can propagate for long distances. (Hungarian suffixes display similar changes.)

5.2.2   Left and right context

Local spelling changes often depend on right context as well as left context; for instance, carry+ed changes "y" to "i" but carry+ing retains "y". Less commonly, long-distance changes can also be triggered by material to the right.[2] Verb stems in the Australian language Warlpiri display a regressive change of "i" to "u" triggered by a tense suffix containing a nasal "u"; thus the imperative form of *throw* is kiji-ka, but the past-tense form is kuju-rnu (Nash, 1980:84). As illustrated, this harmony process can affect more than one "i" in the verb stem. It can also propagate through the element -rni that can appear between the verb stem and the tense ending. (Warlpiri also has a different long-distance harmony process that operates from left to right.)

Other languages provide further examples of long-distance changes that are conditioned by material to the right. Kay and Kaplan (1982) mention a vowel-change process in Icelandic that causes vowels in the middle of a word to depend on the vowels in a following suffix. The inflectional system of German also involves vowel changes. Poser (1982:131ff) discusses an extreme example of long-distance right-to-left harmony that occurs in the lan-

---

[1] For details of this process, see Underhill (1976), Clements and Sezer (1982), and numerous references cited therein.

[2] Many current analyses of vowel harmony take it to be a fundamentally nondirectional process, even in languages in which it always appears to operate from left to right. For example, in Turkish it appears that the influence of root vowels on affix vowels always proceeds from left to right in Turkish, but this is because Turkish lacks prefixes. Clements and Sezer (1982:246ff) discuss a process of colloquial Turkish in which a vowel is inserted between the initial letters of certain words. The choice of vowel is determined by the usual harmony rules of Turkish, but operating from right to left in this case. See also Poser (1982).

guage Chumash. The process that he describes changes "s" to "š" through-out the entire word when an "š" occurs in a suffix; thus s+lu+sisin+waš (*3rd pers.+all+grow awry+past*) becomes šlušišinwaš (*it is all grown awry*).

5.2.3 Right context and processing ambiguity

The existence of changes that depend on right context implies that the lexical-surface correspondence for a particular character position cannot al-ways be determined when the position is first seen in a left-to-right scan. However, spelling-change processes with right context are not crucial to this difficulty. The same kind of *local ambiguity* can arise even when spelling changes do not depend on right context.

For example, for purposes of discussion we can remove the dependence of the y-to-i change on right context by considering a rule system in which "y" always changes to "i" after "p".[3] Even though the rule no longer depends on right context, there can still be uncertainty about how analysis should proceed. A surface string beginning spi... might correspond to a lexical string spy... as in spies, but it could equally well correspond to spi... as in spider or spiel. In general, analysis may proceed several characters beyond a choice point before it becomes apparent which hypothesis is correct. This is especially true with a large system vocabulary: in the above example, a system that did not know any spi... words could immediately rule out spi... in favor of spy..., but a system with more complete coverage would have to look further into the input before it could identify the correct choice.

5.2.4 Reduplication

Many languages display an interesting process called *reduplication,* in which consonants, vowels, syllables, roots, or other subunits of words are re-peated under certain conditions. Nash (1980:136ff) describes a reduplication process in Warlpiri that copies the first two syllables of a verb and has various

---

[3]If "y" always changes to "i" after "p", what justification could there be for saying that spy and not spi is the correct underlying form? None is presented in this trivial constructed example, but in an actual language, there could be evidence from a variety of sources: suffixes beginning with "y"; harmony processes; rules that create or destroy the "p" that triggers the change; rules that are triggered by the "y" before it changes; and so forth.

semantic effects. For example, he cites the sentence

> pirli ka   parnta-parnta-rri-nja-mpa   ya-ni
> hill   PRES   crouch-REDUP   INF-across   go-NONPAST
> *The mountain extends in a series of humps.*

in which the verb stem `parntarri-` has undergone reduplication.[4]
Lieber's (1980:234ff) discussion of several reduplication processes in the language Tagalog provides other examples. One Tagalog reduplication process
copies the first consonant and vowel of the stem, making the copied vowel
short; another is similar, but makes the copied vowel long; a third process
copies the first syllable and part or all of the second, lengthening the copied
vowel of the second syllable. See also McCarthy's (1982:193f) treatment of
reduplication in Classical Arabic.[5]

In many formal systems it happens that reduplication processes are
harder to treat than the other kinds of spelling changes in this section, and
the KIMMO system is no exception. Since reduplication processes find no
easy treatment in the systems we're examining here, they will be ignored in
the rest of this chapter.

5.3 Two-Level Morphology

Given a description of the root forms, the combinatory patterns, and the
spelling-change rules of a language, the morphological analysis task is well-defined in an abstract sense. However, a practical morphological analyzer also
needs an efficient way to put such knowledge to use. The KIMMO implementation of the two-level model is attractive for this purpose. The spelling-change
rules that typically go along with affixation and inflection are encoded in a
finite-state *automaton component,* while roots and affixes are listed with their
co-occurrence restrictions in a *dictionary component.* The main focus here
will be on the automaton component.

---

[4]The hyphens in the Warlpiri examples are inserted as an analytical aid for the reader,
and do not conform to the standard orthography (Hale 1982:222).

[5]McCarthy's treatment of Arabic is of theoretical interest for at least two reasons:
it helps illuminate the nature of linguistic representations, and it shows a way to derive
many characteristics of Arabic reduplication from universal linguistic principles rather than
language-particular stipulations.

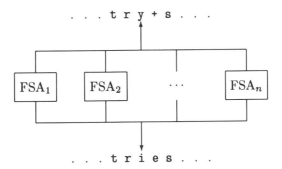

Figure 5.1: The automaton component of the KIMMO system consists of several two-headed finite-state automata that inspect the lexical/surface correspondence in parallel. Each automaton imposes some constraint on the correspondence. The automata move together from left to right. (After Karttunen 1983:176.)

5.3.1   The automaton component

The two-level model is concerned with the representation of a word at two distinct levels, the *lexical* or dictionary level and the *surface* level. At the surface level, words are represented as they might show up in text. At the lexical level, words consist of sequences of stems, affixes, diacritics, and boundary markers that have been pasted together without spelling changes. Thus Karttunen and Wittenburg (1983) represent the surface form `tries` as `try+s` at the lexical level. Similarly, the Warlpiri surface form `kijika` might be represented at the lexical level as `kIjI-ka`, where "I" is a special lexical character that can surface as either "i" or "u" according to harmony rules.[6] The lexical and surface levels are connected by several finite-state transducers that make up the automaton component (figure 5.1).

A specific spelling-change process in the two-level model amounts to a *constraint* on the correspondence between lexical and surface strings. For example, consider a simplified "Y-Change" process that changes "y" to "i"

---

[6]The choice of boundary markers and other special characters for the KIMMO description of a language is up to the grammar-writer. Karttunen and Wittenburg (1983) use "+" as a boundary marker in English, while in the description of Warlpiri, we use "-" for various divisions following our linguistic sources.

before adding "es". Interpreted as a constraint, Y-Change controls the occurrence of the lexical/surface pairs y/y and y/i: lexical "y" must correspond
to surface "i" when it occurs before lexical "+s", which will itself come out
as surface "es" because of other constraints.

Each such constraint is implemented by a finite-state machine with two
scanning heads that move together along the lexical and surface strings. The
machine starts out in state 1 and moves forward by changing state based on
its current state and the pair of characters it is scanning. The following state
table describes the automaton that encodes the Y-Change process:

"Y-Change" 5 5						
	y	y	+	s	=	*(lexical characters)*
	i	y	=	s	=	*(surface characters)*
state 1:	2	4	1	1	1	*(normal state)*
state 2.	0	0	3	0	0	*(require +s)*
state 3.	0	0	0	1	0	*(require s)*
state 4:	2	4	5	1	1	*(forbid +s)*
state 5:	2	4	1	0	1	*(forbid s)*

In this notation, taken from Karttunen (1983) following Koskenniemi, "=" is
a certain kind of wildcard character. The use of ":" rather than "." after
the state-number on some lines indicates that the ":" states are *final states*,
which will accept end-of-input. In order to handle insertion or deletion, it
is also possible to have a null character "0" on one side of a pair, but the
possibility of nulls will not be given full consideration until section 5.7.[7]

In processing the lexical/surface string pair try+s/tries, the automaton would run through the state sequence 1,1,1,2,3,1 and accept the correspondence. In contrast, with the string pair try+s/tryes it would block on
s/s after the state sequence 1,1,1,4,5 because the entry for s/s in state 5
is zero. With the pair try/tri it would not block with any zero entries,
but would still reject the pair because it would end up in state 2, which is
designated as nonfinal.

For present purposes it does not matter whether this particular
Y-Change rule represents the best way to capture the relevant spelling alternations. Instead, the point is to illustrate how a two-level automaton
implements dependence on right context (+s, in the case at hand). The automaton will initially accept either of the correspondences y/i and y/y, but

---

[7]The actual KIMMO system of Karttunen (1983) does not allow null characters at the
lexical level, but the omission is inessential.

if it processes the y/i correspondence, it will enter a sequence of states that will ultimately block unless the y/i pair is followed by the appropriate lexical context "+s".

The right context for a right-to-left vowel harmony process might seem more difficult to encode because it may be necessary to ignore several intervening consonants, but such a situation actually presents no problem at all. An automaton state can easily ignore irrelevant characters by looping back to itself.

A language will generally exhibit several different spelling-change processes; for example, Karttunen (1983:177) mentions that Koskenniemi's analysis of Finnish uses 21 rules. By and large, these separate processes can be encoded as separate automata in the KIMMO system. In actual processing, the automata that express various spelling-change constraints will all inspect the lexical/surface correspondence in *parallel* (as figure 5.1 suggested). The correspondence will be accepted only if every automaton accepts it—that is, if it satisfies every constraint.[8] Because the automata are connected in parallel rather than in series, there are no "feeding" relationships between two-level automata.[9] A set of several automata can also be compiled into a single large automaton that will run faster than the original set, though its size may be prohibitive (1983:176f).

5.3.2 The dictionary component

The dictionary component of the KIMMO system is divided into sections called *lexicons*, which are all ultimately reachable from a distinguished *root lexicon*. In the dictionary-level processing for words such as **singing**, KIMMO first locates the lexical form **sing** in the root lexicon. The mechanism for indi-

---

[8]If null characters are allowed, the interpretation of "satisfying every constraint" takes on a certain subtlety. See section 5.7.

[9]It is a theoretical claim of the two-level framework that intermediate levels of representation and "feeding" relationships are not necessary—that two levels suffice, in other words. Series connection of the automata would imply the existence of intermediate representation levels at the interface between automata. Beyond the question of computational efficiency, the theoretical claims of the two-level model will not be evaluated here. Possible arguments against them could involve (a) rule orderings with depth > 1; (b) particular analyses in which the availability of only two levels leads to redundancy in the automata; and (c) multi-part alternative representations (*e.g.*, from autosegmental theory) that allow a more illuminating description of various linguistic processes. One possible argument for them could involve the multiplicity of possibilities for rule ordering in a model with intermediate derivational steps.

cating co-occurrence restrictions involves listing a set of continuation lexicons for each entry, and in this case one possibility will be a lexicon that contains +ing. In the actual operation of the KIMMO system, dictionary processing is efficiently interleaved with the operation of the automata in such a way that the two components mutually constrain their operations.

The continuation-class mechanism that the KIMMO dictionary uses to encode co-occurrence restrictions among roots and affixes has only finite-state power; each lexicon corresponds to a state in a transition network. As many people have noticed (*e.g.*, Karttunen (1983:180); Karttunen and Wittenburg (1983:222f)), such a design makes it difficult or impossible to express some morphological constraints. In the future, the KIMMO dictionary component will probably be redesigned in a way that makes it easier to express the difficult constraints. But since the automaton component is our main focus here, we'll say little more about the dictionary component until section 5.8.

5.3.3   Generation and recognition

A KIMMO system does not particularly lean toward either *generating* or *recognizing* the words of a language. Because the machines of the automaton component just express constraints on permissible lexical/surface correspondences, they can serve equally well to determine the lexical form of a surface word (recognition) or to map a lexical stem with affixes into the proper surface form (generation). The only major difference is whether the process is driven by the surface or lexical form. However, the recognition algorithm is slightly more complicated because it uses the lexicon as well as the automata to constrain the analysis of an input word. (As Karttunen (1983:184) points out, it would require only a simple change to run the recognizer without the constraints of the stem lexicon. Such a mode of operation would be useful for stripping recognizable suffixes from unfamiliar roots.)

5.4   The Seeds of Complexity

As we've seen, the KIMMO description of a language involves several finite-state two-level automata and a finite-state dictionary component. The use of finite-state machinery lends the two-level model an air of computational efficiency, since it's well known that some tasks involving deterministic finite-state automata are computationally easy to accomplish. For instance, given a string σ and an automaton A, it's easy to decide whether A accepts σ. Unfortunately, a closer look suggests that a KIMMO generator or recognizer can potentially have a lot of work on its hands. This section sorts out the possible sources of computational difficulty; the next section will push the analysis further in mathematical reductions that tell us how hard generation and recognition could be in the general case.

5.4.1 The lure of the finite-state

At first glance, the KIMMO system raises hopes of unfailing efficiency. Both recognition and generation seem to be a matter of stepping finite-state machines through the input from left to right, a process that takes only a quick array reference or so per character. Any nondeterminism that might arise causes little initial concern, since methods of determinizing finite-state machines are well-known.[10] Lexical lookup can also be done quickly, character by character, interleaved with the speedy left-to-right progress of the automata:

> It is a common technique to represent lexicons as letter trees because it minimizes the time spent on searching for the right entry. The recognizer only makes a single left-to-right pass as it homes in on its target in the lexicon. (Karttunen 1983:178)

The fundamental efficiency of finite-state machines promises to make the speed of KIMMO processing for a language largely independent of the nature of the constraints that the automata encode:

> The most important technical feature of Koskenniemi's and our implementation of the Two-level model is that morphological rules are represented in the processor as automata, more specifically, as finite state transducers .... One important consequence of compiling [the grammar rules into automata] is that the complexity of the linguistic description of a language has no significant effect on the speed at which the forms of that language can be recognized or generated. This is due to the fact that finite state machines are very fast to operate because of their simplicity .... Although Finnish, for example, is morphologically a much more complicated

---

[10] One caveat is necessary: though nondeterministic finite-state recognizers can always be determinized, the conversion process may explode machine size exponentially.

> language than English, there is no difference of the same magnitude in the processing times for the two languages .... [This fact] has some psycholinguistic interest because of the common sense observation that we talk about "simple" and "complex" languages but not about "fast" and "slow" ones. (Karttunen 1983:166f)

If the automaton-based two-level model is to be psycholinguistically interesting in this way, it must be the model itself that wipes out processing difficulty, rather than some accidental property of the constraints that the automata encode. In much the same vein, Lindstedt (1984:171) remarks following Koskenniemi that "it is psycholinguistically interesting to note that the [two-level] rules are equivalent to such computationally simple and effective [*i.e.*, efficient] devices," again picking out the finite-state machinery as the factor responsible for computational efficiency.

In many ways, KIMMO processing *is* efficient; for instance, the recognition algorithm interleaves lexical lookup with the operation of the finite-state machines in an efficient way. But the details raise questions; since the generator and recognizer both do a certain amount of search in familiar cases, the question arises of how much search might theoretically be needed.

5.4.2 Sample recognizer behavior

In sorting out the characteristics of the KIMMO algorithms, it's helpful to consider an example. Figure 5.2 shows the operations that one implementation of the KIMMO recognizer for English goes through when it analyzes the word **spiel**. The sequence of hypothesized lexical forms makes it clear that the recognizer doesn't always glide quickly from left to right as we might hope.

For example, at step 7 the recognizer is considering the lexical string **spy+**, "y" surfacing as "i" and "+" as "e", under the theory that the input word might be a plural form of the noun **spy**—**spies** or **spies**', that is. At step 9 that analysis has failed to pan out and **spy+** is considered again, this time with "+" coming out null on the surface instead of matching the input "e". At step 11 the recognizer has dropped back to the form **spy** that it was considering at step 4, this time taking the root as a verb. All of the **spy** possibilities ultimately fail, and at step 52 the recognizer finally tries **spi** instead, repudiating the incorrect choice that it made in step 3. In step 53 it assumes that the "e" in the lexical form **spie**... might have been deleted, but this idea soon founders. Finally, in step 59 it finds the correct lexical entry `spiel`.

5.4.3 Sources of runtime complexity

Traces like the one in figure 5.2 reveal several factors that combine to determine the overall computational difficulty of an analysis. The recognizer must run the finite-state machines of the automaton component and descend the letter trees that make up a lexicon, it must decide which suffix lexicon to explore after finding a root, and it must discover the correct lexical/surface correspondence.

First of all, some of the recognizer's activities are concerned with the *mechanical operation* of the automata and the letter trees of the lexicon. Running the automata is expected to be fast; there are many well-known fast implementations of finite-state machines, differing somewhat in their time and space requirements. Descending a letter tree should also be easy, in any of its common implementations.

Second, the recognizer often makes unfortunate choices about the path that it should follow through the collection of *lexicons* in the dictionary component. Quite a few nodes in the search tree of figure 5.2 represent choices among alternative lexicons (LLL). For example, at step 11 the recognizer may search any of several lexicons next: the lexicon "I" that encodes the fact that the present indicative of a verb may have no added ending, the lexicon "AG" that contains the agentive ending +er, or one of several other lexicons that contain +ed and other inflectional endings.

The search for a path through the suffix lexicons of the dictionary component can take considerable time in the current KIMMO implementation. However, such wandering can be sharply reduced by merging the lexicons in such a way that several lexicons can be searched in parallel; section 5.8 will explain in detail. Meanwhile, taking this improvement for granted will make it possible to sidestep the problem and focus on other processes. With the merged dictionary, figure 5.3 shows that the number of lexicon–choice alternatives in the search tree for `spiel` is reduced from 8 to 2, cutting the total number of steps from 61 to 29. (These figures count LLL nodes excluding unambiguous choices.) The choice between `spy`–noun and `spy`–verb remains because it would be directly reflected in the output, but the purely internal choices among the lexicons for different verbal endings are eliminated.

Finally, some of the backtracking results from local ambiguity in the construction of the *lexical/surface correspondence*. Even if only one possibility is globally compatible with the constraints imposed by the lexicon and the automata, there may not be enough evidence at every point in processing to choose the correct lexical/surface pair; search behavior results. Figure 5.4 displays the search graphically with an expanded version of the merged-lexicon search tree from figure 5.3, annotated with information about the specific choices the recognizer has at each point.

Thus, after seeing the surface characters spi..., the recognizer did not have enough evidence to choose between the lexical possibilities spy... and spi..., even though only one analysis was possible for the complete input spiel. During exploration of the spy... possibility in the (/V) lexicon, there was uncertainty about the pairs +/0, +/e, e/0, and e/e. It proved unprofitable to explore those regions of the tree in the analysis of spiel, but figure 5.5 shows that the correct analysis can lie in those regions for other words.

Incidentally, the KIMMO machinery is not designed to stop after finding one analysis; it explores the entire search tree as pruned by the automata, thus making search order irrelevant. The reason for continuing the search is that a syntactic analyzer may require access to all interpretations of a morphologically ambiguous input. For instance, the morphological analyzer cannot decide on its own whether flies should be given the features of a noun or a verb. Thus, the KIMMO system returns multiple analyses for

---

Figure 5.2: These traces (facing page) show the steps that the KIMMO recognizer for English goes through while analyzing the surface form spiel. Each line of the table on the left shows the lexical string and automaton states at the end of a step. If some automaton blocked, the automaton states are replaced by an XXX entry. An XXX entry with no automaton name indicates that the lexical string could not be extended because the surface character and lexical letter tree together ruled out all feasible pairs. After an XXX or *** entry, the recognizer backtracks and picks up from a previous choice point, indicated by the parenthesized step number before the lexical string. The tree on the right depicts the search graphically, reading from left to right and top to bottom with vertical bars linking the choices at each choice point. The figures were generated with a KIMMO implementation written in an augmented version of MACLISP based initially on Karttunen's (1983:182ff) algorithm description; the dictionary and automaton components for English were taken from Karttunen and Wittenburg (1983) with minor changes. This implementation searches depth-first as Karttunen's does, but explores the alternatives at a given depth in a different order from Karttunen's.

```
Recognizing surface form "spiel".
 1        s                 1,4,1,2,1,1
 2        sp                1,1,1,2,1,1
 3        spy               1,3,4,3,1,1
 4        "spy" ends,       new lexicon N
 5        "0" ends,         new lexicon C1
 6        spy               XXX extra input
 7 (5)    spy+              1,5,16,4,1,1
 8        spy+              XXX
 9 (5)    spy+              1,6,1,4,1,1
10        spy+              XXX
11 (4)    "spy" ends,       new lexicon I
12        spy               XXX extra input
13 (4)    "spy" ends,       new lexicon P3
14        spy+              1,6,1,4,1,1
15        spy+              XXX
16 (14)   spy+              1,5,16,4,1,1
17        spy+              XXX
18 (4)    "spy" ends,       new lexicon PS
19        spy+              1,6,1,4,1,1
20        spy+e             1,1,1,1,4,1
21        spy+e             XXX
22 (20)   spy+e             1,1,4,1,3,1
23        spy+e             XXX
24 (19)   spy+              1,5,16,4,1,1
25        spy+e             XXX Epenthesis
26 (4)    "spy" ends,       new lexicon PP
27        spy+              1,6,1,4,1,1
28        spy+e             1,1,1,1,4,1
29        spy+e             XXX
30 (28)   spy+e             1,1,4,1,3,1
31        spy+e             XXX
32 (27)   spy+              1,5,16,4,1,1
33        spy+e             XXX Epenthesis
34 (4)    "spy" ends,       new lexicon PR
35        spy+              1,6,1,4,1,1
36        spy+              XXX
37 (35)   spy+              1,5,16,4,1,1
38        spy+              XXX
39 (4)    "spy" ends,       new lexicon AG
40        spy+              1,6,1,4,1,1
41        spy+e             1,1,1,1,4,1
42        spy+e             XXX
43 (41)   spy+e             1,1,4,1,3,1
44        spy+e             XXX
45 (40)   spy+              1,5,16,4,1,1
46        spy+e             XXX Epenthesis
47 (4)    "spy" ends,       new lexicon AB
48        spy+              1,6,1,4,1,1
49        spy+              XXX
50 (48)   spy+              1,5,16,4,1,1
51        spy+              XXX
52 (3)    spi               1,1,4,1,2,5
53        spie              1,1,16,1,6,1
54        spie              XXX
55 (53)   spie              1,1,16,1,5,6
56        spiel             1,1,16,2,1,1
57        "spiel" ends,     new lexicon N
58        "0" ends,         new lexicon C1
59        "spiel"           *** result
60 (58)   spiel+            1,1,16,1,1,1
61        spiel+            XXX

(("spiel" (N SG)))
```

```
---+---+---+LLL+LLL+III+
   |   |   |   |
   |   |   ---+XXX+
   |   |   |
   |   |   ---+XXX+
   |   |   |
   |   LLL+III+
   |   |
   |   LLL+---+XXX+
   |   |   |
   |   |   ---+XXX+
   |   |   |
   |   LLL+---+---+XXX+
   |   |   |   |
   |   |   |   ---+XXX+
   |   |   |   |
   |   |   ---+AAA+
   |   |   |
   |   LLL+---+---+XXX+
   |   |   |   |
   |   |   |   ---+XXX+
   |   |   |   |
   |   |   ---+AAA+
   |   |   |
   |   LLL+---+XXX+
   |   |   |
   |   |   ---+XXX+
   |   |   |
   |   LLL+---+---+XXX+
   |   |   |   |
   |   |   |   ---+XXX+
   |   |   |   |
   |   |   ---+AAA+
   |   |   |
   |   LLL+---+XXX+
   |   |   |
   |   |   ---+XXX+
   |   |
   ---+---+XXX+
       |
   ---+---+LLL+LLL+****+
           |
           ---+XXX+
```

Key to tree nodes:

`---`	normal traversal
LLL	new lexicon
AAA	blocking by automata
XXX	no lexical-surface pairs
	compatible with surface
	char and dictionary
III	blocking by leftover input
***	analysis found

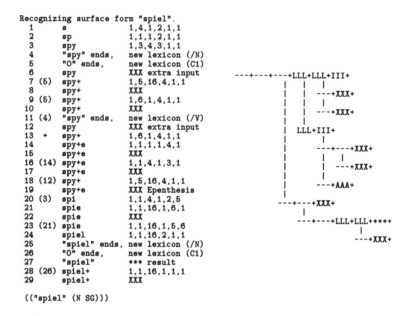

```
Recognizing surface form "spiel".
1        s                    1,4,1,2,1,1
2        sp                   1,1,1,2,1,1
3        spy                  1,3,4,3,1,1
4        "spy" ends,          new lexicon (/N)
5        "0" ends,            new lexicon (C1)
6        spy                  XXX extra input
7 (5)    spy+                 1,5,16,4,1,1
8        spy+                 XXX
9 (5)    spy+                 1,6,1,4,1,1
10       spy+                 XXX
11 (4)   "spy" ends,          new lexicon (/V)
12       spy                  XXX extra input
13 +     spy+                 1,6,1,4,1,1
14       spy+e                1,1,1,1,4,1
15       spy+e                XXX
16 (14)  spy+e                1,1,4,1,3,1
17       spy+e                XXX
18 (12)  spy+                 1,5,16,4,1,1
19       spy+e                XXX Epenthesis
20 (3)   spi                  1,1,4,1,2,5
21       spie                 1,1,16,1,6,1
22       spie                 XXX
23 (21)  spie                 1,1,16,1,5,6
24       spiel                1,1,16,2,1,1
25       "spiel" ends,        new lexicon (/N)
26       "0" ends,            new lexicon (C1)
27       "spiel"              *** result
28 (26)  spiel+               1,1,16,1,1,1
29       spiel+               XXX

(("spiel" (N SG)))
```

Figure 5.3: The dictionary modification that will be described in section 5.8 causes the KIMMO recognizer to make fewer choices among lexicons. These traces show the steps that the recognizer goes through in the analysis of spiel when the merged dictionary is used; the number of lexicon-choice nodes (LLL) is lower than in figure 5.2. The names of the merged lexicons are written in parenthesized form to indicate that each one actually represents a *class* of lexicons in the original dictionary description. A "+" entry in the backtracking column indicates backtracking from an immediate failure in the previous step, which does not require the full backtracking mechanism to be invoked.

morphologically ambiguous inputs. Naturally, it returns only one analysis when the morphological constraints of the automata and the dictionary are sufficient for disambiguation.

In a similar way, when the recognizer analyzes the word rubbish (figure 5.6), it cannot tell after seeing only rubb... whether the lexical string is rubb... as in rubbish or rub+... as in rub+ing ==> rubbing. In fact, it briefly considers the possibility that surface r... might correspond to lexical re'... as in the stress-marked lexical representation re'fer, but it quickly discovers that the right context for licensing the e/0 pair is absent. (Recall from section 5.3.1 how a KIMMO automaton implements a change

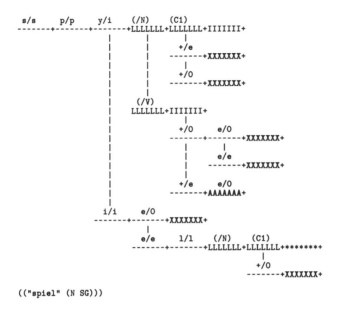

```
   s/s      p/p      y/i     (/N)     (C1)
-------+-------+-------+LLLLLLL+LLLLLLL+IIIIIII+
                      |        |       |
                      |        |      +/e
                      |        |   -------+XXXXXXX+
                      |        |       |
                      |        |      +/0
                      |        |   -------+XXXXXXX+
                      |        |
                      |      (/V)
                      |   LLLLLLL+IIIIIII+
                      |               |
                      |              +/0      e/0
                      |           -------+-------+XXXXXXX+
                      |               |       |
                      |               |      e/e
                      |               |   -------+XXXXXXX+
                      |               |
                      |              +/e      e/0
                      |           -------+AAAAAAA+
                      |
                     i/i      e/0
                  -------+-------+XXXXXXX+
                          |
                         e/e      1/1     (/N)     (C1)
                      -------+-------+LLLLLLL+LLLLLLL+*******+
                                              |
                                             +/0
                                          -------+XXXXXXX+
```

    (("spiel" (N SG)))

Figure 5.4: This expanded version of the search tree from figure 5.3 shows what hypothesis the KIMMO recognizer is entertaining along each path, during the analysis of **spiel** with a merged dictionary.

---

that depends on right context: initially it permits the changed pair in the expectation that the proper right context will be found, and upon processing the changed pair, it enters a state-sequence that will eventually block without the necessary right context.)

In these cases, misguided search subtrees did not get very deep—largely because the relevant spelling-change processes were local in character. Long-distance harmony processes are also possible (section 5.2), and thus there can potentially be a long interval before it's finally determined whether a lexical/surface pair is acceptable. For example, when vowel alternations within a verb stem are conditioned by the occurrence of particular tense suffixes, it may be necessary to see the end of the word before making final decisions about the stem. The possibility of a long period of uncertainty forms the basis of the reductions that probe the worst-case complexity of KIMMO processing.

Since long-distance right context is one factor that helps blow up the search trees, it has been suggested that KIMMO processing in the problem-

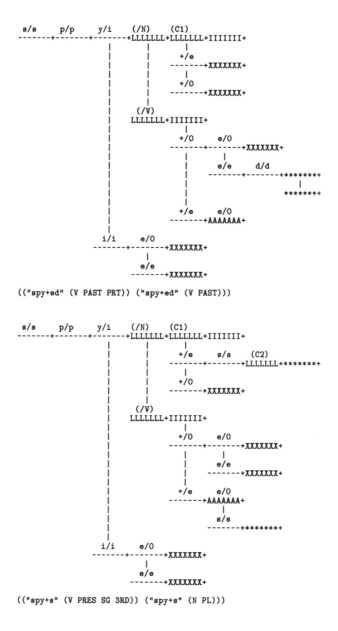

Figure 5.5: The search trees for **spied** and **spies** are similar to the search tree for **spiel** (figure 5.4), but the solutions lie in different regions of the tree; thus none of the three main regions of the tree can be pruned from the search.

```
Recognizing surface form "rubbish".
  1       r            1,1,1,2,1,1      12  +   rub+i       1,1,1,1,2,5
  2       re           1,1,1,1,4,1      13      rub+i       XXX
  3       re'          XXX Elision      14 (6)  rubb        1,1,16,2,1,1
  4 (2)   ru           1,1,4,1,2,1      15      rubbi       1,1,16,1,2,5
  5       rub          1,1,5,2,1,1      16      rubbis      1,4,16,2,1,1
  6       "rub" ends,  new lexicon (/V) 17      rubbish     1,3,16,2,1,1
  7       rub          XXX extra input  18      "rubbish" ends, new lexicon (/N)
  8   +   rub+         1,1,3,1,1,1      19      "0" ends,   new lexicon (C1)
  9       rub+e        XXX Gemination   20      "rubbish"   *** result
 10 (7)   rub+         1,1,2,1,1,1      21 (19) rubbish+    1,6,16,1,1,1
 11       rub+e        XXX Gemination   22      rubbish+    XXX

(("rubbish" (N SG)))
```

Figure 5.6: While analyzing the surface form rubbish, the KIMMO recognizer is temporarily misled (i) by the possibility that a stress-marked lexical "e" (appearing in the lexicon as "e'") might have been deleted at the surface and (ii) by the possibility that the surface "bb" might have resulted from doubling of a single underlying "b". However, in each case the possibility fails to pan out. (Refer to figure 5.2 for an explanation of the table format.)

---

atic cases would be easier if carried out from right to left. But right-to-left processing would make the common case of *left context* difficult instead, and what direction would be appropriate for mixed rule systems in which both left and right context play a role? Jumping ahead a bit, the reductions in section 5.5 imply that no simple fix (such as reversal of direction) will suffice in the general case.

5.4.4 Search and verification

Setting aside until section 5.8 the problem of choosing among alternative lexicons, it's easy to see that the use of finite-state machinery helps control only one of the two remaining sources of complexity. Stepping the automata should be fast, but the finite-state framework doesn't make it easy to guess which lexical/surface pair will ultimately work out when there's more than one choice. The search for the right lexical/surface correspondence may predominate.

In fact, the KIMMO recognition and generation problems bear an ominous resemblance to difficult problems in the class $\mathcal{NP}$ that was defined in section 2.1.2. Informally, such problems have solutions that may be hard to *guess* but are easy to *verify* (in polynomial time):

> [Informally,] we view [a nondeterministic algorithm] as being com-
> posed of two separate stages, the first being a *guessing stage*
> and the second a *checking stage* .... It should be evident that
> a "polynomial time nondeterministic algorithm" is basically a
> definitional device for capturing the notion of polynomial time
> verifiability, rather than a realistic method for solving decision
> problems. (Garey and Johnson 1979:28–29)

This difference in difficulty between guessing and verification seems to fit
the KIMMO framework: the finite-state two-level automata can verify a solution quickly, but it may still be hard to guess the correct lexical/surface
correspondence.

Given some two-level automata and an input, it's not always apparent from local evidence how to build a lexical/surface correspondence that
will satisfy the constraints of the automata. For this reason, the KIMMO
algorithms contain the seeds of complexity. The next sections will exploit
those seeds in mathematical reductions that show KIMMO recognition and
generation to be computationally difficult in the worst case.

5.5 The Complexity of Two-Level Morphology

The reductions in this section show that two-level automata can describe
computationally difficult problems in a very natural way. It follows that the
two-level framework itself can't guarantee computational efficiency. If the
words of natural languages are easy to analyze, the efficiency of processing
must result from some additional property that natural languages have, beyond those that are formally captured in the two-level model.[11] Otherwise,
computationally difficult problems might turn up in the two-level automata
for some natural language, just as they do in the artificially constructed languages here. In fact, the reductions are abstractly modeled on the KIMMO
treatment of harmony processes and other long-distance dependencies (section 5.2) that occur in natural languages.

In connection with the reductions, it's important to remember the distinction between *algorithm complexity* and *problem complexity* (section 1.2.1).

---

[11]For other theoretical discussions of efficient processability, see Berwick and Weinberg (1982) as well as chapter 6, chapter 7, and other chapters of this book.

Here, we're focusing on the difficulty of the general KIMMO processing *problems,* not just the behavior of one set of processing algorithms. In terms of an analogy from mathematics, the KIMMO framework allows "equations" of a certain kind to be set up, and we're concerned with the *intrinsic difficulty* of solving such equations—difficulty that will show up no matter what algorithm we choose. (See chapters 1 and 2 for more discussion.)

We may also question whether the possibility of computational difficulty is inherent in morphology or arises merely from from characteristics of the two-level model. Any formal linguistic model makes explicit a set of assumptions about the nature of the linguistic process and the kind of information that it fundamentally involves. At the same time, the model ignores some details and introduces others that are only artifacts of formalization. Thus, if the formal framework allows problems to arise whose difficulty is too great to be consistent with the apparent difficulty of actual problems, several interpretations are possible. The prevailing opinion about the difficulty of the actual problems may simply be mistaken; formal investigation may have uncovered "worst cases" that were not previously apparent. Alternatively, another natural possibility is that something has been missed in formalization; the natural computational task may have significant features that the formalized version does not capture and exploit effectively. We'll discuss the implications of the reductions more fully in chapter 6.

In any event, all of the reductions in this chapter remind us that problems involving finite-state machines can be hard. Determining membership in a finite-state language may be easy, but using finite-state machines for different tasks such as parsing or transduction can lead to problems that are computationally more difficult.

5.5.1 KIMMO **generation is NP-Hard**

The reductions involve versions of the Boolean satisfiability problem (SAT) as described in section 2.1.1. Each instance of the SAT problem involves a Boolean formula in conjunctive normal form and asks if there's some way of assigning truth-values to the variables so that the formula comes out true. The SAT problem is NP-complete and thus computationally difficult.

It's easy to encode an arbitrary SAT problem as a generation problem in the KIMMO framework. The general problem of mapping from lexical to

```
"u-consistency" 3 3
        u   u   =   (lexical characters)
        T   F   =   (surface characters)
    1:  2   3   1   (u undecided)
    2:  2   0   2   (u true)
    3:  0   3   3   (u false)
```

Figure 5.7: The KIMMO generator system that encodes a SAT formula f should include a *consistency automaton* of this form for every variable u that occurs in f. The consistency automaton constrains the mapping from variables in the lexical string to truth-values in the surface string, ensuring that whatever value is assigned to u in one occurrence must be assigned to u in every occurrence.

surface forms in KIMMO systems is therefore NP-hard, *i.e.*, NP-complete or worse (see section 5.7). Formally, we will define a possible instance of the computational problem KIMMO GENERATION as any pair $\langle A, \sigma \rangle$, where A is the automaton component of a KIMMO system (specified with the notation of Gajek *et al.* (1983)) and σ is a string over the alphabet of the KIMMO system. An actual instance of KIMMO GENERATION will be any possible instance $\langle A, \sigma \rangle$ such that for some σ', the lexical/surface pair σ/σ' satisfies the constraints imposed by the automata in A. Thus $\langle A, \sigma \rangle$ is an instance of KIMMO GENERATION if there is *any* surface string that can be generated from the lexical string σ according to the automata. (As the problem is defined, an algorithm is not required to exhibit the surface strings that can be generated, but only to say whether there are any.)

To encode a SAT problem f as a pair $\langle A, \sigma \rangle$, first construct σ from the CNF formula f by a notational translation. Use a minus sign for negation, a comma for conjunction, and no explicit operator for disjunction. Then the σ corresponding to the formula $(\overline{x} \vee y) \wedge (\overline{y} \vee z) \wedge (x \vee y \vee z)$ is -xy,-yz,xyz. The notation is unambiguous without parentheses because f is required to be in CNF.

Second, construct A (in polynomial time) in three parts. (A varies from formula to formula only when the formulas involve different sets of variables.) The *alphabet specification* should list the variables in σ together with the special characters T, F, minus sign, and comma. The equals sign should be declared as the KIMMO wildcard character, as usual. Several *consistency automata* should be constructed according to figure 5.7. Each consistency

```
"satisfaction" 3 4
        =  =  -  ,      (lexical characters)
        T  F  -  ,      (surface characters)
   1.   2  1  3  0      (no true seen in this group)
   2:   2  2  2  1      (true seen in this group)
   3.   1  2  0  0      (-F counts as true)
```

Figure 5.8: The SAT generator system for any formula should include this *satisfaction automaton*, which determines whether the truth values assigned to the variables cause the formula to come out true. Since the formula is in CNF, the requirement is that the groups between commas must all contain at least one true value. In state 1, no true value has been seen; F cycles, while T goes to state 2 to wait for the comma that begins the next group. State 3 remembers a preceding minus sign so that -F can count as true. Only state 2 is a final state because only state 2 indicates that a true value has occurred.

automaton remembers the truth-value for one variable, so we need one copy of figure 5.7 for each distinct variable in σ. The *satisfaction automaton* should be copied from figure 5.8 and does not change from formula to formula. Figure 5.9 lists the entire SAT generator system A for formulas f that use variables x, y, and z.

The generator system used in this construction is set up so that surface strings are identical to lexical strings, but with truth values substituted for the variables. Thus any surface string generated from σ will directly exhibit a satisfying truth-assignment for f. The consistency automaton for each variable u ensures that the value assigned to u is consistent throughout the string. In state 1, no truth-value has been assigned and either u/T or u/F is acceptable. In state 2, u/T has been chosen once and therefore only u/T can be permitted for other occurrences of u. Similarly, state 3 allows only u/F. No matter what state it's in, the u-consistency automaton just ignores any pair that doesn't involve u, skipping over punctuation marks and other variables. The satisfaction automaton blocks if any disjunction contains only F and -T after truth-values have been substituted for the variables; it will end up in a final state only if the truth-values that have been assigned satisfy every disjunction and hence f.

The net result of the constraints imposed by the consistency and satisfaction automata is that some surface string can be generated from σ just in case the original formula f has a satisfying truth-assignment. Furthermore,

```
    ALPHABET x y z T F - ,

        ANY =
        END
```

```
"x-consistency" 3 3
        x  x  =
        T  F  =
    1:  2  3  1
    2:  2  0  2
    3:  0  3  3

"y-consistency" 3 3
        y  y  =
        T  F  =
    1:  2  3  1
    2:  2  0  2
    3:  0  3  3

"z-consistency" 3 3
        z  z  =
        T  F  =
    1:  2  3  1
    2:  2  0  2
    3:  0  3  3

"satisfaction" 3 4
        =  =  -  ,
        T  F  -  ,
    1.  2  1  3  0
    2:  2  2  2  1
    3.  1  2  0  0

END
```

Figure 5.9: This is the complete KIMMO generator system for solving SAT problems in the variables x, y, and z. The system includes a consistency automaton for each variable in addition to a satisfaction automaton that does not vary from problem to problem.

the pair $\langle A, \sigma \rangle$ can be constructed in time polynomial in the length of f; thus SAT is polynomial-time reduced to KIMMO GENERATION, and the general case of KIMMO GENERATION is at least as hard as SAT.

Technically, this reduction varies both the automaton set and the input string as the problem instance varies—thus raising precompilation questions that we'll consider in section 5.6. However, the automaton set varies only in a limited and regular way. For all satisfiability problems in k variables, a single set of $k + 1$ small automata will do.

Figure 5.10 traces the operation of the KIMMO generation algorithm on a satisfiable formula.

Figure 5.10: The KIMMO generator system of figure 5.9 goes through these steps (facing page) when applied to the encoded version of the (satisfiable) formula $(\overline{x} \vee y) \wedge (\overline{y} \vee z) \wedge (\overline{y} \vee \overline{z}) \wedge (x \vee y \vee z)$. Though only one truth-assignment will satisfy the formula, it takes quite a bit of backtracking to find it. The notation used here for describing generator actions is similar to that used to describe recognizer actions in figure 5.2, but a surface rather than a lexical string is the goal. As in figure 5.6, a "+" entry in the backtracking column indicates backtracking from an immediate failure in the preceding step, which does not require the full backtracking mechanism to be invoked.

Generating from lexical form "-xy,-yz,-y-z,xyz".

#		form	result	#		form	result
1		-	1,1,1,3	38	+	-FF,-FT,-F-T,FFT	3,3,2,2
2		-F	3,1,1,2	39		"-FF,-FT,-F-T,FFT"	*** result
3		-FF	3,3,1,2	40 (3)		-FT	3,2,1,2
4		-FF,	3,3,1,1	41		-FT,	3,2,1,1
5		-FF,-	3,3,1,3	42		-FT,-	3,2,1,3
6		-FF,-T	XXX y-con.	43		-FT,-F	XXX y-con.
7	+	-FF,-F	3,3,1,2	44	+	-FT,-T	3,2,1,1
8		-FF,-FF	3,3,3,2	45		-FT,-TF	3,2,3,1
9		-FF,-FF,	3,3,3,1	46		-FT,-TF,	XXX satis.
10		-FF,-FF,-	3,3,3,3	47 (45)		-FT,-TT	3,2,2,2
11		-FF,-FF,-T	XXX y-con.	48		-FT,-TT,	3,2,2,1
12	+	-FF,-FF,-F	3,3,3,2	49		-FT,-TT,-	3,2,2,3
13		-FF,-FF,-F-	3,3,3,2	50		-FT,-TT,-F	XXX y-con.
14		-FF,-FF,-F-T	XXX z-con.	51	+	-FT,-TT,-T	3,2,2,1
15	+	-FF,-FF,-F-F	3,3,3,2	52		-FT,-TT,-T-	3,2,2,3
16		-FF,-FF,-F-F,	3,3,3,1	53		-FT,-TT,-T-F	XXX z-con.
17		-FF,-FF,-F-F,T	XXX x-con.	54	+	-FT,-TT,-T-T	3,2,2,1
18	+	-FF,-FF,-F-F,F	3,3,3,1	55		-FT,-TT,-T-T,	XXX satis.
19		-FF,-FF,-F-F,FT	XXX y-con.	56 (2)		-T	2,1,1,1
20	+	-FF,-FF,-F-F,FF	3,3,3,1	57		-TF	2,3,1,1
21		-FF,-FF,-F-F,FFT	XXX z-con.	58		-TF,	XXX satis.
22	+	-FF,-FF,-F-F,FFF	3,3,3,1	59 (57)		-TT	2,2,1,2
23		-FF,-FF,-F-F,FFF	XXX satis. nf.	60		-TT,	2,2,1,1
24 (8)		-FF,-FT	3,3,2,2	61		-TT,-	2,2,1,3
25		-FF,-FT,	3,3,2,1	62		-TT,-F	XXX y-con.
26		-FF,-FT,-	3,3,2,3	63	+	-TT,-T	2,2,1,1
27		-FF,-FT,-T	XXX y-con.	64		-TT,-TF	2,2,3,1
28	+	-FF,-FT,-F	3,3,2,2	65		-TT,-TF,	XXX satis.
29		-FF,-FT,-F-	3,3,2,2	66 (64)		-TT,-TT	2,2,2,2
30		-FF,-FT,-F-F	XXX z-con.	67		-TT,-TT,	2,2,2,1
31	+	-FF,-FT,-F-T	3,3,2,2	68		-TT,-TT,-	2,2,2,3
32		-FF,-FT,-F-T,	3,3,2,1	69		-TT,-TT,-F	XXX y-con.
33		-FF,-FT,-F-T,T	XXX x-con.	70	+	-TT,-TT,-T	2,2,2,1
34	+	-FF,-FT,-F-T,F	3,3,2,1	71		-TT,-TT,-T-	2,2,2,3
35		-FF,-FT,-F-T,FT	XXX y-con.	72		-TT,-TT,-T-F	XXX z-con.
36	+	-FF,-FT,-F-T,FF	3,3,2,1	73	+	-TT,-TT,-T-T	2,2,2,1
37		-FF,-FT,-F-T,FFF	XXX z-con.	74		-TT,-TT,-T-T,	XXX satis.

("-FF,-FT,-F-T,FFT")

The generator eventually finds the correct truth-assignment, but only after substantial search (as indicated by the sawtooth pattern in the trace). This example shows that it's *local ambiguity* rather than *global ambiguity* that causes trouble. Here, only one truth-assignment will satisfy the formula, so the string is globally unambiguous—but it takes search to find that answer, because the correct choices aren't obvious during processing when they must be made. Figure 5.11 shows what happens with an unsatisfiable formula.

5.5.2   KIMMO **recognition is NP-Hard**

Like the generator, the KIMMO recognizer can be used to solve computationally difficult problems. KIMMO recognition and KIMMO generation are both NP-hard. To treat the recognizer formally, define a possible instance of the computational problem KIMMO RECOGNITION as any triple $\langle A, D, \sigma \rangle$, where A and σ are as before, and D is the dictionary component of a KIMMO system described as specified in Gajek *et al.* (1983). An actual instance of KIMMO RECOGNITION will be any possible instance $\langle A, D, \sigma \rangle$ such that for some σ', (i) the lexical/surface pair σ'/σ satisfies the constraints imposed by the automata in A as before, and (ii) σ' can be generated by the dictionary component D. Thus $\langle A, D, \sigma \rangle$ is an instance of KIMMO RECOGNITION if σ is a recognizable word according to the constraints of A and D.

Many reductions are possible, but the reduction that we'll sketch here uses the 3SAT problem (section 2.1.1) instead of SAT. It also uses an encoding for CNF formulas that is slightly different from the one used in the generator reduction. To encode a SAT formula f as a triple $\langle A, D, \sigma \rangle$, first construct σ from f by a new notational translation. This time, treat a variable u and its negation $\bar{u}$ as separate, atomic characters. Continue to use a comma for conjunction and no explicit operator for disjunction, but now add a period at the end of the formula. Then the σ corresponding to the formula $(\bar{x} \vee \bar{x} \vee y) \wedge (\bar{y} \vee \bar{y} \vee z) \wedge (x \vee y \vee z)$ is $\overline{x}\overline{x}y,\overline{y}\overline{y}z,xyz.$, a string of 12

Figure 5.11: The KIMMO generator system of figure 5.9 goes through 140 steps (facing page) before verifying that the formula

$$(x \vee y \vee z) \wedge (\bar{x} \vee \bar{z}) \wedge (\bar{x} \vee z) \wedge (\bar{y} \vee \bar{z}) \wedge (\bar{y} \vee z) \wedge (\bar{z} \vee y)$$

has no satisfying truth-assignment.

Generating from lexical form "xyz,-x-z,-xz,-y-z,-yz,-zy".

#		form	result	#		form	result
1		F	3,1,1,1	71		FTT,-T	XXX x-con.
2		FF	3,3,1,1	72	+	FTT,-F	3,2,2,2
3		FFF	3,3,3,1	73		FTT,-F-	3,2,2,2
4		FFF,	XXX satis.	74		FTT,-F-F	XXX z-con.
5	(3)	FFT	3,3,2,2	75	+	FTT,-F-T	3,2,2,2
6		FFT,	3,3,2,1	76		FTT,-F-T,	3,2,2,1
7		FFT,-	3,3,2,3	77		FTT,-F-T,-	3,2,2,3
8		FFT,-T	XXX x-con.	78		FTT,-F-T,-T	XXX x-con.
9	+	FFT,-F	3,3,2,2	79	+	FTT,-F-T,-F	3,2,2,2
10		FFT,-F-	3,3,2,2	80		FTT,-F-T,-FF	XXX z-con.
11		FFT,-F-F	XXX z-con.	81	+	FTT,-F-T,-FT	3,2,2,2
12	+	FFT,-F-T	3,3,2,2	82		FTT,-F-T,-FT,	3,2,2,1
13		FFT,-F-T,	3,3,2,1	83		FTT,-F-T,-FT,-	3,2,2,3
14		FFT,-F-T,-	3,3,2,3	84		FTT,-F-T,-FT,-F	XXX y-con.
15		FFT,-F-T,-T	XXX x-con.	85	+	FTT,-F-T,-FT,-T	3,2,2,1
16	+	FFT,-F-T,-F	3,3,2,2	86		FTT,-F-T,-FT,-T-	3,2,2,3
17		FFT,-F-T,-FF	XXX z-con.	87		FTT,-F-T,-FT,-T-F	XXX z-con.
18	+	FFT,-F-T,-FT	3,3,2,2	88	+	FTT,-F-T,-FT,-T-T	3,2,2,1
19		FFT,-F-T,-FT,	3,3,2,1	89		FTT,-F-T,-FT,-T-T,	XXX satis.
20		FFT,-F-T,-FT,-	3,3,2,3	90	(1)	T	2,1,1,2
21		FFT,-F-T,-FT,-T	XXX y-con.	91		TF	2,3,1,2
22	+	FFT,-F-T,-FT,-F	3,3,2,2	92		TFF	2,3,3,1
23		FFT,-F-T,-FT,-F-	3,3,2,2	93		TFF,	2,3,3,1
24		FFT,-F-T,-FT,-F-F	XXX z-con.	94		TFF,-	2,3,3,3
25	+	FFT,-F-T,-FT,-F-T	3,3,2,2	95		TFF,-F	XXX x-con.
26		FFT,-F-T,-FT,-F-T,	3,3,2,1	96	+	TFF,-T	2,3,3,1
27		FFT,-F-T,-FT,-F-T,-	3,3,2,3	97		TFF,-T-	2,3,3,3
28		FFT,-F-T,-FT,-F-T,-T	XXX y-con.	98		TFF,-T-T	XXX z-con.
29	+	FFT,-F-T,-FT,-F-T,-F	3,3,2,2	99	+	TFF,-T-F	2,3,3,2
30		FFT,-F-T,-FT,-F-T,-FF	XXX z-con.	100		TFF,-T-F,	2,3,3,1
31	+	FFT,-F-T,-FT,-F-T,-FT	3,3,2,2	101		TFF,-T-F,-	2,3,3,3
32		FFT,-F-T,-FT,-F-T,-FT,	3,3,2,1	102		TFF,-T-F,-F	XXX x-con.
33		FFT,-F-T,-FT,-F-T,-FT,-	3,3,2,3	103	+	TFF,-T-F,-T	2,3,3,1
34		FFT,-F-T,-FT,-F-T,-FT,-F	XXX z-con.	104		TFF,-T-F,-TT	XXX z-con.
35	+	FFT,-F-T,-FT,-F-T,-FT,-T	3,3,2,1	105	+	TFF,-T-F,-TF	2,3,3,1
36		FFT,-F-T,-FT,-F-T,-FT,-TT	XXX y-con.	106		TFF,-T-F,-TF,	XXX satis.
37	+	FFT,-F-T,-FT,-F-T,-FT,-TF	3,3,2,1	107	(92)	TFT	2,3,2,2
38		FFT,-F-T,-FT,-F-T,-FT,-TF	XXX satis. nf.	108		TFT,	2,3,2,1
39	(2)	FT	3,2,1,2	109		TFT,-	2,3,2,3
40		FTF	3,2,3,2	110		TFT,-F	XXX x-con.
41		FTF,	3,2,3,1	111	+	TFT,-T	2,3,2,1
42		FTF,-	3,2,3,3	112		TFT,-T-	2,3,2,3
43		FTF,-T	XXX x-con.	113		TFT,-T-F	XXX z-con.
44	+	FTF,-F	3,2,3,2	114	+	TFT,-T-T	2,3,2,1
45		FTF,-F-	3,2,3,2	115		TFT,-T-T,	XXX satis.
46		FTF,-F-T	XXX z-con.	116	(91)	TT	2,2,1,2
47	+	FTF,-F-F	3,2,3,2	117		TTF	2,2,3,2
48		FTF,-F-F,	3,2,3,1	118		TTF,	2,2,3,1
49		FTF,-F-F,-	3,2,3,3	119		TTF,-	2,2,3,3
50		FTF,-F-F,-T	XXX x-con.	120		TTF,-F	XXX x-con.
51	+	FTF,-F-F,-F	3,2,3,2	121	+	TTF,-T	2,2,3,1
52		FTF,-F-F,-FT	XXX z-con.	122		TTF,-T-	2,2,3,3
53	+	FTF,-F-F,-FF	3,2,3,2	123		TTF,-T-T	XXX z-con.
54		FTF,-F-F,-FF,	3,2,3,1	124	+	TTF,-T-F	2,2,3,2
55		FTF,-F-F,-FF,-	3,2,3,3	125		TTF,-T-F,	2,2,3,1
56		FTF,-F-F,-FF,-F	XXX y-con.	126		TTF,-T-F,-	2,2,3,3
57	+	FTF,-F-F,-FF,-T	3,2,3,1	127		TTF,-T-F,-F	XXX x-con.
58		FTF,-F-F,-FF,-T-	3,2,3,3	128	+	TTF,-T-F,-T	2,2,3,1
59		FTF,-F-F,-FF,-T-T	XXX z-con.	129		TTF,-T-F,-TT	XXX z-con.
60	+	FTF,-F-F,-FF,-T-F	3,2,3,2	130	+	TTF,-T-F,-TF	2,2,3,1
61		FTF,-F-F,-FF,-T-F,	3,2,3,1	131		TTF,-T-F,-TF,	XXX satis.
62		FTF,-F-F,-FF,-T-F,-	3,2,3,3	132	(117)	TTT	2,2,2,2
63		FTF,-F-F,-FF,-T-F,-F	XXX y-con.	133		TTT,	2,2,2,1
64	+	FTF,-F-F,-FF,-T-F,-T	3,2,3,1	134		TTT,-	2,2,2,3
65		FTF,-F-F,-FF,-T-F,-TT	XXX z-con.	135		TTT,-F	XXX x-con.
66	+	FTF,-F-F,-FF,-T-F,-TF	3,2,3,1	136	+	TTT,-T	2,2,2,1
67		FTF,-F-F,-FF,-T-F,-TF,	XXX satis.	137		TTT,-T-	2,2,2,3
68	(40)	FTT	3,2,2,2	138		TTT,-T-F	XXX z-con.
69		FTT,	3,2,2,1	139	+	TTT,-T-T	2,2,2,1
70		FTT,-	3,2,2,3	140		TTT,-T-T,	XXX satis.

NIL

```
"u-consistency" 3 5
        T   T   F   F   =     (lexical characters)
        u   ū   u   ū   =     (surface characters)
   1:   2   3   3   2   1     (u undecided)
   2:   2   0   0   2   2     (u true)
   3:   0   3   3   0   3     (u false)
```

Figure 5.12: The KIMMO recognizer system that encodes a 3SAT formula f should include a *consistency automaton* of this form for every variable u that occurs in f. As in the generator reduction, the consistency automaton constrains the mapping from variables to truth-values, ensuring that the value assigned to u is consistent throughout the formula. However, in the recognizer reduction the automaton must also ensure that the values assigned to u and $\bar{u}$ are opposites, since u and $\bar{u}$ are treated as atomic alphabet characters.

---

characters.[12] (With 3SAT, the commas are redundant, but they are retained here in the interest of readability.)

Second, construct A (in polynomial time) in two parts. (As before, A varies from formula to formula only when the formulas involve different sets of variables.) The alphabet specification should list the variables in σ together with their negations and the special characters T, F, comma, and period. The equals sign should again be declared as the KIMMO wildcard character. The consistency automata, still one for each variable in σ, should be constructed as in figure 5.12. There is no satisfaction automaton in this version of the recognizer.

Finally, take D as a constant from figure 5.13. In this reduction, D imposes the satisfaction constraint that was previously enforced by the satisfaction automaton. Formula f will be satisfied iff all of its conjuncts are satisfied, and since f is in 3CNF, that means the truth-values assigned within each disjunction must be TTT, TTF, ..., or any combination of three truth-values except FFF. This is exactly the constraint imposed by the dictionary. (Note that D is the same for every 3SAT problem; it does not grow with the size of the formula or the number of variables.)

---

[12]The version of 3SAT we use here, unlike that in chapter 2, does not require the literals within a clause to be distinct. It is easy to show that this change is inessential; it simplifies the process of padding short clauses.

```
ALTERNATIONS
  ( Root = Root )
  ( Punct = Punct )
  ( # = )
END

LEXICON Root      TTT      Punct      " " ;
                  TTF      Punct      " " ;
                  TFT      Punct      " " ;
                  TFF      Punct      " " ;
                  FTT      Punct      " " ;
                  FTF      Punct      " " ;
                  FFT      Punct      " "

LEXICON Punct     ,        Root       " " ;
                  .        #          " " ;

END
```

Figure 5.13: The 3SAT recognizer system for any formula should include this dictionary component, which ensures that the truth-values assigned to the variables in the surface string will cause the formula to come out true. All combinations of three truth values are listed, except for the value **FFF** that would cause one of the 3CNF disjunctions to be false; the same dictionary component is used for all 3SAT problems. Each lexicon entry specifies the continuation class of lexicons that can follow. For instance, the class **Punct** containing only the lexicon **Punct** is the continuation class of **TTT**, while the class of "." is the empty continuation class **#**. " " is an empty feature set, used because no word features are being recovered in this mathematical reduction. The detailed format of the dictionary component is described in Gajek *et al.* (1983).

Compared to the generator reduction, the roles of the lexical and surface strings are reversed in the recognizer reduction. The surface string encodes f, while the lexical string indicates truth-values for its variables. The consistency automaton for each variable u still ensures that the value assigned to u is consistent throughout the formula, but now it also ensures that u and $\bar{u}$ are assigned opposite values. As before, the net result of the constraints imposed by the various components is that $\langle A, D, \sigma \rangle$ is in KIMMO RECOGNITION just in case f has a satisfying truth-assignment. The general case of KIMMO RECOGNITION is at least as hard as 3SAT, hence at least as hard as SAT or any other problem in $\mathcal{NP}$ (in the sense of polynomial-time reduction).

5.6   The Effect of Precompilation

Since our reductions allow the set of KIMMO automata to vary from formula to formula, questions about *precompilation* arise. The complexity that shows up graphically in traces (*e.g.*, figure 5.10) might reflect only some kind of precompilation complexity, thus blunting the force of the reduction. Perhaps a large grammar-preprocessing cost could be paid just once, allowing KIMMO runtime for a given grammar to be uniformly fast thereafter.

This section examines four aspects of the precompilation question, focusing in part on the kind of "BIGMACHINE precompilation" that's actually been proposed for KIMMO systems. BIGMACHINE precompilation speeds up two-level processing by making each step faster, but the machinery still goes through the same potentially quite numerous steps.

5.6.1   Conversion to GMACHINE/RMACHINE form

The external description of a KIMMO automaton or lexicon is not the same as the form that is used by the generation or recognition algorithm at runtime. Instead, the external descriptions are used to construct internal forms: RMACHINE and GMACHINE forms for automata, and letter trees for lexicons (Gajek *et al.*, 1983). We may thus wonder whether the complexity implied by the reduction might actually apply to the construction of these internal forms. If this were true, then the complexity of the generation problem (for instance) would be concentrated in the construction of the "feasible-pair list" and the GMACHINE.

It is possible to deal with this question directly by reformulating the reduction so that the formal problems and the construction specify machines in terms of their internal (*e.g.*, GMACHINE) forms instead of their external descriptions. The GMACHINEs for the class of machines created in the construction have a very regular structure, and it is easy to build them directly instead of building descriptions in external format. As figure 5.10 also suggested, it is runtime processing that makes translated SAT problems difficult for a KIMMO system to solve.

5.6.2   BIGMACHINE **precompilation**

There is also another kind of preprocessing that we might expect to help. As mentioned in section 5.3.1, it is possible to compile a set of KIMMO automata into a single, large, equivalent automaton that will run faster than the original set. The system will usually run faster with one large automaton than with several small ones, since it has only one machine to step and the speed of stepping a machine is largely independent of its size. (In the worst case the merged automaton is prohibitively large, exponentially larger than the smaller machines (Karttunen 1983:176).)

Gajek *et al.* (1983) use the terms BIGGMACHINE and BIGRMACHINE to refer to the generation and recognition versions of a large merged automaton, and therefore such an automaton will be called a BIGMACHINE. Since it can take exponential time to build the BIGMACHINE for a translated SAT problem, the reduction formally allows the possibility that BIGMACHINE precompilation could make runtime processing uniformly efficient.

In fact, an expensive BIGMACHINE precompilation step doesn't help runtime processing enough to change the fundamental complexity of the algorithms. Recall from section 5.4.3 that the main ingredients of KIMMO runtime complexity are the mechanical operation of the automata, the difficulty of finding the correct lexical/surface pairs, and the necessity of choosing among alternative lexicons. BIGMACHINE precompilation does speed up the mechanical operation of the automata, perhaps by a factor equal to the number of variables. However, the preprocessing step doesn't introduce any *new information* that might help in deciding which pair to choose when there's uncertainty; the BIGMACHINE is as limited as the equivalent smaller automata in its forecasting abilities. Thus BIGMACHINE precompilation speeds up processing, but doesn't represent fundamental redesign.

5.6.3   BIGMACHINE **size and the interaction of constraints**

BIGMACHINE precompilation sheds light on another precompilation question as well. It is known that the compiled BIGMACHINE corresponding to a set of KIMMO automata can be exponentially larger than the original system in the worst case; for example, such blowup occurs if the SAT automata are compiled into a BIGMACHINE. In practice, however, the size of the BIG-

MACHINE varies—thus naturally raising the question of what distinguishes the "explosive" sets of automata from those that behave more tractably.

It is sometimes suggested that the degree of *interaction among constraints* determines the amount of BIGMACHINE blowup. In this view, a large BIGMACHINE for a SAT problem is no surprise, for the computational difficulty of SAT and similar problems results in part from their "global" character. Their solutions generally cannot be deduced piece by piece from local evidence; instead, the acceptability of each part of the solution may depend on the whole problem. In the worst case, the solution is determined by a complex conspiracy among the constraints of the problem. Thus the large BIGMACHINE gives a more "honest" estimate of problem difficulty than the small collection of individual automata.

However, a slight change in the SAT automata demonstrates that BIG-MACHINE size need not correspond to the degree of interaction among the automata. Eliminate the satisfaction automaton from the generator system, leaving only the consistency automata for the variables. Then the system will search not for a *satisfying* truth-assignment but merely for one that is *internally consistent*—that is, one that never assigns both T and F to the same variable in its different occurrences. This change will entirely eliminate the interactions among the automata; each automaton is concerned only with the assignments to its particular variable, and there is no way for an assignment to one variable to influence the acceptability of an assignment to another.

Yet despite the elimination of interactions, the BIGMACHINE must still be exponentially larger than the collection of individual automata. Since the states of the BIGMACHINE must distinguish all the possible truth-assignments to the variables, its size must be exponential in the number of individual automata. In fact, the lack of interaction can actually *increase* the number of states in the BIGMACHINE. Interactions among the automata constrain the combinations of states that can be reached, thus reducing the number of accessible combinations below the mathematical upper limit.

5.6.4   Transducers and determinization

One final precompilation question is whether the nondeterminism involved in constructing the lexical/surface correspondence can't be removed by standard determinization machines techniques for finite-state machines. After all, every nondeterministic finite-state machine has a deterministic counterpart that is equivalent in the sense that it accepts the same language.[13] Aren't KIMMO automata just ordinary finite-state machines operating over an alphabet that happens to consist of pairs of characters?

The KIMMO automata can indeed be viewed in this way when they are being used to *verify or reject* hypothesized pairs of lexical and surface strings.[14] However, in this use they don't need determinizing: they are already deterministic, for there is only one new state listed in each cell of the description of a KIMMO automaton. In the cases of primary interest— generation and recognition—the machines are being used as genuine *transducers* rather than acceptors.

The determinizing algorithms that apply to finite-state acceptors will not work on transducers. Indeed, many finite-state transducers are not determinizable at all. For example, consider the transducer in figure 5.14. On input $xxxxxa$ it must output $aaaaaa$, while on input $xxxxxb$ it must output $bbbbbb$. An equivalent deterministic finite-state transducer is impossible. A deterministic transducer cannot know whether to output a or b upon seeing x. However, it also cannot output nothing and put off the decision until later: being finite-state, it would not in general be able to remember at the end how many occurrences of x there had been, so it would not be able to print the right number of initial occurrences of a or b.

For similar reasons, there is no way to build deterministic finite-state transducers for the SAT problems. Upon seeing the first occurrence of a variable, a deterministic transducer cannot know in general whether it should output T or F. However, it also cannot wait and output a truth-value later, for there might be an unbounded number of occurrences of the variable before there was sufficient evidence to assign the truth-value. A finite-state transducer would not be able in general to remember how many truth-value outputs had been deferred.

The distinction between recognition and transduction pinpoints a weakness in one argument for the two-level model:

> ... fortunately, there are some classes of mechanisms that are inherently simple and that can easily be accomplished on several

---

[13]But not in the sense that it assigns the same parses to the strings of the language, where a parse according to a finite-state machine is the sequence of states traversed—a point related to the impossibility of determinizing transducers.

[14]This statement ignores any subtleties having to do with the processing of nulls, which will be discussed later (section 5.7).

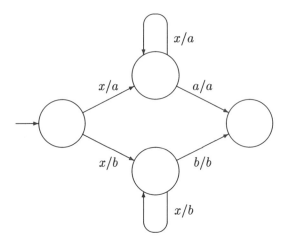

Figure 5.14: This nondeterministic finite-state transducer cannot be determinized. An equivalent deterministic FST would have to wait for the end of the input string before generating any output. However, at that point it would have to remember how many *a*s or *b*s to output in correspondence with the unbounded number of *x*s in the string—an impossible task for a finite-state device.

kinds of devices. Finite state automata have such good qualities (provided that their size remains reasonable). On the one hand, they execute in real time, *i.e.*, the length of the input does not affect the speed (and the computation between input symbols is bounded) ....

[Criterion of] *Reducibility to finite state automata*

A model of the recognition and/or production processes should be simple enough to be simulated with finite-state automata.

A model satisfying this criterion has the advantage that we can speculate that neural networks could perform the same task as the model .... The two-level model rules are implemented as finite state automata, and thus it would be reasonable to claim that they could correspond to simple neural networks processing the rules in real time, just like a hard-wired circuitry transforms a signal implicitly without complex operations. (Koskenniemi 1983:136)

It's easy to see how the difference between KIMMO processing and ordinary finite-state recognizers might seem at first to be a minor distinction, one that we can smooth out by cleverly defining machines over an alphabet of pairs instead of single characters. Unfortunately for the reducibility principle as applied to two-level rules, this method of assimilating KIMMO automata to efficient finite-state recognizers breaks down when the automata are used for their usual purpose of transduction (*i.e.*, generation or recognition).

5.7 The Effect of Nulls

Since KIMMO systems can encode NP-complete problems, the general KIMMO generation and recognition problems are at least as hard as the computationally difficult problems in $\mathcal{NP}$. But could they be even harder? The answer depends on whether null characters are allowed. If null characters are forbidden, the problems are in $\mathcal{NP}$, hence (given the previous NP-hardness result) NP-complete (section 5.7.1). If null characters are completely unrestricted, the problems are PSPACE-complete, thus potentially even harder than the problems in $\mathcal{NP}$ (section 5.7.2). However, the full power of unrestricted null characters is not needed for linguistically relevant processing. Continuing to explore the effect of KIMMO null characters, the final subsection mentions a subtle point—with computational consequences—about the interpretation of the KIMMO constraint-intersection operation when nulls are involved.

5.7.1 NP-Completeness without nulls

The generation and recognition problems for KIMMO automata without nulls are NP-complete. Since section 5.5 showed that the problems were NP-hard, all that remains is to show that a nondeterministic machine could solve them in polynomial time. Only a sketch of the proofs will be given.

Given a possible instance $\langle A, \sigma \rangle$ of KIMMO GENERATION, the basic nondeterminism of the machine can be used to guess the surface string corresponding to the lexical string σ. The automata can then quickly verify the correspondence. The key fact is that if A allows no nulls, the lexical and surface characters must be in one-to-one correspondence. The surface string must be the same length as the lexical string, so the size of the guess can't get out of hand. (If the guess were too large, the machine would not run in polynomial time.)

Given a possible instance $\langle A, D, \sigma \rangle$ of KIMMO RECOGNITION, the machine should guess the lexical string instead of the surface string; as before, its length will be manageable.[15] Now, however, the machine must also guess a path through the dictionary. The number of choice points is limited by the length of the string,[16] while the number of choices at each point is limited by the number of lexicons in the dictionary. Given a lexical/surface correspondence and a lexicon path, the automata and the dictionary component can quickly verify that the lexical/surface string pair satisfies all relevant constraints.

5.7.2 PSPACE-Completeness with unrestricted nulls

If nulls are completely unrestricted, the arguments of section 5.7.1 do not go through. The problem is that unrestricted null characters—modeling unrestricted deletions—allow the lexical and surface strings to differ wildly in length. The time it takes to guess or verify the lexical/surface correspondence may no longer be polynomially bounded in the length of the input string.

In fact, KIMMO RECOGNITION with unrestricted null characters is probably PSPACE-complete. It's easy to show that it's PSPACE-hard— at least as hard as any problem that can be solved in polynomial space— and we'll also sketch an argument for membership in *PSPACE*, which is the other half of the PSPACE-completeness argument. (However, because of diminishing returns we'll stop short of patching up a flaw in the PSPACE-membership argument.) Though the question is open, PSPACE-complete problems are likely to be even harder than NP-complete problems.

> Not only is a PSPACE-complete problem not likely to be in $\mathcal{P}$, it is also not likely to be in $\mathcal{NP}$. Hence a property whose existence question is PSPACE-complete probably cannot even be *ver-*

---

[15]When nulls are allowed as in the next section, the machine must also guess where to insert "0" characters into the surface string. Because of the way the automata operate, the strings that are submitted to the automata for verification must include the nulls.

[16]Nulls in the lexicon do not have the same interpretation as nulls in the automata. Nulls should not occur in the dictionary, except in "null lexicon entries" that are written as "0" in their entirety. Unlike nulls in the automaton component, which are treated as genuine characters by the automata, null lexicon entries are merely a notational device and can be removed in the course of constructing letter trees from the lexicons. Thus the number of choice points in the lexicon data-structure is limited by the length of the lexical string even when nulls are permitted.

ified in polynomial time using a polynomial length "guess." (Garey and Johnson 1979:171)

Thus the worst case of KIMMO RECOGNITION becomes extremely difficult (see chapter 2) if null characters are completely unrestricted.

The easiest PSPACE-completeness reduction for KIMMO RECOGNITION with unrestricted nulls involves the computational problem FINITE STATE AUTOMATA INTERSECTION (Garey and Johnson 1979:266). A possible instance of FSAI is a set of deterministic finite-state automata over the same alphabet. The problem is to determine whether there is any string that is accepted by all of the automata. (Of course, it's easy to decide whether any *particular* string is accepted by all the automata; just submit the string to the various automata separately.)

Given a set of automata over alphabet Σ, construct a corresponding KIMMO RECOGNITION problem as follows. Let a and b be new characters not in Σ, and take the KIMMO alphabet to be $\Sigma \cup \{a, b\}$.[17] Declare "=" as the wildcard character and "0" as the null character.

Then build the rest of the automaton component in two parts. First, include the following "main driver" automaton:

```
"Main Driver" 3 3
        a  b  =    (lexical characters)
        a  b  0    (surface characters)
    1.  2  0  0    (want a)
    2.  0  3  2    (let automata run)
    3:  0  0  0    (got ab; final state)
```

This will accept the surface string *ab*, allowing arbitrary lexical gyrations between a and b as long as they come out null on the surface. Second, for each of the automata in the FSAI problem, translate it directly into a KIMMO automaton by pairing the original characters from Σ with surface nulls. Also add columns for a/a and b/b, with entries zero unless otherwise specified. Bump all of the state numbers up by two. Let the new start state accept only a/a, going to 3 (the old start state). Let only state 2 be a final state, but for every state that was final in the original automaton, give it a transition to 2 on b/b.

[17]The reduction can also be done without a and b, but they are included because the resulting reduction is more reminiscent of ordinary processing problems in which the question arises of how many nulls to hypothesize *between* characters.

Third, let the root lexicon of the dictionary component contain a lexicon entry for each single character in $\Sigma \cup \{a, b\}$. The continuation class of each entry should send it back to the root lexicon, except that the entry for b should list the word-final continuation class # instead. Finally, take ab as the surface string for the KIMMO RECOGNITION problem. Surface a will start up the translated versions of the original automata, which will be able to run freely in between the a and the b because the characters in Σ all get paired with surface nulls. If there is some string that all of the original automata accept, that lexical string will send all of the translated automata into a state where the remaining b is acceptable. On the other hand, if the original intersection is empty, the b will never become acceptable and the recognizer will not accept the string ab.

As an example, consider why the recognizer doesn't just *always* accept our dummy string ab by running through the direct path 1, 2, 3 in order. The driver automaton will accept according to that sequence, but the pair a/a sends each translated automaton into state 3, which corresponds to its old start state. By construction, state 3 of a translated automaton won't accept b/b unless the start state was final in the original automaton. The recognizer can't traverse a lexical/surface pair unless every automaton does, so we can't accept ab "directly" unless the start state of every original automaton was a final state. But in that case, the empty string is a string that the original automata all accept—so the recognizer behaves as desired.

This construction shows that KIMMO RECOGNITION with no restrictions on null characters is at least as hard as any problem in *PSPACE*—that is, it's PSPACE-hard—but for PSPACE-completeness, it's also necessary to show that KIMMO RECOGNITION is *no harder* than problems in *PSPACE*. It is sufficient to use only polynomial space while transforming arbitrary KIMMO RECOGNITION problems into FSAI problems. Given a recognition problem, first convert the dictionary component into a large automaton that (i) constrains the lexical string in the same way the dictionary component does, pairing lexical characters with surface wildcards, but (ii) allows nulls to be inserted freely at the lexical level, in case the other automata permit lexical nulls. The conversion can be performed because the dictionary component is finite-state. Second, convert the input string into an automaton as well. The input-string automaton should (i) constrain the surface string to be exactly the input string, but (ii) allow surface nulls to be inserted freely. Third, expand out all wildcard and subset characters in the automata, then interpret each lexical/surface pair at the head of an automaton column as a single character in an extended alphabet. Given this preparation, it is possible to solve the original recognition problem by solving FSAI for the augmented set of automata. Because the input string is now encoded as an automaton, the intersection of the languages accepted by all the automata consists of all the permissible lexical/surface correspondences that reflect recognition of the input string. The intersection will be nonempty—as FSAI tests—if and only if the input string is recognizable.

As we hinted before, this PSPACE-membership argument has a flaw. The trouble is that the size of the dictionary may increase exponentially when it's converted to a large deterministic automaton, thus causing us to use more than polynomial space in the reduction. In this case it's not particularly instructive to patch up the argument, so we will leave it as it stands.

The PSPACE-hardness proof shows that if null characters are completely unrestricted, it can be very difficult for the recognizer to reconstruct the superficially null characters that may lexically intervene between two surface characters. However, unrestricted nulls surely are not needed for linguistically relevant KIMMO systems. Happily, the complexity problems of this section can be reduced by any restriction that prevents the number of possible nulls between surface characters from getting too large. As a crude approximation to a reasonable constraint, the above reduction could be ruled out by forbidding entire lexicon entries to come out null on the surface.[18] A suitable restriction would make the KIMMO generation and recognition problems only NP-complete rather than PSPACE-complete.

5.7.3   The intersection of constraints

The null characters ("0") that can appear in a KIMMO automaton allow the recognizer to advance without consuming any characters from the input word. For example, in analyzing the word hoed as hoe+ed, the automata advance as if the surface string were hoo0ed (see Karttunen and Wittenburg 1983:220), postulating surface nulls freely as required by the constraints of the system. In this section we continue to explore the computational effects of KIMMO null characters, noting that the interpretation of "0" as the empty string involves some subtlety when multiple constraints are involved.

---

[18]Recall from footnote 16 that an entry "0" in the dictionary is not the same as a dictionary entry that is entirely deleted at the surface by the automata.

Internal to a KIMMO automaton, "0" is treated the same as any other character, but "0" is effectively deleted at the interface to the surface string or the dictionary component. Abstractly speaking, the treatment of nulls by the KIMMO recognizer involves two steps: (i) null characters are inserted freely into the surface string to produce a form like ho00ed; (ii) this augmented string is used to run the automata. Thus, a KIMMO automaton can be considered to define both an *internal* constraint (relating the augmented strings with "0" characters inserted) and an *external* constraint (relating the strings as they stood before "0" insertion).

This distinction becomes important when there is more than one automaton in a KIMMO system. The notion of "satisfying every constraint" could refer to intersecting either the *internal* or the *external* versions of the constraints defined by the automata. If the external languages are intersected, different automata can disagree about the placement of nulls. (This corresponds to interpreting null characters as ordinary empty strings (epsilons, ϵ), since the number of occurrences of the empty string between any two characters is indeterminate.) On the other hand, if the internal forms of the constraints are intersected, all the automata must agree on the number of nulls and their positions.

The actual KIMMO system performs *internal* intersection of the constraints defined by the automata. Ron Kaplan[19] has pointed out that this subtle distinction in the interpretation of KIMMO nulls has computational consequences. If the various constraints of a KIMMO system were subject to external rather than internal intersection, thus interpreting KIMMO nulls as ordinary epsilons, then BIGMACHINE precompilation would not be generally possible.

Since BIGMACHINE precompilation produces a single large finite-state transducer as output, the intersection operation that it implicitly implements must always map finite-state constraints into finite-state constraints. External intersection does not have this property, and therefore BIGMACHINE precompilation would not be generally possible if external intersection were used. Specifically, Kaplan has called attention to the following finite-state

---

[19]Kaplan's remarks were made in a talk presented to the Workshop on Finite-State Morphology, Center for the Study of Language and Information, Stanford University, July 29–30, 1985.

relations over lexical/surface pairs:

$$A = (a/b)^*(0/c)^*$$
$$\text{and} \quad B = (0/b)^*(a/c)^*$$

Each of these relations is easy to encode in a KIMMO automaton, but their external intersection

$$A \cap B = \{a^n/b^n c^n\}$$

cannot be defined by any KIMMO automaton, large or small, despite its finite-state origins.

This example makes crucial use of the fact that external intersection allows different automata to disagree about the placement of nulls; under internal intersection (*e.g.*, in the current KIMMO system) no nontrivial lexical/surface pair satisfies both of the constraints. For instance, A will reject the external string pair aa/bbcc except as aa00/bbcc, while B will reject it except as 00aa/bbcc. Since internal intersection requires all automata to agree about the placement of nulls, aa/bbbb will be rejected under internal intersection.

The computational consequences of the distinction between internal and external intersection become more severe when KIMMO systems are generalized slightly. For example, if KIMMO automata are generalized to use three levels instead of two, and if certain other small changes are made, then the recognition problem becomes computationally *undecidable* under external intersection.[20]

5.8 Improving KIMMO Dictionary Efficiency

One final matter remains. Despite the fact that navigation through the lexicons of the dictionary component can account for quite a bit of backtracking in the current KIMMO system, the previous sections gave little attention to that problem. Instead, section 5.4.3 promised that the dictionary component could be changed in such a way that most of the choice points would be eliminated. This section explains how.

---

[20]The relevant reduction involves Post's Correspondence Problem, but we will not describe it here.

5.8.1 Subdivisions of the dictionary

Naturally, there would be no need to choose among alternative lexicons if the dictionary were not subdivided. In the existing KIMMO system, subdivisions are needed for two reasons. First, the continuation-class mechanism is the only means for expressing co-occurrence restrictions among roots and affixes, and a continuation class is a set of lexicons. Second, incorrect dictionary search paths can be recognized and pruned more quickly when suffixes are stored separately from roots.

The existing continuation-class mechanism makes the lexicon the finest unit of discrimination between suffixes. If a, x, y are dictionary entries such that the sequence ax is possible but ay is not, this constraint will be impossible to capture unless x and y are listed in separate lexicons; if they are in the same lexicon, it will be impossible for the continuation class of a to include x but not y. Thus the need to express co-occurrence restrictions leads to the use of multiple lexicons. For example, Karttunen and Wittenburg (1983:224) must list -ed and -er in separate lexicons because of such contrasts as doer/*doed. In the special case of separated dependencies, the weakness of the current continuation-class mechanism leads to a large amount of duplicated structure in the multiple lexicons that must be constructed (Karttunen 1983:180).

Small lexicons are also advantageous for pruning search, since it can become apparent very early that no acceptable suffix starts out with the letters at hand. For instance, if none of the suffixes that can attach to the current word start with "a", it is pointless to search beyond an "a" in the input (ignoring spelling-change rules here). If the legal suffixes for the current class of word are stored in a separate lexicon, the letter-tree version of the lexicon will not be searched beyond an "a". However, if they are listed with many other suffixes such as -able, the search will not be aborted until later—possibly not until the end of a suffix, when the combinatory features of the suffix can be checked.

Unfortunately, multiple lexicons slow analysis down quite a bit in the current version of KIMMO. Each of the lexicons in a continuation class is searched separately. The first few characters beyond a lexicon choice point tend to get reanalyzed several times, with that portion of the lexical/surface correspondence worked out afresh each time. If x, y above are stems (N, V, *etc.*) instead of suffixes—that is, if a is a prefix—then the *root* lexicon becomes subdivided. In such a situation, the separate searching of the different portions of the root lexicon becomes especially serious. Much storage is also wasted (Karttunen and Wittenburg 1983:221f).

In some cases, however, the current finite-state lexicon structure cannot capture the proper co-occurrence restrictions even if duplication and inefficiency can be tolerated. Prefixes generally apply only to words of particular classes, thus making it necessary to have separate lexicons for the various classes of words involved. But because prefixes and suffixes can productively form new words of various classes (for instance, `-ize` forms verbs), it may not be possible for a lexicon to list them all. Formally speaking, if both prefixes and suffixes (i) are fully productive, (ii) can change the categories of words arbitrarily, and (iii) can attach to only particular categories of words, then separated dependencies can arise that exceed the power of a finite-state lexicon structure. In such cases, context-free rules of some kind might be better suited to the hierarchical word-structures that are involved. Alternatively, it might be preferable to subdivide the problem by enforcing only crude finite-state combinatorial constraints while figuring out the lexical/surface correspondence, then filtering the analyses in a more sophisticated way afterward.

5.8.2   Merging the lexicons

The number of separate lexicon searches can obviously be reduced if there is only one lexicon. Roots and affixes can all be listed together, with the combinatory possibilities of various elements indicated by a feature system. Such a feature system can be used whether or not the existing finite-state dictionary framework is replaced with something more powerful.

Within the existing framework, each lexicon name can be interpreted as a feature; the continuation class of each entry is then taken to specify the possible lexicon features of its immediate successor in the word. Alternatively, a more powerful framework might be modeled after the linguistic framework of Lieber (1980). Context-free machinery of some kind could implement the recovery of hierarchical structure, the application of Lieber's feature-percolation conventions, and the enforcement of combinatory restrictions. Common grammar-processing techniques could be used to predict at each boundary the set of permissible combinatorial features (the continuation class) of the next segment of input.

As noted, however, merging the lexicons in this way has the disadvantage that it prolongs some dictionary searches that would have failed early when the lexicons were divided. At modest cost in time and space, this disadvantage can be eliminated by adding bit vectors to the internal letter-tree form of the lexicon. The bit vector associated with a link in the letter tree indicates which classes of words or affixes can be found in the subtree below. Bit vectors should also be associated with the *outputs* of the tree.

The bit-vector scheme makes it possible to search in parallel through all of the lexicons in a continuation class. The implementation will no longer interpret a continuation class in terms of the individual letter trees of several lexicons; instead, a continuation class will correspond to an encoded set of lexicon names for use in descending the single merged letter-tree. Before descending a branch (or using an output), it is necessary to check whether there is a non-null intersection between the lexicons comprising the desired continuation class and the lexicons accessible down the branch. On many computers, this test can be carried out in a single instruction, if the number of lexicons in the dictionary is small (*e.g.,* ≤ 32). Search should terminate if the intersection is null. With the "virtual" split lexicons provided by the bit-vector scheme, a failing search can terminate just as early in the lexical string as it will with lexicons that have individual letter-trees; figure 5.15 shows an idealized illustration. In an actual system, the dictionary would have more finely divided lexicons than N and V, especially for suffixes.

An implementation of this dictionary scheme was used to generate the traces shown in figure 5.3 and succeeding figures. Without the merged dictionary, the recognizer for English locates a suffix in the continuation class /V by doing a separate letter-tree descent for each of the lexicons P3, PS, PP, PR, I, AG, and AB. With the merged dictionary, the recognizer needs only one letter-tree descent in the virtual lexicon $(/V) = \{P3, PS, PP, PR, I, AG\}$, thus reducing the number of steps needed to analyze an input. Finely divided lexicons (hence continuation classes with several members) are typically necessary for capturing co-occurrence restrictions even in approximate form, and consequently the merged dictionary almost always speeds up recognizer operation. Finally, even though it takes extra space to augment links and outputs with bit-vectors, the merged dictionary can also save space by sharing structure among what would otherwise be separate letter trees.

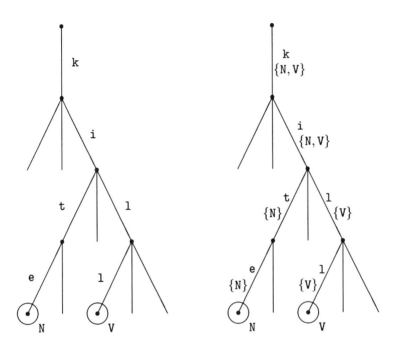

Figure 5.15: If separate letter trees for nouns and verbs are merged as on the left, failing searches may be prolonged unnecessarily. Assuming that no nouns are accessible down the kil... branch of the merged tree, it is useless to traverse that branch if only a noun is acceptable in the current context. However, the fruitlessness of the branch may not be apparent until the end of an entry (*e.g.*, kill) is reached and category features are available. In the letter tree on the right, each link has been augmented with a bit-vector that indicates the classes of entries that are accessible down the link. The bit-vectors enable the system to terminate a failing search without going any further down the tree than it would with unmerged lexicons. In this case, the kil... subtree would not be searched because the intersection of {V} and {N} is null.

Chapter 6

Constraint Propagation in KIMMO Systems

The two-level model of morphological processing appears at first to guarantee efficiency because of its finite-state basis. Yet, as we saw in the previous chapter, the processing machinery can end up doing a lot of search. The difficult Boolean satisfiability problem (SAT) for formulas in N variables can be encoded within the KIMMO framework using only $N + 1$ small automata. The combinatorial search that's involved in determining satisfiability becomes readily visible in the resulting processing traces (see figure 5.10).

But like other measuring instruments, the tools of complexity theory produce results that require interpretation. A reduction that uncovers NP-completeness in a formalized grammatical system might convince us that the natural problem can also be difficult and processing machinery must provide for combinatorial search. Instead, we might suspect that the grammatical model is too general and appropriate constraints would rule out difficult problems. Or, if we independently believe the model has machinery that is too limited, we could even suspect that extensions would expand the sources of computational difficulty beyond NP-completeness.

The best interpretation of a reduction is one that helps us fit the properties of our theoretical apparatus more closely to those of natural language. The *causes* of unexpected complexity in processing—as illuminated by reductions—are ripe areas for closer scrutiny, often suggesting constraints that can rein in the excess power of a grammatical formalism.[1] Because many of our reductions show formalized problems to require more instead of less processing than natural problems might purportedly receive, we will focus on

---

[1]In this chapter, the terms "grammar" and "grammatical" encompass phonological as well as syntactic processes.

the case of unexpected difficulty (and in fact on unexpected NP-completeness, which we will assume requires combinatorial search). However, unexpected simplicity can be equally illuminating, potentially exposing underlying assumptions that are unrealistically restrictive.[2]

Strengthened grammatical constraint represents perhaps the cleanest way to exorcise computational difficulty, for it can produce a theory that is linguistically more restrictive as well as computationally more tractable. We'll see in the first part of this chapter that such an outcome is not always possible; the best grammatical formalism will sometimes allow computational difficulty to arise. But even when grammatical theory fails to reduce worst-case complexity, natural problems may still typically have special properties that make them unlike the mathematical problems used in reductions. Such special properties—though not grammatically guaranteed—can support specialized processing methods that succeed on "ordinary" examples but fail on pathologically difficult ones. Thus, some properties of language are reflected in the processing machinery rather than in the grammatical formalism.[3]

The latter part of this chapter will sketch a processing method for two-level morphology that uses *constraint propagation* in an attempt to reflect the special features of *local information flow* and *linear separability* that we suspect are typical of natural morphological-analysis problems. More difficult computational problems such as SAT do not have such a local character, but instead have a globally interconnected character that makes them hard to solve.

6.1   Interpreting Unexpected Complexity

The SAT problems used in the two-level reductions of chapter 5 seem more like puzzles than like ordinary linguistic problems, and it is thus possible that their structure is *unnatural* in some significant way—that similar problems are not likely to turn up in the analysis of Finnish, Turkish, or Warlpiri. If this is true, the reductions say less about the difficulty of morphological analysis than about natural constraints that aren't expressed in the two-

---

[2]For instance, if we consider context-free grammars with preterminals, there are some grammars that become susceptible to the efficient *LALR* processing method (Aho and Ullman 1977:219ff) only if lexical ambiguity is disallowed or restricted.

[3]Another way to describe this situation is simply to say that the theory of grammatical performance is nontrivial, hardly a surprising notion.

level framework. Since difficult SAT problems seem no more linguistically essential than recognizing prime numbers, additional grammatical principles might rule out such problems without compromising linguistic analyses. The computational difficulties of the two-level framework would then have been traced to a surfeit of expressive power.

This view has merit: like most linguistic models, the two-level model should indeed be strengthened with additional principles. The constraints of the model are linguistically weak because they permit many analytic styles of varying character and abstractness. Though the model appears to push linguistic analyses toward increased concreteness because it eliminates intermediate levels of representation, two-level analyses frequently use a wide range of diacritics that make them no less abstract than other analyses.[4] Tighter restrictions on analytic style would strengthen the scientific content of the two-level theory and perhaps firm up the notion of increased concreteness. They would also decrease the general "programming language" capabilities of the formalism, which are the raw material for reductions.

Note, however, that additional constraints of this kind are justified on standard linguistic grounds; they do not spring specifically from complexity considerations. Many linguistically motivated constraints and representational choices have implications for computational complexity (see Berwick and Weinberg 1984). Conversely, complexity analysis often suggests where missing constraints may lie. But in general, we can't always remove computational difficulties through constraints on the grammatical formalism. The best theory of grammatical knowledge will sometimes permit grammatical "equations" that *are* hard to solve. If we go beyond linguistically motivated constraints on the grammatical formalism, we may clutter grammatical theory with constraints that belong elsewhere. Deeply center-embedded structures are the standard example: although the unacceptability of such constructions is a genuine property of natural language, our picture of how sentences are put together becomes complicated and apparently distorted if the grammar is modified so as not to generate them. The unacceptability of center-embedding probably results from the finite nature of performance mechanisms rather than from grammatical knowledge.

For similar reasons, the computational difficulties that arise from *lexical ambiguity*—a key ingredient of many linguistic reductions—probably won't

---

[4]There is a large literature on variants of the "abstractness controversy" in phonology; see, *e.g.*, chapter 6 of Kenstowicz and Kisseberth (1979).

be tamed by grammatical constraints.[5] Homonyms (or homographs), zero-derived forms, and other confusing complications make the set of possible feature-specifications for a surface word unpredictable rather than linguistically principled; even if the grammar supports deterministic parsing given word categories, uncertainty will enter the parsing process from the dictionary in a haphazard way.[6] The cases that are hard to process probably won't form a linguistically principled class, arising as they do from the interaction with grammar of accidental coincidences in the dictionary. Hence, they probably won't be cured by reasonable constraints on grammatical theory. There are valid constraints that ease worst-case processing—but if we were to insist on such constraints for removing all difficult problems, the accidental nature of some difficulties would necessarily clutter the grammatical model with extraneous factors.

Thus, linguistic scrutiny will sometimes suggest that the complexity of a formalized problem is not an artifact of loose formalism, but fairly reproduces the potential complexity of the natural problems that mentally representable grammars define. If we do conclude that the grammatical framework correctly captures the language user's syntactic knowledge, the reductions serve to highlight worst-case situations that were not otherwise apparent. They show us that grammatical knowledge of the relevant form—in the presence of homonyms or other superficial coincidences—can be difficult to put to use, potentially demanding computationally intensive methods.

Given such a residue of true difficulty, lightweight processing methods may seem out of the question—for the difficult cases require a computational blunderbuss such as backtracking search. One could even envision backtracking search as a perfect performance model; perhaps inputs that humans analyze easily require little backtracking, but inputs that humans find difficult engage search machinery more extensively. But the invocation of search as a performance theory should incite wariness, for such fortuitous results would not come about automatically. To control, guide, and prune the search, a general search procedure can use a variety of methods based on many different kinds of information. Different methods will give different difficulty

---

[5]Lexical ambiguity is a contributor to complexity that will accompany almost any linguistic feature system, even though the possible systems span an enormous range from small sets of binary features to hierarchical f-structures (chapter 4) and beyond.

[6]Indeed, the lexicon is traditionally conceived as the quintessential repository of unpredictable information; see, *e.g.,* Kenstowicz and Kisseberth (1979:31ff). In general, however, there's no way to tell an accidental property from a principled one except by doing linguistics.

predictions, and a method that matches human performance may be quite elusive; computers and humans often don't stumble in the same way. (Of course, even a perfect match with human performance would be scant scientific advantage if it were achieved merely by mechanical tuning of myriad free parameters and stipulated costs.)

However, there are both practical and theoretical reasons why we should resort to combinatorial search only as a fallback position.[7] Full-blown search algorithms are costly in natural-language processing; in many computer languages increased programming effort is required to set up the necessary loops or state-saves, and of course the search itself may take substantial processing time.[8] Indeed, the design of an augmented transition network (ATN) system often involves various arc-ordering schemes that are introduced to help contain the potential for combinatorial explosion.[9] Also, once processing procedures are set up for search, it's easy to end up using that mechanism even for aspects of a linguistic problem that would easily succumb to other methods.

In theoretical terms as well, the adoption of brute-force search leaves unexplained the oft-cited rapidity with which humans process most linguistic inputs, though the domain of such rapid processing is actually unclear. More generally, unless a great deal more is said about algorithm details, it cannot predict the detailed topography of human performance, as we noted above. And most seriously from our point of view, general search procedures implicitly assume that the natural problem has no *special structure* that would support more specialized processing methods—despite all the principles, representational details, nooks, and crannies of grammatical theory. Thus, if we fall back on search too easily, we may miss interesting linguistic properties and processing strategies that we could have found with more investigation. This is true even if the amount of search is tolerable in practice—especially

---

[7]It's an empirical question whether human linguistic processing involves such search, and we cannot legislate the answer; but we do wish to guard against adopting a combinatorial search algorithm simply because it's easy to think of.

[8]We have seen a version of the commercially available Q&A natural-language system for the PC that makes this computational cost immediately apparent: the system displays its backtracking activity visibly by highlighting the part of the sentence it's working on.

[9]ATNs are a grammatical formalism in which parsing corresponds to traversing a path through a network of nodes and arcs. The "augmentations" involve the setting and testing of various registers during arc traversal. See Woods (1970) and Bates (1978). Experience with the search behavior of ATN systems suggests that it is common for such systems to do more backtracking on seemingly simple sentences than one might expect.

true, because we'd like to know why such computational power is needed if it never gets used.

In fact, however, extreme difficulty in the hardest grammatically determined problems does not dictate the design of our processing methods. If the possibility of hard-to-process inputs leads us to propose search-based machinery for all inputs, we have implicitly assumed continuity of processing method across the whole range of possible inputs. Yet there might be no continuity at all between fluent processing and the deciphering of puzzles like BUFFALO BUFFALO BUFFALO and THE BOAT FLOATED NEARBY SANK; Marcus (1980:203ff) and many others have proposed that various kinds of difficult sentences may receive different processing from more typical ones.[10]

Thus, if ordinary processing methods are tailored to the most difficult situations, we can easily miss the forest for the trees—preparing for the rare worst cases, but missing streamlined strategies that would work in the usual case. We may certainly consider bullet-proof search machinery that takes extreme difficulty as its guiding example, but we may also explore less powerful methods that usually work but break down on the hardest problems.[11]

For instance, consider the interaction of feature agreement and lexical ambiguity. We've seen that it can be deadly in the worst case (chapter 3) and probably won't be tamed by purely grammatical constraints (p. 164). Yet the fact that *agreement* is involved can suggest a processing strategy that doesn't involve guessing. One effect of a feature-agreement constraint is that evidence of feature values will generally be manifested at more than one point in a sentence. For instance, if subject and verb must agree in features and both are unambiguously inflected, feature values can be read off at either point. Of course, not every surface form is unambiguously marked; in English,

---

[10]The central hypothesis of generative grammar is that a mentally represented grammar forms the basis of a speaker/hearer's linguistic abilities, but it does not follow that speakers must use a single, uniform processing algorithm that relates the grammar to all the sentences it characterizes mathematically. We can easily imagine performance strategies that—despite clear knowledge of grammatical principles—will sometimes be unable to work out the consequences those principles have for particular sentences.

[11]Fodor, Bever, and Garrett (1974) discuss some such methods under the heading of performance strategies. In addition, many processing methods that have been proposed in the psycholinguistic literature will fail in various situations. In the computational literature, it is more common to consider algorithms that always succeed with grammars from some well-defined class.

"sheep" could be singular or plural.[12] And in general, the most difficult situations for the processing machinery are those in which reliable surface cues are missing. (The famous difficult sentence "BUFFALO[5]" from section 3.4 in chapter 3 certainly lacks surface cues about syntactic categories.) But it's uncommon—though grammatically possible—for both subject and verb to be wholly unmarked, and thus a promising strategy is to delay the assignment of features to ambiguous words, relying on agreement to fill them in later when unambiguous evidence is found.

Such a strategy replaces powerful computational machinery with a more limited form of inference, in effect requiring all deduced feature values to be ultimately "grounded" in clear features of the input. Thus, it implicitly assumes that the structure of ordinary problems will allow such limited procedures to succeed. The strategy breaks down on "puzzles" that cannot be unraveled without guessing. The constraint-propagation method that we sketch for two-level morphology has similar properties.

6.2   Modular Information Structure

Whatever representations and processing methods we choose, their success must be grounded in what we will call the "information structure" of the task, a concept more abstract than a particular algorithm. For instance, given the task of evaluating fully parenthesized arithmetic expressions such as $((2 + 2) \times 3)$, a significant feature of its information structure is that the parentheses exactly reflect the nesting of operations, thus telling us when each operation can be performed in a linear scan. This feature does not force any particular processing method—we could write an algorithm that pays particular attention to parentheses, we could base our efforts on a context-free grammar and a shift-reduce parser, or we could use Earley's algorithm instead—but it does underwrite the correctness of certain conclusions an algorithm could potentially draw from parenthesis count. In this chapter, we seek a specialized processing method that will work on two-level systems for natural languages while avoiding the combinatorial search that seems necessary for solving general SAT problems and the like; therefore, we must ask what it is about the information structure of natural problems that would

---

[12]Even here, singular and plural will usually be distinguished by the choice of determiner, but sequences like "that sheep ..." remain ambiguous since *that* could be either a singular determiner or a complementizer.

make such a specialized method possible. In syntax, for instance, we might investigate under what conditions the sequence NP–V forms a reliable surface cue for imposing a clausal interpretation, much as parentheses were reliable cues in our arithmetical problem. Similarly, syntactic locality principles can underwrite the design of a parser that has a limited window of information for making syntactic decisions.[13]

Ultimately, sophisticated processing methods will require detailed understanding of what information depends on other information according to linguistic theory. But at a coarse level, a *modular information structure* may be one characteristic that differentiates natural morphological-analysis problems from difficult SAT problems. Making this idea precise is rather tricky, for the KIMMO systems that encode SAT problems are modular in the sense that they involve various independent KIMMO automata assembled in the usual way. However, the essential notion is that the Boolean satisfaction problem has a more interconnected and "global" character than morphological analysis.[14] The solution to a satisfaction problem generally cannot be deduced piece by piece from local evidence. Instead, the acceptability of each part of the solution may depend on the whole problem. In the worst case, the solution is determined by a complex conspiracy among the problem constraints instead of being composed of independently derivable subparts. There is little alternative to running through the possible cases in a combinatorial way.

A SAT-style conspiracy seems unlikely for two-level analysis problems.[15] We believe the various complicating processes will usually operate in separate domains—defined for instance by separate feature-groups—instead of conspiring closely together. For instance, a significant characteristic of vowel

---

[13]Berwick and Weinberg (1984, 1985) discuss such a parser, which is a refinement of Marcus's (1980) parser. See also Berwick (1985) on the implications of such a limited parsing window for language acquisition.

[14]See section 2.4.3 for a related notion of modularity in graph problems.

[15]We have not determined whether such a conspiracy should be grammatically possible. If the current two-level model were correct and complete, it would be possible, and it would also be possible in some versions of the autosegmental model. In this chapter we attempt to use performance methods rather than grammatical constraints to rule out such a situation. However, this does not imply any position on the question of whether the ultimate shape of phonological theory will allow NP-complete processing problems, for an investigation of performance methods could ultimately lead to new grammatical constraints. Note that the phonological changes affecting the lexical/surface correspondence in two-level systems are generally less arbitrary than the dictionary mapping that takes an entry to its possible syntactic categories, so that we cannot use the same argument we used regarding lexical ambiguity to conclude that difficulty related to the mapping will probably remain with us.

harmony is that it usually *ignores* intervening consonants, as if vowels and consonants were internally represented in separate domains.[16] Along such lines, the modern theory of *autosegmental phonology* separates many different kinds of phonological information onto independent representational planes that flesh out a central skeleton of featureless slots.[17] Though the computational implications of autosegmental theory are not yet clear, we believe autosegmental representations are likely to support processing methods that work more by superposition than by trying out solutions to intertwined and conspiratorial constraints.

The properties of linear separability and superposition that characterize a modular information structure represent two necessary components of a divide-and-conquer strategy. In this chapter we are using the terms informally, but separability refers to the ability to divide a problem into relatively independent subproblems that can be solved by themselves, while superposition refers to the ability to combine the resulting solutions to solve the original problem. A collection of KIMMO automata may not be modular in the sense of these properties despite being modular in other ways, for here we focus on modularity that is strong enough to support *modular processing.*

For modular processing, it must be possible to make some decisions without making assumptions about others, continuing with a chain of inference that ultimately solves the whole problem. A few examples will suggest why natural-language processing problems might typically be so arranged. In English, when generating from the lexical string `try+s` with a left-to-right scan, it's unclear what to do with the "y" when it's first seen, but before long, there's enough context in the input to decide the matter. With a Warlpiri lexical string that we can write as `pIrrI#kIjI-rn<u2>`, a long-distance right-to-left assimilation process is operating between the special "u" vowel in the suffix and the vowels of the stem, with the result that the surface form is `pirri-kuju-rnu`.[18] We can't tell at first whether the stem vowels should come out as "i" or "u", but here again the choice is decided when we see the right piece of information—there's really no need to guess. The same

---

[16]This oversimplifies matters, since some vowels may also be ignored and there may be consonants that block harmony. The picture is somewhat cleaner when both vowels and consonants are decomposed into distinctive features.

[17]See Halle (1985) and references cited therein for an introduction to the substantial body of literature on autosegmental phonology.

[18]See Nash (1980) for a description of this assimilation process. The notation `<u2>` for the special "u" is particular to our two-level system for Warlpiri.

abstract pattern of inference shows up in the "easy" SAT formula

$$(\overline{y} \vee z) \wedge (x \vee y) \wedge \overline{x},$$

for which the unique satisfying assignment follows piece by piece from specific evidence. The conjunct $\overline{x}$ forces x to be false, so y must be true, so finally z must be true. In contrast, the formula

$$(x \vee y \vee z) \wedge (\overline{x} \vee \overline{z}) \wedge (\overline{x} \vee z) \wedge (\overline{y} \vee \overline{z}) \wedge (\overline{y} \vee z) \wedge (\overline{z} \vee y)$$

does not yield in the same way. Since there are no obvious forced conclusions, it takes some form of *arguing by cases* to figure out that it's unsatisfiable—and that's just what combinatorial search amounts to.

A general search procedure implicitly allows for a nonmodular problem structure in which nothing follows from clear evidence on its own and any analytic decision may depend on any other decision. For example, this assumption shows up in the KIMMO treatment of a right-to-left long-distance harmony process that changes some character x into character y if it is eventually followed by y. When a y is first seen in a surface word, the system can't tell whether the corresponding lexical/surface pair should be y/y or— assuming another y will turn up—the pair x/y instead. Faced with such a choice, it chooses a possibility and arranges for rejection if the required right context never shows up. In the event of rejection, the system carries out backtracking until it eventually returns to the erroneous choice point.[19] Another choice is then made, but the entire analysis to the right of the choice point will be recomputed. This recomputation reveals the implicit assumption that a decision may depend on other decisions to its left, while the procedure of taking each choice forward to see if it is ultimately rejected makes it clear that a decision may depend on other decisions to its right.

6.3   A Constraint Propagation Method

How—in contrast—can we design processing methods that make more specific assumptions about the structure of the problem? The remaining sections of this chapter explore a *constraint propagation method* for two-level generation that represents one such attempt. The method was chosen because

---

[19]Although the phrasing of this section suggests a depth-first search order as used by Karttunen (1983), it applies equally well to the breadth-first order that is simulated in some implementations by "task records."

it reflects a rough version of the modularity properties that we suspect are found in the two-level systems for natural languages. The informal idea of *local information flow* is reflected in the fact that processing decisions at each point in the constraint-propagation network are made based on the states of neighboring nodes. Information propagates over long distances only when it causes a change at every point along its path. The idea of *linear separability* is reflected in the design of the network, which allows two automata to communicate only by ruling out a lexical/surface pair. Informally speaking, this arrangement prevents the automata from conspiring too closely. Guiding the design of the machinery is the assumption that analyses can generally be built up, piece by piece, by the individual automata through local processes. In more difficult cases the constraints of the automata are enforced only approximately, with some nonsolutions accepted (as is usual with this kind of method).

The constraint propagation method is one species of a limited and local inference process that is rather different from combinatorial search. Such a limited process cannot solve problems with the global structure of the most difficult SAT problems; roughly speaking, it succeeds only when the solution can fall into place through a chain of limited and local inferences without guessing.[20] Preliminary tests suggest that the constraint-propagation method for KIMMO generation works for English, Turkish, and Warlpiri. When applied to the SAT generator system of chapter 5, the method succeeds on formulas that are "easy" in the sense mentioned earlier (p. 170), but fails (as desired) on "hard" ones.[21] Thus, in a limited way, the tests support the hypothesis that conspiratorial SAT problems have an unnatural information structure compared to natural two-level analysis—that the natural problems may support less powerful inference methods than general search.

Our general approach contrasts with many other potentially valid responses to processing difficulties. The constraint-propagation method does not represent the restriction to finite memory capacity of a "competence algorithm" that can process any grammatical sentence, as in the well-known work of Miller and Chomsky (1963). Neither does it involve changing the

---

[20]Strictly speaking, constraint propagation can solve such problems if they are translated into constraint networks that are exponentially large. Nonpolynomial translations are implicitly disallowed throughout this discussion, whether or not they are explicitly mentioned.

[21]Note that "easy" in this chapter is not the same as "solvable in polynomial time"; for instance, 2SAT formulas can be hard in the present sense.

expressive range of the formal framework.[22] Instead, it allows problems that
have perfectly well-defined solutions from the viewpoint of the grammatical
framework, but are too difficult for the processing machinery to solve—just
as it can be hard to find the solution of some perfectly well-defined mathematical equation. To emphasize this fact, we will refrain from calling the
constraint-propagation method an algorithm.[23]

We'll use a SAT generator system from chapter 5 for illustration; it is
repeated for reference in figure 6.1. This system encodes satisfiability for formulas in three variables x, y, and z—arguably an unnaturally difficult problem compared to natural-language morphology, bearing in mind our caveats.
The KIMMO generation algorithm backtracks extensively while using these
automata to determine truth-assignments for formulas (recall figures 5.10
and 5.11).

6.3.1 Waltz's constraint propagation

Our constraint propagation method is based on Waltz's similar method
for determining the interpretation of lines in drawings—whether they are con-
vex interior edges, boundaries, and so forth.[24] The goal of Waltz's procedure
is to assign a label to each line and junction in the drawing, consistent with
physical constraints on how line types can come together at junctions. However, the program does not search through all the possible combinations of
labels. Instead, it decouples the combinations and only constrains the possibilities for each junction *locally,* based on the possibilities for neighboring
junctions. In part (a) of figure 6.2, the possibilities at *A* require the line *AB*
to be labeled with either plus or minus. That constrains the possibilities at

---

[22] We do hope that extensions of this work will ultimately help guide the way to revisions
of the formal framework. We are particularly interested in the graph separability notions
of section 2.4.3, which might suggest ways to reorganize the constraints of the framework
in computationally effective ways. But as we've explained, we expect that some special
properties of language are the subject of grammatical theory proper, while other properties
are best attributed to characteristics of the processing or acquisition machinery. In other
words, not every constraint of natural language has to be captured in the grammatical
framework itself.

[23] The program certainly implements an algorithm for a certain technical task known
as constraint propagation under arc consistency, but according to technical usage, it does
not represent an algorithm for solving KIMMO generation and recognition problems. An
algorithm for a problem is generally required to solve all of its instances.

[24] See Winston (1984), Freuder (1978), Mackworth (1977), and Mackworth and
Freuder (1985) for an introduction to Waltz's constraint propagation method, which he
described in his 1972 Ph.D. thesis.

```
ALPHABET x y z T F - ,

    ANY =
    END
```

```
"x-consistency" 3 3
      x  x  =
      T  F  =
1:    2  3  1
2:    2  0  2
3:    0  3  3

"y-consistency" 3 3
      y  y  =
      T  F  =
1:    2  3  1
2:    2  0  2
3:    0  3  3

"z-consistency" 3 3
      z  z  =
      T  F  =
1:    2  3  1
2:    2  0  2
3:    0  3  3

"satisfaction" 3 4
      =  =  -  ,
      T  F  -  ,
1.    2  1  3  0
2:    2  2  2  1
3.    1  2  0  0

END
```

Figure 6.1: Repeated from Chapter 5, this is a KIMMO generator system for solving SAT problems in the variables x, y, and z. In the consistency automata, state 2 remembers a truth-assignment of T, state 3 of F; the initial state 1 is uncommitted. In the satisfaction automaton, state 2 indicates that a true value has been seen in a disjunction (between commas), while the initial state 1 indicates that none has; state 3 implements treatment of the negation sign "-".

B, and the line BC must be labeled with an arrow pointing in one direction or the other. The necessity of an arrow reduces C to a unique labeling as shown. In turn, the possibilities at B and A become uniquely determined as well, producing the labeling in part (b). Because constraint propagation of this kind uses simple, local criteria to rule out possibilities from an initial labeling of polynomial size, it takes only polynomial time (section 6.4).

In contrast, the problem of solving Waltz-style scene labeling problems exactly is NP-complete and thus seems to demand exponential search.[25] Since Waltz's procedure is a polynomial-time method, immediately we see that it can't always solve the line labeling problem. The constraint-propagation method we're considering imposes on the scene labeling a form of local consistency that's technically known as *arc consistency* (Mackworth 1977:103),

---

[25]Mackworth and Freuder (1985:65) note that the NP-complete problem of graph coloring has the same general form as a Waltz-style labeling problem. Kirousis and Papadimitriou (1985) show that an exact solution to Waltz's more specific problem is also NP-complete. It follows that all known methods of solving it will take exponential time. Kirousis and Papadimitriou also claim that Waltz's procedure takes exponential time in the worst case, while we have characterized it as a polynomial-time method. This discrepancy results from a difference in what we mean by Waltz's procedure; we include only the constraint-propagation step, while Kirousis and Papadimitriou also include the use of backtracking search after constraint propagation to remove remaining ambiguities.

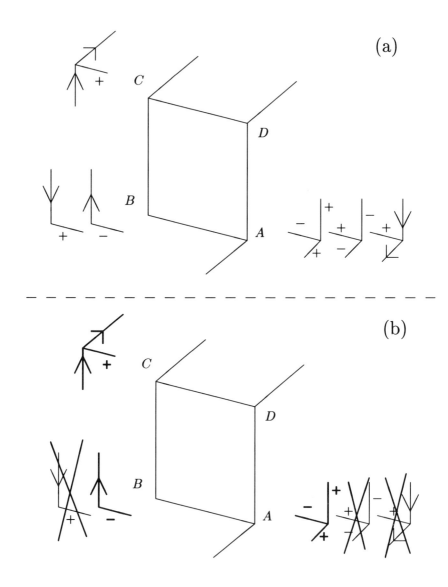

Figure 6.2: This fragment of a scene-analysis problem illustrates the operation of Waltz's constraint propagation procedure. As shown in part (a), junction A initially does not have a unique labeling, but limits the possible labelings for junction B to two. Given the labelings at B, only one labeling is possible for junction C. Constraint from the single possibility at C then reduces the possibilities at B and A as shown by the canceled possibilities in part (b). See Winston (1984) for an explanation of the labels.

and local consistency won't always rule out every nonsolution. As Mackworth and Freuder (1985:66) note,

> [Network consistency algorithms] do not solve a constraint satisfaction problem completely but they eliminate once and for all local inconsistencies that cannot participate in any global solutions. These inconsistencies would otherwise have been repeatedly discovered by any backtracking solution.

Thus, constraint propagation can be less computationally intensive than backtracking search but recovers the exact solution of a problem only when local constraint suffices to completely determine a globally acceptable solution. Otherwise, some nonsolutions may not be ruled out. For example, Freuder (1978:959) cites the example of a fully connected three-node network that expresses a graph coloring problem. Each node must be labeled as red or green, and a line between nodes must have different colors at its two ends. In this network, constraint propagation fails to rule anything out, even though with only two colors available the coloring problem obviously can't have any solution. The same thing happens with SAT problems that are too hard for our two-level constraint propagation method to solve; section 6.4 gives an example.

6.3.2   The two-level constraint tableau

If we interpret KIMMO generation by analogy with Waltz's scene analysis problem, our goal is to label each character position with a lexical/surface pair, consistent with the constraints from the automata. When it's unclear which pair to choose, the standard algorithm picks a possible choice and continues. This method enforces the constraints of the system exactly, but as we've seen, it ends up searching through the possible combinations of choices—a potentially exponential number of *combinations of truth-values*, in the satisfiability problem.[26] The constraint-propagation procedure constrains the possibilities at each character position in a weaker and less precise way, based only on the possibilities for adjacent positions.

Instead of a line drawing, we will use a tableau like the one shown in figure 6.3 to represent the constraint propagation network. The upright

---

[26]This is true regardless of whether the search is carried out depth-first or breadth-first. See Karttunen (1983:184) on the difference in search order between Karttunen's KIMMO algorithms and the equivalent procedures originally presented by Koskenniemi.

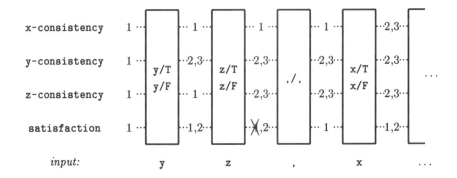

Figure 6.3: The constraint-propagation method produces this representation when processing the first few characters of the formula yz,x-y-z,-x,-y using the automata from Figure 6.1. At this point no truth-values have been definitely determined. One possible state of the satisfaction automaton after the z-position has been crossed out because it will be eliminated by constraint propagation.

rectangles represent character positions and are labeled with lexical/surface pairs; for instance, at this early stage of processing, the y-position is labeled with the two possibilities y/T and y/F. The dotted lines joining each rectangle to its neighbors represent the operation of the automata and are labeled with automaton states; for instance, the dotted lines in the top row indicate that the x-consistency automaton stays in state 1 until the first x-position is reached. At that point it may enter either state 2 or state 3, depending on whether the x-position is labeled with x/T or x/F.

Pursuing the analogy with Waltz's scene analysis method, we can establish a correspondence between the two problems. The labeling of junctions in a line drawing corresponds to the labeling of character positions with lexical/surface pairs. The propagation of information along the lines connecting junctions corresponds to propagation between adjacent columns along the dotted lines of the tableau. The underlying constraint that justifies the propagation of information is also similar in the two problems. In a line drawing, information flows along lines because the junctions at the two ends of a line must label it consistently; the elimination of a possible label at one end can reduce possibilities at the other. In the tableau of figure 6.3, there is constraint because at each character position the automata must start off in the same states where the previous position left them; they can change state only while stepping over a lexical/surface pair. Thus, if we reduce the possible states an automaton may be in after processing position i, we also reduce possibilities for position $i + 1$, and conversely.

In addition, there is one route for information flow that has no direct counterpart in the scene-analysis domain. As the tableau suggests, the pair set for a position is common to all the automata; each pair in the pair set must be acceptable to every automaton. If one automaton has concluded that there cannot be a surface "**g**" at some position, it makes no sense to let another automaton assume there might be one. The automata are therefore partially coupled through the lexical/surface pairs, and effects may propagate to other automata when one automaton eliminates a pair from consideration. However, this propagation will occur only if more than one automaton distinguishes among the possible pairs at a given position. For example, a machine concerned solely with consonants would not be affected by new information about the identity of a vowel.

Like constraint propagation in a line drawing, constraint propagation in the tableau of figure 6.3 proceeds from an underconstrained initial labeling by eliminating impossible labels. However, with the tableau it is the transitions of the two-level automata rather than the constraints of the physical world that limit the ways labels may come together. A possibility τ for a transition of an automaton at character position i may be ruled out in any of three ways. The starting state of τ may not be a possible ending state at position $i - 1$; the ending state of τ may not be a possible starting state at position $i + 1$; the lexical/surface pair associated with τ may be ruled out by some other automaton or by the input character. Since all of these ways of ruling out transitions are important, for implementation purposes it is convenient to represent each two-level automaton as simply a set of transitions, each one being a triple ⟨old state, pair, new state⟩. Figure 6.4 shows the triples corresponding to a portion of figure 6.3.

6.3.3   Inference through constraint propagation

Return now to figure 6.3. When the tableau is initially constructed from left to right, it appears that the satisfaction automaton can be in either state 1 or state 2 after the z-position is processed. State 1 indicates that no true value has been seen, and it is possible if both **y** and **z** are taken to be false. State 2 indicates that some true value has been seen, and it is possible if either **y** or **z** is taken to be true. But when the next position—the

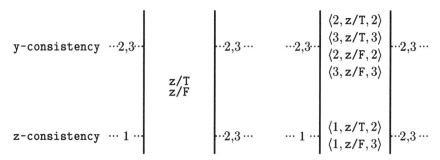

Figure 6.4: When the active transitions of each automaton are represented by triples, it is easy to enforce the constraints that relate the left and right state-sets and the pair set. The left configuration is excerpted from figure 6.3; the right configuration shows the underlying triples. The set of triples for the y-consistency automaton could easily be represented in more concise form.

comma in the formula—is considered, it becomes clear that y and z cannot both be false if the formula is to be satisfied. Mechanically, what happens is that the satisfaction automaton will not accept a comma from state 1 (see figure 6.1). Consequently, state 1 is not a possible label along the dotted line that connects the z-position and the comma position. For this reason, state 1 has been shown as canceled in the figure. However, the elimination of state 1 causes no further effects at this point because neither y nor z is yet forced to have a definite value.

The deductions that occur at the end of the easy formula -x,xyz,-y are more interesting. The state-numbers in the tableau of figure 6.5 are not perspicuous, but if we run through what happens, the satisfaction automaton can't end up in state 1 because that state is nonfinal. Therefore, the transition on y/T that takes the automaton into state 1 is also ruled out. No other possible transition accepts y/T, so the pair itself is ruled out at the last position; the system has inferred that y must be false. But if y can't be true, then the y-consistency automaton can't be in state 2—which serves only to remember y's being true—and that cancellation propagates leftward as shown in figure 6.6.

Propagation continues beyond the edge of the figure, but one of its effects off to the left is to make false the y in the clause xyz. More precisely, the possibility y/T is ruled out for the y-position, leaving only y/F. Since x was already false due to the earlier clause -x, z is the only term in the clause that could still be true. In figure 6.7, that situation shows up in the

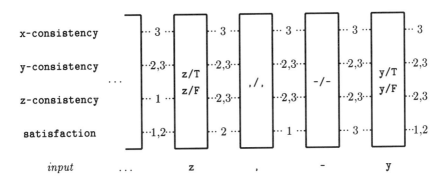

Figure 6.5: This figure depicts the right-hand end of the constraint-propagation tableau that is used for processing the formula -x,xyz,-y according to the automata in figure 6.1. At this point, the states at the right edge have not been subjected to the constraint that they must be final states. The lack of nondeterminism in the x-consistency automaton reflects the fact that the previously processed clause -x forces x to be false.

state of the satisfaction automaton at the left edge of the figure before z is processed. State 2 is no longer possible at that point because the automaton definitely cannot have seen a true value in the clause. However, state 1 will not accept the pair z/F; only z/T remains, and the system has inferred that z must be true. Rightward propagation through the z-consistency automaton now occurs. Eventually, the constraint network settles down to the satisfying truth-assignment -F,FFT,-F for the formula.

6.3.4   Details of the tableau

As the figures have suggested, the constraint propagation method involves constructing a rectangular tableau with one row for each automaton and one column for each input character. However, more columns are required when the automata permit the null characters that two-level systems use for insertion and deletion. An additional column must be added anywhere a lexical or surface null might occur. In addition, since the final analysis might not include the null, an additional pair 0/0 should be added to each column that may involve a null. Any automaton state is considered to loop back to itself on 0/0, thus making 0/0 transparent to the automata. Given this transparency, it is necessary to guard against inserting an infinite sequence of

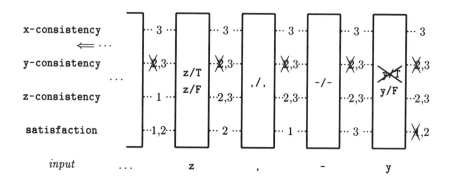

Figure 6.6: Constraint propagates leftward in the tableau of figure 6.5 when constraint from the end of the formula is taken into account. State 1 of the satisfaction automaton is eliminated because it is nonfinal, with the pair y/T and then state 2 of the y-consistency automaton being ruled out as a result. Propagation continues beyond the left edge of the figure, as indicated by the arrow.

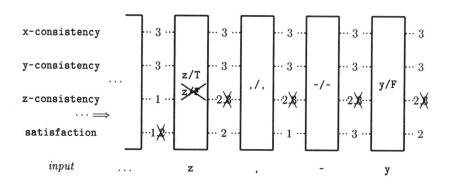

Figure 6.7: After the propagation begun in figure 6.6 has marked the y in the clause xyz as false, additional conclusions follow because z is the only remaining disjunct in the clause that might be true. Mechanically, what happens is that state 2 of the satisfaction automaton is ruled out at the left edge of this figure. The pair z/F is then eliminated because satisfaction state 1 will not accept it. The conclusion that z/T is the correct pair then propagates rightward through the z-consistency automaton. The possibilities that were eliminated in figure 6.6 have been erased from this figure.

0/0 pairs when building the network, and some restrictions on the automata are probably needed.[27]

The left edge of the tableau is constrained by the requirement that every automaton must start off in state 1. Similarly, the states at the right edge are constrained to be final states. The lexical/surface pairs that label columns of the tableau must match the corresponding input characters; for instance, the character "y" in a generation problem might allow the lexical/surface pairs y/y and y/i. In the interior of the tableau, the constraints among labels are as previously explained. A possible state for an automaton between columns i and $i + 1$ is ruled out when any of the following conditions hold:

- The only possible predecessor of the state (given the possible pairs at column i) is ruled out between columns $i - 1$ and i.

- The only possible successor of the state (given the possible pairs at column $i + 1$) is ruled out between columns $i + 1$ and $i + 2$.

- Every pair that allows a transition out of the state is eliminated from the possible pairs at $i + 1$.

- Every pair that allows a transition into the state is eliminated from the possible pairs at i.

Similarly, a pair is ruled out whenever any automaton becomes unable to traverse it given the possible starting and ending states for the transition. If sets of triples are used, the requirement is that the left state-set, right state-set, and center pair-set projections of a triple set must agree with the state sets to the left and right and with the pair set for the position, respectively.

6.4 Constraint Propagation Characteristics

Arc consistency in constraint networks—the general form of what Waltz's constraint propagation method achieves—can be attained in time linear in the number of edges in the network.[28] The constraint propagation method for two-level generation that we have sketched inherits from Waltz's labeling procedure the characteristics that prevent combinatorial blowup:

---

[27]It is not clear what restrictions would best serve. The current implementation attacks the problem with certain runtime tests, but has the disadvantage that the tests will reject some *inputs* instead of restricting the automata themselves, as we would prefer.

[28]See Mackworth and Freuder (1985:66) for details.

- The size of the constraint propagation tableau is limited. Excluding the columns that may be added to handle nulls, there is only one column per input character. The additional columns for nulls can be limited by reasonable restrictions on the automata, since natural two-level systems do not require unrestricted null characters.

- The initial possibilities at each point in the tableau are limited and noncombinatorial. The triples at some position for an automaton can do no worse than to encode the whole automaton, and there will usually be only a few triples reflecting the small portion of the automaton that deals with the particular character found in the input. It is particularly significant that the number of triples does not grow exponentially as more automata are added.

- Possibilities are eliminated monotonically, so the limited number of initial possibilities guarantees a limited number of eliminations.

- After initialization, propagation to the neighbors of a visited element takes place only if a possibility is eliminated, so the limited number of eliminations guarantees a limited number of visits.

- Limited effort is required for each propagator visit.

With a suitable restriction on nulls, the constraint propagation method runs in time polynomial in the size of the automata and input. However, we have not performed a full analysis of our preliminary implementation, in part because many details are subject to change. For instance, it would be desirable to replace the weak notion of monotonic possibility-elimination with some (stronger) notion of indelible construction of representation, based if possible on phonological features. It is also desirable to vary the geometry of the tableau in order to reduce the distance that information must be propagated through the representation. The trace that will be shown in figure 6.8 takes longer than necessary to implement vowel harmony; information propagates through unaffected consonant positions in addition to vowel positions.

From another perspective, the constraint propagation method avoids combinatorial explosion by using only an *imprecise summary* of the search space. The KIMMO machinery applied to a k-variable SAT problem explores a search space whose elements are k-tuples of truth-values for the variables, represented in the form of k-tuples of automaton states. The search space distinguishes among 2^k possible combinations in general; the KIMMO machinery considers the elements of the search space one at a time, and in the worst case it will enumerate all the elements.

Instead of considering the tuples in this space individually, the constraint propagation method summarizes whole sets of tuples in slightly imprecise form. To take a tiny example, we could summarize the set of tuples

$$\langle T, F \rangle \qquad \langle F, T \rangle \qquad \langle T, T \rangle$$

with a single vector listing the possibilities for each variable: $\langle \{T, F\}, \{T, F\} \rangle$. The summary is imprecise because it does not record the fact that the possibility $\langle F, F \rangle$ is excluded. However, if we work directly with the summary to constrain the variables individually—instead of multiplying out the combinations the summary represents and considering them one by one—the size is $2k$ instead of 2^k, at the price of more limited inferential power. In the two-level tableau, the imprecision that arises from listing the possible states of each automaton instead of enumerating combinations of states represents a *decoupling* of the automata that allows the state-possibilities for different automata to be adjusted individually. Note that in the most modular case in which the automata truly do not interact, the summary is exact because the search space contains all possible combinations. Also, the summary is exact when the possibilities have been reduced to a unique labeling, since the "summary" then identifies a single point in the search space.

The relative decoupling of the automata and the fact that constraint propagation is a network relaxation technique suggest that a significantly parallel implementation is feasible (but see caveats below and in chapter 2). However, it is uncertain whether the constraint-propagation method enjoys an advantage on serial machines. It is clear that the KIMMO machinery does combinatorial search while the constraint-propagation machinery does not, but we have not investigated such questions as whether an analog to BIGMACHINE, precompilation method (Gajek *et al.* 1983) is possible for the constraint-propagation method. BIGMACHINE precompilation speeds up the KIMMO machinery at a potentially large cost in storage space, though it does not reduce the amount of search. KIMMO problems are often tractable in practice, and thus we value our preliminary constraint-propagation method more as a probe into modularity properties of natural problems than as a practical speedup technique. A better understanding of such properties can lead to processing methods that are more specialized than general search, but also more specialized than the constraint propagation method we have described, which is applied to two-level problems in a somewhat mechanical way.

In addition, a parallel implementation of constraint propagation cannot be viewed as a panacea, for the problem encoded in a constraint propagation network may sometimes be inherently serial (Kasif 1986) and therefore subject to only limited parallel speedup. It is easy to imagine a constraint network in which information must reverberate through large regions of the network, triggering a chain of successive conclusions all along the way, before the final solution is determined. In such a case, the sequential information structure of the problem prevents parallel computation from reaching conclusions sooner than in a serial model. As we mentioned above, figure 6.8 shows our current constraint propagation method propagating information further than we would like, a situation that could be remedied by changing the geometry of the tableau.

The constraint-propagation method sketched here for KIMMO *generation* has been tested with previously constructed KIMMO automata for English, Warlpiri, and Turkish. Preliminary results suggest that the method works. However, the corresponding method for *recognition* cannot be tested on the KIMMO automata that are available to describe various languages unless the method is extended to support the KIMMO dictionary. Existing language descriptions rely heavily on the dictionary when used for recognition, and consequently an attempt to do recognition without the dictionary produces meaningless results. For instance, without constraints from the dictionary, the machinery may freely insert suffix-boundary markers "+" almost anywhere; the automata typically do not seriously constrain their occurrence.

Figure 6.8 shows the columns visited by the program when running the Warlpiri generator on a typical example, in this case a past-tense verb form ('scatter-PAST') taken from Nash (1980:85). The special lexical characters "I" and "<u2>" implement a right-to-left vowel assimilation process. The last two occurrences of "I" surface as "u" under the influence of "<u2>", but the boundary "#" blocks assimilation of the first two occurrences. Here the propagation of constraints has gone backwards twice, once to resolve each of the two sets of "I" characters. The final result is ambiguous because our automata optionally allow underlying hyphens to appear on the surface, in accordance with the way morpheme boundaries are indicated in many articles on Warlpiri.

The generation and recognition programs have also been run on mathematical SAT formulas, with the desired result that they can handle "easy"

```
0 1 2 3 4 5
  1 2 3 4
    2 3 4 5 6 7 8 9 10 11 12 13
                7 8 9 10 11 12
                8 9 10 11 12 13 14
pIrrI#kIjI-rn<u2>: result ambiguous, pirri{0,-}kuju{-,0}rnu
```

Figure 6.8: This display shows the columns visited by the constraint-propagation program when the Warlpiri generator is used on the form pIrrI#kIjI-rn<u2> 'scatter-PAST'. Each reversal of direction begins a new line. Leftward movement in this program always begins with a position adjacent to the current position, but it is an accidental property of this example that rightward movement does also. The final result is ambiguous because the automata are written to allow underlying hyphens to appear optionally on the surface. A more refined constraint-propagation method would visit fewer columns by using a different tableau geometry.

---

but not "difficult" formulas as described above.[29] For the easy formula

$$(\overline{y} \vee z) \wedge (x \vee y) \wedge \overline{x}$$

constraint propagation determines the solution

$$(\overline{T} \vee T) \wedge (F \vee T) \wedge \overline{F}.$$

In contrast, the hard formula

$$(x \vee y \vee z) \wedge (\overline{x} \vee \overline{z}) \wedge (\overline{x} \vee z) \wedge (\overline{y} \vee \overline{z}) \wedge (\overline{y} \vee z) \wedge (\overline{z} \vee y)$$

produces a different result; constraint propagation fails to make any deductions about the values of variables, merely producing the trivial result that each variable must be either true or false, and certainly failing to notice that the formula is unsatisfiable:

$$(\{T,F\} \vee \{T,F\} \vee \{T,F\}) \wedge (\overline{\{T,F\}} \vee \overline{\{T,F\}})$$
$$\wedge (\overline{\{T,F\}} \vee \{T,F\}) \wedge (\overline{\{T,F\}} \vee \overline{\{T,F\}})$$
$$\wedge (\overline{\{T,F\}} \vee \{T,F\}) \wedge (\overline{\{T,F\}} \vee \{T,F\})$$

If it is true that natural-language problems have a special modular structure that distinguishes them from other logically possible problems, making

---

[29]Recall again that the current classification of formulas as "easy" is different from polynomial-time satisfiability. In particular, the restricted problem 2SAT can be solved in polynomial time by resolution, but not every 2SAT formula is "easy" in the current sense.

them more like the easy problem than the hard one, constraint propagation represents an appropriate preliminary step toward processing methods that exploit that structure.

Chapter 7

The Complexity of ID/LP Parsing

Standard context-free rules specify not only the constituents of each phrase-type but also the order in which those constituents occur. This might seem natural for describing languages with relatively fixed word order; not only does *S* dominate *NP* and *VP*, but *NP* and *VP* must also typically appear in that order. Yet CFG rules quickly become clumsy when languages with more free word order are considered; each possible order for the daughters of a node must be described in a separate rule.[1] Many languages can be described more concisely if constraints on dominance and linear order are factored apart as in the *ID/LP grammar formalism* (Gazdar *et al.* 1985). In the simple case of unconstrained constituent order, the CFG technique of listing all orders misses an obvious generalization.

In similar fashion, much of modern linguistic theory attributes surface complexity to interacting subsystems of constraints. It is therefore of interest to know how such modular theories can be put to use in processing. Must we multiply out the various effects to produce something like a huge CFG? An ID/LP parsing algorithm by Shieber (1983) shows how ID and linear precedence (LP) constraints can be used *directly* in parsing—without using an expanded intermediate "object grammar."

The direct parsing algorithm is a straightforward extension of Earley's (1970) algorithm, and for this reason it seems at first to have the same runtime bound (Shieber 1983:14f). However, this chapter shows that this underestimates the difficulty of ID/LP parsing. ID/LP parsing is actually

---

[1] In this brief introduction, we are of course ignoring transformations and other devices that could produce a variety of surface orders from a single underlying rule. We also ignore the numerous other shortcomings of a strict context-free framework.

NP-complete, and the worst-case runtime of the direct parsing algorithm is actually *exponential* in grammar size. As we'll see, the growth of parser data structures causes the difficulty.

Some computational and linguistic implications follow (sections 7.8 and 7.9). It is important to note that despite the potential for combinatorial explosion, Shieber's algorithm remains better than the alternative of parsing an expanded object grammar. In addition, our analysis provides insight into the kind of constraint that must be provided by various components of a larger grammatical system if computational difficulty is to be avoided. We will conclude this chapter (section 7.10) with a brief discussion of how UCFGs might be restricted to reduce processing difficulty.

7.1 Separating ID and LP Constraints

It is common in recent linguistic theories for various surface characteristics of a language to be described in terms of several different kinds of under-lying constraints. ID/LP grammars involve immediate dominance rules and linear order constraints; more broadly, GPSG systems can also involve feature relationships and metarules (Gazdar *et al.* 1985), which we consider in chapter 8. The tree adjunction grammars of Kroch and Joshi (1985) separate the statement of local constraints from the projection of those constraints to larger structures. The GB-framework of Chomsky (1981:5) identifies the subtheories of bounding, government, θ-marking, binding, Case, and control. When several independent constraints are involved, a system that explicitly multiplies out their effects is large, cumbersome, and uninformative.[2] If carried out properly, the disentanglement of different kinds of constraints can result in shorter and more illuminating language descriptions.

With any such modular framework, two questions immediately arise: how can the various constraints be put back together in parsing, and what are the computational characteristics of the process? One approach is to compile a large "object grammar" that expresses the combined effects of the constraints in a more familiar format such as an ordinary context-free grammar (CFG). The context-free object grammar can then be parsed with Earley's (1970) algorithm or any of several other well-known procedures with known computational characteristics.

---

[2]See Barton (1984) for discussion.

However, in order to apply this method, it is necessary to expand out the effects of *absolutely everything* that falls outside the strict context-free format: rule schemas, metarules, immediate dominance rules, linear precedence constraints, feature instantiations, case-marking constraints, *etc.* The standard algorithms operate on CFGs, not on extended variants of them. Unfortunately, the object grammar may be huge after the effects of all nonstandard devices have been expanded out. Estimates of the object-grammar size for typical systems vary from hundreds or thousands up to trillions of rules (Shieber 1983:4) or beyond (chapter 8).[3] With some formalisms, the context-free object-grammar approach is not even possible because the object grammar would be infinite (Shieber 1985:145). Grammar size matters beyond questions of elegance and clumsiness, for it typically affects processing complexity. Berwick and Weinberg (1982) argue that the effects of grammar size can actually *dominate* complexity for a relevant range of input lengths.

Given the disadvantages of multiplying out the effects of separate systems of constraints, Shieber's (1983) work on *direct parsing* leads in a welcome direction. Shieber considers how one might do parsing with ID/LP grammars, which involve two orthogonal kinds of rules. ID rules constrain *immediate dominance* irrespective of constituent order ("a sentence can be composed of V with NP and SBAR complements"), while LP rules constrain *linear precedence* among the daughters of any node ("if V and SBAR are sisters, then V must precede SBAR"). Shieber shows how Earley's (1970) algorithm for parsing CFGs can be adapted to use the constraints of ID/LP grammars directly, without the combinatorially explosive step of converting the ID/LP grammar into standard context-free form. Instead of multiplying out all of the possible surface interactions among the ID and LP rules, Shieber's algorithm applies them one step at a time as needed. Surely this should work better in a parsing application than applying Earley's algorithm to an expanded grammar with trillions of rules, since the worst-case time complexity of Earley's algorithm is proportional to the square of the grammar size!

Shieber's general approach is on the right track. On pain of having a large and cumbersome rule system, the parser designer should first look to linguistics to find the correct set of constraints on syntactic structure, then discover how to apply some form of those constraints in parsing without multiplying out all possible surface manifestations of their effects.

---

[3]The lower estimate is from an anonymous referee for *Computational Linguistics*, but we suspect it measures the size of a grammar that has not been fully expanded into context-free form; see the last sections of chapter 8 for discussion.

Nonetheless, nagging doubts about computational complexity remain. Although Shieber (1983:15) claims that his algorithm is identical to Earley's in time complexity, it seems almost too much to hope for that the size of an ID/LP grammar should affect the time complexity of ID/LP parsing in exactly the same way that the size of a CFG affects the time complexity of CFG parsing. An ID/LP grammar G can enjoy a huge size advantage over a context-free grammar G' for the same language; for example, if G contains only the rule $S \rightarrow_{\text{ID}} abcde$, the corresponding G' contains $5! = 120$ rules. In effect, the claim that Shieber's algorithm has the same time complexity as Earley's algorithm means that this tremendously increased brevity of expression comes free (up to a constant). The supporting argument in Shieber's article is not sufficiently complete to allay these doubts:

> We will not present a rigorous demonstration of time complexity, but it should be clear from the close relation between the presented algorithm and Earley's that the complexity is that of Earley's algorithm. In the worst case, where the LP rules always specify a unique ordering for the right-hand size of every ID rule, the presented algorithm reduces to Earley's algorithm. Since, given the grammar, checking the LP rules takes constant time, the time complexity of the presented algorithm is identical to Earley's .... That is, it is $O(|G|^2 n^3)$, where $|G|$ is the size of the grammar (number of ID rules) and n is the length of the input. (1983:14f)

Many questions remain; for example, why should a situation of maximal constraint represent the worst case?[4]

Although the expressive economy of ID/LP grammars raises suspicions, we cannot conclude from the mere fact of representational succinctness that such grammars are difficult to parse (see section 2.3.4 of chapter 2). Instead, we must investigate the complexity of ID/LP parsing in more detail—and the following sections do just that. In brief, the outcome is that Shieber's direct-parsing algorithm usually *does* have a time advantage over the use of Earley's algorithm on the expanded CFG, but that the algorithm blows up in the worst case. The claim of $O(|G|^2 n^3)$ time complexity is mistaken; in fact, the worst-case time complexity of ID/LP parsing cannot be bounded by any polynomial in the size of the grammar and input, unless $\mathcal{P} = \mathcal{NP}$. ID/LP parsing is NP-complete.

---

[4]See section 7.6; it is in fact the *best* case.

As it turns out, the complexity of ID/LP parsing has its source in the immediate-domination rules rather than the linear precedence constraints. Consequently, the precedence constraints will be neglected. Attention will be focused on *unordered context-free grammars* (UCFGs), which are exactly like standard context-free grammars except that when a rule is used in a derivation, the symbols on its right-hand side are considered to be unordered and hence may be written in any order. UCFGs represent the special case of ID/LP grammars in which there are no LP constraints. Shieber's ID/LP algorithm can be used to parse UCFGs simply by assuming permissive LP constraints.

ID rules and similar devices have a history that goes beyond their current revival within GPSG theory. Before moving on to technical details, we will briefly place them in historical context.

7.2 Free-Order Devices in Modern Linguistics

Some languages (such as English) place fairly rigid constraints on word and constituent order, while other languages (such as Warlpiri) permit extremely free variation. Thus, two main approaches to formalizing word-order facts immediately suggest themselves. Within the *Aspects* model of transformational grammar, fixed word order was taken as basic and scrambling rules were used to account for free order. Ross (1967) proposes a scrambling transformation for Latin, while Nash (1980:157ff) reports that Hale's earliest work on Warlpiri attempted to apply scrambling and other rules to that language as well.[5] Alternatively, ordering restrictions could be accounted for by imposing constraints on a system that is fundamentally unordered in some sense. ID/LP grammars represent one version of this notion, but numerous others of varying character have also been proposed.

Following a distinction introduced by Emmon Bach, Nash (1980:148ff) classifies several free-word-order systems as either *L-systems* or *M-systems*. Both L-systems and M-systems involve rules that have roughly the same superficial form as UCFG rules, for instance $S \rightarrow \{NP, VP\}$, but the two kinds of systems differ in how the rules are applied. In an M-system, the

---

[5]Hale's account is described in a mimeographed 1967–68 work, "Preliminary remarks on Walbiri grammar."

rules produce ordered phrase-structure trees in the usual sense; the daughters of any node are ordered, although the order in which they appear is not restricted by the rules. UCFGs as we have defined them are M-systems. L-systems, on the other hand, produce hierarchical but unordered phrase-structure trees—sometimes called *wild trees*—in which no daughter of a node is considered to precede any other.[6] The linear order that ultimately appears results from other processes:

> [Some L-system proponents] have been primarily studying languages (Russian and Sanskrit) which exhibit considerable variation in the allowable word-order of surface sentences. Others who have been concerned with languages with less freedom of word-order have also proposed base rules of the L-system type, but [have] also had to discuss the *linearization* process, whereby specific orders are assigned to the "wild trees." In addition to stratificational grammarians ... one might include here ... Relational and Arc-Pair Grammarians (Postal, Perlmutter, and others, who use a relation of Linear Precedence) [as well as others] .... [Others] see the modifier-head relationship as the main ... determinant of word-order within a given language .... [Still others see] linearization as governed by functional and discourse factors .... [or by] the nature of the mechanisms which process sentences. (Nash 1980:149)

Nash also mentions proposals to the effect that languages may include both ordered and unordered rules or constituents.

However, languages such as Dyirbal and Warlpiri exhibit freedom of word-order beyond what can be captured with either L-systems or M-systems (including ID rules). Neither kind of system permits an arrangement in which elements of different constituents are intermingled, and further scrambling rules would therefore be needed just as in transformational analyses. However, it is possible to interpret wild trees in a way that allows linearization to intermingle the elements of constituents. Nash (1980:151) uses the term *Boas/Moulton-mobile* for an interpretation of wild trees that allows the unordered tree of an L-system to project onto a two-dimensional plane as if it were the shadow of a three-dimensional mobile. This interpretation al-

---

[6]Chomsky (1965:124ff) criticizes such systems on grounds that they do not appear to provide an adequate basis for the (transformational) mapping to surface structure, among other defects.

lows intermingling, though it is unclear how to capture the restrictions on order that do exist. (See Nash (1980) and Hale (1981) on the possibility of "discontinuous constituents" in Warlpiri.) Yngve (1960) allowed a type of phrase-structure rule with which discontinuous constituents could be generated directly; related proposals have quite often been made, typically in connection with verb–particle constructions.

We see from these passages that ID rules and similar devices have been of interest primarily for the treatment of languages in which the order of words or constituents is relatively free. However, ID rules in conjunction with LP constraints can also be used for languages with stricter requirements on ordering, and the separation of ID and LP constraints may potentially capture generalizations that would go unexpressed with standard context-free rules. (An ID/LP grammar on its own still does not permit the degree of free word order that produces discontinuous constituents.)

7.3 Generalizing Earley's Algorithm

Shieber's algorithm for parsing ID/LP grammars (here, UCFGs) generalizes Earley's algorithm by modifying the *progress datum* that tracks progress through a rule. The Earley algorithm uses the position of a dot to track linear advancement through an ordered sequence of constituents. The major predicates and operations on such dotted rules are these:

- A dotted rule is *initialized* with the dot at the left edge, as in the dotted rule $X \rightarrow .ABC$.

- A dotted rule is *advanced* across a terminal or nonterminal that was predicted and has been located in the input by simply moving the dot to the right. For example, $X \rightarrow A.BC$ is advanced across a B by moving the dot to obtain $X \rightarrow AB.C$.

- A dotted rule is *complete* iff the dot is at the right edge. For example, $X \rightarrow ABC.$ is complete.

- A dotted rule *predicts* a terminal or nonterminal iff the dot is immediately before the terminal or nonterminal. For example, $X \rightarrow A.BC$ predicts B.

UCFG rules differ from CFG rules only in that the right-hand sides represent unordered multisets (that is, sets with repeated elements allowed). It is thus appropriate to use successive accumulation of set elements in place of linear advancement through a sequence. In essence, Shieber's algorithm replaces the standard operations on dotted rules with corresponding operations on what will be called dotted UCFG rules:[7]

- A dotted UCFG rule is *initialized* with the empty multiset before the dot and the entire multiset of right-hand elements after the dot, as in $X \rightarrow \{\}.\{A, B, C\}$.

- A dotted UCFG rule is *advanced* across a terminal or nonterminal that was predicted and has been located in the input by simply moving one element from the multiset after the dot to the multiset before the dot. For example, $X \rightarrow \{A\}.\{B, C\}$ is advanced across a B by moving the B to obtain $X \rightarrow \{A, B\}.\{C\}$. Similarly, $X \rightarrow \{A\}.\{B, C, C\}$ may be advanced across a C to obtain $X \rightarrow \{A, C\}.\{B, C\}$.

- A dotted UCFG rule is *complete* iff the multiset after the dot is empty. For example, $X \rightarrow \{A, B, C\}.\{\}$ is complete.

- A dotted UCFG rule *predicts* a terminal or nonterminal iff the terminal or nonterminal is a member of the multiset after the dot. For example, $X \rightarrow \{A\}.\{B, C\}$ predicts B and C.

Given these replacements for operations on dotted rules, Shieber's algorithm operates in the same way as Earley's algorithm. As usual, each state in the parser's state sets consists of a dotted rule tracking progress through a constituent plus the interword position defining the constituent's left edge (Earley 1970:95, omitting lookahead). The left-edge position is also referred to as the *return pointer* because of its role in the *complete* operation of the parser.

7.4   The Advantages of Direct Parsing

The first question to ask is whether Shieber's direct-parsing algorithm saves anything. Is it faster to use direct parsing on a UCFG than to use Earley's algorithm on the corresponding expanded CFG? Consider the UCFG G_1 that has only the single rule $S \rightarrow abcde$. The corresponding CFG G_1' has 120 rules

---

[7]Shieber's representation differs in some ways from the representation used here, which was developed independently by E. Barton. The differences are generally inessential, but see note 9.

spelling out all the permutations of *abcde*: $S \rightarrow abcde$, $S \rightarrow abced$, and so forth. If the string *abcde* is parsed by using Shieber's algorithm directly on G_1, the state sets of the parser remain small:[8]

$$S_0 : \quad [S \rightarrow \{\}.\{a, b, c, d, e\}, 0]$$
$$S_1 : \quad [S \rightarrow \{a\}.\{b, c, d, e\}, 0]$$
$$S_2 : \quad [S \rightarrow \{a, b\}.\{c, d, e\}, 0]$$
$$S_3 : \quad [S \rightarrow \{a, b, c\}.\{d, e\}, 0]$$
$$S_4 : \quad [S \rightarrow \{a, b, c, d\}.\{e\}, 0]$$
$$S_5 : \quad [S \rightarrow \{a, b, c, d, e\}.\{\}, 0]$$

In contrast, consider what happens if the same string is parsed using Earley's algorithm on the expanded CFG with its 120 rules. As figure 7.1 illustrates, the state sets of the Earley parser are much larger. In state set S_1, the Earley parser uses $4! = 24$ states to spell out all the possible orders in which the remaining symbols $\{b, c, d, e\}$ could appear. Shieber's modified parser does not spell them out, but uses the single state $[S \rightarrow \{a\}.\{b, c, d, e\}, 0]$ to summarize them all. Direct parsing should thus be faster, since both parsers work by successively processing all of the states in the state sets.

Similar examples show that the Shieber parser can enjoy an arbitrarily large advantage over the use of the Earley parser on the expanded CFG. Instead of multiplying out all surface appearances ahead of time to produce an expanded CFG, Shieber's algorithm works out the possibilities one step at a time, as needed. This can be an advantage because not all of the possibilities may arise with a particular input.

7.5 Combinatorial Explosion with Direct Parsing

The answer to the first question is Yes, then: it can be more efficient to use direct parsing than to use the Earley parser on an expanded "object grammar." The second question to ask is whether Shieber's parser *always* enjoys a large advantage. Does the algorithm blow up in difficult cases?

In the presence of lexical ambiguity, direct parsing is susceptible to combinatorial explosion. Consider the following UCFG, G_2, in which x is

---

[8] The states related to the auxiliary start symbol and endmarker that are added by some versions of the Earley parser have been omitted for simplicity.

(a) $[S \rightarrow \{a\}.\{b, c, d, e\}, 0]$

(b)

$[S \rightarrow a.edcb, 0]$	$[S \rightarrow a.ecbd, 0]$
$[S \rightarrow a.decb, 0]$	$[S \rightarrow a.cebd, 0]$
$[S \rightarrow a.ecdb, 0]$	$[S \rightarrow a.ebcd, 0]$
$[S \rightarrow a.cedb, 0]$	$[S \rightarrow a.becd, 0]$
$[S \rightarrow a.dceb, 0]$	$[S \rightarrow a.cbed, 0]$
$[S \rightarrow a.cdeb, 0]$	$[S \rightarrow a.bced, 0]$
$[S \rightarrow a.edbc, 0]$	$[S \rightarrow a.dcbe, 0]$
$[S \rightarrow a.debc, 0]$	$[S \rightarrow a.cdbe, 0]$
$[S \rightarrow a.ebdc, 0]$	$[S \rightarrow a.dbce, 0]$
$[S \rightarrow a.bedc, 0]$	$[S \rightarrow a.bdce, 0]$
$[S \rightarrow a.dbec, 0]$	$[S \rightarrow a.cbde, 0]$
$[S \rightarrow a.bdec, 0]$	$[S \rightarrow a.bcde, 0]$

Figure 7.1: The use of the Shieber parser on a UCFG can enjoy a large advantage over the use of the Earley parser on the corresponding expanded CFG. After having processed the terminal *a* while parsing the string *abcde* as discussed in the text, the Shieber parser uses the single state shown in (a) to keep track of the same information for which the Earley parser uses the 24 states in (b).

---

five-ways ambiguous:

$$
\begin{aligned}
&S \rightarrow ABCDE \\
&A \rightarrow a \mid x \\
&B \rightarrow b \mid x \\
&C \rightarrow c \mid x \\
&D \rightarrow d \mid x \\
&E \rightarrow e \mid x
\end{aligned}
$$

What happens if Shieber's algorithm is used to parse the string $xxxxa$ according to this grammar? After the first three occurrences of x have been processed, the state set of Shieber's parser will reflect the possibility that *any three* of the phrases A, B, C, D, and E might have been encountered in the input and *any two* of them might remain to be parsed. There will be $\binom{5}{3} = 10$ states reflecting progress through the rule expanding S, in addition to 5 states reflecting phrase completion and 10 states reflecting phrase prediction (not shown):

$$S_3 : \quad [S \to \{A, B, C\}.\{D, E\}, 0] \quad [S \to \{A, B, D\}.\{C, E\}, 0]$$
$$[S \to \{A, C, D\}.\{B, E\}, 0] \quad [S \to \{B, C, D\}.\{A, E\}, 0]$$
$$[S \to \{A, B, E\}.\{C, D\}, 0] \quad [S \to \{A, C, E\}.\{B, D\}, 0]$$
$$[S \to \{B, C, E\}.\{A, D\}, 0] \quad [S \to \{A, D, E\}.\{B, C\}, 0]$$
$$[S \to \{B, D, E\}.\{A, C\}, 0] \quad [S \to \{C, D, E\}.\{A, B\}, 0]$$

In cases like this, Shieber's algorithm enumerates all of the combinations of k elements taken i at a time, where k is the rule length and i is the number of elements already processed. Thus it can be combinatorially explosive.

But it is important to note that even in this case, Shieber's algorithm wins out over parsing the expanded CFG with Earley's algorithm. After the same input symbols have been processed, the state set of the Earley parser will reflect the same possibilities as the state set of the Shieber parser: any three of the required phrases might have been located, while any two of them might remain to be parsed. However, the Earley parser has a less concise representation to work with. In place of the state involving $S \to \{A, B, C\}.\{D, E\}$, for instance, there will be $3! \cdot 2! = 12$ states involving $S \to ABC.DE$, $S \to BCA.ED$, and so forth.[9] Instead of a total of 25 states, the Earley state set will contain $135 = 12 \cdot 10 + 15$ states.

In the above case, although the parser could not be sure of the *categorial identities* of the phrases parsed, at least there was no uncertainty about the *number* of phrases and their *extent*. We can make matters even worse for the parser by introducing uncertainty in those areas as well. Let G_3 be the result of replacing every x in G_2 with the empty string ϵ:

$$S \to ABCDE$$
$$A \to a \mid \epsilon$$
$$B \to b \mid \epsilon$$
$$C \to c \mid \epsilon$$
$$D \to d \mid \epsilon$$
$$E \to e \mid \epsilon$$

Then an A, for instance, can be either an a or nothing. Before any input has been read, the first state set S_0 in Shieber's parser must reflect the possibility

---

[9]In contrast to the representation illustrated here, Shieber's representation actually suffers to some extent from the same problem. Shieber (1983:10) uses an ordered sequence instead of a multiset before the dot; consequently, in place of the state involving $S \to \{A, B, C\}.\{D, E\}$, Shieber would have the $3! = 6$ states involving $S \to \alpha.\{D, E\}$, where α ranges over the six permutations of ABC.

that the correct parse may include *any of the* $2^5 = 32$ *possible subsets* of A, B, C, D, and E as empty initial constituents. For example, S_0 must include $[S \rightarrow \{A, B, C, D, E\}.\{\}, 0]$ because the input might turn out to be the null string. Similarly, it must include $[S \rightarrow \{A, C, E\}.\{B, D\}, 0]$ because the input might turn out to be *bd* or *db*. Counting all possible subsets in addition to other states having to do with predictions, completions, and the parser's start symbol, there are 44 states in S_0. (There are 338 states in the corresponding state when the expanded CFG G_3' is used.)

7.6   The Source of the Difficulty

Why is Shieber's algorithm potentially exponential in grammar size despite its "close relation" to Earley's algorithm, which has time complexity polynomial in grammar size? The answer lies in the size of the state space that each parser uses. Relative to grammar size, Shieber's algorithm involves a much larger bound than Earley's algorithm on the number of states in a state set. Since the main task of the Earley parser is to perform *scan, predict,* and *complete* operations on the states in each state set (Earley 1970:97), an explosion in the size of the state sets will be fatal to any small runtime bound.

Given a CFG G_a, how many possible dotted rules are there? Resulting from each rule $X \rightarrow A_1 \ldots A_k$, there are $k+1$ possible dotted rules. Then the number of possible dotted rules is bounded by $|G_a|$, if this notation is taken to mean the number of symbols that it takes to write G_a down. An Earley state is a pair $[r, i]$, where r is a dotted rule and i is an interword position ranging from 0 to the length n of the input string. Because of these limits, no state set in the Earley parser can contain more than $O(|G_a| \cdot n)$ (distinct) states.

The limited size of a state set allows an $O(|G_a|^2 \cdot n^3)$ bound to be placed on the runtime of the Earley parser. Informally, the argument (due to Earley) runs as follows. The *scan* operation on a state can be done in constant time; the *scan* operations in a state set thus contribute no more than $O(|G_a| \cdot n)$ computational steps. All of the *predict* operations in a state set taken together can add no more states than the number of rules in the grammar, bounded by $|G_a|$, since a nonterminal needs to be expanded only once in a state set regardless of how many times it is predicted; hence the *predict* operations need not take more than $O(|G_a| \cdot n + |G_a|) = O(|G_a| \cdot n)$ steps. Finally, there are the *complete* operations to be considered. A given completion can do no worse than advancing every state in the state set indicated by the return pointer. Therefore, k completions require at most k^2 steps; the *complete* operations in a state set can take no more than $O(|G_a|^2 \cdot n^2)$ steps. Overall, then, it takes no more than $O(|G_a|^2 \cdot n^2)$ steps to process one state set and no more than $O(|G_a|^2 \cdot n^3)$ steps for the Earley parser to process them all.

In Shieber's parser, though, the state sets can grow much larger relative to grammar size. Given a UCFG G_b, how many possible dotted UCFG rules are there? Resulting from a rule $X \rightarrow A_1 \ldots A_k$, there are not $k + 1$ possible dotted rules tracking linear advancement, but 2^k possible dotted UCFG rules tracking accumulation of set elements. In the worst case, the grammar contains only one rule and k is on the order of $|G_b|$; hence the number of possible dotted UCFG rules for the whole grammar is not bounded by $|G_b|$, but by $2^{|G_b|}$. (The bound can be reached; recall that exponentially many dotted rules are created in the processing of G_3 from section 7.5.)

Informally speaking, the reason why Shieber's parser sometimes suffers from combinatorial explosion is that there are exponentially more possible ways to progress through an unordered rule expansion than an ordered one. When disambiguating information is scarce, the parser must keep track of all of them. In the more general task of parsing ID/LP grammars, the most tractable case occurs when constraint from the LP relation is strong enough to force a unique ordering for every rule expansion. Under such conditions, Shieber's parser reduces to Earley's. However, the case of strong constraint represents the *best case* computationally, rather than the *worst case* as Shieber (1983:14) suggests.

7.7 ID/LP Parsing is Inherently Difficult

The worst-case time complexity of Shieber's direct-parsing algorithm is exponential in grammar size rather than quadratic as Shieber (1983:15) believed. Did Shieber choose a poor algorithm, or is ID/LP parsing inherently difficult in the general case? In fact, the simpler problem of *recognizing* sentences according to unrestricted UCFGs is NP-complete.[10] Consequently, unless $\mathcal{P} = \mathcal{NP}$, *no* general algorithm for ID/LP parsing can have a runtime bound that is polynomial in the size of the grammar and input.

---

[10]Recall that recognition is simpler than parsing because a recognizer is not required to *recover the structure* of an input string, but only to decide whether the string is *in the language* generated by the grammar: that is, whether or not there *exists* a parse.

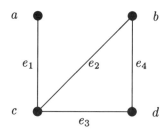

Figure 7.2: This graph illustrates a trivial instance of the vertex cover problem. The set $\{c, d\}$ is a vertex cover of size 2.

The proof of NP-completeness involves reducing the vertex cover problem (Garey and Johnson 1979:46) to the UCFG recognition problem. By careful construction of the grammar and input string, it is possible to "trick" the parser into solving this known hard problem. Recall from Chapter 2 that the vertex cover problem involves finding a small set of vertices in a graph with the property that every edge of the graph has at least one endpoint in the set. Figure 7.2 shows a trivial example.

To construct a grammar that encodes the question of whether the graph in figure 7.2 has a vertex cover of size 2, first take the vertex names a, b, c, and d as the alphabet. Take $START$ as the start symbol. Take H_1 through H_4 as special symbols, one per edge; also take U and D as special dummy symbols.

Next, write the rules corresponding to the edges of the graph. Edge e_1 runs from a to c, so include the rules $H_1 \rightarrow a$ and $H_1 \rightarrow c$. Encode the other edges similarly. Rules expanding the dummy symbols are also needed. Dummy symbol D will be used to soak up excess input symbols, so $D \rightarrow a$ through $D \rightarrow d$ should be rules. Dummy symbol U will also be used to soak up excess input symbols, but U will be allowed to match only when there are four occurrences in a row of the same symbol (one occurrence for each edge). Take $U \rightarrow aaaa$, $U \rightarrow bbbb$, and $U \rightarrow cccc$, and $U \rightarrow dddd$ as the rules expanding U.

Now, what does it take for the graph to have a vertex cover of size $k = 2$? One way to get a vertex cover is to go through the list of edges and underline one endpoint of each edge. If the vertex cover is to be of size 2, the underlining must be done in such a way that only two distinct vertices are ever touched in the process. Alternatively, since there are 4 vertices in all,

$$START \quad \rightarrow \quad H_1 H_2 H_3 H_4 UU DDDD$$

$$
\begin{aligned}
H_1 &\rightarrow a \mid c \\
H_2 &\rightarrow b \mid c \\
H_3 &\rightarrow c \mid d \\
H_4 &\rightarrow b \mid d
\end{aligned}
$$

$$
\begin{aligned}
U &\rightarrow aaaa \mid bbbb \mid cccc \mid dddd \\
D &\rightarrow a \mid b \mid c \mid d
\end{aligned}
$$

Figure 7.3: For $k = 2$, the construction described in the text transforms the vertex cover problem of figure 7.2 into this UCFG. A parse exists for the string *aaaabbbbccccdddd* iff the graph in the previous figure has a vertex cover of size ≤ 2.

---

the vertex cover will be of size 2 if there are $4 - 2 = 2$ vertices left *untouched* in the underlining process. This method of finding a vertex cover can be translated into a UCFG rule as follows:

$$START \rightarrow H_1 H_2 H_3 H_4 UU DDDD$$

That is, each H-symbol is supposed to match the name of one of the endpoints of the corresponding edge, in accordance with the rules expanding the H-symbols. Each U-symbol is supposed to correspond to a vertex that was left untouched by the H-matching, and the D-symbols are just there for bookkeeping. Figure 7.3 lists the complete grammar that encodes the vertex cover problem of figure 7.2.

To make all of this work properly, take

$$\sigma = aaaabbbbccccdddd$$

as the input string to be parsed. (In general, for every vertex name x, include in σ a contiguous run of occurrences of x, one occurrence for each edge in the graph.) The grammar encodes the underlining procedure by requiring each H-symbol to match one of its endpoints in σ. Since the right-hand side of the $START$ rule is unordered, the grammar allows an H-symbol to match anywhere in the input, hence to match any vertex name (subject to interference from other rules that have already matched). Furthermore, since there is one occurrence of each vertex name for every edge, all of the edges could conceivably be matched up with the same vertex; that is, it's impossible to run out of vertex-name occurrences. Consequently, the grammar will allow either endpoint of an edge to be "underlined." The parser will have to figure out which endpoints to choose—in other words, which vertex cover to select. However, the grammar also requires two occurrences of U to match somewhere. U can only match four contiguous identical input symbols that have not been matched in any other way, and thus if the parser chooses a vertex cover that is too large, the U-symbols will not match and the parse will fail. The proper number of D-symbols is given by the length of the input string, minus the number of edges in the graph (to account for the H_i-matches), minus k times the number of edges (to account for the U-matches): in this case, $16 - 4 - (2 \cdot 4) = 4$, as illustrated in the *START* rule.

The net result of this construction is that in order to decide whether σ is in the language generated by the UCFG, the parser must in effect search for a vertex cover of size 2 or less.[11] If a parse exists, an appropriate vertex cover can be read off from beneath the H-symbols in the parse tree; conversely, if an appropriate vertex cover exists, it indicates how to construct a parse. Figure 7.4 shows the parse tree that encodes a solution to the vertex cover problem of figure 7.2.

The construction shows that VERTEX COVER is reducible to UCFG recognition. Furthermore, the construction of the grammar and input string can be carried out in polynomial time. Consequently, UCFG recognition and the more general task of ID/LP parsing must be computationally difficult. Appendix A gives a more careful and detailed treatment of the reduction and its correctness.

7.8   Computational Implications

The reduction of VERTEX COVER shows that the ID/LP parsing problem is NP-complete. Unless $\mathcal{P} = \mathcal{NP}$, the time complexity of ID/LP parsing cannot be bounded by any polynomial in the size of the grammar and input.[12] An immediate conclusion is that complexity analysis must be done carefully: despite its similarity to Earley's algorithm, the direct parsing algorithm does

---

[11]If the vertex cover is *smaller* than expected, the D-symbols will soak up the extra contiguous runs that could have been matched by more U-symbols.

[12]Even assuming $\mathcal{P} \neq \mathcal{NP}$, it does not *follow* that the time complexity must be *exponential*, though it seems likely to be. There are functions such as $n^{\log n}$ that fall between polynomials and exponentials. See Hopcroft and Ullman (1979:341).

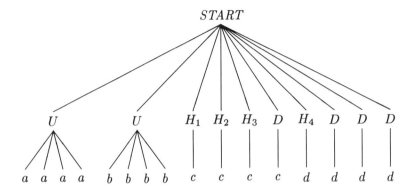

Figure 7.4: The grammar of figure 7.3, which encodes the vertex-cover problem of figure 7.2, generates the string $\sigma = aaaabbbbcccddd$ according to this parse tree. The vertex cover $\{c, d\}$ can be read off from the parse tree as the set of elements dominated by H-symbols.

not have complexity $O(|G|^2 \cdot n^3)$. For some choices of grammar and input, its internal structures undergo exponential growth. Other consequences also follow.

7.8.1   Parsing the object grammar

Even in the face of its combinatorially explosive worst-case behavior, Shieber's algorithm should not be cast aside. Despite the fact that it sometimes blows up, it still has an advantage over the alternative of parsing the expanded "object grammar." One interpretation of the NP-completeness result is that the general case of ID/LP parsing is inherently difficult; hence it should not be surprising that Shieber's algorithm for solving that problem can sometimes suffer from combinatorial explosion. More significant is the fact that parsing with the expanded CFG blows up in cases that should *not* be difficult. There is nothing inherently difficult about parsing the language that consists of all permutations of the string *abcde*, but while parsing that language the Earley parser can use 24 states or more to encode what the Shieber parser encodes in only one (section 7.4). To put the point another way, the significant fact is not that the Shieber parser can blow up; it is that the use of an expanded CFG blows up *unnecessarily.*

7.8.2   Is precompilation possible?

The present reduction of VERTEX COVER to ID/LP parsing involves constructing a grammar and input string that *both* depend on the problem to be solved. Consequently, the reduction does not rule out the possibility that through clever programming one might concentrate most of the computational difficulty of ID/LP parsing into a separate *precompilation* stage, dependent on the grammar but independent of the input. According to this optimistic scenario, the entire procedure of preprocessing the grammar and parsing the input string would be as difficult as any NP-complete problem, but after precompilation, the time required for parsing a particular input would be bounded by a polynomial in grammar size and sentence length.

Regarding the case immediately at hand, Shieber's modified Earley algorithm has no precompilation step.[13] The complexity result implied by the reduction thus applies with full force; any possible precompilation phase has yet to be proposed. Moreover, it is by no means clear that a clever precompilation step is even *possible;* it depends on exactly how $|G|$ and n enter into the complexity function for ID/LP parsing. If n enters as a *factor* multiplying an exponential, precompilation cannot help enough to ensure that the parsing phase will run in polynomial time. See section 2.3 of chapter 2 for discussion of this point.

In a related vein, suppose the precompilation step is conversion from ID/LP to CFG form and the runtime step is the use of the Earley parser on the expanded CFG. Although the precompilation step does a potentially exponential amount of work in producing G' from G, another exponential factor can still show up at runtime because $|G'|$ in the complexity bound $|G'|^2 n^3$ is exponentially larger than the original $|G|$.

7.8.3   Polynomial-time parsing of a fixed grammar

As noted above, both grammar and input in the current VERTEX COVER reduction depend on the vertex cover problem to be solved. The

---

[13]Shieber (1983:15 n. 6) mentions a possible precompilation step, but it is concerned with the LP relation rather than the ID rules.

NP-completeness result would be strengthened if there were a reduction that used the same fixed grammar for all vertex cover problems, for it would then be possible to prove that a precompilation phase would be of little avail. However, unless $P = \mathcal{N}P$, it is impossible to design such a reduction. Since grammar size is not considered to be a parameter of a fixed-grammar parsing problem, the use of the Earley parser on the object grammar constitutes a polynomial-time algorithm for solving the fixed-grammar ID/LP parsing problem.

Any fixed ID/LP grammar can therefore be parsed in "cubic time" by the strategy of using the expanded object grammar. However, this observation represents exactly the wrong way to look at the complexity of ID/LP parsing; it is little more than an accounting trick if we attain polynomial-time processing merely by shifting to the fixed-grammar viewpoint. The ID/LP framework allows ID/LP grammars that would expand into huge object grammars G', and if $|G'|^2 \cdot n^3$ complexity is too slow, it doesn't get any faster when $|G'|^2$ is regarded as a constant. Recall from our examples that parsing with the object grammar can often be *slower* than direct parsing—hence the object grammar leads in the wrong direction if we're interested in processing efficiency.

The same idea sometimes comes up as a slightly different question. Can't we have our cake and eat it too by using the ID/LP grammar G directly when we want to see linguistic generalizations, but parsing the object grammar G' when we want efficient parsing? After all, the Earley algorithm runs in cubic time based on the length of the input string, and its dependence on grammar size is only $|G'|^2$.

In response, we stress once again that using the object grammar doesn't help. The reduction shows that it's not always easy to process the ID/LP form of the grammar, but it is no easier to use the Earley algorithm on the expanded form. As our examples have illustrated, both the Shieber parser and the Earley parser for a given ID/LP grammar can end up with state sets that contain large numbers of elements. The object grammar does not promote efficient processing; the Shieber parser operating on the ID/LP grammar can often do *better* than the Earley parser operating on the object grammar, because of its more concise representation (section 7.5).

The Earley-algorithm grammar-size factor $|G'|^2$ looks smaller than the Shieber factor $2^{|G|}$ until one recalls that G' can be exponentially larger than G. Hiding the factor $2^{|G|}$ inside $|G'|$ doesn't make it any smaller. Thus ID/LP parsing can in the worst case take a great many steps even if we parse with the object grammar, which might mistakenly be thought to be more efficient than direct parsing. It's unlikely that ID/LP parsing can be accomplished quickly over the whole range of grammars allowed by the formalism.

In contrast, a much more helpful reaction is to understand the sources of complexity and determine their status in natural languages. We've seen that nothing in the ID/LP framework guarantees efficient parsability. However, section 9.1.2 of chapter 9 argues that *substantive* properties of natural languages may bound the length of ID rules—a principal source of complexity— thus reducing the computational difficulties associated with UCFG parsing (but see section 7.10 for cautionary notes).

7.8.4   The power of the UCFG formalism

The VERTEX COVER reduction also helps pin down the computational power of the UCFG formalism. As G_1 and G_1' in section 7.4 illustrated, a UCFG (or an ID/LP grammar) can enjoy considerable brevity of expression compared to the equivalent CFG. The NP-completeness result illuminates this property in two ways. First, the result shows that this brevity of expression is sufficient to allow an instance of any problem in $\mathcal{NP}$ to be stated in a UCFG that is only polynomially larger than the original problem instance. In contrast, if an attempt is made to replicate the current reduction with a CFG rather than a UCFG, the necessity of spelling out all the orders in which the H-, U-, and D-symbols might appear makes the CFG more than polynomially larger than the problem instance. Consequently, the attempted reduction fails to establish NP-completeness, which indeed does not hold. Second, the result shows that the increased expressive power of UCFGs does not come free; although the general CFG recognition problem can be solved in polynomial time, unless $\mathcal{P} = \mathcal{NP}$ the general UCFG recognition problem cannot be.

The details of the reduction show how powerful a single UCFG rule can be. If the UCFG formalism is extended to permit ordinary CFG rules in addition to rules with unordered expansions, the grammar that expresses a vertex cover problem needs only *one* UCFG rule, although that rule may need to be arbitrarily long. The complexity of ID/LP parsing drops as maximum rule length is reduced—although the succinctness advantage of the ID/LP grammar drops as well. This seems to suggest that computational difficulties could be banished by adopting a binary-branching syntactic analysis, but section 7.10 argues that matters are not so simple.

7.8.5 The role of constraint

Finally, the discussion of section 7.6 illustrates the way in which the *weakening of constraints* can often make a problem computationally *more difficult*. It might erroneously be thought that weak constraints represent the best case in computational terms, for "weak" constraints sound easy to verify. However, frequently the weakening of constraint multiplies the number of possibilities that must be considered in the course of solving a problem. In the case at hand, the removal of constraints on the order in which constituents can appear causes the dependence of parsing complexity on grammar size to grow from $|G|^2$ to $2^{|G|}$.

7.9 Linguistic Implications

The key factors that cause difficulty in ID/LP parsing are familiar to linguistic theory. GB-theory and GPSG both permit the existence of constituents that are empty on the surface, and thus in principle they both allow the kind of pathology illustrated by G_3 in section 7.5, subject to amelioration by additional constraints. Similarly, every current theory acknowledges lexical ambiguity, a key ingredient of the vertex cover reduction. But although the reduction illuminates the power of certain mechanisms and formal devices, the direct implications of the NP-completeness result for grammatical theory are few.

The reduction does expose the weakness of attempts to link context-free generative power directly to efficient parsability. Consider, for instance, Gazdar's (1981:155) claim that the use of a formalism with only context-free power can help explain the rapidity of human sentence processing:

> Suppose ... that the permitted class of generative grammars constituted a subset of those phrase structure grammars capable only of generating context-free languages. Such a move would have two important metatheoretical consequences, one having to do with learnability, the other with processability .... We would have the beginnings of an explanation for the obvious, but largely ignored,

fact that humans process the utterances they hear very rapidly.
Sentences of a context-free language are provably parsable in a
time which is proportional to the cube of the length of the sentence or less.

As the arguments and examples in this chapter have illustrated, *context-free
generative power does not guarantee efficient parsability*. Every ID/LP grammar technically generates a context-free language, but the potentially large
size of the corresponding CFG means that we can't count on that fact to give
us efficient parsing. Thus it is impossible to sustain this particular argument
for the advantages of such formalisms as GPSG over other linguistic theories; instead, GPSG and other modern theories seem to be (very roughly)
in the same boat with respect to complexity. To the extent that this holds,
the linguistic merits of various theories are more important than complexity results. (For further discussion, see Berwick (1982), Berwick and Weinberg (1982, 1984), and the other chapters of this book.)

The reduction does not rule out the use of formalisms that decouple ID
and LP constraints; note that Shieber's direct parsing algorithm wins out
over the use of the object grammar. However, if we assume that natural
languages are in some sense efficiently processable (EP), then computational
difficulties in processing a formalism *do* indicate that the formalism itself does
not tell the whole story. If a grammatical formalism can encode problems
that are not EP—but natural-language problems *are* EP—then necessarily
the natural problems must obey *missing constraints* not accounted for in our
formal system.

Such missing constraints may indicate that the formalism is too general and should be restricted. In this interpretation, the missing constraints
tell us that the range of possible languages has been incorrectly characterized: the additional constraints that guarantee efficient parsability remain
unstated. Since the *general* case of parsing ID/LP grammars is computationally difficult, if the *linguistically relevant* ID/LP grammars are to be
efficiently parsable, there must be additional factors that guarantee a certain amount of constraint from some source.[14] Constraints beyond the bare

---

[14]In the GB-framework of Chomsky (1981), for instance, the syntactic expression of unordered θ-grids at the $\overline{X}$ level is constrained by the principles of Case theory. In a related
framework, the limited possibilities for projection from "lexical-conceptual structure" to
syntactic argument structure combine with Case-assignment rules to severely restrict the
possible configurations (Guerssel *et al.* 1985; Levin and Rappaport 1985). See also chapter 4 and related earlier work (Berwick 1982) for a discussion of constraints that could be

ID/LP formalism are justified on linguistic grounds as well; limits on subcategorization may help alleviate the computational difficulty of ID/LP parsing
(see section 7.10). Note also that the *subset principle* of language acquisition
(see Berwick and Weinberg 1984:233) would lead the language learner to start
off with strong order constraints, to be weakened only in response to positive
evidence.

However, as we explained in chapter 6, the problem of accounting for
the missing constraints is subtle. It is not always appropriate to restrict the
formal grammatical framework; a substantive theory of *performance* may be
needed instead. In this interpretation, the missing constraints reflect the
properties of processing machinery instead of being embodied in the grammatical formalism itself. It might turn out that the principles and parameters of the best grammatical theory permit languages that are not efficiently
parsable in the worst case—just as grammatical theory permits sentences
that are deeply center-embedded (Miller and Chomsky 1963).[15] In such a
situation, difficult languages or sentences would not be expected to turn up
in general use, precisely *because* they would be difficult to process.[16] The
factors that guarantee efficient parsability would not be part of grammatical theory because they would result from extragrammatical factors, *i.e.*, the
resource limitations of the language-processing mechanisms.

A performance-based account is not automatically available, depending
as it does on a detailed account of processing mechanisms. For example, in
the Earley parser, the difficulty of parsing a construction can vary widely with
the amount of lookahead used (if any). Like any other theory, an explanation
based on resource limitations must make the right predictions about which
constructions will be difficult to parse.

---

placed on another grammatical formalism—lexical-functional grammar—to avoid a similar
intractability result.

[15]Indeed, one may not conclude *a priori* that all the sentences of every language permitted
by linguistic theory are algorithmically parsable *at all* (Chomsky 1980). This is true for a
variety of reasons. Imagine, for instance, that linguistic theory allowed the strings ruled
out by *filters* to be specified by complex enumerators. Then the strings of a language would
be defined in part by *subtracting off* a recursively enumerable (r.e.) set, which could lead
to nonrecursiveness because the complement of an r.e. set is not always r.e. But even if
nonrecursive, the set of strings would be perfectly well-defined.

[16]It is often anecdotally remarked that languages that allow relatively free word order
tend to make heavy use of inflections. A rich inflectional system can supply parsing constraints that make up for the lack of ordering constraints; thus the situation we do *not*
find is the computationally difficult case of weak constraint. This relates to the notion of
terminal-string distinguishability that we will discuss in section 7.10.

In the same way, the *language-acquisition procedure* could potentially be the source of some constraints relevant to efficient parsability. Perhaps not all of the languages permitted by the principles and parameters of syntactic theory are *accessible* in the sense that they can potentially be constructed by the language-acquisition component. It is to be expected that language-acquisition mechanisms will be subject to various kinds of limitations just as all other mental mechanisms are. Again, however, a definite proposal is required before we may conclude that accessible languages are efficiently parsable.

7.10   Restricting the Power of UCFGs

We conclude our discussion of UCFGs by considering factors that might limit their processing difficulty. In the previous section, we mentioned that other components of current linguistic theories might provide constraints that reduce the number of possibilities a parser must consider. Here we consider two factors that might make UCFG systems themselves more tractable. Our reduction relies heavily on the fact that the parts of a surface string may be highly ambiguous, thus suggesting a constraint of *terminal-string distinguishability*. The reduction also uses a very long UCFG rule, thus suggesting that *binary-branching analyses* might banish computational difficulty.

We noted in section 7.6 that the state sets of the UCFG parser blow up because there are exponentially more possible ways to progress through an unordered rule expansion than an ordered one. Suppose our UCFG rule is $X \to A_1, \ldots, A_5$ and we have already seen A_1 and A_4. The dotted UCFG rule reflecting this state of affairs will be

$$X \to \{A_1, A_4\}.\{A_2, A_3, A_5\},$$

which allows either an A_2, an A_3, or an A_5 to come next. Computational difficulty arises when the next region of input is *ambiguous* so that we can't tell which A_i we actually have. In the face of ambiguity, the parser must advance our single dotted rule in three different ways reflecting the three possibilities:

$$X \to \{A_1, A_4, A_2\}.\{A_3, A_5\}$$
$$X \to \{A_1, A_4, A_3\}.\{A_2, A_5\}$$
$$X \to \{A_1, A_4, A_5\}.\{A_2, A_3\}$$

As parsing continues, such ambiguity can allow the possibilities to build up exponentially.

Limits on ambiguity cut down the difficulty of UCFG parsing. For instance, in chapter 2 we mentioned that *terminal-symbol UCFGs* would be easy to process. In a terminal-symbol UCFG, the right-hand side of an unordered rule must consist of terminal elements only (without lexical ambiguity). The rule $X \rightarrow A_1, \ldots, A_5$ would thus be impossible; the closest we could come would be $X \rightarrow a_1, \ldots, a_5$. It's easy to see that direct parsing can't blow up with such a restricted rule; only terminals such as a_3 may appear on the right-hand side of a rule, and we can always tell whether a_3 or a_5 comes next in the input. There will still be exponentially many ways to progress through a dotted UCFG rule, but now we can be sure that the parser won't have to consider them all. Because of the restriction to terminals, at each step the parser will know exactly what to do.

Terminal-symbol UCFGs are too restricted to be useful; unless we have rules with ordered as well as unordered right-hand sides, a derivation in a terminal-symbol UCFG can't even include more than one rule. However, terminal-symbol UCFGs do suggest a less restrictive constraint that will also wipe out computational difficulty. First, let us note that *structural ambiguity* can be just as bad as *lexical ambiguity* in its computational effects. Returning to our rule $X \rightarrow A_1, \ldots, A_5$, we might have A_3 analyzing the substring xxx as $[x[xx]]$ and A_5 analyzing it as $[[xx]x]$. If xxx comes next in the input and the parser is expecting either A_3 or A_5, the parser will be unable to tell which one it has. What we need is a constraint of *terminal-string distinguishability* that rules out any troublesome sort of ambiguity.

More precisely, we require nonterminals A and B to be *distinguishable* if they occur as nonterminals on the unordered right-hand side of the same rule. The exact definition of distinguishability is somewhat tricky, and in this brief discussion we will not completely perfect the notion. We may begin by saying that two distinguishable nonterminals may never derive the same terminal string; this rules out the cases we discussed above. However, this constraint is not strong enough. If A derives only x and B derives only xb, then A and B can never derive the same terminal string; yet the parser can still have trouble if the remaining input starts with xb, since it can't tell whether an A or a B really comes next. Therefore, let us say that A and B are distinguishable if A never derives a terminal string α such that B derives some $\alpha\beta$, and similarly for B. (The weaker constraint treated only the case where

β is null.) We assert (without proof) that UCFGs satisfying the constraint of terminal-string distinguishability are computationally tractable.[17]

This constraint is unlikely to be achievable in general because of the pervasiveness of structural ambiguity and the the unpredictable effects of lexical ambiguity (see chapter 6 for discussion). However, closed-class items in prominent positions—such as unambiguous morphological markings or un-ambiguous prepositions—can make many natural grammars tractable. For instance, if an ID rule lists a V, a PP headed by *from*, and another PP headed by *with*, the two PPs are distinguishable; if *with* is next in the input, we can easily tell which PP is coming up.

The advantage of another promising constraint—a restriction to *binary-branching* syntactic analyses—proves less clear. Our demonstration that UCFG recognition is NP-complete relies crucially on rules with unbounded right-hand sides. If UCFG rule length were bounded, both the computa-tional difficulty and the succinctness advantage of UCFGs would be limited to a polynomial factor. Even the inefficient method of parsing with the ob-ject grammar would be polynomial in grammar size (though see the caveats in section 1.4.1). Binary-branching tree structure is generated by rules of severely limited length; thus, at first blush, the binary-branching analyses of Kayne (1981), Barss and Lasnik (1986), and others seem computationally advantageous.

However, linguistic considerations make this conclusion premature. The above argument for the computational advantages of binary branching applies only to the bare UCFG framework, and we will argue below that the reduced rule length of binary-branching analyses will probably be accompanied by a compensating augmentation in other mechanisms. Recall that a reduction establishes the difficulty of a problem over a fairly wide range of variation in serial machine models, representational choices, and so forth. This means that any formalism that can achieve the *effect* of long UCFG rules will be just as difficult to process as one that allows long UCFG rules, so long as only a polynomial overhead is involved in achieving that effect. If we can encode a UCFG-style constraint, it doesn't actually matter whether our trees are binary-branching or not. For instance, consider the flat trees that are generated by the UCFG rule $X \rightarrow A_1, \ldots, A_n$. If we switch to a system that places X at the top of a deeper, binary-branching tree, but use polynomial-

---

[17]The proper notion of distinguishability may shade off into the notion of *bounded context parsing* (see Berwick 1985).

sized *feature constraints* to ensure that the tree must contain exactly one of each of the A_i, we will be in the same computational boat as before—despite a binary-branching analysis.

The linguistic significance of this point lies in the fact that the UCFG rule $X \rightarrow A_1, \ldots, A_n$ would not be proposed in the first place unless it were in some way justified by the facts of the language under description. In the simplest case, the language might demand *exactly one* or *at most one* of each of the A_i; with similar effect, it might link the A_i to different semantic roles in some way. For example, whether or not we adopt a binary-branching analysis of double-object constructions, we still must have some means of relating a double-object verb to its objects in the proper way. Therefore, all other things being equal, a switch to a binary-branching analysis would *necessarily* be accompanied by a corresponding augmentation in feature constraints or other mechanisms. It is unlikely that more than polynomial-sized feature augmentations would be needed, and hence our reduction could almost surely be replicated in the augmented binary-branching formalism.

We see from this example that if a reduction in rule length is to be computationally beneficial, it must result from a reduction in the range over which co-occurrence restrictions must be enforced; a merely *mechanical* shift to analyses with reduced branching is not sufficient. In fact, natural-language grammars may obey substantive constraints that do limit the effective range of ID rules rather than merely their mechanical length; they may also typically have properties that promote distinguishability. See section 9.1.2 of chapter 9 for further discussion.

If such substantive constraints do exist, the complexity of UCFG processing might have quite different implications from the computational difficulties associated with agreement and ambiguity (chapter 3). We argued in chapters 3 and 6 that the theory of grammar must permit difficulty to arise from lexical ambiguity; the haphazard nature of lexical ambiguity makes it difficult to rule out on any principled basis. If a small and principled bound can be placed on rule length, the effect of UCFG rules on object-grammar size can—in contrast—be limited to a polynomial blowup. However, recall the caveats in section 1.4.1, and note that the increase in object-grammar size due to *feature systems* (chapter 8) will usually far overshadow the effect of UCFG rules in any case.

Chapter 8

Sources of Complexity in GPSG Theory

An important goal of computational linguistics has been to use linguistic theory to guide the construction of computationally efficient real-world natural-language processing systems. The linguistic theory of generalized phrase structure grammar (GPSG) holds out considerable promise as an aid in this task. The precise formalisms of GPSG offer the prospect of a direct and transparent guide for parser design and implementation. Furthermore, and more importantly, GPSG's weak context-free generative power suggests an efficiency advantage for GPSG-based parsers. Because context-free languages can be parsed in polynomial time, it seems plausible that GPSGs can also be parsed in polynomial time. This would in turn seem to help explain the rapidity of human language processing.[1]

In this chapter, we argue that the informal argument from weak context-free generative power to efficient parsing does not hold up. In the process, we illustrate how complexity analysis at many levels can pinpoint sources of intractability in linguistic theory. We begin by examining the computational complexity of metarules and the feature system of GPSG and show that each of these systems can lead to computational intractability. Next, we prove that the universal recognition problem for current GPSG theory is EXP-POLY hard, and assuredly intractable.[2] That is, it is an exponential polynomial time hard problem to decide for an arbitrary GPSG and input string whether

---

[1] This argument is due to Gazdar (1981:155); see section 7.9 for details. Similar assumptions can be found in Joshi (1985:226) and Peterson (1985:315).

[2] We use the universal recognition problem because it more accurately reflects the difficulty of processing a grammatical formalism, as explained in section 1.4.4. Ristad (1985) has previously proven that the universal recognition problem for the GPSGs of Gazdar (1981) is NP-hard and likely to be intractable, even under severe metarule restrictions.

the string is in the language generated by the grammar. This result puts GPSG-Recognition in a complexity class occupied by few naturally arising problems: GPSG-Recognition is harder than the traveling salesman problem, context-sensitive language recognition, or winning the game of chess on an $n \times n$ board. The complexity classification shows that the fastest recognition algorithm for GPSGs must take exponential time or worse. In all cases, the reductions are used to pinpoint sources of complexity in GPSG and to suggest linguistically and computationally motivated restrictions (see chapter 9).

8.1   The GPSG Formal System

A generalized phrase structure grammar contains five language-particular components: immediate dominance rules, metarules, linear precedence constraints, feature co-occurrence restrictions (FCRs), and feature specification defaults (FSDs). GPSG theory also provides four language-universal components: a theory of syntactic features, principles of universal feature instantiation, principles of semantic interpretation, and formal relationships among various components of the grammar.[3] In this section, we provide a brief and linguistically motivated overview of the theory.

8.1.1   Syntactic categories

Syntactic categories (nonterminals) in GPSG are partial functions that map features to atomic feature values or to syntactic categories. They encode subcategorization, agreement, unbounded dependency, and other syntactically significant information. Categories may also be thought of as sets of *feature specifications*. A feature specification is a tuple [*feature feature-value*] where *feature* is an atomic symbol and *feature-value* is either an atomic symbol or a syntactic category. Thus, [N +] indicates that the atomic-valued "nominal" feature has the "+" value, while [SLASH {[BAR 2]}] indicates that the "slash" feature has the category {[BAR 2]} as its value. In the GPSG system, {[N +], [V -], [BAR 2]} is an *NP*, {[N -], [V +], [BAR 2], [SUBJ -]} is a *VP*, and {[N -], [V +], [BAR 2], [SUBJ +]} is a verb phrase with a subject, or an *S*. Some features are morphologically realized; for example, in

---

[3]This work is based on current GPSG theory as presented in Gazdar, Klein, Pullum, and Sag (1985), hereafter GKPS. The reader is urged to consult that work for a formal presentation and thorough exposition of current GPSG theory. Sells (1986) contains an overview of the theory.

the GKPS grammar for English, a category bearing the feature specification [PFORM with] must dominate a prepositional phrase headed by the preposition *with*. We adopt the abbreviatory conventions found in the GPSG literature: syntactic categories may be abbreviated up to ambiguity. Thus, a noun phrase containing the additional feature specifications [CASE NOM] and [POSS +] might written *NP*[CASE NOM,POSS +] or even as *NP*[NOM,+POSS] because the atomic feature value NOM may only be associated with the CASE feature. The SLASH feature is abbreviated with a trailing slash ('/') character: *VP*[VFORM PAS,SLASH *NP*] is usually written *VP*[PAS]/*NP*. A numerical value appearing inside square brackets ([32], for example) denotes a SUBCAT value, while a numerical value that precedes a set of square brackets *V2*[NEG +] is a BAR value. For example, the category *V0*[2] abbreviates the category {[N -], [V +], [BAR 0], [SUBCAT 2]}. Appendix B contains a list of GPSG category abbreviations. To reduce confusion, we will not abbreviate syntactic categories in any formal proofs.

The set K of syntactic categories is specified inductively by listing a set *Feat* of features, a set *Atom* of atomic-valued features, a set A of atomic feature values, a function ρ that defines the range of each atomic-valued feature, and a set R of restrictive predicates on categories (feature co-occurrence restrictions). The *category-valued features* in $(Feat - Atom)$ allow categories to be freely contained within other categories, subject to FCRs (below) and the restrictive principle of *finite feature closure*, which prevents a category-valued feature f from taking categories in which f already appears. That is, the feature specification $[f\ C]$ is legal only "if f is not in the domain of C, or in the domain of any C' contained in C, at any level of embedding" (GKPS:36).

A category C_1 *extends* a category C_2 (written $C_1 \sqsupseteq C_2$) if and only if two conditions hold. For every *atomic* feature specification f in C_2, it must be true that $C_1(f) = C_2(f)$, and for every *category-valued* feature specification f in C_2, it must be true that $C_1(f) \sqsupseteq C_2(f)$. For example, {[N +], [V -], [BAR 2], [POSS +]} $\sqsupseteq$ *NP*, and *VP* $\not\sqsupseteq$ *S*.

As one might imagine, not every set of feature specifications that satisfies finite feature closure is a possible syntactic category. For example, there are no passive prepositional phrases, and a noun phrase cannot bear the [PFORM with] specification, which is reserved for prepositional phrases. *Feature co-occurrence restrictions* (FCRs) express these and similar constraints in GPSG. FCRs are restrictive predicates on categories, constructed by standard Boolean combination of feature specifications. All legal categories must satisfy all FCRs. For example,

$$\text{FCR 1: [INV +]} \supset (\text{[AUX +]} \wedge \text{[VFORM FIN]})$$

requires any category that bears the [INV +] feature specification to also bear the specifications [AUX +] and [VFORM FIN].

8.1.2   Immediate Dominance rules

As we saw in chapter 7, the immediate dominance/linear precedence format factors out two independent relations that compose phrase structure. An ID rule is a context-free production

$$C_0 \rightarrow C_1, C_2, \ldots, C_k$$

whose left-hand side (LHS) is the mother category and whose right-hand side (RHS) is an unordered multiset of daughter categories, some of which may be designated as *head daughters*. The LHS *immediately dominates* the unordered RHS in a tree of depth one (a *local tree*). (Chapter 7 contains an independent discussion of immediate dominance rules.)

8.1.3   Metarules

Informally, metarules together with features perform much of the linguistic work done by transformations in transformational grammar. Unlike transformations, which can operate on entire trees, the domain of metarules is restricted to local trees (trees of depth one) involving a lexical head. Therefore, metarules express generalizations about the subcategorization possibilities of lexical heads. (In the next chapter, we further constrain metarules to express *only* lexical generalizations.) Formally, metarules are functions that take *lexical ID rules*—ID rules with a lexical head—to sets of lexical ID rules. They have fixed input and output patterns containing a distinguished multiset variable W in addition to constants. If an ID rule matches the input pattern under some specialization of the metavariable W, then the metarule generates an ID rule corresponding to the metarule's output pattern under the same specialization of W. For example, the passive metarule

$$VP \rightarrow W, NP$$
$$\Downarrow \qquad\qquad (8.1)$$
$$VP[\texttt{PAS}] \rightarrow W, (PP[\texttt{by}])$$

says that "for every ID rule in the grammar which permits a VP to dominate an NP and some other material, there is also a rule in the grammar which permits the passive category $VP[\texttt{PAS}]$ to dominate just the other material from the original rule, together (optionally) with a $PP[\texttt{by}]$" (GKPS:59).

The complete set of ID rules in a GPSG is the maximal set that can be arrived at by taking each metarule and applying it to the set of rules that did not themselves arise from the application of that metarule. This maximal set is called the *finite closure* $FC(M, R)$ of a set R of lexical ID rules under a set M of metarules.

8.1.4 Local trees

The ID rules obtained by taking the finite closure of the metarules on the ID rules are *projected* into local phrase structure trees. Local trees are projected from ID rules by mapping the categories in a rule into legal extensions of those categories in the projected local tree.

$$C_0 \rightarrow C_1, C_2, \ldots, C_k$$

projects to the local tree

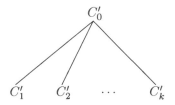

where for all i, $0 \leq i \leq k$, C_i' extends C_i. Because the RHS of an ID rule is unordered, the C_i' could appear in any order (subject to linear precedence constraints).

Principles of *universal feature instantiation* (UFI) constrain this projection by requiring categories in a local tree to agree in certain feature specifications when it is possible for them to do so. Intuitively, principles of UFI determine how feature specifications "flow" through a tree; more abstractly, they constrain the distribution of structural linguistic relations. For example, the head feature convention (HFC) requires the mother to agree with all head features that the head daughters agree on, if agreement is possible. The HFC expresses $\overline{\text{X}}$-theory, requiring a phrase to be the projection of its head, and it plays a central role both in the GPSG account of coordination phenomena and in the complexity analysis of this chapter. Two other principles of UFI, which we mention here but do not use below, are the *control agreement principle* and the *foot feature principle*. The control agreement principle represents the GPSG theory of predicate–argument relations; informally, it requires predicates to agree with their arguments (for example, verb phrases must agree with their subject NPs in English). The foot feature principle provides a partial account of gap–filler relations in the GPSG system, including parasitic gaps and the binding facts of reflexive and reciprocal pronouns; it plays a role strikingly similar to that of Pesetsky's (1982) path theory and Chomsky's (1986) binding and chain theories.[4] Informally, the foot feature principle ensures that certain syntactic information is not lost. Local trees are further constrained by FSDs, FCRs, and LP statements.

Finally, local trees are assembled to form phrase structure trees, which are terminated by lexical elements.

8.1.5   An example of projection

Let the features $\{\text{N}, \text{V}, \text{BAR}\}$ and $\{\text{NEG}, \text{POSS}\}$ be head features and non-head features, respectively. Let the symbol H mark head daughters. Then the ID rule

$$\{\, [\text{N } -], [\text{V } +], [\text{BAR } 2] \,\} \rightarrow \text{H} [\text{BAR } 0], \mathit{NP}$$

---

[4]The possibility of expressing the control agreement and foot feature principles as local constraints falls out from the central role of c-command, or equivalently unambiguous paths, in binding theory. C-command is a local relation, in fact the primary source of locality in phrase structure (see Berwick and Wexler 1982). Similarly, the possibility of encoding multiple gap–filler relations in one feature specification of one category corresponds to the "no crossing" constraint of path theory. Pesetsky (1982:556) compares the predictions of path theory and principles of UFI when the two diverge in cases of double extraction (for example, *a problem that$_i$ I know who$_j$ to* [$_\alpha$ *talk to* e_j *about* e_i]) from coordinate structures. He concludes that "the apparent simplicity of the slash category solution fades when more complex cases are considered."

can project to this local tree:

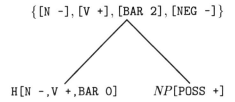

$$\{[\text{N } -], [\text{V } +], [\text{BAR 2}], [\text{NEG } -]\}$$

$$\text{H}[\text{N } -, \text{V } +, \text{BAR 0}] \qquad NP[\text{POSS } +]$$

The constrained mapping of ID rules into local trees is at the heart of GPSG. The constraints subdivide into absolute constraints on local trees (due to FCRs and LP-statements) and relative constraints on the mapping from rules to local trees (stemming from FSDs and universal feature instantiation). The absolute constraints are all language-particular and thus not inherent in the formal framework of GPSG. The relative constraints, of which only universal instantiation might be universal, do not apply to fully specified ID rules and consequently are not strongly inherent in the framework either.[5] In summary, GPSG local trees are only as constrained as ID rules are.

The only constraint strongly inherent in GPSG theory (when compared to context-free grammars) is finite feature closure. This limits the number of GPSG nonterminal symbols to be finite and bounded.[6]

8.2   Complexity of GPSG Components

To identify sources of computational complexity in GPSG theory, we consider the isolated complexity of the metarule finite closure operation and the rule-to-tree projection, using the finite closure membership and category membership problems, respectively. The *finite closure membership* problem is to determine if an ID rule is in the finite closure of a set of metarules M on a

---

[5]We use "strongly inherent" to mean "unavoidable by virtue of the formal framework." Note that the use of problematic feature specifications in universal feature instantiation means that this constraint is dependent on other, more parochial components (*e.g.,* FCRs). Appropriate choice of FCRs or ID rules will abrogate universal feature instantiation, thus rendering it implicitly language particular too.

[6]On the one hand, this formal constraint is extremely weak, because the theory of syntactic features licenses more than 10^{775} syntactic categories. See footnote 7 directly below for an extended discussion. On the other hand, this formal constraint has an interesting range of desirable empirical consequences, including the fact that GPSGs are not truly closed under union, concatenation, or substitution. Thus, the finite feature closure constraint expresses a little-noticed mathematical property of natural language.

set of ID rules R. The *category membership* problem is to determine whether
a category C or any legal extension of C is in the set K of all categories based
on the function ρ and the sets A, *Feat* and R. Note that both problems must
be solved by any GPSG-based parsing system when computing the ID rule
to local tree mapping.

Both problems are likely to be computationally intractable: finite closure
membership is NP-hard and category membership is PSPACE-hard. Chapter 7 contains a proof that the recognition problem for ID/LP grammars is
NP-hard. The components of GPSG theory are computationally difficult, as
is the theory as a whole.

Assumptions.   In the following problem definitions, we allow syntactic categories to be based on arbitrary sets of features and feature values. In actual-
ity, GPSG syntactic categories are based on fixed sets and a fixed function ρ.
Therefore, the set K of permissible categories is finite, and a large table containing K could, in principle, be given.[7] We generalize to arbitrary sets and
an arbitrary function ρ to prevent such a solution while preserving GPSG's
theory of syntactic features. No other modifications to the theory are made.

An ambiguity in GKPS is how FCRs apply to embedded categories.[8]
Following Ivan Sag (personal communication), we make the natural assumption here that FCRs apply equally at top level and to embedded categories.

8.2.1   Metarules revisited

In the *finite closure membership* problem for GPSG metarules, we are
given an ID rule r, a set M of metarules, and a set R of ID rules. The problem

---

[7]This suggestion is of no practical significance, because the actual number of GPSG
syntactic categories is extremely large. The total number of categories, given the 25 atomic
features and 4 category-valued features, is:

$$\left|K = K^4\right| \quad = \quad 3^{25}((1+3^{25})((1+3^{25})((1+3^{25})(1+3^{25})^1)^2)^3)^4$$
$$= \quad 3^{25}(1+3^{25})^{64} > 3^{1625} > 10^{775}$$

See page 234 for details. Many of these categories will be linguistically meaningless, but all
GPSGs will generate all of them and then filter some out in consideration of FCRs, FSDs,
universal feature instantiation, and the other admissible local trees and lexical entries in
the GPSG. Although the FCRs in some grammars may reduce the number of categories,
FCRs are a language-particular component of the grammar. The vastness of the category
space is *inherent* in the GPSG framework.

[8]If a category C is defined for a category-valued feature f (*e.g.*, $f =$ **SLASH**) and
$C(f) = C_e$, then C_e is said to be an (immediately) embedded category.

is to decide whether there exists any $r' \in FC(M, R)$ such that $r' \sqsupseteq r$. In *strict* finite closure membership the question is simply whether $r \in FC(M, R)$.

The cleanest possible complexity proof for metarule finite closure would fix the GPSG (with the exception of metarules) for a given problem, and then construct metarules dependent on the specific problem instance. However, metarules cannot be cleanly separated from the GPSG system. Metarules take ID rules as input and produce other ID rules as their output; if we were to separate metarules from their inputs and outputs, there would be nothing left to study. Although the use of a dummy initial ID rule would allow us to fix the initial set of ID rules on which finite closure operates, metarules would still be inextricably bound to the feature system.

The best complexity proof for metarules, then, would fix the GPSG except for the metarules, their input, and the feature system. We ensure that the input is not inadvertently performing some computation by requiring the one ID rule R allowed in the reduction to be fully specified, with only one 0-level category on the left-hand side and one unanalyzable terminal symbol on the right-hand side. Furthermore, no FCRs, FSDs, or principles of universal feature instantiation will be used. These are exceedingly severe constraints. The ID rules generated by this formal system will be the finite closure of the lone ID rule R under the set M of metarules.

The insight underlying the following reduction is that metarules are production systems: we can use them to simulate Turing machine transitions on a TM tape as represented by ID rules. The polynomial-time reduction restriction limits us to constructing at most a polynomial number of metarules, while metarule finite closure restricts each metarule to at most one application in a given computation: metarules by themselves are only capable of simulating a polynomial time TM computation. But the finite closure operation on metarules gives the GPSG formal system the power of nondeterminism because all possible permutations of metarules are applied; using this power, we can use a metarule system to simulate any nondeterministic polynomial-time computation.

Theorem 4: Finite Closure Membership is NP-hard.

Proof. We will reduce the known NP-complete problem 3SAT to FC-Membership in polynomial time. Assume as input a 3CNF formula f of length n using the m variables $x_1, \ldots, x_m$.

The metarule closure operation will be applied to a single ID rule R whose mother category will represent the variables and clauses of the formula f. We will also construct a set M of metarules that generate possible truth-assignments for the variables and then compute the truth-value of f given those assignments. The result of the construction will be that another ID rule A will have some extension in $FC(M, R)$ iff f is satisfiable.

Let w be the string of literals in the formula f. In general w_j will denote the jth symbol in the string w. Because f is a 3SAT formula, $|w|$ will be a multiple of 3 and we can pick out the literals of the ith clause as w_{3i-k} where k ranges over $0 \leq k \leq 2$. Then construct R, A, and M as follows.

1. Let R be the rule

$$R: \qquad S \rightarrow \texttt{<satisfiability>}$$

where $\texttt{<satisfiability>}$ is a terminal symbol and the category S on the left-hand side is used in part to encode the variables in f. S contains specifications for three kinds of features. The feature x_i represents the Boolean variable x_i, and has an initial truth-value of 0. Similarly, the feature c_i represents the truth-value of the ith clause in the formula f, and it too has the initial value 0. Finally, the [STAGE 1] specification simply starts off the assignment-generation process. Specifically,

$$\begin{aligned} S \;=\; & \{\,[x_i \; 0] : 1 \leq i \leq m\,\} \\ & \cup \{\,[c_i \; 0] : 1 \leq i \leq \tfrac{|w|}{3}\,\} \\ & \cup \{\,[\texttt{STAGE 1}]\,\} \end{aligned}$$

2. Let A be the rule

$$A: \qquad \{\,[\texttt{STAGE 3}]\,\} \rightarrow \texttt{<satisfiable>}$$

where $\texttt{<satisfiable>}$ is another terminal symbol. This rule is our "test rule," which the metarules will place in $FC(M, R)$ iff the formula f is satisfiable.

3. Construct the set M of metarules in four parts.

   (a) Use m metarules to generate all possible assignments to the variables. For every i, $1 \leq i \leq m$, M should include the following metarule:

$$\{\,[x_i \; 0], [\texttt{STAGE 1}]\,\} \rightarrow W$$
$$\Downarrow \qquad\qquad\qquad (8.2)$$
$$\{\,[x_i \; 1], [\texttt{STAGE 1}]\,\} \rightarrow W$$

If one of these metarules applies, it will change the value assigned to x_i from 0 to 1. Because any subset of these rules can apply one by one to the original rule R before the next metarule (below) shuts off the process, any possible truth-assignment to the variables can wind up encoded on the left-hand side of the modified rule. Also, because categories are formally *functions* from features to feature values, there is no way a variable can be assigned both values at the same time.

(b) Use one metarule to stop the generation of truth-assignments:

$$\{\,[\text{STAGE 1}]\,\} \rightarrow W$$
$$\Downarrow \qquad \qquad (8.3)$$
$$\{\,[\text{STAGE 2}]\,\} \rightarrow W$$

(c) Use $|w|$ metarules to determine whether the assignment that has been generated makes the clauses come out true. For each clause in f there will be three metarules, one for each of its three literals. i will be the clause number and k will indicate which literal of the ith clause is being considered. Because the literals of a clause are combined with *OR*, the three metarules for clause i are designed to change feature c_i from 0 (not satisfied) to 1 (satisfied) if any of its literals are true. Finally, a positive literal comes out true when its variable is true, while a negative literal comes out true when its variable is false. Formally, we include the following metarules for all i, $1 \leq i \leq \frac{|w|}{3}$:

- If $w_{3i-k} = x_j$ for some j, use this metarule to watch for x_j being true:

$$\{\,[x_j \ 1],\,[c_i \ 0],\,[\text{STAGE 2}]\,\} \rightarrow W$$
$$\Downarrow \qquad \qquad (8.4)$$
$$\{\,[x_j \ 1],\,[c_i \ 1],\,[\text{STAGE 2}]\,\} \rightarrow W$$

- If $w_{3i-k} = \overline{x}_j$ for some j, use this metarule instead to watch for x_j being false:

$$\{\,[x_j \ 0],\,[c_i \ 0],\,[\text{STAGE 2}]\,\} \rightarrow W$$
$$\Downarrow \qquad \qquad (8.5)$$
$$\{\,[x_j \ 0],\,[c_i \ 1],\,[\text{STAGE 2}]\,\} \rightarrow W$$

(d) Finally, use one final metarule to check whether all of the clauses
have been satisfied in stage 2. Let the category

$$C = \{ [c_i \ 1] : 1 \le i \le \tfrac{|w|}{3} \}$$

and include the following metarule in M:

$$C \cup \{ [\texttt{STAGE 2}] \} \to W$$
$$\Downarrow \qquad\qquad (8.6)$$
$$\{ [\texttt{STAGE 3}] \} \to \texttt{<satisfiable>}$$

Because of this metarule, some extension of the rule A will be
included in $FC(M, R)$ iff some assignment generable in stage 1
satisfied all the clauses in stage 2.

The reduction constructs $\theta(|w|)$ metarules of size $\theta(\log(|w|))$, and clearly
may be performed in polynomial time; the reduction time is essentially the
number of symbols needed to write down the GPSG. Note that the *strict* finite closure membership problem is also NP-hard. One need only add a polynomial number of metarules to "change" the feature values of the mother node
C to some canonical value when $[\texttt{STAGE 3}] \in C$: for example, all to 0 with the
exception of STAGE. Let $D = \{ [y_i \ 0] : 1 \le i \le m \} \cup \{ [c_i \ 0] : 1 \le i \le \tfrac{|w|}{3} \}$.
Then the canonical version of A would be

$$A : \qquad D \cup \{ [\texttt{STAGE 3}] \} \to \texttt{<satisfiable>}$$

and we could use the strict finite closure membership problem. □

The major source of intractability is the nondeterminism of the finite
closure operation itself. Informally, each metarule can more than double the
number of ID rules. By chaining metarules—that is, by applying the output
of a metarule to the input of the next metarule—finite closure can increase
the number of ID rules exponentially.[9]

However, it is crucial to realize that our reduction is not concerned with
the number of ID rules *per se*. An obvious way of testing finite metarule

---

[9]More precisely, the metarule finite closure operation can increase the size of a GPSG G
worse than exponentially: from $|G|$ to $\theta(|G|^{2|G|})$. Given a set of ID rules R of symbol size
n, and a set M of m metarules, each of size p, the symbol size of $FC(M, R)$ is $\theta(n^{2m}) = \theta(|G|^{2|G|})$. Each metarule has $\theta(n)$ different ways of matching the productions in R,
inducing $\theta(n + p)$ new symbols per match; each metarule can therefore square the ID rule
grammar size. There are m metarules, so finite closure can create an ID rule grammar
with $\theta(n^{2m})$ symbols.

closure membership is to begin by listing all the ID rules that the metarules produce, and the exponential blowup that metarules can accomplish clearly makes that procedure difficult. But our reduction goes beyond any particular testing method to show that the *problem* of testing finite closure membership is inherently difficult: *any algorithm* for solving the problem will be computationally intractable, regardless of whether it works by actually generating the ID rules. Our reduction is more than a trivial observation on the representational economy of metarules, for taken alone, representational economy is not sufficient to establish that metarule systems are difficult to process (see section 2.3.4). To determine processing difficulty, we must look more closely.

8.2.2 Theory of syntactic features

We next show that the complex feature system employed by GPSG leads to computational intractability. The underlying insight for the following complexity proof is the nearly direct equivalence between alternating Turing machines (ATMs) and syntactic categories in GPSG (see figure 8.3 below). The nodes or configurations of an ATM computation correspond to 0-level syntactic categories, and the ATM computation tree corresponds to a full, n-level syntactic category. The finite feature closure restriction on categories, which limits the depth of category nesting, will limit the depth of the corresponding ATM computation tree. Finite feature closure constrains us so that in polynomial time we can specify (at most) a polynomially deep, polynomially branching tree. This is exactly equivalent to a polynomial time ATM computation, and by Chandra and Stockmeyer (1976), also equivalent to a deterministic polynomial space-bounded Turing machine computation.

As a consequence of the above insight, one would expect the GPSG Category membership problem to be PSPACE-hard. The actual proof is considerably simpler when framed as a reduction from the quantified Boolean formula (QBF) problem, a known PSPACE-complete problem.

Quantified Boolean formulas

The QBF problem, a paradigmatic PSPACE-complete problem, is defined as follows.

Quantified Boolean formulas (QBF) are built from variables, the operators ∨, ∧, and ¬, parentheses, and the quantifiers ∃

("there exists") and ∀ ("for all"). When defining QBFs recursively, we find it useful simultaneously to define *free* occurrences of variables (occurrences to which no quantifier applies), *bound* occurrences of variables (occurrences to which a quantifier applies), and the scope of a quantifier (those occurrences to which the quantifier applies).

1. If x is a variable, then it is a QBF. The occurrence of x is free.

2. If E_1 and E_2 are QBFs, so are $\neg(E_1)$, $(E_1) \vee (E_2)$, and $(E_1) \wedge (E_2)$. An occurrence of x is free or bound, depending on whether the occurrence is free or bound in E_1 or E_2. Redundant parentheses can be omitted.

3. If E is a QBF, then $\exists x(E)$ and $\forall x(E)$ are QBFs. The scopes of $\exists x$ and $\forall x$ are all free occurrences of x in E. (Note that there may also be bound occurrences of x in E; these are not part of the scope.) Free occurrences of x in E are bound in $\exists x(E)$ and $\forall x(E)$. All other occurrences of variables in E are free or bound, depending on whether they are free or bound in E.

A QBF with no free variables has a value of either **true** or **false**, which we denote by the Boolean constants 1 and 0. The value of such a QBF is determined by replacing each subexpression of the form $\exists x(E)$ by $E_0 \vee E_1$ and each subexpression of the form $\forall x(E)$ by $E_0 \wedge E_1$, where E_0 and E_1 are E with all occurrences of x in the scope of the quantifier replaced by 0 and 1, respectively. (Hopcroft and Ullman 1979:343f)

In the *QBF problem*, we are given a formula of the form

$$Q_1 y_1 Q_2 y_2 \ldots Q_m y_m F(y_1, y_2, \ldots, y_m)$$

where the Q_i are quantifiers in $\{\forall, \exists\}$, the y_i are Boolean variables, and F is a Boolean formula containing no variables except the y_i. The problem is to determine whether the formula is true; for instance, we could solve the problem by cycling through the values 0 and 1 for each variable. In our proofs, we will assume without loss of generality that F is in conjunctive normal form with exactly three literals per clause (3CNF).

Hopcroft and Ullman (1979:344) give the following example of a QBF instance:

$$\forall x[\forall x[\exists y(x \lor y)] \land \neg x]$$

To see whether this is true, we write it as $\forall x E$ and evaluate the truth of E with the free occurrences of x in E set to the values 0 and 1 in turn.

(a) First we set x to 0. Considering the first clause of E, which is $\forall x[\exists y(x \lor y)]$, we find that it has no free occurrences of x because of the inner quantifier $\forall x$. Thus, we proceed to evaluate the inner quantifier as well, substituting 0 and 1 for this inner x to get the subformulas $\exists y(0 \lor y)$ and $\exists y(1 \lor y)$. In each case the formula is true, because we can always take $y = 1$ to satisfy the existential quantifier. Therefore, $\forall x[\exists y(x \lor y)]$ is true. Returning to the second clause of E, which is $\neg x$, we note that it also comes out true because x is set to zero. Thus E is true in this case.

(b) Next we set x to 1. Because the first clause of E has no free occurrences of x, it comes out true as before. However, the second clause $\neg x$ of E is now false. Thus E is false in this case.

Our formula is $\forall x E$, so these results make it false. In contrast, if the QBF were

$$\forall x[\forall x[\exists y(x \lor y)] \lor \neg x]$$
$$\text{or} \quad \exists x[\forall x[\exists y(x \lor y)] \land \neg x]$$

then it would be true.

Note that a QBF instance might allow an arbitrary number of alternating quantifiers. Intuitively, this is what makes the satisfiability of QBF formulas so hard even to *verify*. A 3SAT problem over m variables corresponds to a restricted QBF with all existential quantifiers,

$$\exists x_1 \exists x_2 \ldots \exists x_m E$$

where E is a quantifier-free 3CNF formula, and this means that once we have the right set of values for for $x_1 \ldots x_m$ we can verify the satisfiability of the formula simply by plugging in the values and evaluating E left-to-right.[10] In contrast, if E could itself contain an arbitrary number of alternating quantifiers as with general QBF, it could take exponential time to verify the truth of E after $x_1 \ldots x_n$ were plugged in. The truth of an existentially quantified

---

[10]See Garey and Johnson (1979:165–166).

formula can be verified by finding one true instance, but universal quantifiers amount to AND-branches, in which every branch must be fully evaluated.

Garey and Johnson (1979:171) sketch the following demonstration that QBF is PSPACE-complete (where we have made minor notational changes to retain compatibility with Hopcroft and Ullman (1979)):

> That QBF is in *PSPACE* follows from the fact that we can check whether [the formula] is true by cycling through all possible truth-assignments for the variables $y_1, y_2, \ldots, y_m$ and evaluating $[F]$ for each. Recording the current assignment, testing $[F]$, and keeping track of where we are in the process can all be done in polynomial space, even though exponential time will be required to examine all 2^m truth-assignments. That each language $L' \in PSPACE$ can be transformed to QBF follows from an analog to Cook's theorem, in which one simulates a polynomial space bounded computation instead of a polynomial time bounded computation.

Reduction from QBF to GPSG category membership

Now we reduce the QBF problem to the GPSG category membership problem, thereby proving that the latter problem is PSPACE-hard.

Let a *specification* of a set K of syntactic categories consist of several arbitrary components $\langle Feat, Atom, \rho, R \rangle$: *Feat* is a set of features, *Atom* $\subseteq$ *Feat* is a set of atomic-valued features, ρ is a function on *Atom* that defines the range of each atomic-valued feature, and R is a set of FCRs, where all of these components are equivalent to those defined in chapter 2 of GKPS. The *category membership problem* is: Given a specification for a set K of syntactic categories, and given a category C, determine whether there is any $C' \in K$ that extends C.

Theorem 5: Category-Membership is PSPACE-hard.

Proof. By reduction from QBF. On input formula

$$\Omega = Q_1 y_1 Q_2 y_2 \ldots Q_m y_m F(y_1, y_2, \ldots, y_m)$$

we construct an instance P of the category membership problem in poly-nomial time, such that $\Omega \in QBF$ if and only if P is true.

Following the definition of QBF truth-value on page 228, we will con-sider a quantified Boolean formula as a strictly balanced binary tree that has quantifiers associated with its internal nodes. The ith quantifier Q_i represents pairs of subtrees $\langle T_1, T_0 \rangle$ such that (1) T_1 and T_0 each immediately dominate subtrees representing the quantifiers $Q_{i+1} \ldots Q_m$, and (2) the ith variable y_i is 1 in T_1 and 0 in T_0. All nodes at level i in the whole tree correspond to the quantifier Q_i. The leaves of the tree are different instantiations of the formula F corresponding to the quantifier-determined truth-assignments to the m variables. A leaf node is labeled **true** if the fully instantiated formula F that it represents is true. An internal node in the tree at level i is labeled **true** if

1. $Q_i =$ "∃" and either daughter is labeled **true**, or

2. $Q_i =$ "∀" and both daughters are labeled **true**.

Otherwise, the node is labeled **false**.

Similarly, a category can easily be understood as a tree. The atomic-valued features in a category constitute a node in the tree, and a category C dominates its embedded categories—that is, C immediately dominates all categories C' such that for some category-valued feature f, $C(f) = C'$.

In this reduction, we use categories that correspond to the nodes of a quantifier tree. Atomic-valued features represent the m variables, the clauses of F, the quantifier associated with the tree node, and the truth label of the node. Category-valued features encode domination in the quantifier tree; for each quantifier Q_k, there will be two category-valued features q_k, q'_k to represent the pair $\langle T_1, T_0 \rangle$ of subtrees. FCRs maintain quantifier-imposed variable truth-assignments "down the tree," calculate the truth labelings of leaves according to F, and calculate the truth labelings of internal nodes according to quantifier meaning.

Given the QBF Ω as described, let w be the string of formula literals in the quantifier-free 3CNF Boolean formula F, and let w_i denote the ith symbol in this string. We will construct a specification $P = \langle Feat, Atom, \rho, R \rangle$ for a set K of permissible categories, with the end result that the category $\{[\text{LABEL } 1]\}$ has some extension in K iff Ω is true.

We begin by defining the set of possible 0-level categories, which encode the formula F and the truth-assignments for its variables. Let w be the string of formula literals in F. Then the feature w_i represents the formula literal w_i in w, y_j represents the variable y_j in Ω, and c_i represents the truth-value of the ith clause in F. As before, $|w|$ will be a multiple of 3 and we will often pick out the literals of the ith clause as w_{3i-k} where $k = 0, 1, 2$. Then we define *Feat*, *Atom*, and ρ as follows:

$$
\begin{aligned}
Atom &= \{\text{LEVEL}, \text{LABEL}\} \\
&\cup \{w_i : 1 \leq i \leq |w|\} \\
&\cup \{y_j : 1 \leq j \leq m\} \\
&\cup \{c_i : 1 \leq i \leq \tfrac{|w|}{3}\} \\
Feat &= Atom \cup \{q_k, q'_k : 1 \leq k \leq m\} \\
\rho(f) &= \begin{cases} \text{the set } \{k : 1 \leq k \leq m+1\}, \text{ if } f = \text{LABEL} \\ \text{the set } \{0, 1\}, \text{ if } f \in Atom \text{ otherwise} \end{cases}
\end{aligned}
$$

We then finish the reduction by constructing the set R of FCRs, which will constrain both the form and content of the quantifier trees:

1. We need FCRs to create strictly balanced binary trees with correct values for the feature LEVEL. For all k, $1 \leq k \leq m$, include the following FCR:
$$
\begin{aligned}
[\text{LEVEL } k] &\equiv \\
&[q_k \; \{[y_k \; 1], [\text{LEVEL } k+1]\}] \wedge \\
&[q'_k \; \{[y_k \; 0], [\text{LEVEL } k+1]\}]
\end{aligned}
$$

2. We need FCRs to ensure that all 0-level categories are labeled with truth-values. For each clause-number i, $1 \leq i \leq \frac{|m|}{3}$, and for all internal levels k, $1 \leq k \leq m$, include the following FCRs:
$$
\begin{aligned}
[c_i] &\equiv [w_{3i-2}] \wedge [w_{3i-1}] \wedge [w_{3i}] \\
[\text{LABEL}] &\equiv [c_i] \\
[\text{LABEL}] &\equiv [y_k]
\end{aligned}
$$

3. Only satisfiable assignments are to be permitted. Include the following FCR:
$$
[\text{LEVEL } 1] \supset [\text{LABEL } 1]
$$

4. Internal nodes must be labeled with truth-values determined by quantifier meaning. For all internal levels k, $1 \leq k \leq m$, there are two cases. If $Q_k = \text{``}\forall\text{''}$ then include these FCRs:
$$
\begin{aligned}
[\text{LEVEL } k] \wedge [\text{LABEL } 1] &\equiv [q_k \; \{[\text{LABEL } 1]\}] \wedge [q'_k \; \{[\text{LABEL } 1]\}] \\
[\text{LEVEL } k] \wedge [\text{LABEL } 0] &\equiv [q_k \; \{[\text{LABEL } 0]\}] \vee [q'_k \; \{[\text{LABEL } 0]\}]
\end{aligned}
$$

Otherwise, $Q_k = \text{``}\exists\text{''}$ and include these FCRs instead:
$$
\begin{aligned}
[\text{LEVEL } k] \wedge [\text{LABEL } 1] &\equiv [q_k \; \{[\text{LABEL } 1]\}] \vee [q'_k \; \{[\text{LABEL } 1]\}] \\
[\text{LEVEL } k] \wedge [\text{LABEL } 0] &\equiv [q_k \; \{[\text{LABEL } 0]\}] \wedge [q'_k \; \{[\text{LABEL } 0]\}]
\end{aligned}
$$

Recall that the category-valued features q_k and q'_k represent the quantifier Q_k. In the category value of q_k, the formula variable $y_k = 1$ everywhere, while in the category value of q'_k, $y_k = 0$ everywhere.

5. We must preserve value assignments "down the tree." For every internal level k, $1 \leq k \leq m$, and for every level i that is above it in the tree ($1 \leq i < k$), include the following FCRs to preserve the values that have already been assigned:

$$[y_i \ 1] \supset [q_k \ \{[y_i \ 1]\}] \wedge [q'_k \ \{[y_i \ 1]\}]$$
$$[y_i \ 0] \supset [q_k \ \{[y_i \ 0]\}] \wedge [q'_k \ \{[y_i \ 0]\}]$$

6. We must relate the quantifier-determined variable truth-assignments to the literals of the clauses, taking negation into account. For each literal-number i, $1 \leq i \leq |w|$, there are two cases. If $w_i = y_k$ for some k, the literal is not negated and the following FCRs should be included:

$$[y_k \ 1] \supset [w_i \ 1]$$
$$[y_k \ 0] \supset [w_i \ 0]$$

Otherwise $w_i = \bar{y}_k$ for some k and these FCRs should be included instead:

$$[y_k \ 1] \supset [w_i \ 0]$$
$$[y_k \ 0] \supset [w_i \ 1]$$

7. Finally, we need FCRs to verify the guessed variable assignments in leaf nodes (level $k + 1$). Compute the truth-values of the clauses by including these FCRs for every clause-number i, $1 \leq i \leq \frac{|w|}{3}$:

$$[c_i \ 0] \equiv [w_{3i-2} \ 0] \wedge [w_{3i-1} \ 0] \wedge [w_{3i} \ 0]$$
$$[c_i \ 1] \equiv [w_{3i-2} \ 1] \vee [w_{3i-1} \ 1] \vee [w_{3i} \ 1]$$

Also, F is false if any clause is false, so include this FCR for every clause-number i as well:

$$[\text{LEVEL } m+1] \wedge [c_i \ 0] \supset [\text{LABEL } 0]$$

Finish relating the truth of F to the truth of its clauses by including this longer FCR:

$$[\text{LEVEL } m+1] \wedge [c_1 \ 1] \wedge [c_2 \ 1] \wedge \cdots \wedge [c_{|w|/3} \ 1] \supset [\text{LABEL } 1]$$

The reduction constructs $\theta(|w|)$ features and $\theta(m^2)$ FCRs of size $\theta(\log m)$ in a simple manner, and consequently may be seen to be polynomial time. $\square$

The primary source of intractability in the theory of syntactic features is the large number of possible syntactic categories (arising from finite feature closure) in combination with the computational power of feature co-occurrence restrictions.[11] FCRs of the "disjunctive consequence" form $[f \ v] \supset [f_1 \ v_1] \vee \cdots \vee [f_n \ v_n]$ compute the direct analog of Satisfiability: when several such FCRs are used together, the GPSG effectively must try all n feature-value combinations.

8.3 Complexity of the GPSG Recognition Problem

Two membership problems for separate formal devices of GPSG were considered above in an attempt to isolate sources of complexity in GPSG theory. In this section we consider the universal recognition problem for GPSG theory as a whole. We begin by discussing the class *EXP-POLY* of problems solvable in exponential-polynomial time, a class of provably exponential time problems. Then we show that the universal recognition problem for GPSGs is EXP-POLY time-hard.

8.3.1 Exponential-polynomial time and alternating Turing machines

So far, we have discussed problems that *probably* have no polynomial time solution. However, there are classes of problems that are even harder; they take provably exponential time to solve. "Natural" problems in these classes are hard to come by, though they do exist. As a mathematical example, consider what is called *the theory of real numbers with addition*. This

---

[11]Finite feature closure admits a surprisingly large number of possible categories. Given a specification $\langle Feat, Atom, \rho, R \rangle$ of K, let $a = |Atom|$ and $b = |Feat - Atom|$. Assume that all atomic features are binary: a feature may be $+$, $-$, or undefined and there are 3^a 0-level categories. The b category-valued features may each assume $\theta(3^a)$ possible values in a 1-level category, so $\left|K^1\right| = \theta(3^a(3^a)^b)$. More generally,

$$\left|K = K^b\right| = \theta(3^{(a\sum_{i=0}^{b} \frac{b!}{(b-i)!})}) = \theta(3^{(a \cdot b! \sum_{i=0}^{b} \frac{1}{i!})}) = \theta(3^{a \cdot b! \cdot e}) = \theta(3^{a \cdot b!})$$

where $\sum_{i=0}^{b} \frac{1}{i!}$ converges to $e \approx 2.7$ very rapidly and $a, b = \theta(|G|)$; $a = 25, b = 4$ in GKPS. The smallest category in K will be 1 symbol (null set), and the largest, maximally specified, category will be of symbol-size $\log|K| = \theta(a \cdot b!)$.

is a language that consists of statements, some of which are true and others false. For example, for the real numbers $\Re$, we have that $\forall x \exists y (y > x)$ is true, because for every real number we can find a larger one. In contrast, $\exists y \forall x (x > y)$ is false, because for every real number we can find a smaller one. More specifically, the theory of reals is specified by giving a domain, $\Re$; a set of operators, $+$, $=$; and set of predicates, here $>$; some constants, 0, 1; the quantifiers $\forall$ and $\exists$; a stock of variables x, y, and so forth; and axioms that tell us how to give the meaning of the operators and predicates by defining a language of true expressions over these elements. We can now ask exactly how hard it is to find out whether an expression in this language is true or not. A very famous result is that one version of this kind of first-order language, number theory, is undecidable. The theory of reals is not as hard as that, but it is still exponentially hard; it is decidable in nondeterministic exponential time $\theta(2^{cn})$ (see Hopcroft and Ullman (1979:354–362)).

Other examples of exponential time complexity are of more direct relevance to linguistics. One example is of some linguistic interest, though now outdated; the second is a problem that we will actually exploit in the next section to analyze the complexity of current GPSG theory.

The linguistically relevant example is from Rounds (1975). Rounds studied various versions of transformational grammar, as presented in Chomsky's (1965) *Aspects of the Theory of Syntax*. This outdated version of transformational grammar contained a set of context-free *base rules* generating an initial set of phrase structure trees that could be manipulated by later *transformations*. Transformations could add, move, or delete arbitrarily large tree segments; this is what gives them enormous computational power. Indeed, Peters and Ritchie (1973) show in effect that every Turing machine computation can be simulated by some transformational grammar. It is important to note that this is *not* the modern theory of transformational grammar (so-called government-binding theory or GB theory), in which transformations are more constrained.

Adding restrictions to this older version of transformational grammar cuts down this power somewhat. Rounds (1975) showed that every language recognizable in exponential time can be generated by a transformational grammar that satisfies two additional constraints. The first is *recoverability of deletions*: every transformation that deletes material must leave behind enough information so that the original, pre-transformed structure can be recovered, given a list of the transformations that have been applied.

For example, if we take a transformation that deletes the embedded subject under identity with the matrix subject and apply it to the sentence *John likes John to win*, then the result will be *John likes to win*, and this deletion is recoverable because of the identity condition. The second condition, called the *terminal-length nondecreasing constraint*, basically ensures that the length of the string being developed by a sequence of transformations grows monotonically. More precisely, if a transformation applies to some subtree t with a bottom fringe of elements (yield) w, then the resulting yield must be at least as great as the length of any prior output yield from a transformation applying to a subtree of t. The preceding example obeys the terminal-length nondecreasing constraint because the first embedded sentence, *John to win*, is of length three and is shorter than the length four terminal string of the next higher cycle, *John likes to win*. Rounds's result is interesting because few "natural" problems are known that take provably exponential time. However, from a linguistic point of view the result is outdated, since the version of transformational grammar employed has long been superseded.[12]

Current transformational theory no longer relies on arbitrary deletion transformations of the sort that result in exponential-time recognition complexity. Berwick (1984) presents a review of these older results and a discussion of how more recent transformational theory sidesteps the computational difficulties of the *Aspects* model. However, a precise formalization of current transformational theory (GB theory) has yet to be carried out, and so a formal complexity analysis of GB theory also remains to be done. Berwick (1984) gives a preliminary indication that the GB languages are context-sensitive, but this can only be regarded as a tentative result.

The class *EXP-POLY* consists of *all* problems that can be solved in exponential-polynomial time on a deterministic machine. Just as with the class $\mathcal{NP}$, there are problems that are *complete* for the class, and any problem that is complete for exponential-polynomial time is as hard as the hardest problems in *EXP-POLY*. Because some problems in *EXP-POLY* take provably exponential time to solve, that means any EXP-POLY-complete problem must take exponential time to solve also. *EXP-POLY* can be defined as follows, where $DTIME(F(n))$ is the class of problems solvable in time $F(n)$ on

---

[12]Rounds did not argue whether the nondecreasing constraint actually held for natural languages; in fact, he pointed out some counterexamples. For example, the sentence *The meat is easy to cook, bring to the table, and eat* seems to actually violate the condition.

a deterministic Turing machine:

$$EXP\text{-}POLY = \{DTIME(c^{f(n)}) : c > 0 \text{ and } f(n) \text{ is a polynomial}$$
$$\text{function in } n \}$$

Note that this class includes the problems solvable in time 2^n, 3^{n^3}, $30^{n^{56}}$ and so forth. We will use this class in the next section when we analyze the complexity of generalized phrase structure grammars.

Recall that the class $\mathcal{NP}$ consists of the problems that are solvable in polynomial time on a nondeterministic Turing machine. The class EXP-$POLY$ also corresponds naturally to a particular kind of generalized Turing machine. Chandra and Stockmeyer (1976) demonstrate that EXP-$POLY$ is the same as the class of problems solvable in polynomial *space* on a machine called an *alternating Turing machine* (ATM). To understand what an ATM is, it is helpful to contrast deterministic and nondeterministic Turing machines and show how ATMs generalize nondeterministic TMs.

Consider the sequence of configurations a deterministic Turing machine moves through on its way to successfully recognizing an input string x. As we saw in chapter 2, the machine starts in some initial configuration C_0 (read head at some starting position, some set of tape contents, and finite-state control in an initial state). Then, because it is deterministic, it moves on through configurations C_1, C_2, and so forth until it reaches a final (accepting) configuration. We may therefore picture the configuration sequence as a straight line (figure 8.1). The machine recognizes the input string x if and only if such a derivation sequence exists.

Now consider an accepting computation sequence for a nondeterministic TM. Instead of a straight line, it looks like an OR-tree that is rooted at the initial configuration C_0 (figure 8.2). At any step, the machine can take one of a finite number of nondeterministic branches, leading to new next-state configurations; these configurations in turn may branch. A computation succeeds if there is *any* path from root C_0 to a final (accepting) configuration somewhere along the fringes of the tree. It is possible that some of these paths may fail or never terminate, but for the machine to recognize an input, only one sequence needs to reach an accepting configuration after some finite number of steps.

There is another way of saying the same thing. We may imagine that a final configuration labels itself **true**, while any other node propagates the value **true** upward if any daughter has it. Then the computation succeeds

if the root somehow ever becomes labeled **true**. In this picture, all the tree
nodes are OR-nodes or existential nodes because a node gets labeled **true** if
any of its daughters is labeled **true**. This is similar to the QBF form for SAT
(p. 229).

An alternating Turing machine generalizes this OR-tree to an AND/OR-
tree. As before, an OR-node is labeled **true** if any of its daughters are labeled
true, but an AND-node is labeled **true** only if *all* of its daughters are labeled
true. Levels of AND-nodes and OR-nodes alternate as in figure 8.3. Clearly,
this subsumes the QBF problems that were discussed earlier.

More precisely, an alternating Turing machine is like a nondeterministic
TM, except that some subset of its states will be referred to as *universal
states*, and others as *existential states*. A nondeterministic TM is an alternating TM with no universal states.

Definition: A k-tape alternating Turing machine is an 11-tuple:[13]

$$M = < Q, \Sigma, \Gamma, \$, \#, k, \sigma, q_0, Final, U, E >$$

where

$Q, q_0, Final$	=	set of states, initial state, set of accepting states
Σ, Γ	=	input, tape alphabets, $\Sigma \subseteq \Gamma$
$\$, \#$	=	endmarker, blank symbol, $\$, \# \in \Gamma - \Sigma$
U	=	set of universal states,
		$U \subseteq Q$, U disjoint from $Final$ and E
E	=	set of existential states,
		$E \subseteq Q$, E disjoint from $Final$ and U
k	=	number of read-write tapes, $k \geq 1$
Q'	=	$U \cup E$
δ	=	next-move relation, where
		$\delta \subseteq (Q' \times \Gamma^{k+1}) \times (Q \times \Gamma^k \times \{Left, Right\}^{k+1})$
$Left$	=	-1
$Right$	=	$+1$

The ATM has a read-only input tape, with the input $w \in \Sigma^*$ written as
$\$w\$$ and the reading head initialized to the first symbol of w. The k work
tapes are one-way infinite and are initially blank. A *configuration* of the

---

[13]This definition is based on Chandra and Stockmeyer (1976). We have taken the work
tapes to be one-way infinite instead of two-way infinite, in addition to making other minor
changes.

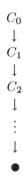

Figure 8.1: The accepting computation sequence for a deterministic TM is simply a straight line. The accepting state is indicated by a large dot.

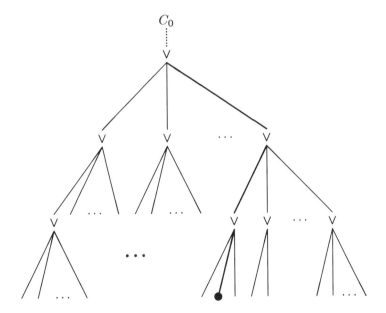

Figure 8.2: A nondeterministic Turing machine computation corresponds to an OR-tree. The computation succeeds if *any* accepting state can be reached, as indicated by the OR-symbols ($\vee$) in the tree nodes. Here, the accepting state is symbolized by a large dot and the accepting path is marked by a dark line. There could be more than one accepting state.

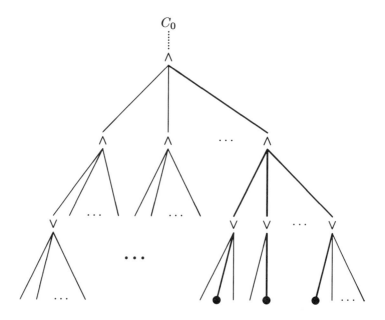

Figure 8.3: An alternating Turing machine computation corresponds to an AND/OR-tree. The subcalculation at an OR-level (∨) succeeds if any of its daughters succeed just as in figure 8.2, but the subcalculation at an AND-level (∧) does not succeed unless *all* of its daughters do. In this tree, accepting states are symbolized by large dots and the essential branches of the computation—making up a *pruned computation tree* as defined on page 242—are marked by dark lines. Note that the rightmost daughter of C_0 is an AND-node, which requires every daughter to succeed.

ATM consists of the state together with the head positions and contents of the $k + 1$ tapes. A move of the ATM consists of reading one symbol from the input tape and moving the heads left/right as allowed by δ, in addition to changing the state of the machine. The directions *Left* and *Right* have the numerical values $+1$ and -1 for convenience in proofs. We have defined δ to exclude transitions from accepting states. In addition, we assume well-behaved machines that never attempt to move the tape heads beyond the limits of the tapes.[14] We say a configuration of M is *existential, universal,* or

---

[14]The input tape is limited to the input string with its endmarkers. The work tape is limited to positive head positions, and when we know a space bound, it will of course be limited by the space bound at the upper end.

accepting if the state of the TM in that configuration is; in this formalization, an accepting configuration does not need any special tape contents, but only an accepting machine state.[15]

For configurations C of M, let the sequence $Next_M(C) = (C_0, \ldots, C_{k-1})$ enumerate in some standard order the possible successor configurations of C according to δ. k is bounded above by the number of pairs in the relation δ, which we may write as $|\delta|$.

The *computation* of an alternating TM M on an input w is a possibly infinite tree where the nodes correspond to ATM configurations. In essence, each node contains a copy of possible configuration that is reachable from the configuration above it. However, to build a possibly infinite tree the nodes must be made mathematically distinct. This is accomplished by defining each node as a pair $\langle x, C \rangle$ where C is the configuration and x is a tree position. Technically, the tree position is a string of numbers that identify a position in the tree by listing which branch to take at each node; the numbers are all between 0 and $|\delta| - 1$. The root position is the empty string, so the root node of the tree is $\langle \epsilon, C_0 \rangle$ where C_0 is the initial configuration. The daughters of any node $\langle x, C \rangle$ are given by $NextNode_M(x, C)$ where

$$NextNode_M(x, C) = \{\langle xi, C_i \rangle : Next_M(C) = (\ldots, C_i, \ldots)\}.$$

The concatenation xi identifies a unique daughter of the position x by adding another branch number at the end.

The criterion for acceptance in an ATM computation tree is as follows. Let N be the set of nodes in the computation tree of ATM M on input w. We label the nodes of the tree either **true** or **false** according to different rules depending on whether they are accepting, universal, or existential. A labeling $L : N \to \{\textbf{true}, \textbf{false}\}$ is said to be *acceptable* if the labeling of each node $\langle x, C \rangle$ is given by one of these three cases:

1. C is an accepting configuration and $L(x, C) = \textbf{true}$.

2. C is an existential configuration and

$$L(x, C) = \bigvee_{\langle xi, C' \rangle \in NextNode_M(x, C)} L(xi, C')$$

---

[15] In this formalization a machine does not "halt and reject"; instead, it can enter a distinguished nonfinal state that simply loops back to itself. Other formalizations exist.

3. C is a universal configuration and

$$L(x,C) = \bigwedge_{\langle xi,C'\rangle \in NextNode_M(x,C)} L(xi,C').$$

To forestall up some technical complications, in this case we also require that $NextNode_M(x,C)$ must be nonempty.

By convention, $\bigvee$ of an empty set is **false**. M is defined to *accept* the input w if and only if $L(\epsilon,C_0) = $ **true** for all acceptable labelings L. Note that alternating TMs without universal states operate exactly as nondeterministic TMs do.

We can define a *pruned computation tree* of an ATM as a computation tree from which inessential subtrees have been omitted—in another words, a minimal accepting computation subtree. Four conditions define the pruning.

(a)   Every subtree that is labeled **false** in any acceptable labeling must be omitted.

(b)   For every universal node, all of its daughter subtrees must be retained.

(c)   For every existential node, exactly one of its daughter subtrees must be retained.

(d)   The pruned computation tree must be finite and must include the root node of the full computation tree.

It is not too hard to see that an ATM computation will possess some pruned computation tree iff it succeeds, because the pruned tree includes exactly enough of the full tree to prove that the computation succeeds. In figure 8.3, the dark branches identify a pruned computation tree.

Chandra and Stockmeyer (1976) show that

$$ASPACE(S(n)) = \bigcup_{c>0} DTIME(c^{S(n)})$$

where $ASPACE(S(n))$ is the class of problems solvable in space $S(n)$ on an ATM and $DTIME(F(n))$ is the class of problems solvable in time $F(n)$ on a deterministic Turing machine. Therefore, if $f(n)$ is the class of all polynomial functions, this means that the problems solvable in polynomial space on an ATM is the same as the class of problems solvable in exponential-polynomial time on a deterministic TM. It is quite hard to think of natural problems that are this difficult, but as we show in the next section, generalized phrase structure grammar recognition is exponential-polynomial time-hard, and so includes problems at least as hard as those in this class. (GPSG-Recognition could still be harder than this.)

8.3.2 GPSG-Recognition is EXP-POLY time-hard

The following proof reduces instances of polynomial space-bounded alternating Turing machines to instances of GPSG-Recognition.

Theorem 6: GPSG-Recognition is EXP-POLY time-hard.

Proof. By direct simulation of ATM M on input w.[16] Let M be a one-tape alternating Turing machine with polynomial space bound $S(n)$; let w be its input. Given these reduction inputs, we will construct a GPSG G in polynomial time such that M accepts w iff

$$\$0w_11w_22\ldots w_n(n)\$(n+1) \in L(G).$$

By Chandra and Stockmeyer (1976), the class of problems solvable in polynomial space $S(n)$ on an ATM is exactly equivalent to the class of problems solvable in exponential polynomial time on a DTM. Therefore, given our following proof, we have the immediate result that GPSG-Recognition is $DTIME(c^{S(n)})$-hard, for all constants c, or EXP-POLY time-hard.

The basic plan of the reduction is to reproduce a *pruned computation tree* of the ATM as the *parse tree* of the GPSG. The GPSG will assign this elaborate structure to the empty string and not to the machine input. However, before the ATM simulation starts there will be some auxiliary structure that copies the machine input w into the features that represent the ATM input tape. The actual input that is presented to the grammar will therefore include an encoded version of w in addition to the "very long empty string" over which the computation tree is built.

---

[16]Without loss of generality, we use a 1-tape ATM, so

$$\delta \subseteq (Q' \times \Gamma \times \Gamma) \times (Q \times \Gamma \times \{Left, Right\} \times \{Left, Right\}).$$

Also, in the reduction, note that the word *input* refers to three completely distinct objects. The *ATM input string w* is the string which may or may not be in the language generated by the ATM. The *GPSG input string x* is the string which may or may not be in the language generated by the GPSG; x and w are *never* the same. The *reduction input* is the problem instance $\langle M, w \rangle$, i.e., the ATM M and its input string w. It is important not to confuse the three distinct uses by believing, for example, that the GPSG accepts the same language as the ATM. They cannot accept the same language in principle.

Configurations of the ATM will be encoded as zero-level syntactic categories. Because the amount of tape the machine can use is bounded by the known quantity $S(|w|)$, we can use a separate feature to record the contents of each tape square. We also need three features to encode the ATM head position and current state. In a polynomial-time reduction, we are limited to specifying a polynomial number of features (for tape squares) and feature-values (for head positions), and that is why the reduction will be limited to polynomial space bounded ATM computations ($S(n)$ a polynomial).

The immediate domination (ID) rules of the GPSG will encode the next-move relation δ of the ATM. The category corresponding to any configuration C can dominate the category corresponding to C' in a local tree iff δ licenses the transition $\langle C, C' \rangle$. However, the details depend on whether the configuration C is universal or existential. The reduction preserves the invariant that a nonterminal in the grammar can be terminated iff the configuration that it represents must be labeled **true** in the ATM computation. Consequently, the local tree for a universal configuration must include *every* successor configuration as a daughter. In contrast, the local tree for an existential configuration must merely include *some* successor configuration as a daughter. Nonterminals corresponding to halted, accepting configurations are terminated by the empty string.

Let $Next_M(C) = (C_0, \ldots, C_p)$. If C is a universal configuration, we would like to include the ID rule $C \rightarrow C_0, \ldots, C_p$; if C is an existential configuration, we would like to include $k + 1$ rules of the form $C \rightarrow C_i$. However, we cannot use such rules directly in a polynomial-time reduction; there are far too many possible configurations, and we would need at least one rule for each. Instead, we must set up the features that encode the configurations in such a way that the ID rules only have to encode the relation δ, which is much smaller than the $Next_M(\cdot)$ function. Each δ-transition of the ATM licenses many transitions between configurations because δ does not care about the tape squares in a configuration that the machine is not currently scanning. In the same way, each ID rule of the constructed GPSG will project into a large number of local trees. The unchanged portion of a tape will not be transferred from a configuration to its successor by the ID rule, but will be transferred by the head feature convention (HFC, a principle of universal feature instantiation). All features that represent tape squares are declared to be head features and all daughter categories in the constructed ID rules are head daughters. Consequently, the HFC will transfer the tape contents of the mother to the daughters except when prevented by the tape-writing activity specified by the next-move relation.

Proceeding to the details of the reduction, we will now describe the features that will be used to represent M-configurations:

STATE:	the state of the machine
INPUTPOS:	the head position of the read-only input tape
WORKPOS:	the head position of the read-write work tape
INPUT$_i$:	the contents of the ith square of the input tape
WORK$_i$:	the contents of the ith square of the work tape

In addition, the feature PHASE will be used to separate functionally distinct regions of the parse tree. [PHASE READ] categories are involved in reading the input string, [PHASE RUN] categories participate in the direct ATM simulation, and the [PHASE START] category links the READ and RUN phases.

As we have mentioned, the input string that is presented to the GPSG has the form

$$\$0w_1 1 w_2 2 \ldots w_n (n) \$ (n+1)$$

where the w_i are the characters of the machine input, the "$\$$" characters are endmarkers, and $0, \ldots, (n+1)$ are regarded as additional characters. We must copy $\$w\$$ onto the input tape of the simulated machine. For every character index i, $1 \leq i \leq |w|$, and for every possible character $a \in \Sigma$, include the following lexical rule for the lexical item ai:

$$\langle ai, \{ [\text{PHASE READ}], [\text{INPUT}_i \ a] \} \rangle$$

In addition, for every index over a wider range, $0 \leq i \leq |w| + 1$, include this lexical rule for the endmarker:

$$\langle \$i, \{ [\text{PHASE READ}], [\text{INPUT}_i \ \$] \} \rangle$$

Once these rules are constructed, they will work for other inputs w' of length $|w'| \leq |w|$ as well as for w. That is why endmarkers in the middle of w have been allowed in the copying rules.

Together with the specially formatted grammar input, these rules set up the input tape of the simulated ATM. We must also initialize the features that encode the work tape contents, the machine state, and the tape head positions. We can complete the initialization by defining the top-level category

START so that it provides the correct values for these features:

$$\text{START} \;=\; \{\,[\text{INPUTPOS } 1], [\text{WORKPOS } 1]\,\}$$
$$\cup \{\,[\text{STATE } q_0], [\text{PHASE START}]\,\}$$
$$\cup \{\,[\text{WORK}_j \text{ \#}] : 1 \leq j \leq S(|w|)\,\}$$

Then we use the following two ID rules to link things up:

$$\text{START} \rightarrow \{\,[\text{PHASE RUN}]\,\}, \{\,[\text{PHASE READ}]\,\}$$
$$\{\,[\text{PHASE READ}]\,\} \rightarrow \{\,[\text{PHASE READ}], [\text{PHASE READ}]\,\}$$

(Here all daughters are head daughters.) The [PHASE READ] rule allows the input-reading portion of the tree to branch as many times as necessary to cover the input characters.

In our formal model of ATMs, the machine halts and accepts if it ever enters an accepting state $q \in Final$. Thus, for every such state we need a null-transition ID rule that will terminate the simulated computation tree. For every $q \in Final$, the following ID rule should be included:

$$\{\,[\text{STATE } q]\,\} \rightarrow \epsilon$$

However, the most important ID rules are still to come; they encode the next-move relation δ of the machine. Recall that

$$\delta \subseteq (Q' \times \Gamma \times \Gamma) \times (Q \times \Gamma \times \{Left, Right\} \times \{Left, Right\})$$

is a relation between tuples

$$\langle \text{state, input tape symbol, work tape symbol} \rangle$$

on the one hand and tuples

$$\langle \text{new state, new work tape symbol,}$$
$$\text{input head movement, work head movement} \rangle$$

on the other hand. Strictly speaking, δ is not a function, because no action or more than one action may be legal given the state of the machine and the currently scanned tape symbols. However, it is convenient to use functional notation for the *set* of actions licensed by δ in a situation, and we will write

$$\delta(q, a, b) \;=\; \{\langle q', b', d_I, d_W \rangle :$$
$$\langle\langle q, a, b \rangle, \langle q', b', d_I, d_W \rangle\rangle \in \delta\}.$$

With this notation, we may specify the ID rules that encode δ. A set of rules will be specified for every state $q \in Q'$ and all tape symbols a and b, thus covering all of δ. No rules are to be constructed when $\delta(q, a, b) = \emptyset$. For $q \in Q'$ with $\delta(q, a, b) \neq \emptyset$ there are two cases depending on whether q is existential or universal. In either case, the construction must be carried out for all possible input-head positions i $(0 \leq i \leq |w| + 1)$ and work-head positions j $(1 \leq j \leq S(|w|))$:

(a) If q is in E (an existential state), include an instance of the following ID rule for every $\langle q', b', d_I, d_W \rangle \in \delta(q, a, b)$:

$$\{\,\texttt{[INPUTPOS } i\texttt{]}, \texttt{[INPUT}_i\ a\texttt{]}, \texttt{[WORKPOS } j\texttt{]}, \texttt{[WORK}_j\ b\texttt{]},$$
$$\texttt{[STATE } q\texttt{]}, \texttt{[PHASE RUN]}\,\} \rightarrow$$
$$\{\,\texttt{[INPUTPOS } i + d_I\texttt{]}, \texttt{[INPUT}_i\ a\texttt{]},$$
$$\texttt{[WORKPOS } j + d_W\texttt{]}, \texttt{[WORK}_j\ b'\texttt{]},$$
$$\texttt{[STATE } q'\texttt{]}, \texttt{[PHASE RUN]}\,\}$$

Each of these rules propagates the value on the input tape, changes the value on the work tape, moves the heads, and changes the automaton state; note that all have the same left-hand side. Because several such rules are included, only one daughter computation has to succeed. The daughter in the rule is a head daughter.

(b) If q was not in E, it must be in U instead (a universal state). For this case, let $L \rightarrow R_1, \ldots, L \rightarrow R_p$ be the rules that would have been constructed according to case (a) if q had been an existential state. Then include the rule

$$L \rightarrow R_1, \ldots, R_p$$

instead of those rules. Again, every daughter in the rule is a head daughter.

With these rules, the construction is almost finished; only a few loose ends remain. The syntactic categories used in our GPSG are formally specified as follows:

$$
\begin{aligned}
Feat \;\; = \;\; & \{\texttt{STATE}, \texttt{INPUTPOS}, \texttt{WORKPOS}, \texttt{PHASE}\} \\
& \cup \{\texttt{INPUT}_i : 0 \le i \le |w| + 1\} \\
& \cup \{\texttt{WORK}_j : 1 \le j \le S(|w|)\} \\
Atom \;\; = \;\; & Feat \\
\end{aligned}
$$

$$
\rho(f) \;\; = \;\; \begin{cases}
Q, \text{ if } f = \texttt{STATE} \\
\text{the set } \{i : 0 \le i \le |w| + 1\}, \text{ if } f = \texttt{INPUTPOS} \\
\text{the set } \{j : j \le j \le S(|w|)\}, \text{ if } f = \texttt{WORKPOS} \\
\Sigma \cup \{\$\}, \text{ if } f = \texttt{INPUT}_i \text{ for some } i \\
\text{the ATM tape alphabet } \Gamma, \text{ if } f = \texttt{WORK}_j \text{ for some } j \\
\text{the set } \{\texttt{START}, \texttt{READ}, \texttt{RUN}\}, \text{ if } f = \texttt{PHASE}
\end{cases}
$$

The set of head features is defined to consist of the $\texttt{INPUT}_i$ features and the $\texttt{WORK}_j$ features. In addition, we need feature co-occurrence restrictions to ensure full specification of all non-null categories. For every $f \in Atom$, include the FCR $[\texttt{STATE}] \supset [f]$.

Inspection of the construction steps shows that the reduction may be performed in polynomial time in the size of the simulated ATM. (Note that the grammar we construct encodes only the *description* of the machine that produces the computation tree—not the potentially infinite computation tree itself.)

No metarules or LP statements are needed, although metarules could have been used instead of the head feature convention. Both devices are capable of transferring the contents of the ATM tape from the mother to the daughter(s). One metarule would be needed for each tape square/tape symbol combination in the ATM.

GKPS definition 5.14 of admissibility guarantees that admissible trees must be terminated.[17] By the construction above, a [PHASE RUN] node can be terminated only if it represents an accepting configuration. In particular, a [PHASE RUN] node cannot be terminated by a lexical rule, because all

---

[17]The admissibility of nonlocal trees is defined as follows (GKPS:104):

Let R be a set of ID rules. Then a tree t is *admissible from* R if and only if

1. t is terminated, and
2. every local subtree in t is either terminated or locally admissible from some $r \in R$.

constructed lexical rules are [PHASE READ]. This means the only admissible trees are accepting ones whose yield is the input string followed by a very long empty string. □

8.3.3   Sources of intractability

The two sources of intractability in GPSG theory spotlighted by this reduction are null-transitions in ID rules and universal feature instantiation (in this case, the head feature convention). Grammars with unrestricted null-transitions can assign elaborate phrase structure to the empty string, which is linguistically undesirable and computationally costly. The reduction must construct a GPSG G and input string x in polynomial time such that $x \in L(G)$ iff $w \in L(M)$, where M is a PSPACE-bounded ATM with input w. The polynomial time constraint prevents us from making either x or G too big. Null-transitions allow the grammar to simulate the polynomial space ATM computation (and indirectly an exponential-polynomial time TM computation) with an enormously long derivation string that is subsequently erased. If the G were unable to erase the derivation string, G would accept only strings that were exponentially larger than M and w—hence too big to write down in polynomial time.

The head feature convention transfers head feature values from the mother to the head daughters just in case they don't conflict. In the reduction we use head features to encode the ATM tape and thereby use the HFC to transfer the tape contents from one ATM configuration C (represented by the mother) to its immediate successors $C_0, C_1, \ldots, C_p$ (the head daughters). The configurations $C, C_0, C_1, \ldots, C_p$ have identical tapes, with the critical exception of one tape square. If the HFC enforced absolute agreement between the head features of the mother and head daughters, we would be unable to simulate the polynomial space ATM computation in this manner.

8.4   A Paradox Resolved

At first glance, a proof that GPSG-Recognition is EXP-POLY hard appears to contradict the fact that context-free languages can be recognized in $O(n^3)$ time by a wide range of algorithms. To see why there is no contradiction, we must first explicitly state the argument from weak context-free generative power, which we will call the *efficient processability* argument.

The main thrust of the EP argument runs as follows:

- Any GPSG can be converted into a weakly equivalent context-free grammar (CFG).

- CFG recognition can be accomplished in polynomial time.

- Therefore, GPSG recognition can also be accomplished in polynomial time.

The argument continues:

- If the conversion is fast, then GPSG recognition is fast. However, even if the conversion is slow, recognition with the "compiled" CFG will still be fast; we may justifiably lose interest in doing recognition with the original, slow GPSG.

The EP argument is misleading because it ignores both the effect conversion has on grammar size and the effect grammar size has on recognition speed. Crucially, grammar size affects recognition time in all known CFG recognition algorithms. The only grammars *directly* usable by context-free parsers—hence the only grammars for which rapid parsing results carry over—are those composed of those composed of *context-free productions* with *atomic nonterminal symbols*. For GPSG, this corresponds to the set of admissible local trees, and this set is astronomical; it is

$$\theta(3^{m!}m^{2m+1}) \tag{8.7}$$

in a GPSG G of size m.[18,19] In the worst case, every symbol in $FC(M,R)$ is underspecified, and every category in K extends every symbol in the $FC(M,R)$ grammar. Because there are

$$\theta(3^{m \cdot m!})$$

possible syntactic categories, and $\theta(m^{2m})$ symbols in $FC(M,R)$, the number of admissible local trees (= atomic context-free productions) in G is

$$\theta(3^{m!}m^{2m+1}).$$

---

[18]As we saw above, the metarule finite closure operation can increase the ID rule grammar size from $|R| = \theta(|G|)$ to $\theta(m^{2m})$ in a GPSG G of size m.

[19]We ignore the effects of ID/LP format on the number of admissible local trees here, but note in passing that if we expanded out all admissible linear precedence possibilities in $FC(M,R)$, the resultant "ordered" ID rule grammar would be of size $\theta(m^{2m}!)$.

In other words, it is astronomical. This mathematical analysis is vindicated in practice. Phillips and Thompson (1985:252) observe that in their parser based on the GPSGs of Gazdar (1982), "To expand the [GPSG] grammar completely ... would be ridiculously wasteful of space and time. (The toy grammar of English we use with GPSGP [their parser], of 29 phrase-structure rules and four metarules, which expands to 85 rules, is equivalent to several tens of millions of context-free rules.)" Similarly, Shieber (1983:137) notes that typical post-Gazdar (1982) GPSG systems contain "literally trillions" of derived rules. In appendix B, we estimate that the GKPS grammar for English contains more than 10^{33} admissible local trees.

The Earley recognizer for context-free grammars runs in time $\theta(|G'|^2 \cdot n^3)$ where $|G'|$ is the size of the CFG G' and n the input string length, so a GPSG G of size m will be recognized in time

$$\theta(3^{2 \cdot m! m^{2m+1}} \cdot n^3) \tag{8.8}$$

The hyperexponential term will dominate the Earley algorithm complexity in the reduction above because m is a function of the size of the ATM we are simulating. Even if the GPSG is held constant, the stunning derived grammar size in formula 8.7 turns up as an equally stunning "constant" multiplicative factor in 8.8, which in turn will dominate the real-world performance of the Earley algorithm for all expected inputs (that is, any that can be written down in the universe), every time we use the derived grammar. This class of hyperexponential functions c^{n^n} grows at a frightening rate—in the mathematical worst case, if a GPSG with 2 symbols recognized a given sentence in .001 second, a grammar with 3 symbols would recognize the same sentence in 2.5 hours, and a grammar with a mere 4 symbols could take at least 10^{63} centuries.[20]

Pullum (1985) has suggested that "examination of a suitable 'typical' GPSG description reveals a ratio of only 4 to 1 between expanded and un-expanded grammar statements," strongly implying that GPSG is efficiently

---

[20]Evans (1985:237) experiences the real-world intractability of GPSG-Recognition first hand in his GPSG-based parser, and proposes to manage it by eliminating lexical ambiguity and by keeping both grammar and input string size as small as possible: "The attempts to overcome the time and space problems have only been partially successful .... The only remedies seem to be, keep phrases as short as possible (for example, do not try to test large noun phrases inside complex sentences if it can be avoided—use proper nouns instead), make sure no words are duplicated in the lexicon, keep the number of ID rules currently loaded down where possible ...."

processable as a consequence.[21] But this "expanded grammar" is not adequately expanded, that is, it is not composed of *context-free productions with unanalyzable nonterminal symbols*. In fact, Pullum's "expanded grammar" appears to be the output of metarule finite closure, and CFG results would show this grammar to be tractable only if the grammar were directly usable by the Earley algorithm exactly as context-free productions are: all nonterminals in the context-free productions would have to be unanalyzable. But the categories and ID rules of the metarule finite closure grammar do not have this property. Nonterminals in GPSG are decomposable into a complex set of feature specifications and cannot be made atomic, in part because not all extensions of ID rule categories are legal. For example, the categories *VP*[INV +,VFORM PAS] and *VP*[INV +,VFORM FIN] are not legal extensions of *VP* in English due to the FCR [INV +] ⊃ [AUX +] ∧ [VFORM FIN], while *VP*[INV +,AUX +,VFORM FIN] is. FCRs, FSDs, LP statements, and principles of universal feature instantiation—all of which contribute to GPSG's intractability—must all still apply to the rules of this expanded grammar.

Even if we ignore the significant computational complexity introduced by the machinery mentioned in the previous paragraph (that is, syntactic features, FCRs, FSDs, ID/LP format, null-transitions, and metarules), *GPSG will still not obtain an efficient processability result*. This is because the head feature convention alone ensures that the universal recognition problem for GPSGs will be NP-hard and likely to be intractable. Chapter 3 contains a proof. This result should not be surprising, given that (1) principles of universal feature instantiation in current GPSG theory replace the metarules of earlier versions of GPSG theory, and (2) metarules are known to cause intractability in GPSG. Thus, Pullum's informal tractability arguments are a particular instance of the more general EP argument and are equally misleading.

Although known grammar conversion procedures increase both grammar size and recognition time for the GPSG, the preceding discussion does not in principle preclude the existence of an efficient compilation step. If the compiled grammar is truly fast and assigns the same structural descriptions as the uncompiled GPSG, and it is possible to compile the GPSG in practice,

---

[21]This *substantive* argument does not appear to fit in with the (GKPS:4) goal of a purely *formal* investigation of linguistics: "The universalism [of natural language] is, ultimately, intended to be entirely embodied in the formal system, not expressed by statements made in it." It is difficult to respond precisely to the claims made in Pullum (1985), since the abstract is (necessarily) brief and consists of assertions not supported by factual documentation or clarifying assumptions.

then the complexity of the universal recognition problem would not accurately reflect the real cost of parsing. But the existence or nonexistence of efficient compilation functions does not affect either our scientific interest in the universal grammar recognition problem or the power and relevance of a complexity analysis. If complexity theory classifies a problem as intractable, we learn that something more must be said to obtain tractability. Further, any efficient compilation step, if it exists at all, must itself be costly. Until a definite proposal for compilation is forthcoming, we conservatively assume that one does not exist.

In fact, it may not be possible to construct an efficient compilation procedure for GPSGs, because it would be both extremely powerful and extremely general. Note that the GPSG we constructed in the preceding reduction will actually accept *any* input x of length less than or equal to $|w|$ if and only if the ATM M accepts it using $S(|w|)$ space. We prepare an input string x for the GPSG by converting it to the string $\$0x_11x_22\dots x_n(n)\$(n+1)$; for example, *abadee* is accepted by the ATM if and only if the string $\$0a1b2a3d4e5e6\$7$ is accepted by the GPSG. Trivial changes in the grammar allow us to permute and "spread" the characters of x across an infinite class of strings in an unbounded number of ways; for example, $\$0\gamma_1x_ii\gamma_2\dots\gamma_ax_11\gamma_b\dots\gamma_n\$(n+1)$ where each γ_j is a string over an alphabet which is distinct from the σi alphabet. Although the flexibility of this construction results in a more complicated GPSG, it argues powerfully against the existence of any efficient compilation procedure for GPSGs. Any efficient compilation procedure must perform more than an exponential polynomial amount of work (GPSG-Recognition takes at least EXP-POLY time) on at least an exponential number of inputs (all inputs that fit in the $|w|$ space of the ATM's read-only tape). More importantly, the required compilation procedure will convert *any* exponential-polynomial time bounded DTM into a polynomial-time DTM for the class of inputs whose membership can be determined within an arbitrary (fixed) exponential-polynomial time bound. Simply listing the accepted inputs will not work because both the GPSG and TM may accept an infinite class of inputs. Such a compilation procedure would be extremely powerful.[22]

As we noted in chapter 2, it is misleading to believe that succintness and expressive economy automatically cause intractability. The fact that GPSGs can succinctly encode some CFGs does not bear on the complexity of the GPSG recognition *problem*; all it says is that straightforward use of CFG

---

[22]An expensive compilation step may pose particular difficulties for language acquisition; see section 2.3.3.

recognition *algorithms* will fail to be efficient for GPSGs, because a GPSG is weakly equivalent to a very large CFG, and CFG size affects recognition time. The complexity result, on the other hand, firmly establishes that no current or future algorithm for GPSG-Recognition will be efficient. To take a linguistic example in which succintness and intractability diverge, the iterating coordination schema (ICS) of GPSG is an unbeatably succinct encoding of an infinite set of context-free rules; yet from a complexity viewpoint, the ICS is trivial to process with a slightly modified Earley algorithm.

8.5　Relevance of the Complexity Result

In this chapter, we argued that *there is nothing in the GPSG formal framework that guarantees computational tractability*: proponents of GPSG must look elsewhere for an explanation of efficient processability, if one is to be given at all. The crux of the matter is that the complex components of GPSG theory interact in intractable ways, and that weak context-free generative power does not guarantee tractability when grammar size is taken into account. A faithful implementation of the GPSG formalisms of GKPS will be provably intractable, and any expectations computational linguistics might have held in this regard are not fulfilled by current GPSG theory. This formal property of GPSGs is straightforwardly interesting to GPSG linguists, because "an important goal of the GPSG approach to linguistics [is] the construction of theories of the structure of sentences under which significant properties of grammars and languages fall out as theorems as opposed to being stipulated as axioms" (GKPS:4).

A computational analysis of the sort provided here plays a fundamentally positive role; it can offer significant formal insights into linguistic theory and human language, and suggest improvements in linguistic theory and real-world parsers. The insights gained may be used to revise the linguistic theory so that it is both stronger linguistically and weaker formally. In the next chapter, we revise GPSG theory. Briefly, some changes suggested by our reductions are unit feature closure; the elimination of FCRs and FSDs; the elimination of null-transitions in ID rules; unit metarule closure; and no problematic feature specifications in the principles of universal feature instantiation. Not only do these restrictions alleviate most of GPSG's computational intractability, but they increase the theory's linguistic constraints and reduce the number of unnatural grammars licensed by the theory.

Chapter 9

Revised Generalized Phrase Structure Grammar

The central goal of this chapter is to show how the insights of computational complexity theory can strengthen linguistic theory and ensure that powerful formal devices are well-motivated linguistically. We use the insights of the preceding chapter's reductions to construct a *revised* generalized phrase structure grammar (R-GPSG) that is both stronger linguistically and weaker formally. In all cases, we strive to prevent overgeneration, improve empirical coverage, and strengthen linguistic universalism through formal constraint.

Accordingly, R-GPSG replaces finite closure (a source of overgeneration) with unit closure everywhere, revises principles of universal feature instantiation to alleviate the computational problems noted in the previous chapter, and restricts metarules so that they express lexical redundancy alone. We weaken the theory formally by eliminating all *spurious* sources of complexity noted in chapter 8, and by preventing the unmanageable and highly unpredictable interaction of GPSG's formal devices. There are no disjunctive consequence FCRs or FSDs, no null-transitions in ID rules, and no "problematic" feature specifications in the principles of universal feature instantiation. R-GPSG recasts the extensional definitions of GPSG as constructive ones; it also attempts to isolate each formal component and its effects from the other components. In order to effect this revision, we always try to make the most restrictive statement possible while maintaining empirical coverage. Another guiding principle in this work has been to reduce nondeterminism everywhere.

We began the revision process by unilaterally expunging all apparently unnecessary sources of linguistic and computational complexity. We then worked through Gazdar, Klein, Pullum, and Sag (1985), hereafter GKPS, attempting to reproduce their analysis of English, often failing, and revising R-GPSG accordingly. Not every computationally troublesome feature was eliminated, however; as we argued in chapters 3 and 6, some potential difficulties represent genuine properties of natural language and should not be ruled out by the formal framework.

9.1 Formal Presentation

R-GPSG solves some of the computational and theoretical problems inherent in GPSG by strengthening the GPSG metagrammar and weakening the class of rule systems that can be written in the GPSG metagrammar. R-GPSG constrains the ID rules themselves, in addition to constraining the projection of ID rules into local trees. R-GPSG, like GPSG, determines phrase structure from underspecified ID rules and lexical elements. Features must be licensed by an ID rule, a simple default (SD), principles of universal feature sharing, or lexical elements. Crucially, the theory is easier to understand because every component (and its effects) may be understood in isolation from the other components.

This section presents the R-GPSG formal system. In the previous chapter, we sketched the formalism's underlying linguistic motivation.

9.1.1 Theory of syntactic features

As in GPSG, R-GPSG categories are sets of feature specifications, and may also be thought of as partial functions from features to feature values, which may be categories or atomic feature values.[1] *Unit feature closure*, a fundamental constraint on syntactic categories, restricts the values of category-valued features to be only categories composed solely of atomic-valued features. For example, in the category 9.1 the category-valued feature

---

[1] A promising direction for future work is to specify the set K^0 using complex symbol rules similar to those of Chomsky (1965:79–83), rather than the function ρ. This would increase both the theory's linguistic universalism and its empirical coverage without increasing the theory's computational complexity significantly. Complex symbol rules could make the features {NFORM, PFORM, VFORM} universally mutually exclusive, for example, thereby increasing linguistic universalism. If we included the ±ABSTRACT feature, R-GPSG would be strengthened empirically because it could exclude abstract subjects of verbs like *eat, admire*. Similarly, the theory would be additionally strengthened if it included the features {±HUMAN, ±ANIMATE, ±COUNT, ...}.

SLASH contains a category-valued feature AGR and therefore is not a possible R-GPSG category, although it is permissible in the theory of GKPS. The category 9.2, on the other hand, is legal in both theories.

$$\{\,[\texttt{N -}],[\texttt{V +}],[\texttt{BAR 2}],[\texttt{SUBJ +}],$$
$$[\texttt{SLASH } \{[\texttt{N +}],[\texttt{V -}],[\texttt{BAR 2}], \tag{9.1}$$
$$[\texttt{AGR } \{[\texttt{N +}],[\texttt{V +}],[\texttt{ADV +}]\}]\}]\}$$

$$\{\,[\texttt{N -}],[\texttt{V +}],[\texttt{BAR 2}],[\texttt{SUBJ +}]$$
$$[\texttt{SLASH } \{[\texttt{N +}],[\texttt{V -}],[\texttt{BAR 2}]\}], \tag{9.2}$$
$$[\texttt{AGR } \{[\texttt{N +}],[\texttt{V +}],[\texttt{ADV +}]\}]\}$$

A *specification* is a 4-tuple $\langle Atom, Cat, A, \rho \rangle$ where $Atom$, Cat, and A are finite sets of atomic-valued features, category-valued features, and feature values, respectively. ρ is a function from atomic-valued features to permissible feature values, $\rho : Atom \to 2^A$. An atomic-valued feature f may assume the distinguished values noBind or unBound in addition to those values determined by $\rho(f)$. A noBind value indicates that the given feature may not receive a value in the given category. $\langle Atom, Cat, A, \rho \rangle$ *specify* the finite sets K^0 of 0-level categories and K of categories,

$$K^0 = \{C \in [Atom \to A] : \forall f \in \text{DOM}(C)[C(f) \in \rho(f)]\}$$

$$\tag{9.3}$$

$$K = \{C_1 \cup C_2 : C_1 \in K^0 \text{ and } C_2 \in K^{0(Cat)} \text{ such that}$$
$$\forall f \in Atom[C_1(f) \in \rho(f) \wedge \forall f_c \in Cat[C_2(f_c)(f) \in \rho(f)]]\}$$

where $Y^{(X)}$ is the set of all partial functions from X to Y and $\text{DOM}(C)$ is the set $\{x : \exists y[\langle x, y \rangle \in C]\}$.

A category C' is an *extension* of C (written $C' \sqsupseteq C$) if and only if $\forall f \in \text{DOM}(C)$, $[(f \in Atom \wedge C'(f) = C(f)) \vee (f \in Cat \wedge C'(f) \sqsubseteq C(f))]$.

Let $S \subseteq K$ be a set of categories, and $C \in K$ be a category. C is an *upper bound* for S iff $\forall C' \in S, C' \sqsupseteq C$. C is the *unification* of S iff C is an upper bound for S and for all C' in K, if C' is an upper bound for S, then $C' \sqsupseteq C$.

9.1.2 Grammatical rules

Like GPSG, R-GPSG factors phrase structure into the distinct relations of immediate dominance (ID) and linear precedence (LP). R-GPSG ID rules have exactly one mother and at least one head daughter, which must dominate more than the empty string. R-GPSG possesses the exhaustive constant partial ordering (ECPO) property: all expansions of all categories obey the same partial ordering of linear precedence.

Immediate dominance

Formally, a headed ID rule is a 3-tuple $r \in \langle C \times \{C^+\}_m \times \{C^*\}_m \rangle$ whose first element is the mother category, whose second element is a multiset of head daughter categories, and whose third element is a multiset of non-head daughter categories. The mother and all head daughters are implicitly specified for [NULL noBind].[2] For example, the R-GPSG headed ID rule 9.4 is abbreviated as 9.5 and corresponds to the GKPS ID rule 9.6.

$$\langle \{ [V +], [N -], [BAR 2] \},$$
$$\{ \{ [SUBCAT 2] \} \}_m, \tag{9.4}$$
$$\{ \{ [N +], [V -], [BAR 2] \} \}_m \rangle$$

$$V2 \rightarrow [SUBCAT 2] : N2 \tag{9.5}$$

$$V2 \rightarrow H[SUBCAT2], N2 \tag{9.6}$$

A *lexical ID rule* is a headed ID rule whose second element (head daughters) contains a category specified for the **SUBCAT** feature. A *lexical element* is a tuple whose first element is a syntactic category and whose second element is a terminal symbol string. There is only one lexical element for the null string, and it is universal across all grammars:

$$X2 [SLASH \; X2_1, NULL \; +]_1 \rightarrow \epsilon \tag{9.7}$$

Co-subscripting indicates that the two $X2$ categories share all feature specifications, with the exception of [NULL +] (more on this below).

Linear precedence

An LP statement is a tuple of category predicates $P_1 \prec P_2$ such that no daughter category C_2 ever precedes a category C_1 in an ordered S-rule

---

[2] Any daughter category C in an ID rule may be closed under positive Kleene closure (written $(C)^+$), in which case it represents any natural number of categories identical to C. This work contains an incomplete account of positive Kleene closure categories.

production where $P_1 \sqsupseteq C_1$ and $P_2 \sqsupseteq C_2$ (see p. 268 below). LP statements are identical to those of GPSG and are written, for example,

$$\texttt{[SUBCAT]} \prec \neg \texttt{[SUBCAT]}.$$

Tractability of ID/LP grammars

The R-GPSG ID/LP formalism does not contain formal constraints sufficient to guarantee polynomial-time recognition. Instead, we use the insights of chapter 7 to choose two substantive constraints that can ensure the ID/LP formalism does not significantly contribute to the complexity of the R-GPSG recognition problem (although other formal devices may). The constraint of *terminal-string distinguishability* tames the interaction between ID/LP rules and ambiguity, but cannot be truly guaranteed because of lexical ambiguity. The constraint of *short ID rules* limits the combinatorial blowup that ID rules can produce, though it is important that the short rules reflect genuinely bounded constraint and thus do not use some other mechanism to get the effect of longer rules.

First, the ID/LP reduction assumes a CFG in which it is difficult to distinguish different nonterminals by their terminal strings. If distinct nonterminals had easily distinguishable yields (in the sense of section 7.10), then incorrect Earley-algorithm *predict* operations would be detected quickly and locally, and the ID/LP parsing algorithm of Shieber (1983) would not blow up. This is difficult to guarantee in general ID/LP grammars; certain head features make it easier to enforce in R-GPSG, though lexical ambiguity still prevents complete enforcement.

Head features make it easier to achieve terminal-string distinguishability in R-GPSGs than in UCFGs, given the uncontroversial substantive assumption that certain head features must be morphologically realized in the lexicon. The idea starts from the observation that a $PP\texttt{[to]}$ and a $PP\texttt{[from]}$ are clearly distinguishable by their *PFORM* features. Ignore lexical ambiguity for a moment. Then a set $\mathcal{D}$ of head feature specifications can be selected such that if two categories differ in a feature value from $\mathcal{D}$, their terminal strings will be different. A subset of *HEAD* is the obvious candidate for $\mathcal{D}$, because the head feature convention (HFC) will guarantee that phrases which differ in head features will also differ in the lexical entries possible for the heads of those phrases.[3] For example, two categories must have different terminal strings in GKPS grammar for English if they differ in their COMP, CONJ, NFORM, NULL, INV, PFORM, or VFORM specifications—again ignoring lexical ambiguity. (This is also true for the R-GPSG grammar for English in appendix B.)

Lexical ambiguity clouds the picture because—for instance—a single surface word might potentially have either VFORM or NFORM features. As we've noted several times, the set of possible syntactic categories for a surface word is largely influenced by accidental factors and therefore constraints on its composition are difficult to guarantee. (However, closed-class items such as prepositions seem anecdotally to be less affected by lexical ambiguity.) Despite these limitations, we believe distinguishability will often mitigate the potential difficulty associated with ID rules.

The second substantive factor that will often render ID rules tractable in practice is the linguistically justified use of *short ID rules*. The UCFG reduction of chapter 7 critically relies on ID rules with unbounded right-hand sides. ID/LP grammars with bounded rules can be parsed in time polynomial in the grammar size.[4]

However, as we explained in section 7.10, short rules do not necessarily help in a system that has additional mechanisms beyond the bare ID/LP formalism that can allow the *effects* of long ID rules to be encoded. Thus, we must argue for short ID rules that reflect a linguistic bound on the *kind of constraint* that ID rules express.

Unbounded ID rules have two effects: each of the RHS nonterminals appears exactly once in the "flat" phrase structure licensed by the rule, and the RHS nonterminals may appear in any linear order in the structure. We'll argue below that phrase structure branching may be strictly bounded in natural language. Given the caveats of section 7.10, however, it is more important to

---

[3] As we shall see below, the head feature convention in R-GPSG can ensure distinguishability because head features, once introduced, cannot be altered by the HFC or deleted with null-transitions, because phrasal heads cannot be deleted once introduced. The use of problematic feature specifications in the GPSG head feature convention means that distinguishability cannot be ensured in that theory. Similarly, unrestricted null-transitions in GPSG prevent that theory from enforcing distinguishability.

[4] If the length bound for natural language grammars is the constant b, then any ID/LP grammar G can be converted into a strongly-equivalent CFG G', of size $\theta(|G| \cdot b!) = \theta(|G|)$ by simply expanding out the (constant number of) linear precedence possibilities. In the GKPS and R-GPSG grammars for English, $b = 3$ because double object constructions ([*give NP NP*], for example) are assigned a flat, ternary branching structure. (We ignore the iterating coordination schema, which licenses rules with unbounded right-hand sides.)

note that in addition, the linguistic idealizations of unbounded ID rules seem unnatural.

The unbounded ID rule idealization permits grammars to group an un-limited number of syntactic categories in a nonhierarchical fashion, much like a finite set—the grammar does not naturally express hierarchical or linear relationships among categories, but it does *count* them. Natural languages, however, seem to have exactly opposite properties: categories participate in stringent hierarchical relationships, and never in relationships of quantity. Even languages with free word order are often highly structured. At first glance, modifiers (adjectives, adverbials, adjuncts) may appear to fit the unbounded ID/LP idealization: they are unbounded, their order doesn't generally matter, and they lack internal structure cross-linguistically. Yet no natural language constrains the distribution of modifiers by quantity, as un-bounded ID/LP systems would lead us to expect. (In GPSG and R-GPSG, a phrase of type *XP* with optional arguments such as adjuncts is assigned the structure [*XP Adjunct*]; thus the adjuncts are not mentioned in the main ID rules for phrases.)

The conclusion that natural languages do not count in the manner of long ID rules is only tentative because there are arguments on the other side. In particular, languages do "count" in the sense that they establish a one-to-one correspondence between θ-roles and arguments of predicators, perhaps a large number of θ-roles depending on how we analyze rather peripheral arguments that might be marked with semantically meaningful prepositions. However, if this conclusion is correct, the agreement grammar reduction of chapter 3 and the ID/LP reduction of chapter 7 have rather different roles: we argued that difficulties with agreement and ambiguity represented a fact of language, but difficulties with ID/LP grammars may serve instead to expose the unnatural possibilities allowed by an ID/LP system.

Fortunately, reductions of both types are equally useful to the linguist. In this chapter, we attempt to combine the insights offered by the reductions when constructing our new formal system (R-GPSG); we wish to maintain the natural character of agreement grammars while eliminating the arguably unnatural possibility of long ID rules.[5] Note that ID rules in GPSGs for

---

[5]A particularly low bound on rule length—a restriction to binary branching—is inde-pendently motivated by the linguistic arguments of Kayne (1981). In that work, Kayne argues that the path from a governed category to its governor (for example, from an anaphor to its antecedent) must be unambiguous—informally put, "an unambiguous path is a path such that, in tracing it out, one is never forced to make a choice between two

natural languages are likely to be strictly bounded, due in part to bounded subcategorization frames in the lexical component of GPSG and in part to the GKPS definition of semantic types.

To summarize, R-GPSG does not formally guarantee that distinct categories result in different terminal strings. Actual grammars for natural languages are likely to have this property up to lexical ambiguity (by the claims above), motivating R-GPSG to adopt two substantive constraints that ensure ID/LP format does not contribute to recognition intractability. First, a member f of the feature set D must be lexically realized so that different values for f guarantee differing terminal strings. Second, ID rules are strictly bounded in length.

9.1.3   Metarules

Metarules map lexical ID rules to lexical ID rules. Metarules serve, intuitively, "to express generalizations about the subcategorization possibilities of lexical heads" (GKPS:59). The only differences between the formulation of metarules given here and the one in GKPS are (1) R-GPSG uses *unit closure* instead of finite closure, and (2) R-GPSG metarules are only able to affect nonhead daughters. The former constraint simplifies the theory, while the latter constraint strengthens it: unlike GPSG metarules, R-GPSG metarules are *only* able to express generalizations about the syntactic selection properties of lexical heads.[6]

(or more) unused branches, both pointing in the same direction" (Kayne 1981:146). The unambiguous path requirement sharply constrains fan-out in phrase structure trees because n-ary branching, for $n > 2$, is only possible when none of the n sister nodes must govern any other nodes in the phrase structure tree. Government plays a central role in many linguistic relations: case is only assigned under government, lexical heads govern their complements, traces of movement are governed, and so on. Kayne argues that for these and other reasons, phrase structure trees must be *binary*-branching. Barss and Lasnik (1986) present independent arguments for binary-branching double object constructions. From this conceptually appealing assumption, which replaces c-command in the government-binding theory of Chomsky (1981), Kayne provides a uniform cross-linguistic account of the principles of particle and derived nominal constructions that uses only existing government-binding machinery (ECP, case filter, bounding). It is interesting to note that both arguments for binary branching—our complexity result and Kayne's linguistic reasons—have in part a motivation that has computational consequences: the desire to eliminate ambiguity. We might speculate that binary-branching constraints like Kayne's could reduce ambiguity (and search) in recovering phrase structure and anaphor-antecedent relations, but see caveats in section 7.10.

[6]One result of (1) only allowing metarules to affect nonhead daughters and (2) implicitly specifying the heads of all ID rules for [NULL noBind] is that no head daughter may ever

With the aid of some auxiliary definitions, we will now formally define the operation of metarules in R-GPSG.

Definition: Correspondence

If C_1, C_2 are categories, C_2 *corresponds to* C_1 iff

1. $C_1 \mid \{\mathtt{N}, \mathtt{V}\} = C_2 \mid \{\mathtt{N}, \mathtt{V}\}$, and

2. $\text{DOM}(C_1) \subseteq \text{DOM}(C_2)$

At most two terms can occur on a metarule's right-hand side, and one must be the distinguished metarule variable W.

Definition: Pattern and Target

A metarule *pattern* is a pair $\langle P_0, P_1 \rangle$ where P_0 and P_1 are categories.

A metarule *target* is a tuple $\langle \alpha_0, \{\alpha_1, \ldots, \alpha_k\}_m \rangle$ where

1. α_0 corresponds to P_0,

and for $1 \leq i \leq k$,

2. at most one of the α_i is the variable W, and

3. at most one of the α_i corresponds to P_1 (if present)

Definition: Pattern Matching

A pattern $\langle P_0, P_1 \rangle$ *matches* a headed ID rule

$$C_0 \rightarrow C_1, \ldots, C_j : C_{j+1}, \ldots, C_n$$

iff

1. P_0 matches C_0,

2. if P_1 is present, there is some C_k, $j < k \leq n$, such that P_1 matches C_k, and

3. W matches and *is bound to* the multiset consisting of the categories $C_{j+1}, \ldots, C_n$, minus the occurrence of C_k that was matched by P_1 if $l \leq j$.

---

be specified for [NULL +]. This constraint ensures that the empty string does not have elaborate phrase structure in any R-GPSG. The constraint both crucially contributes to the tractability of R-GPSG recognition and expresses the substantive linguistic constraint that elaborate phrase structure must be lexically realized.

where a category P matches a category C if and only if $C \sqsupseteq P$, and the variable W matches any multiset of categories.

Definition: Category and Variable Determination

Let r be an input headed ID rule of the form $C_0 \rightarrow C_1, \ldots, C_j :$ $C_{j+1}, \ldots, C_n$ and let m be a metarule with a target of the form $\langle \alpha_0, \{\alpha_1, \ldots, \alpha_k\}_m \rangle$.

1. If a category α in the target corresponds to P in the pattern, and P matches the category C_i, $j < i \leq n$, in rule r, then (α, m, r) determines the category

$$C' = \alpha \cup (C_i \mid (\text{DOM}(C_i) - \text{DOM}(\alpha)))$$

2. If a category α in the target does not correspond to a P in the pattern, then (α, m, r) determines the category α

3. If α is the variable W, and W in the pattern of m is bound to $\{C_a, \ldots, C_b\}_m$, then (α, m, r) determines the same multiset $\{C_a, \ldots, C_b\}_m$

Note that a metarule may determine more than one ID rule per input ID rule because a metarule pattern may match an ID rule in more than one way.

Definition: Rule Determination

Given a metarule m with a target of the form $\langle \alpha_0, \{\alpha_1, \ldots, \alpha_k\}_m \rangle$ and a headed ID rule r, then (m, r) determines a rule

$$r' = C_0 \rightarrow C_1, \ldots, C_j : C_{j+1}, \ldots, C_n$$

iff

1. C_0 is determined by (α_0, m, r), and

2. $\forall i, j < i \leq n$, C_i is present if and only if $\exists q, 1 \leq q \leq k$ and C_i is determined by (α_q, m, r), and

3. $\forall i, 1 \leq i \leq j$, C_i is present if and only if it was present as a head in rule r.

Definition: The Metarule Relation

Let m be a metarule with pattern p and target t. Then m induces the relation

$$f_m = \{\langle R, R' \rangle: \quad R \text{ and } R' \text{ are sets of lexical ID rules}$$
$$\text{and } R' = \{r': \exists r \in R, \quad p \text{ matches } r \text{ and}$$
$$(m, r) \text{ determines } r'\}$$

The unit closure ($UC(M, R)$) of a set R of lexical ID rules under a set M of metarules is defined below. The complete set of headed ID rules defined by a GPSG is the set of initial rules R plus the set of rules resulting from applying each metarule to each rule of R exactly once.

<u>Definition:</u> Unit Closure

$$UC(\emptyset, R) = R;$$
$$UC(M, R) = \bigcup_{m \in M} f_m(R).$$

Given a set of ID rules R whose size is n symbols, and given a set M containing m metarules each of size p, the symbol-size of $UC(M, R)$ is $\theta((n + p)n \cdot m) = \theta(|G|^3)$. Each metarule can match the productions in R $\theta(n)$ different ways, inducing $\theta(n + p)$ new symbols per match, and there are m metarules.

9.1.4 Simple defaults

Simple defaults are, at heart, abbreviatory devices or markedness conventions akin to the feature co-occurrence restrictions and feature specification defaults of GPSG. Unlike FCRs and FSDs, however, they are constructive, easy to understand, and computationally tractable. Each SD is applied (and may be understood) independently of all other R-GPSG components, including other SDs.

An SD contains a predicate and a consequent. The consequent is a list of feature specifications. A predicate is the normal Boolean combination $(\&, \lor, \neg)$ of truth-values and feature specifications such that if a category C bears or extends a given feature specification, that feature specification is true of C, else false. If the predicate is true of a given category C in an S-rule and the consequent includes only unbound (and unlinked) features, then the feature specifications listed in the consequent are instantiated on C. SDs only apply to top-level categories (that is, not to a category C' embedded in a category C such that $\exists f \in Cat$ with $C(f) = C'$).

Consider the following simple default:

$$SD \; 1: \; \textit{if} \; [\text{SUBCAT}] \; \textit{then} \; [\text{BAR 0}]$$

If the target category C in an S-rule is specified for the SUBCAT feature, but unspecified for the BAR feature, then R-GPSG will force the feature specification [BAR 0] on C.

Simple defaults are applied to S-rules as part of the process of converting ID rules to S-rules. The SD application process obeys principles of universal feature sharing, and results in a set of S-rules. Each SD is applied to every category of every rule exactly once, in the order specified by the grammar. Given a list of simple defaults whose symbol size is p, and given an ID rule grammar of n symbols, the resultant S-rule grammar can at most contain $\theta(n \cdot p)$ symbols (reached if every SD were true of every category and every category consisted of a lone symbol).

9.1.5   Universal feature sharing

Principles of universal feature sharing (UFS) all preserve a simple invariant across all S-rules. They are monotonic; that is, they never delete or alter existing feature specifications. The head feature convention (HFC), for example, ensures that the mother agrees exactly with all head feature specifications that the head daughters agree on, regardless of where the specifications come from.

Principles of UFS are first applied when converting ID rules to S-rules. After this conversion, each principle always applies, even during the application of SDs.

ID rule conversion

All ID rules resulting from metarule unit closure are converted into equivalent S-rules before being used to derive terminal strings. First, principles of universal feature sharing are applied to the ID rules. Last, simple defaults are applied, satisfying the principles of UFS (see figure 9.1). The resultant S-rules are used to derive utterances in the language generated by the R-GPSG.

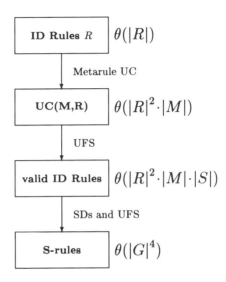

Figure 9.1: This diagram shows internal organization of an R-GPSG G with ID rules R, metarules M, and simple defaults S. The θ-bounds show the effect of various devices on derived grammar symbol size.

ID rule conversion is clearly polynomial time, given the speed with which simple defaults are applied. Metarule unit closure can at most cube the grammar symbol size. The conversion process (*i.e.*, SD application) can at most multiply this grammar's symbol size by $|G|$ without increasing the number of productions in the grammar. Therefore, in the worst case an R-GPSG G can determine a set of S-rule productions P, where $|P| = \theta(|G|^4)$.[7]

Informally, S-rules are headed ID rules whose component categories share certain feature specifications. Any change in the feature value of a shared feature specification affects all feature specifications that share the given feature value. Shared feature specifications may be tentative or obligatory. A category C containing an *obligatory* feature specification is specified

---

[7]On the effect of metarules, recall from note 9 of chapter 8 that each metarule can account for $O(|G|^2)$ output rules and there are $O(G)$ metarules; thus we get a total of $O(|G|^3)$ output rules under unit closure. This is in contrast to the exponential effect of finite closure. As for SDs, they do not increase the number of productions in the grammar but add features to the categories in the productions. At worst an SD can be of size $O(|G|)$ and affect all categories, thus producing a uniform $O(|G|)$ blowup.

for the given feature. A *tentative* feature specification indicates that the containing category C is currently undefined for the given feature. If, however, C becomes specified for the feature, the tentative specification becomes obligatory. We write $C(f)$ to denote the value of a feature f in a category C.

Two atomic feature values v_1, v_2 may be *linked* with respect to an S-rule r (abbreviated "link(v_1, v_2, r)"). The result is that future references or modifications to either value, by any mechanism, return the value v_1 if $v_1 = v_2$. Otherwise, the linking fails and the S-rule is discarded. Two categories C_1, C_2 may also be linked with respect to an S-rule r. Future references to either category return the category $C_1 \sqcup C_2$, and future references to a value $C_i(f)$ contained in either C_1 or C_2 return the result of linking the values $C_1(f)$ and $C_2(f)$. In all cases, we indicate linking by co-subscripting.

An *ordered S-rule production* (ordered production) is an S-rule whose daughters are completely linearly ordered, *i.e.*, a string of daughter categories rather than multisets of head and nonhead daughters.[8] An ordered production is *LP-acceptable* if all LP statements in the R-GPSG are true of it.

If a feature specification is linked to another specification, or made to assume a value directly in a category, we say that the feature specification has been *forced* on the category.

Head feature convention

The head feature convention (HFC) enforces the invariant that the mother is in absolute agreement with all head features on which the head daughters agree, adding features minimally to accomplish this (see details below). It operates all the time. *HEAD* contains exactly those features that must be equivalent on the mother and head daughters of an S-rule.

$$HEAD \quad = \quad \{\text{AGR, ADV, AUX, INV, LOC, N, NFORM, PAS, PAST,}$$
$$\text{PER, PFORM, PLU, PRD, V, VFORM}\}$$

In order to properly account for feature sharing in the Binary and Iterating Coordination Schemata, binary head (*BHEAD*) features are considered to be head features for the purposes of the HFC in all nonlexical, multiply headed S-rules.

---

[8]Positive Kleene closure categories must be "expanded" here because of LP constraints and principles of UFS.

$$BHEAD = \{\text{BAR}, \text{SUBJ}, \text{SUBCAT}, \text{SLASH}\}$$

Head Feature Convention

1. Any head feature specification (HFS) that is forced on the mother of an S-rule is also forced on all of the mother's head daughters (by linking).

2. Any HFS that is forced on a head daughter in an S-rule is also forced on the mother by linking, *if* all other head daughters are similarly specified.

3. The **BAR** value on a head daughter must be less than or equal to the **BAR** value on the mother.

The third clause of the HFC partially enforces $\overline{\text{X}}$-theory.[9]

The control agreement principle

The control agreement principle (CAP) only operates during ID rule to S-rule conversion.

$$CONTROL = \{\text{SLASH}, \text{AGR}\}$$

1. *VP*s are predicates (at least in English).[10]

2. The control feature of C_i, where $C_i(\text{BAR}) \neq 0$, is f if and only if

---

[9]A formal statement of the HFC follows. $HFC(r, r')$ is true for an ID rule $r = C_0 \to C_1, \ldots, C_j : C_{j+1}, \ldots, C_n$ and an ordered S-rule production $r' = C_0' \to C_1', \ldots, C_j' : C_{j+1}', \ldots, C_n'$ iff

(a) $\forall f \in (\text{DOM}(C_0') \cap F_A), \forall i, 1 \leq i \leq j,$
   $[(f \in \text{DOM}(C_i')) \wedge (C_i'(f) = C_0'(f))]$

(b) $\forall f \in F_A, [\exists v \in \rho(f)$
   $[(\forall i, 1 \leq i \leq j, [f \in \text{DOM}(C_i') \wedge C_i'(f) = v]) \supseteq (C_0'(f) = v)]]$

(c) $(\text{BAR} \in \text{DOM}(C_0') \wedge C_0'(\text{BAR}) = x) \supseteq (\forall i, 1 \leq i \leq j, [C_i'(\text{BAR}) \leq x])$

where $F_A = HEAD \cup BHEAD$ if r is a multiply-headed nonlexical ID rule, $F_A = HEAD$ otherwise.

[10]GKPS define predicates to include infinitival verb phrases and instantiations of *XP*[+PRD] such as predicative nominals and adjective phrases, but we simplify here. In that theory, only head feature specifications and inherited foot feature specification determine the semantic types relevant to the definition of control. R-GPSG simplifies this by considering only inherited feature specifications. Alternatively, every time the HFC forces a feature specification, we could recompute control relations and proceed from there.

(a) $f = $ SLASH and $f \in$ DOM(C_i), or

(b) SLASH $\notin$ DOM(C_i) and $f = $ AGR.

3. Control is calculated when ID rules are converted into S-rules. A category C_1 is controlled by C_2 in a rule whose mother is C_0 if and only if $C_1(f) = C_2$, $C_2 = NP$, and

   (a) the rule is $C_0 \rightarrow C_1 : C_2$ (*i.e.*, C_1 is the head daughter) where f is the control feature of C_i.

   (b) the rule is $C_0 \rightarrow C_3 : C_1, C_2$ where $C_0 = C_1 = VP$.

4. **Control Agreement Principle**
   In an S-rule $r = C_0 \rightarrow C_1, \ldots, C_j : C_{j+1}, \ldots, C_n$,

   (a) If C_i controls C_k and f_k is the control feature of C_k, then link$(C_k(f_k), C_i, r)$ obligatorily.

   (b) If there exists a nonhead C_i that is a predicative category with no controller, then link$(C_i(f_i), C_0(f_0), r)$ obligatorily, where f_i, f_0 are the control features of C_i, C_0 respectively.

In the theory of GKPS, the control agreement principle is capable of enforcing a control relation between the two daughters of the rule

$$S \rightarrow X2, \text{H}[\text{-SUBJ}]$$

but in R-GPSG, this rule must be stated as

$$S \rightarrow X2[\text{-SUBJ,AGR } X2] : X2$$

if we wish to enforce the control relation between the two daughters. Because control relations in R-GPSG are static, this control relation exists even if $X2 \neq NP$. Fortunately, no lexical entry will ever be specified for [AGR AP], and therefore any "questionable" control relations involving an $X2$ other than NP are ignored at the lexical insertion level.

The foot feature principle

Any *FOOT* feature specification that is instantiated on a daughter category is also instantiated on the mother category. The specification is identical to an instantiation of the same feature on other daughter categories. The foot feature principle (FFP) ensures that (1) the existence of inherited foot features on any category of an S-rule blocks instantiation of those foot features on any other component category of the rule, and (2) inherited foot features are equivalent (up to linking) across all component categories of the rule. The second condition may be too strong.

The FFP operates all the time. Given that the empty string can be dominated only by a category of the form α[NULL +, SLASH α], the FFP ensures that every gap will have a unique filler; the direct consequence is that R-GPSG phrase structure obeys recoverability of deletions, by virtue of its formal framework.

Definition: Free Features

A feature f is said to be *free in* the ID rule $r = C_0 \rightarrow C_1, \ldots, C_j :$
$C_{j+1}, \ldots, C_n$ iff $\forall i,\ 0 \leq i \leq n,\ f \notin \text{DOM}(C_i)$.

Foot Feature Principle

1. When converting ID rules into S-rules, if a foot feature f is not free in an S-rule r, then obligatorily noBind all unbound occurrences of f in r.

2. When SLASH is forced on the mother, force it on all non-lexical head daughters.

3. When a foot feature f is forced onto a daughter, force it onto the mother.

4. When a foot feature f is forced onto a mother, tentatively force it on all nonhead daughters; and if f was obligatorily forced, then obligatorily force f on at least one daughter.

Condition 4 of the FFP introduces indeterminacy and computational complexity, but it is unavoidable given our desire to abstract away from parsing strategies. The complexity is introduced only for the foot features RE and WH, not for SLASH.

Condition 2 springs from the necessity of accounting for certain parasitic gap facts according to the traditional GPSG analysis of clausal structure. A change in analysis along the lines of Chomsky (1981) might simplify this component of the theory (more below). The problem arises in sentences of the form

Kim wondered [$_S$ which authors [$_{S/NP}$ reviewers of _ always detested _]]

$$(9.8)$$

where the parasitic gap is introduced by a binary nonlexical rule 9.9

$$S \rightarrow X2\,[\text{-SUBJ,AGR}\ X2] : X2 \qquad (9.9)$$

rather than a ternary lexical rule like other parasitic gaps. Instantiating SLASH on the $X2$ nonhead daughter must force the identical SLASH specification on the mother and head daughter. SLASH isn't a head feature in R-GPSG, so there is no other way to accomplish this.

A possible solution is to make S the maximal projection of I (inflection) rather than {[V +], [N -], [SUBJ +]}, that is, replace 9.9 with

$$I2 \quad \rightarrow \quad \{[\text{SUBCAT } 49]\} : X2, VP$$

or

$$I2 \quad \rightarrow \quad X1 : X2$$
$$I1 \quad \rightarrow \quad \{[\text{SUBCAT } 49]\} : VP$$

In both cases the CAP or FFP would ensure that (1) AGR was transferred from $I0$[49] to the $X2$ sister and (2) we could only instantiate SLASH on $X2$ if we also instantiated it on the VP. It might be possible to simplify the HFC, CAP, and FFP if we made this change. Clause 2 of the FFP could be dropped, for example.[11]

Tractability of UFS. The "tractability" of universal feature sharing stems in part from the demands of monotonicity and absolute agreement. At the very most, UFS can force every feature on every node of a phrase structure "tree" constructed from S-rules in a derivation (an *S-tree*, hereafter). No work is ever duplicated or undone, so we force at most $(|Cat| + 1) \cdot |Atom|$ features on each node of an S-tree for a polynomial amount of total work per S-tree. (There are $O(n)$ nodes in an S-tree for an utterance of length n.) Absolute feature agreement means that we can never transfer the unaltered portion of a TM tape from mother to daughter, as was done in the Exp-Poly time

---

[11] These speculations are rough and require consideration of how they fit in with existing ID rules, metarules, UFS, and SDs. For example, we must introduce a cliticization rule for English, and thereby retreat from the GPSG goal of constructing a monostratal linguistic theory.

hard reduction for GPSG Recognition. However, we do not claim that the universal R-GPSG recognition problem is in $\mathcal{P}$. It is, in fact, NP-complete (see below).

9.1.6 R-GPSG phrase structure

In this section, we provide a concise formal definition of an R-GPSG and the language it generates.[12]

A *revised generalized phrase structure grammar* (R-GPSG) is a 8-tuple:

$$G = \langle \langle Atom, Cat, A, \rho \rangle, V_T, \langle F_H, F_B, F_C, F_F \rangle, R, L, M, D, Start \rangle$$

The first element specifies a set K of syntactic categories. V_T is a finite terminal alphabet. F_H, F_B, F_C, F_F are sets of head, binary head, control, and foot features, respectively. $F_H, F_B \subseteq Atom \cup Cat$ and $F_C \cup F_F \subseteq Cat$. $R, L, M,$ and D are finite sets of ID rules, LP statements, metarules, and simple defaults, respectively. *Start* is the distinguished start category. Let P be the finite set of S-rule productions determined by G, each member of which has one of the forms:

1. $C \to a$, where $C \in K$ and $a \in V_T$,

2. $C_0 \to C_1, \ldots, C_j : C_{j+1}, \ldots, C_n$, where each $C_i \in K$.

An S-rule $r' = C_0' \to C_1', \ldots, C_j' : C_{j+1}', \ldots, C_n'$ is the extension of an S-rule $r = C_0 \to C_1, \ldots, C_j : C_{j+1}, \ldots, C_n$ iff

1. $\forall i,\ 0 \le i \le n,\ [C_i' \sqsupseteq C_i]$, and

2. the pair (r, r') satisfies the HFC, CAP, and FFP (see above).

If P contains an S-rule $A \to \gamma$ with an extension $A' \to \gamma'$ that is an LP-acceptable ordered production, then for any $\alpha, \beta \in (K \cup V_T)^*$, we write $\alpha A' \beta \Longrightarrow \alpha \gamma' \beta$. Let $\overset{*}{\Longrightarrow}$ be the reflexive transitive closure of $\Longrightarrow$. The language $L(G)$ generated by G is

$$L(G) = \{\ x \mid x \in V_T^* \text{ and } \exists C \in K[(C \sqsupseteq Start) \wedge C \overset{*}{\Longrightarrow} x]\}$$

---

[12]Note that this formulation fails to account for positive Kleene closure categories in ID rules.

9.2   Linguistic Analysis of English

This section reproduces some of the more intricate or troublesome linguistic analyses of GKPS. To reproduce their comprehensive analysis of English in toto would be a disservice to that work and beyond the scope of this work. Instead, in appendix B we provide an R-GPSG (roughly) empirically equivalent to the GKPS GPSG for English and urge the reader to consult that work for the accompanying linguistic exposition.

Examples of three linguistic phenomena (explicative pronouns, topicalization, and parasitic gaps) suffice to illustrate R-GPSG's formalisms. Following that, we extend the grammar along the lines suggested by Gazdar (1981) to handle rightward movement. In all cases, we indicate linking by co-subscripting.

9.2.1   Explicative pronouns

First, we account for the distribution of the explicative pronouns *it* and *there* in infinitival constructions on the basis of postulated ID rules and principles of universal feature sharing (see the (GKPS:115–121) analysis). The feature specification [AGR *NP*[NFORM α]] is abbreviated as $+\alpha$ below, where α is it, there, or NORM.

The R-GPSG for English includes the ID rules 9.10,

$$a.\ S \rightarrow X2\,[\text{-SUBJ},\text{AGR}\ X2] : X2$$
$$b.\ VP \rightarrow [\text{13}] : VP\,[\text{INF}]$$
$$c.\ VP \rightarrow [\text{16}] : (PP\,[\text{to}]),\ VP\,[\text{INF}] \qquad (9.10)$$
$$d.\ VP \rightarrow [\text{17}] : NP,\ VP\,[\text{INF}]$$
$$e.\ VP\,[\text{AGR}\ S] \rightarrow [\text{20}] : NP$$

the simple defaults 9.11,

$$a.\ SD1:\ \textit{If}\ [\text{+V},\text{-N},\text{-SUBJ}]\ \textit{Then}\ [\text{NORM}\ +]$$
$$b.\ SD2:\ \textit{If}\ [\text{SUBCAT}]\ \textit{Then}\ [\text{BAR}\ 0] \qquad (9.11)$$

the extraposition metarule 9.12,

$$X2\,[\text{AGR}\ S] \rightarrow W$$
$$\Downarrow \qquad (9.12)$$
$$X2\,[\text{+it}] \rightarrow W, S$$

and the lexical entries 9.13. All other nouns are specified for [NFORM NORM] by their lexical entries.

$$NP\,[\text{PRO},\text{-PLU},\text{NFORM it}] \to it$$
$$NP\,[\text{PRO},\text{NFORM there}] \to there \tag{9.13}$$

From the ID rules in 9.10, R-GPSG constructs the following S-rules.

$$a.\ VP\,[\text{AGR}_1] \to V0\,[13,\text{AGR}_1] : VP\,[\text{INF},\text{AGR}_1]$$
$$b.\ VP\,[\text{AGR}_1] \to V0\,[16,\text{AGR}_1] : (PP\,[\text{to}]), VP\,[\text{INF},\text{AGR}_1] \tag{9.14}$$

The absence of a controlling category allows the CAP to link the AGR values of the mother and predicative *VP*[INF] daughter. The HFC then links the AGR values of the mother and lexical head daughter. SD1 specifies the head daughter for [BAR 0], but SD2 cannot affect the linked AGR values.

$$VP\,[\text{AGR}_1\ NP[\text{NORM}]] \ \to \ V0\,[14,\text{AGR}_1\ NP[\text{NORM}]] :$$
$$V2\,[\text{INF},\ \text{AGR}_1\ NP[\text{NORM}]]$$

The CAP and HFC operate identically as in 9.14, except that the [+NORM] specification is inherited from the ID rule 9.10b and propagated through the S-rule by the CAP and HFC.

$$VP\,[\text{AGR}_2\ NP[\text{NORM}]] \ \to \ V0\,[17,\text{AGR}_2\ NP[\text{NORM}]] :$$
$$NP_1, VP\,[\text{INF},\ \text{AGR}_1\ NP] \tag{9.15}$$

The *NP* daughter controls its *VP*[INF] sister, and the CAP links the AGR value of the *VP* to its sister *NP*. SD2 specifies the mother for [+NORM], and the HFC forces this specification on the head daughter.

The rules 9.16 introduce [+it] and [+there] specifications. Note that 9.16a is the result of the extraposition metarule on the ID rule 9.10e.

$$a.\ VP\,[\text{+it}] \to [20] : NP, S$$
$$b.\ VP\,[\text{+it}] \to [21] : (PP\,[\text{to}]), S\,[\text{FIN}] \tag{9.16}$$
$$c.\ VP\,[\text{AGR}\ NP[\text{+there},\text{PLU }\alpha]] \to [22] : NP\,[\text{PLU }\alpha]$$

The rules in 9.16 may only be linked to the *VP* daughters introduced by the S-rules 9.14 and 9.15 in a "tree" of (or derivation using) S-rules (compare their AGR values). The grammar claims that explicative pronouns only occur in utterances generated using the rules in 9.16, in combination with the "extending" S-rules 9.14 and 9.15. This describes the following facts from GKPS

(p. 120):

$$\left\{ \begin{array}{c} \text{It} \\ \text{*There} \\ \text{*Kim} \end{array} \right\} \text{[continues [to bother [Lou] [that Robin was chosen]]]}$$

$$(9.17)$$

$$\left\{ \begin{array}{c} \text{*It} \\ \text{There} \\ \text{*Kim} \end{array} \right\} \text{[appeared (to us) [to be [nothing in the park]]]} \quad (9.18)$$

$$\text{Leslie [believed} \left\{ \begin{array}{c} \text{it} \\ \text{*there} \\ \text{*Kim} \end{array} \right\} \text{[to bother [us] [that Lee lied]]]} \quad (9.19)$$

$$\text{We [believed} \left\{ \begin{array}{c} \text{*it} \\ \text{there} \\ \text{*Kim} \end{array} \right\} \text{[to be [no flaws in the argument]]]} \quad (9.20)$$

9.2.2   Topicalization

The rule 9.21a expands clauses and rule 9.21b introduces unbounded dependency constructions (UDCs) in English.

$$\begin{array}{l} a.\ S \rightarrow X2\,[\text{-SUBJ},\text{AGR}\ X2] : X2 \\ b.\ S \rightarrow X2\,[\text{+SUBJ},\text{SLASH}\ X2] : X2 \end{array} \qquad (9.21)$$

In both cases the nonhead $X2$ daughter controls the head daughter, and the CAP links the value of the head daughter's control feature with the $X2$ daughter, creating the S-rules 9.22.

$$\begin{array}{l} a.\ S \rightarrow VP\,[\text{AGR}_1\ X2] : X2_1 \\ b.\ S \rightarrow S\,[\text{SLASH}_2\ X2] : X2_2 \end{array} \qquad (9.22)$$

In the following discussion, [3s] and [3p] abbreviate [PER 3,-PLU] and [PER 3,+PLU], respectively. Consider the topicalization structure in figure 9.2, taken from GKPS (p. 145).

Note that it is impossible to extract any constituent out of the $X2$ daughter in 9.22b because the FFP has forced [SLASH noBind] on the mother and $X2$ daughter. This explains the unacceptability of 9.23 in R-GPSG, which is permissible in the theory of GKPS.

$$* \text{ New York [[the girl from } \_ \text{] [we want } \_ \text{ to succeed]]} \qquad (9.23)$$

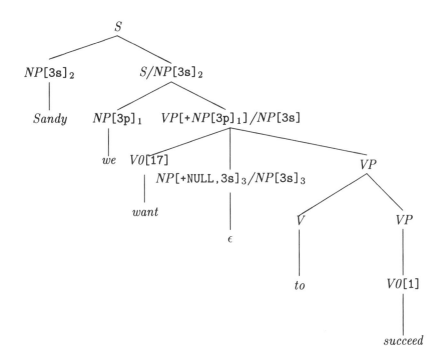

Figure 9.2: This is a typical topicalization structure in R-GPSG. Co-subscripted categories share all absent feature specifications.

9.2.3   Parasitic gaps

Simple parasitic gaps, that is, those introduced in verb phrases by lexical rules, present no problem for R-GPSG because the FFP demands all instantiations of **SLASH** on daughters to be equal to each other and equal to the **SLASH** instantiation on the mother.

$$
\begin{array}{l}
VP/NP \\
\quad V0\,[13] \\
\quad NP/NP \\
\quad PP\,[\texttt{to}]/NP
\end{array}
\qquad (9.24)
$$

Kim wondered which models

$$\text{Sandy} \left\{ \begin{array}{l} [\text{ had sent } [\text{ pictures of } \_] [\text{ to } \_]] \\ [\text{ had sent } [\text{ pictures of } \_] [\text{ to Bill }]] \\ [\text{ had sent } [\text{ pictures of Bill }] [\text{ to } \_]] \end{array} \right\} \quad (9.25)$$

The FFP insists nonlexical heads be instantiated for SLASH if any nonhead daughter is, thereby explaining the unacceptability of 9.26 and the acceptability of 9.27.

a. * *S/NP*

    NP/NP

    VP

b. * Kim wondered which authors [[reviewers of _] [always detested sushi]]

(9.26)

a. S/NP

    NP/NP

    VP/NP

b. Kim wondered which authors [[reviewers of _] [always detested _]]

(9.27)

This analysis of parasitic gaps exactly follows the one presented in GKPS on matters of fact. These facts may be questionable, however. Some sentences considered acceptable in GKPS (for example, *Kim wondered which models Sandy had sent pictures of to Bill* and *Kim wondered which authors reviewers of always detested*) are marginal for some native English speakers. Note that both sentences are marked unacceptable in the GB framework because of subjacency violations.

9.2.4 Rightward dependencies

GKPS observe that "a treatment of rightward dependencies along the lines suggested by Gazdar (1981) will interact with the rules responsible for [(9.28)] to produce the relevant examples [(9.29)]" (GKPS:125).

a. How ready (for us) to leave are they?

b. How eager (for the students) to take the exam did you say they were?

(9.28)

a. How ready are they (for us) to leave?

b. How eager did you say they were (for the students) to take the exam?

(9.29)

This reference to Gazdar's (1981) analysis appears to be at odds with the GKPS goal of constructing a linguistic theory where "the universalism [of natural language] is, ultimately, intended to be entirely embodied in the formal system, not expressed by statements made in it" (GKPS:4).

Consider the approach advocated in Gazdar (1981:177–178, emphasis added):

> As is well known, rightward displacement of constituents is subject to a constraint having to do with "heaviness": roughly speaking, the heavier the displaced constituent, the better the sentence sounds. This fact is hard to capture in the formalism of generative grammar (whether phrase structure or transformational) and it seems reasonable, and probably not controversial, to suppose that *it may be a fact that ought to be captured not in that formalism, but rather in one's model of language perception and/or production* .... If the boundedness of rightward dependencies is a by-product of parser operation, then it need not be built into the syntactic rules which permit such dependencies.

Gazdar (1981) proposes the schema 9.30a to account for rightward displacement, where α is any clausal category and β is any phrasal category. The R-GPSG equivalent is the ID rule 9.30b, which is identical to the rule 9.21b that introduces unbounded dependencies.

$$a.\ \alpha \rightarrow \alpha/\beta\ \beta$$
$$b.\ S \rightarrow X2\,[\text{+SUBJ},\text{SLASH}\ X2] : X2 \tag{9.30}$$

The problem, of course, is that existing LP statements prevent rightward movement of noun phrases, adjective phrases, and prepositional phrases. Neither R-GPSG nor GPSG can provide a clean formal account of rightward dependencies. Following the spirit of the Gazdar (1981) analysis, R-GPSG must provide a substantive parser-based account for the phrase structure of rightward dependencies.[13]

---

[13]This account might take the form of a rule "if we have two constituents *S/X2* and *X2* and can't complete the parse, then guess right-node-raising structure and attach the two together in a clause."

9.3 Complexity of R-GPSG Recognition

We now prove that the *universal recognition problem* for R-GPSGs is NP-complete. We conclude by arguing that this result reflects positively on the empirical adequacy of R-GPSG linguistic theory.

Theorem 7: R-GPSG Recognition is NP-complete.

The proof is identical in all essential respects to the 3SAT reduction in chapter 3 that shows AG Recognition is NP-complete, and for that reason is not reproduced here (see Ristad (1986) for details).

Two minor differences must be considered. First we examine the complexity of converting R-GPSG ID rules into the S-rules that are actually used in the reduction. Then we account for null-transitions in R-GPSG.

The set P of S-rule productions (corresponding to the AG productions in the chapter 3 proof) is computed by applying the simple defaults (while respecting the principles of UFS) to the metarule unit closure $UC(M,R)$. This can be done in deterministic polynomial time (see above), and $|P| = \theta(|G|^6)$. There are no metarules, LP statements, or simple defaults in the reduction grammar.

Recall that the only ϵ-production is the lexical element for the category $X\mathcal{2}[\texttt{SLASH } X\mathcal{2}_1, \texttt{NULL } +]_1$. Null-transitions in R-GPSG may, at the worst, convert the extension of a branching production to a nonbranching one in the derivation because no head daughter may bear the [+NULL] specification: they may in effect be "compiled" out of the derivation when we choose an ordered extension to expand the nonterminal A'. As with agreement grammars, each branching S-rule production can be separated from its closest branching production in the derivation by a run of at most $|P|$ nonbranching productions, and the shortest derivation of x will be of length $\theta(|P| \cdot |x|)$.

The reduction demonstrates that intractability in R-GPSG arises from a particularly deadly combination of feature agreement and ambiguity. Underspecification of categories can be costly. This suggests that limiting the number of head features or the scope of their agreement will mitigate the intractability. An efficient recognition algorithm might approximate grammaticality by failing to transfer all head features through coordinate structures (for example, letting them assume default values instead), or by aborting a parse in the face of excessive lexical or structural ambiguity.

In chapter 6 we proposed a constraint-based computational solution to intractability in a two-level morphological analyzer. Intractability arises from unbounded agreement processes in that system, and we believe that similar techniques based on constraint propagation can be adapted to create an efficient *approximate* parsing algorithm for coordinate structures in R-GPSG. Tuples of features would correspond to constraint-propagation nodes, while tuples of sets of feature-values would correspond to node labels; features could receive multiple values in this implementation. Nodes would be connected by both R-GPSG phrase structure (ID rules) and principles of universal feature sharing.

The proof also demonstrates that even if we ignore the significant computational complexity introduced by most of the GPSG machinery (that is, the control agreement principle, foot feature principle, FCRs, FSDs, ID/LP format, ϵ-transitions, and metarules), GPSG will still not obtain an efficient parsability result. The head feature convention *alone* ensures that the universal recognition problem for GPSG (and R-GPSG) is NP-hard and likely to be intractable. This result is not surprising, because the HFC in current GPSG theory functionally replaces some metarules in earlier versions of GPSG and metarules are known to cause intractability.

Appendix A

UCFG Recognition is NP-Complete

This appendix contains the details of a careful reduction of the vertex cover problem to the UCFG recognition problem. This version of the reduction establishes that the difficulty of UCFG recognition is not due either to the possibility of empty constituents (ϵ-rules, null-transitions) or to the possibility of repeated symbols in rules (*i.e.*, to the use of multisets rather than sets). Consequently, it is somewhat different from and more complex than the one sketched in chapter 7.

A.1   Defining Unordered Context-Free Grammars

In this section we formalize the informal characterization of UCFGs that was given in chapter 7.

Definition: An *unordered CFG* (UCFG) is a quadruple $\langle N, \Sigma, R, S \rangle$, where:

(a) N is a finite set of *nonterminals*.

(b) Σ disjoint from N is a finite, nonempty set of *terminal symbols*.

(c) R is a nonempty set of *rules* $\langle A, \alpha \rangle$, where $A \in N$ and $\alpha \in (N \cup \Sigma)^*$. The rule $\langle A, \alpha \rangle$ may be written as $A \to \alpha$.

(d) $S \in N$ is the *start symbol*.

Convention: The grammar G and its components N, Σ, R, S need not be explicitly mentioned when clear from context.

Convention: Unless otherwise noted,

(a) $A, A', A_i, \ldots$ denote elements of N;

(b) $a, a', a_i, \ldots$ denote elements of Σ;

(c) $X, Y, X', Y', X_i, Y_i, \ldots$ denote elements of $N \cup \Sigma$;

(d) $\sigma, u, u', u_i, \ldots$ denote elements of Σ^*;

(e) $\alpha, \beta, \gamma, \varphi, \psi$ denote elements of $(N \cup \Sigma)^*$.

Definition: $G = \langle N, \Sigma, R, S \rangle$ is ϵ-*free* iff for every $\langle A, \alpha \rangle \in R$, $|\alpha| \neq 0$.

Definition: $G = \langle N, \Sigma, R, S \rangle$ is *branching* iff some rule branches, *i.e.*, for some $\langle A, \alpha \rangle \in R$, $|\alpha| > 1$.

Definition: $G = \langle N, \Sigma, R, S \rangle$ is *duplicate-free* iff no rule RHS contains a duplicated element, *i.e.*, for every $\langle A, \alpha \rangle \in R$, $\alpha = Y_1 \ldots Y_n$ and for all $i, j \in [1, n]$, $Y_i = Y_j$ iff $i = j$.

Definition: $G = \langle N, \Sigma, R, S \rangle$ is *simple* iff it is ϵ-free, duplicate-free, and branching.

Note. The notion of a simple UCFG is introduced in order to help pin down the source of any computational difficulties associated with UCFGs. For example, since simple UCFGs are restricted to be duplicate-free, a difficulty that arises with simple UCFGs cannot result from the possibility that a symbol may occur more than once on the right-hand side of a rule.

Definition: In a derivation, $\varphi A \psi \underset{G}{\Rightarrow} \varphi \alpha \psi$ (by r) just in case (for some) $r = \langle A', Y_1 \ldots Y_n \rangle \in R$ and for some permutation ρ of $[1, n]$, $A = A'$ and $\alpha = Y_{\rho(1)} \ldots Y_{\rho(n)}$. If $\varphi \in \Sigma^*$, also write $\varphi A \psi \underset{G}{\Rightarrow}_{\text{lm}} \varphi \alpha \psi$.

Definition: $L(G) = \{ \sigma \in \Sigma^* : S \Rightarrow^* \sigma \}$.

Definition: An n-step *derivation* of ψ from φ is a sequence $(\varphi_0, \ldots, \varphi_n)$ such that $\varphi_0 = \varphi$, $\varphi_n = \psi$, and for all $i \in [0, n-1]$, $\varphi_i \Rightarrow \varphi_{i+1}$. If it is also true for all i that $\varphi_i \Rightarrow_{\text{lm}} \varphi_{i+1}$, say that the derivation is *leftmost*.

A.2   Defining the Computational Problems

Here we define particular versions of the vertex cover and UCFG recognition problems, which will be the subject of our reduction.

Definition: A possible instance of the problem VERTEX COVER is a triple $\langle V, E, k \rangle$, where $\langle V, E \rangle$ is a finite graph with at least one edge and at least

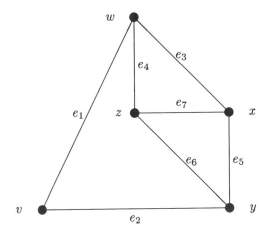

$$
\begin{aligned}
V &= \{v, w, x, y, z\} \\
E &= \{e_1, e_2, e_3, e_4, e_5, e_6, e_7\} \\
&\quad \text{with the } e_i \text{ as indicated} \\
k &= 3
\end{aligned}
$$

Figure A.1: The triple $\langle V, E, k \rangle$ is an instance of VERTEX COVER. The set $V' = \{v, x, z\}$ is a vertex cover of size $k = 3$.

---

two vertices, $k \in \mathbf{N}$, and $k < |V|$.[1] VERTEX COVER itself consists of all possible instances $\langle V, E, k \rangle$ such that for some $V' \subseteq V$, $|V'| \leq k$ and for all edges $e \in E$, at least one endpoint of e is in V'. (Figure A.1 gives an example of a VERTEX COVER instance.)

Fact: VERTEX COVER is NP-complete (Garey and Johnson 1979:46; see also section 2.2.2 of chapter 2).

Definition: A possible instance of the problem SIMPLE UCFG RECOGNITION is a pair $\langle G, \sigma \rangle$, where G is a simple UCFG and $\sigma \in \Sigma^*$. SIMPLE UCFG RECOGNITION itself consists of all possible instances $\langle G, \sigma \rangle$ such that $\sigma \in L(G)$.

Notation: Take $\|\cdot\|$ to be any reasonable measure of the encoded input length for a computational problem; continue to use $|\cdot|$ for set cardinality and string length. It is reasonable to require that if S is a set, $k \in \mathbf{N}$, and $|S| > k$,

---

[1] This formulation differs trivially from the one cited by Garey and Johnson.

then $\|S\| > \|k\|$; that is, the encoding of numbers is better than unary. It is also reasonable to require that $\|\langle \ldots, x, \ldots \rangle\| \geq \|x\|$.

A.3 UCFG Recognition is in NP

Here we show that a nondeterministic machine can easily guess the derivation of a string. We begin by setting a bound on the length of the required derivation.

Lemma A.3.1: Let $(\varphi_0, \ldots, \varphi_k)$ be a shortest leftmost derivation of φ_k from φ_0 in a branching ϵ-free UCFG. If $k > |N| + 1$ then $|\varphi_k| > |\varphi_0|$.

Proof. There exists some sequence of rules $\langle A_0, \alpha_0 \rangle, \ldots, \langle A_{k-1}, \alpha_{k-1} \rangle$ such that for all $i \in [0, k-1]$, $\varphi_i \Rightarrow_{\mathrm{lm}} \varphi_{i+1}$ by $\langle A_i, \alpha_i \rangle$. Since G is ϵ-free, $|\varphi_{i+1}| \geq |\varphi_i|$ always.

Case 1. For some i, $|\alpha_i| > 1$. Then $|\varphi_{i+1}| > |\varphi_i|$. Hence $|\varphi_k| > |\varphi_0|$.

Case 2. For every i, $|\alpha_i| = 1$. Then there exist u, γ such that for every $i \in [0, k-2]$, there is $A_i' \in N$ such that $\varphi_{i+1} = uA_i'\gamma$. Suppose the A_i' are all distinct. Then $|N| \geq k-1$, hence $|N|+1 \geq k$, hence $|N|+1 > |N|+1$, which is impossible. Hence for some $i, j \in [0, k-2]$, $i < j$, $A_i' = A_j'$. Hence $\varphi_{i+1} = \varphi_{j+1}$, since $[1, 1]$ has only one permutation. Then $(\varphi_0, \ldots, \varphi_i, \varphi_{j+1}, \ldots, \varphi_k)$ is a leftmost derivation of φ_k from φ_0 and has length less than k, which is also impossible.

Then $|\varphi_k| > |\varphi_0|$. $\square$

Corollary A.3.2: If G is a branching ϵ-free UCFG and $\sigma \in L(G)$ then σ has a leftmost derivation of length at most $|\sigma| \cdot m$, where $m = |N| + 2$.

Proof. Let $(\varphi_0, \ldots, \varphi_k)$ be a shortest leftmost derivation of σ from S. Suppose $k > |\sigma| \cdot m$. Consider the subderivations

$$(\varphi_0, \ldots, \varphi_m)$$
$$(\varphi_m, \ldots, \varphi_{2m})$$
$$\vdots$$
$$(\varphi_{(|\sigma|-1)\cdot m}, \ldots, \varphi_{|\sigma|\cdot m})$$
$$(\varphi_{|\sigma|\cdot m}, \ldots, \varphi_k).$$

Each one except the last has m steps and $m > |N| + 1$. Then by lemma,

$$\left|\varphi_{|\sigma|\cdot m}\right| > \left|\varphi_{(|\sigma|-1)\cdot m}\right| > \cdots > |\varphi_m| > |\varphi_0| = 1.$$

Then $|\sigma| \geq 1 + |\sigma|$, which is impossible. Hence $k \leq |\sigma| \cdot m$. $\square$

Lemma A.3.3: Π = SIMPLE UCFG RECOGNITION is in the computational class $\mathcal{NP}$.

Proof. Let $G = \langle N, \Sigma, R, S \rangle$ be a simple UCFG and $\sigma \in \Sigma^*$. Consider the following nondeterministic algorithm with input $\langle G, \sigma \rangle$:

> *Step 1.* Write down $\varphi_0 = S$.
>
> *Step 2.* Perform the following steps for i from 0 to $|\sigma| \cdot m - 1$, where $m = |N| + 2$.

(a)   Express φ_i as $u_i A_i \gamma_i$ by finding the leftmost nonterminal, or loop if impossible.

(b)   Guess a rule $\langle A_i, Y_{i,1} \ldots Y_{i,k_i} \rangle \in R$ and a permutation ρ_i of $[1, k_i]$, or loop if there is no such rule.

(c)   Write down $\varphi_{i+1} = u_i Y_{i,\rho_i(1)} \ldots Y_{i,\rho_i(k_i)} \gamma_i$.

(d)   If $\varphi_{i+1} = \sigma$ then halt.

> *Step 3.* Loop.

It should be apparent that the algorithm runs in time at worst polynomial in $\|\langle G, \sigma \rangle\|$; note that the length of φ_i increases by at most a constant amount on each iteration.

Assume $\langle G, \sigma \rangle \in \Pi$. Then σ has a leftmost derivation of length at most $|\sigma| \cdot m$ by Corollary A.3.2; hence the nondeterministic algorithm will be able to guess it and will halt. Conversely, suppose the algorithm halts on input $\langle G, \sigma \rangle$. On the iteration when the algorithm halts, the sequence $(\varphi_0, \ldots, \varphi_{i+1})$ will constitute a leftmost derivation of σ from S; hence $\sigma \in L(G)$ and $\langle G, \sigma \rangle \in \Pi$.

Then there is a nondeterministic algorithm that runs in polynomial time and accepts exactly Π. Hence $\Pi \in \mathcal{NP}$. $\square$

A.4   UCFG Recognition is NP-complete

We now continue with the main part of the proof, which shows NP-hardness by reducing the vertex cover problem. Together with the result of the previous section, this shows NP-completeness.

Lemma A.4.1: Let $\langle V, E, k \rangle = \langle V, \{e_i\}, k \rangle$ be a possible instance of VERTEX COVER. Then it is possible to construct, in time polynomial in $\|V\|$, $\|E\|$, and k, a simple UCFG $G(V, E, k)$ and a string $\sigma(V, E, k)$ such that

$$\langle G(V, E, k), \sigma(V, E, k) \rangle \in \text{SIMPLE UCFG RECOGNITION}$$
$$\text{iff} \quad \langle V, E, k \rangle \in \text{VERTEX COVER.}$$

Proof. Construct $G(V, E, k)$ as follows. Let the set N of nonterminals consist of the following symbols not in V:

$$\begin{aligned}
&START, U, D,\\
&H_i \text{ for } i \in [1, |E|],\\
&U_i \text{ for } i \in [1, |V| - k],\\
&D_i \text{ for } i \in [1, |E| \cdot (k - 1)].
\end{aligned}$$

$\|N\|$ will be at worst polynomial in $\|E\|$, $\|V\|$, and k for a reasonable length measure. Define the terminal vocabulary Σ to consist of subscripted symbols as follows:

$$\Sigma = \{a_i : a \in V, i \in [1, |E|]\}.$$

Designate $START$ as the start symbol. Include the following as members of the rule set R:

(a)   Include the rule

$$START \rightarrow H_1 \ldots H_{|E|} U_1 \ldots U_{|V|-k} D_1 \ldots D_{|E| \cdot (k-1)}.$$

(b)   For each $e_i \in E$, include the rules

$$\{H_i \rightarrow a_i : a \text{ an endpoint of } e_i\}.$$

(c)   For each $i \in [1, |V| - k]$, include the rule $U_i \rightarrow U$. Also include the rules

$$\{U \rightarrow a_1 \ldots a_{|E|} : a \in V\}.$$

(d)   For each $i \in [1, |E| \cdot (k - 1)]$, include the rule $D_i \rightarrow D$. Also include the rules

$$\{D \rightarrow a : a \in \Sigma\}.$$

Take $G(V, E, k)$ to be $\langle N, \Sigma, R, START \rangle$. (Figure A.2 shows the result of applying this construction to the VERTEX COVER instance of figure A.1.)

Let $h : [1, |V|] \rightarrow V$ be some standard enumeration of the elements of V. Construct $\sigma(V, E, k)$ as $h(1)_1 \ldots h(1)_{|E|} \ldots h(|V|)_1 \ldots h(|V|)_{|E|}$; thus $\sigma(V, E, k)$ will have length $|E| \cdot |V|$.

$START \rightarrow$
$\qquad H_1 H_2 H_3 H_4 H_5 H_6 H_7 U_1 U_2 D_1 D_2 D_3 D_4 D_5 D_6 D_7 D_8 D_9 D_{10} D_{11} D_{12} D_{13} D_{14}$

H_1	$\rightarrow$	$v_1 \mid w_1$	H_2	$\rightarrow$	$v_2 \mid y_2$	H_3	$\rightarrow$	$w_3 \mid x_3$
H_4	$\rightarrow$	$w_4 \mid z_4$	H_5	$\rightarrow$	$x_5 \mid y_5$	H_6	$\rightarrow$	$y_6 \mid z_6$
H_7	$\rightarrow$	$x_7 \mid z_7$						

U_1	$\rightarrow$	U	U_2	$\rightarrow$	U	U_3	$\rightarrow$	U
U_4	$\rightarrow$	U						

$$U \rightarrow v_1 v_2 v_3 v_4 v_5 v_6 v_7 \mid w_1 w_2 w_3 w_4 w_5 w_6 w_7 \mid x_1 x_2 x_3 x_4 x_5 x_6 x_7$$
$$\mid y_1 y_2 y_3 y_4 y_5 y_6 y_7 \mid z_1 z_2 z_3 z_4 z_5 z_6 z_7$$

D_1	$\rightarrow$	D	D_2	$\rightarrow$	D	D_3	$\rightarrow$	D
D_4	$\rightarrow$	D	D_5	$\rightarrow$	D	D_6	$\rightarrow$	D
D_7	$\rightarrow$	D	D_8	$\rightarrow$	D	D_9	$\rightarrow$	D
D_{10}	$\rightarrow$	D	D_{11}	$\rightarrow$	D	D_{12}	$\rightarrow$	D
D_{13}	$\rightarrow$	D	D_{14}	$\rightarrow$	D			

$$D \rightarrow v_1 \mid v_2 \mid v_3 \mid v_4 \mid v_5 \mid v_6 \mid v_7 \mid w_1 \mid w_2 \mid w_3 \mid w_4 \mid w_5 \mid w_6 \mid w_7$$
$$\mid x_1 \mid x_2 \mid x_3 \mid x_4 \mid x_5 \mid x_6 \mid x_7 \mid y_1 \mid y_2 \mid y_3 \mid y_4 \mid y_5 \mid y_6 \mid y_7$$
$$\mid z_1 \mid z_2 \mid z_3 \mid z_4 \mid z_5 \mid z_6 \mid z_7$$

Figure A.2: The construction described in Lemma A.4.1 produces this grammar when applied to the VERTEX COVER problem of figure A.1. The H-symbols ensure that the solution that is found must hit each of the edges, while the U-symbols ensure that enough elements of V remain untouched to satisfy the requirement $|V'| \leq k$. The D-symbols are dummies that absorb excess input symbols. A shorter grammar than this will suffice if the grammar is not required to be duplicate-free.

It is easy to see that $\|\langle G(V, E, k), \sigma(V, E, k)\rangle\|$ will be at worst poly-nomial in $\|E\|$, $\|V\|$, and k for reasonable $\|\cdot\|$. It will also be possible to *construct* the grammar and string in polynomial time. Finally, note that given the definition of a possible instance of VERTEX COVER, the gram-mar will be branching, ϵ-free, and duplicate-free, hence simple.

Now suppose $\langle V, E, k\rangle \in$ VERTEX COVER. Then there exist $V' \subseteq V$ and $f : E \to V'$ such that $|V'| \leq k$ and for every $e \in E$, $f(e)$ is an endpoint of e. E is nonempty by hypothesis and V' must hit every edge, hence $|V'|$ cannot be zero. Construct a parse tree for $\sigma(V, E, k)$ according to $G(V, E, k)$ as follows.

Step 1. Number the elements of $V - V'$ as $\{x_i : i \in [1, |V - V'|]\}$. For each x_i where $i \leq |V| - k$, construct a node dominating the substring

$$(x_i)_1 \ldots (x_i)_{|E|}$$

of $\sigma(V, E, k)$ and label it U. Then construct a node dominating only the U-node and label it U_i. Note that the available symbols U_i are numbered from 1 to $|V| - k$, so it is impossible to run out of U-symbols. Also, $|V'| \leq k$ and $V' \subseteq V$, hence $|V - V'| \leq |V| - k$, so all of the U-symbols will be used. Finally, note that $U \to a_1 \ldots a_{|E|}$ is a rule for any $a \in S$ and that $U_i \to U$ is a rule for any U_i.

Step 2. For each $e_i \in E$, construct a node dominating the (unique) occurrence of $f(e_i)_i$ in $\sigma(V, E, k)$ and label it H_i. Step 2 cannot conflict with step 1 because $f(e_i) \in V'$, hence $f(e_i) \notin V - V'$. Different parts of step 2 cannot conflict with each other because each one affects a symbol with a different subscript. Also note that $f(e_i)$ is an endpoint of e_i and that $H_i \to a_i$ is a rule for any $e_i \in E$ and a an endpoint of e_i.

Step 3. Number all occurrences of terminals in $\sigma(V, E, k)$ that were not attached in step 1 or step 2. For the ith such occurrence, construct a node dominating the occurrence and label it D. Then construct another node dominating the D-node and label it D_i. Note that the stock of D-symbols runs from 1 to $(k-1) \cdot |E|$. Exactly $(|V| - k) \cdot |E|$ symbols of $\sigma(V, E, k)$ were accounted for in step 1. Also, exactly $|E|$ symbols were accounted for in step 2. The length of $\sigma(V, E, k)$ is $|V| \cdot |E|$, hence exactly

$$\begin{aligned} |V| \cdot |E| - (|V| - k) \cdot |E|) - |E| &= |V| \cdot |E| - |V| \cdot |E| + k \cdot |E| - |E| \\ &= (k-1) \cdot |E| \end{aligned}$$

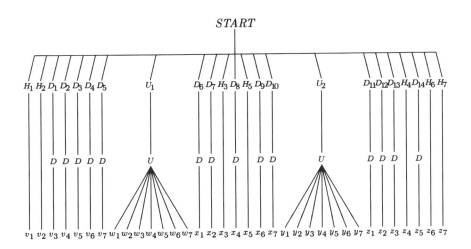

Figure A.3: This parse tree shows how the grammar shown in figure A.2 can generate the string $\sigma(V, E, k)$ constructed in Lemma A.4.1 for the VERTEX COVER problem of figure A.1. The corresponding VERTEX COVER solution $V' = \{v, x, z\}$ and its intersection with the edges can be read off by noticing which terminals the H_i nodes dominate. The H_i and D_i nodes are all daughters of the root node.

symbols remain at the beginning of step 3. $D \rightarrow a$ is a rule for any $a \in \Sigma$; $D_i \rightarrow D$ is a rule for any D_i.

Step 4. Finally, construct a node labeled $START$ that dominates all of the H_i, U_i, and D_i nodes constructed in steps 1, 2, and 3. The rule

$$START \rightarrow H_1 \ldots H_{|E|} U_1 \ldots U_{|V|-k} D_1 \ldots D_{|E| \cdot (k-1)}$$

is in the grammar. Note also that nodes labeled $H_1, \ldots, H_{|E|}$ were constructed in step 2, nodes labeled $U_1, \ldots, U_{|V|-k}$ were constructed in step 1, and nodes labeled $D_1, \ldots, D_{|E| \cdot (k-1)}$ were constructed in step 3. Hence the application of the rule is in accord with the grammar. Then $\sigma(V, E, k) \in L(G)$. (Figure A.3 illustrates the application of this parse-tree construction procedure to the grammar and input string derived from the VERTEX COVER example in figure A.1.)

Conversely, suppose $\sigma(V, E, k) \in L(G)$. Then the derivation of $\sigma(V, E, k)$ from *START* must begin with the application of the rule

$$START \rightarrow H_1 \ldots H_{|E|} U_1 \ldots U_{|V|-k} D_1 \ldots D_{|E| \cdot (k-1)}$$

and each H_i must later be expanded as some subscripted terminal $g(H_i)$. Define $f(e_i)$ to be $g(H_i)$ without the subscript; then by construction of the grammar, $f(e_i)$ is an endpoint of e_i for all $e_i \in E$. Define $V' = \{f(e_i): e_i \in E\}$; then it is apparent that $V' \subseteq V$ and that V' contains at least one endpoint of e_i for all $e_i \in E$. Also, each U_i for $i \in [1, |V| - k]$ must be expanded as U, then as some substring $(a_i)_1 \ldots (a_i)_{|E|}$ of $\sigma(V, E, k)$.[2] Since the substrings dominated by the H_i and U_i must all be disjoint, and since there are only $|E|$ subscripted occurrences of any single symbol from V in $\sigma(V, E, k)$, there must be $|V| - k$ distinct elements of V that are not dominated in any of their subscripted versions by any H_i. Then $|V - V'| \geq |V| - k$. Since in addition $V \subseteq V'$, $|V'| \leq k$. Then $\langle V, E, k \rangle \in$ VERTEX COVER. $\square$

Theorem 8: SIMPLE UCFG RECOGNITION is NP-complete.

Proof. SIMPLE UCFG RECOGNITION is in the class $\mathcal{NP}$ by Lemma A.3.3, hence a polynomial-time reduction of VERTEX COVER to SIMPLE UCFG RECOGNITION is sufficient. Let $\langle V, E, k \rangle$ be a possible instance of VERTEX COVER. Let G be $G(V, E, k)$ and σ be $\sigma(V, E, k)$ as constructed in Lemma A.4.1. Note that G is simple.

The construction of G and σ can, by lemma, be carried out at time at worst polynomial in $\|E\|$, $\|V\|$, and k. Also by lemma, $\langle G, \sigma \rangle$ is in SIMPLE UCFG RECOGNITION iff $\langle V, E, k \rangle \in$ VERTEX COVER. k is not polynomial in $\|k\|$ under a reasonable encoding scheme. However, $|E| > k$, hence $\|E\| \geq \|k\|$; also $\|\langle V, E, k \rangle\| \geq \|E\|$, hence $\|\langle V, E, k \rangle\| \geq k$, all by properties assumed to hold of $\|\cdot\|$. Then G and σ can in fact be constructed in time at worst polynomial in $\|\langle V, E, k \rangle\|$.

Hence the VERTEX COVER problem is polynomial-time reduced to SIMPLE UCFG RECOGNITION. $\square$

---

[2]The grammar would allow the substring $(a_i)_1 \ldots (a_i)_{|E|}$ to appear in any permutation, but in $\sigma(V, E, k)$ it appears only in the indicated order.

Appendix B

An R-GPSG for English

B.1 Number of CF Productions for English

For both GPSG and R-GPSG, the only grammar *directly* usable by the Earley algorithm, that is, with the same complexity as a context-free grammar, is the set of admissible local trees. We estimate the number of local trees in the following "typical" R-GPSG for English and show, in accordance with earlier estimates (Shieber 1983:137), that this set is astronomical. Any recognition procedure that explicitly calculates or uses the set of admissible local trees can only result in a slower recognition time than one that does not.

Consider the simplest ID rule B.1 in the R-GPSG for English.

$$VP \rightarrow [1] : \tag{B.1}$$

The *VP* mother may receive multiple values (or remain unspecified) for the atomic-valued features CASE, GER, NEG, POSS, REMOR, WHMOR, AUX, INV, LOC, PAST, PER, PLU, PRD, or VFORM. Assume that each feature is binary. Then 3^{14} possible extensions of the *VP* are licensed, because each feature may be +, −, or unspecified. *VP* may also receive many AGR specifications in which the atomic-valued features CASE, COMP, GER, NEG, αFORM, POSS, REMOR, WHMOR, ADV, AUX, INV, LOC, N, PAST, PER, PLU, SUBJ, V may receive multiple values or be undefined. The daughter's feature values are fixed by the lexicon and the HFC, so the ID rule B.1 corresponds to $3^{14} \cdot 3^{19} = 3^{33}$ unanalyzable context-free productions. The GPSG equivalent of B.1 corresponds to significantly more context-free productions due to the combinatorial possibilities of embedded categories in GPSG.

The ID rule B.2 is slightly more complicated.

$$VP \rightarrow [2] : NP \tag{B.2}$$

The *VP* mother in B.2 may bear all of the features of the VP mother in the rule B.1, plus it may also bear the category-valued features SLASH or WH, or RE, because these FOOT features can be instantiated on the NP daughter. ID rule B.2 therefore corresponds to approximately $3^{14} \cdot (3^{19})^3 = 3^{71} > 10^{33}$ unanalyzable context-free productions. We would expect that only some of these 10^{33} context-free productions are really legitimate rules of an English R-GPSG. Even if we were able to exclude the invalid extensions from consideration, the R-GPSG for English would still contain an astronomical number of context-free productions.

Significantly underspecified ID rules such as the binary coordination schema correspond to an even greater number of context-free productions. In the following estimate, the three mutually-exclusive atomic head features NFORM, PFORM, VFORM are counted as one feature, and the features NULL, CONJ, COMP are ignored since their distribution is extremely limited. We must also ignore the positive Kleene star categories of the iterating coordination schema, because any ID rule containing them corresponds to an infinite number of context-free productions.

The 12 atomic head features can receive any value on either head daughter $(= (3^{12})^2)$ and the 9 non-head atomic features can receive any value on any of the three categories in the rule $(= (3^9)^3)$. Because the foot features WH and SLASH are mutually exclusive, there are effectively 3 category-valued features: the head feature AGR may take 3^{12+9} values on either head daughter $(= (3^{21})^2)$, while the two foot feature may each take 3^{21} possible values on only one category $(= (3^{21})^2)$. Thus, the binary coordination schema corresponds to

$$(3^{12})^2 \cdot (3^9)^3 \cdot (3^{21})^2 \cdot (3^{21})^2 = 3^{135} \geq 10^{64}$$

context-free rules. In short, even the highly constrained R-GPSG framework licenses an astronomical number of context-free productions.

B.2   Tricks and Remaining Problems

Here we discuss some of the more subtle aspects of converting the FCRs and FSDs of the GKPS grammar for English into R-GPSG.

We duplicate *FSD 7:* [BAR 0] $\supseteq$ ¬[VFORM PAS], which prevents random lexical categories from assuming a passive alternate, in a complicated way. We introduce a new *HEAD* feature ±PAS to indicate passive sentences and verb phrases, and no longer allow the VFORM feature to take PAS as a value. We also include four SDs to ensure that VFORM and PAS are mutually exclusive, and that PAS only appears in [+V,-N] categories. While this solution allows us to avoid both the implicit disjunctive consequence of FSD 7 and the morass of problematic feature specifications, it is linguistically dubious. R-GPSG claims that human languages can have passive categories that are also finite, infinitival, and so on. On the other hand, this is just as odd as the GPSG/R-GPSG claim that some human languages can specify a category for VFORM, NFORM, and PFORM simultaneously.

The solution to this problem is to introduce finer internal structure in feature specifications. A more intricate version of the tree-like theory of features proposed in Gazdar and Pullum (1982) or the complex-symbol rules of Chomsky (1965) appear to be more linguistically and computationally desirable for these reasons.

FCR 10: [+INV,BAR 2] $\supseteq$ [+SUBJ] prevents [+INV] from "dripping through" the *VP* by the HFC. Note that [+INV] is only introduced on the mother *V2*[+SUBJ] category of lexical ID rules, and that the only instance of *V2*[+SUBJ] as the head daughter of a (potential) *VP* is in the ID rule B.3:

$$V2 \rightarrow X2 : X2\,[\text{+ADV}] \tag{B.3}$$

We include the simple default *SD: If* [-SUBJ] *Then* [-INV] to prevent [+INV] from rising through any daughter *VP*s. Alternately, we could replace B.3 with B.4, which could be linguistically incorrect.

$$V2\,[\text{-INV}] \rightarrow X2 : X2\,[\text{+ADV}] \tag{B.4}$$

Lastly, GKPS (p. 73, n.2) says that the category *S*[VFORM PAS] is invalid in English, yet GKPS fail to enforce this constraint in their GPSG for English. If it is actually desirable to rule out the suspect category, then include *SD: If* [+SUBJ] *then* [-PAS].

B.3   R-GPSG Features and Rules

```
;-----------------SYNTACTIC FEATURES------------------

BAR       {0,1,2}
CASE      {ACC,NOM}
COMP      {for,that,whether,if}
CONJ      {and,both,but,neither,either,nor,or}
GER       {+,-}
NEG       {+,-}
NULL      {+,-}
POSS      {RECP,REFL}
SUBCAT    {1,...,48,for,that,whether,if,
             and,both,either,neither,but,nor,or,not}
SUBJ      {+,-}
REMOR     {RECP,REFL}
WHMOR     {R,Q,FR,EX}

; HEAD features

AGR       {}
ADV       {+,-}
AUX       {+,-}
INV       {+,-}
LOC       {+,-}
N         {+,-}
NFORM     {there,it,NORM}
PAS       {+,-}
PAST      {+,-}
PER       {1,2,3}
PFORM     {to,by,for,about,of,with}
PLU       {+,-}
PRD       {+,-}
V         {+,-}
VFORM     {BSE,FIN,INF,PRP,PSP}

; FOOT features

RE        {}         ;to be ignored also
SLASH     {}
WH        {}
```

```
;----------------ABBREVIATIONS-----------------------

S  ::= [+V,-N,+SUBJ,BAR 2]
VP ::= [+V,-N,-SUBJ,BAR 2]
NP ::= [-V,+N,BAR 2]
AP ::= [+V,+N,BAR 2]
PP ::= [-V,-N,BAR 2]
V  ::= [+V,-N]
N  ::= [+N,-V]
A  ::= [+N,+V]
P  ::= [-N,-V]


+it    ::= [AGR NP[NFORM it]]
+there ::= [AGR NP[NFORM there]]
+NORM  ::= [AGR NP[NFORM NORM]]
+Q     ::= [WH NP[WHMOR Q]]
+R     ::= [WH NP[WHMOR R]]
Deg    ::= {[SUBCAT 23,BAR noBind]}
~F     ::= [F noBind]



;----------------SIMPLE DEFAULTS----------------------

If [SUBCAT] Then [BAR 0]
If [SUBCAT] Then [SLASH noBind]
If (~[+PAS] & ~[PRP] & [+V,-N] Then [-PRD]
If [+SUBJ,WH] Then [COMP noBind]
If [+SUBJ,INF] Then [COMP for]
If [+V,-N,-SUBJ] Then [AGR NP[NFORM NORM]]
If [SLASH] Then [WH noBind]
If [WH] Then [SLASH noBind]
If A1 Then [WH noBind]
If VP then [WH noBind]
If true Then [-NULL]
If true Then [CONJ noBind]
If [-SUBJ] Then [-INV]
If [VFORM] Then [-PAS]
If [+PAS] Then [VFORM noBind]
If [SUBCAT] & [+V,-N] Then [-PAS]
If [-V] | [+N] Then [PAS noBind]

; to duplicate FCR 5, which appears to be useless . . . .
If [+SUBJ] | (~[FIN] & [VFORM]) Then [-PAST]

; these four are all questionable
```

```
If true Then [-INV]   ; means extraposed S's must be matrix S's
If true Then [CASE NOM] ;BUT no case defaults should be allowed
If [+N,-V,BAR 2] Then [CASE ACC] ; no case defaults should be allowed
If [+SUBJ] Then [-PAS] ; GKPS p.73 footnote 2 implies this is needed


;----------------ID RULES----------------------------

VP -> [1] : %(die eat sing run succeed weep occur
   dine elapse grow look)
VP -> [2] : NP %(sing love close prove succeed
   abandon enlighten castigate slap eat devour grow bring trade)
VP -> [3] : NP, PP[to] %(give sing throw hand trade)
VP -> [4] : NP, PP[for] %(buy cook reserve save trade)
VP -> [5] : NP, NP %(spare hand give buy trade)
VP -> [6] : NP, PP[+LOC] %(put place stand)
VP -> [7] : X2[+PRD] %(be)
; Sells (1986:130) suggests VP[+AUX] -> [7] : X2[+PRD] instead
VP -> [8] : NP, S[FIN] %(persuade convince tell)
VP -> [9] : (PP[to]), S[FIN] %(concede admit)
VP -> [10] : S[BSE] %(prefer desire insist)
VP -> [11] : (PP[of]), S[BSE] %(require)
VP[INF,+AUX,AGR NP] -> [12] : VP[BSE] %(to)
VP -> [13] : VP[INF] %(continue tend seem want)
VP -> [14] : V2[INF,+NORM] %(prefer intend)
VP -> [15] : VP[INF,+NORM] %(try attempt want)
VP -> [16] : (PP[to]), VP[INF] %(seem appear)
VP -> [17] : NP, VP[INF] %(believe expect)
VP -> [18] : NP, VP[INF,+NORM] %(persuade force)
VP -> [19] : (NP), VP[INF,+NORM] %(promise)
VP[AGR S] -> [20] : NP %(bother amuse)
VP[+it] -> [21] : (PP[to]), S[FIN] %(seem appear)
VP[AGR NP[there,PLU_1]] -> [22] : NP[PLU_1] %(be)
VP -> [40] : S[FIN]   %(believe say regret)
VP -> [43] : S[+Q]    %(wonder ask inquire)
VP[+it] -> [44] : NP, S[+R]     %(be)
VP[+it] -> [44] : X2, S[FIN]/X2   %(be)
VP -> [45] : PP[of]   %(approve)
VP -> [48], X2[-SUBJ,CONJ and] :   %(come go)
VP -> X2[-SUBJ] : AP[+ADV] %   ;is this too constrained?
VP -> X2[-SUBJ] : X2[+ADV] %   ;adverbial adjuncts to VP
S -> X2[+SUBJ] : X2[+ADV] %    ;adverbial adjuncts to S
VO[+NEG] -> XO[+AUX] : [SUBCAT not,~BAR] %   ; "was not"


A2 -> X1 : (Deg) %
```

```
AP[-ADV] -> X1 : (AP[+ADV]) %
A1 -> [24] : PP[about] %(angry glad curious)
A1[AGR S] -> [25] : PP[to] %(apparent obvious certain)
A1 -> [26] : S[FIN] %(afraid aware amazed)
A1 -> [27] : S[BSE] %(insistent adamant determined)
A1 -> [28] : VP[INF] %(likely certain sure)
A1 -> [29] : V2[INF,+NORM] %(anxious eager)
A1 -> [42] : V2[INF]/NP[-NOM] %(easy)


;Spec ::= determiners, possessive phrases, limited set of quantifying
;          APs (e.g. many, few)
; N1 -> X1 : Modifier

NP -> X1 : Spec %
NP[+SUBJ] -> X1 : NP[+POSS] % ; X1 prevents multi-DET or -gerunds
            ; [+SUBJ] says i have a subject, allowing refl/recip
            ; to work properly. Multiple-possesives must be allowed.
NP[+POSS] -> X1  : "'s" %
N1 -> X1 : PP[+POSS] %
N1 -> X1 : PP %
N1 -> X1 : S[+R] %
N1 -> X1 : NO %  ;for noun-noun modification
N1 -> [30] : %(death disappearance laughter)
N1 -> [31] : PP[with], PP[about] %(argument consultation conversation)
N1 -> [32] : S[COMP that] %(belief implication proof notion idea)
N1 -> [33] : S[BSE,COMP that] %(request insistence proposal)
N1 -> [34] : V2[INF] %(plan wish desire)
N1 -> [35] : PP[of] %(king sister inside love seduction criticism)
N1 -> [36] : PP[of], PP[to] %(gift announcement surrender)
N1 -> [37] : PP[of,+GER] %(dislike admission memory habit prospect)


;Mod ::= almost, totally, immediately, right, three feet, nearly
;Mod bears the SUBCAT feature and so precedes X1 in PP -> X1 : Mod
;perhaps P1[+POSS] should be PP[+POSS]?

PP -> X1 : Mod %
P1 -> [38] : NP %(to underneath in beside)
P1 -> [39] : PP[of] %(out forward in_front in_back)
P1[+POSS] -> [41] : NP[+POSS] %(of)


S[COMP noBind] -> X2[-SUBJ,AGR X2] : X2 %
S[COMP noBind] -> X2[+SUBJ]/X2 : X2 %
S[COMP that,FIN] -> S[COMP noBind] : [SUBCAT that] %
S[COMP that,BSE] -> S[COMP noBind] : [SUBCAT that] %
```

```
S[COMP whether] -> S[COMP noBind] : [SUBCAT whether] %
S[COMP if] -> S[COMP noBind] : [SUBCAT if] %
S[COMP for,INF] -> S[COMP noBind] : [SUBCAT for] %


; iterating coordination schema, * means positive transitive closure +
X -> [CONJ and], X* : %
X -> [CONJ noBind], [CONJ and]* : %
X -> [CONJ neither], [CONJ nor]* : %
X -> [CONJ or], X* : %
X -> X, [CONJ or]* : %

; binary coordination schema
X -> [CONJ both], [CONJ and] : %
X -> [CONJ either], [CONJ or] : %
X -> X, [CONJ but] : %

[BAR_1,SUBJ_2,SUBCAT_3,CONJ and] ->
[BAR_1,SUBJ_2,SUBCAT_3] : [SUBCAT and] %
[BAR_1,SUBJ_2,SUBCAT_3,CONJ both] ->
[BAR_1,SUBJ_2,SUBCAT_3] : [SUBCAT both] %
[BAR_1,SUBJ_2,SUBCAT_3,CONJ but] ->
[BAR_1,SUBJ_2,SUBCAT_3] : [SUBCAT but] %
[BAR_1,SUBJ_2,SUBCAT_3,CONJ neither] ->
[BAR_1,SUBJ_2,SUBCAT_3] : [SUBCAT neither] %
[BAR_1,SUBJ_2,SUBCAT_3,CONJ nor] ->
[BAR_1,SUBJ_2,SUBCAT_3] : [SUBCAT nor] %
[BAR_1,SUBJ_2,SUBCAT_3,CONJ or] ->
[BAR_1,SUBJ_2,SUBCAT_3] : [SUBCAT or] %


;------------------LP STATEMENTS----------------------

[SUBCAT] << [SUBCAT {unbound,noBind}]
[+N] << P2 << V2
[CONJ {both,either,neither,noBind}] << [CONJ {and,but,nor,or}]


;------------------METARULES-----------------------

; passive metarule
!VP -> W, NP! => !VP[+PAS] -> W, (PP[by])!

; subject-aux inversion metarule
!V2[-SUBJ] -> W! => !V2[+INV,+AUX,+SUBJ,FIN] -> W, NP!
```

```
; extraposition metarule
!X2[AGR S] -> W! => !X2[+it] -> W, S!

;complement omission metarule
![+N,BAR 1] -> W! => ![+N,BAR 1] -> !

; slash termination metarule 1
!X -> W, X2! => !X -> W, X2[+NULL]!

; slash termination metarule 2
!X -> W, V2[+SUBJ,FIN]! => !X/NP -> W, V2[-SUBJ]!


;--------------------SOME LEXICAL RULES-----------------------

; universal lexical rule,
; where two X2's are linked for all features but NULL
<"", X2[+NULL]_1/X2_1>

<"quickly", A[+ADV]>
<"excessively", A[+ADV]>
<"aren't", V[+AUX,+NEG,PER 1,-PLU,+INV]>

<"that", [SUBCAT that,~BAR]>
<"whether", [SUBCAT whether,~BAR]>
<"if", [SUBCAT if,~BAR]>
<"for", [SUBCAT for,~BAR]>
<"both", [SUBCAT both,~BAR]>
<"either", [SUBCAT either,~BAR]>
<"neither", [SUBCAT neither,~BAR]
<"and", [SUBCAT and,~BAR]>
<"but", [SUBCAT but,~BAR]>
<"nor", [SUBCAT nor,~BAR]>
<"or", [SUBCAT or,~BAR]>

<"it", NP[PRO,-PLU,NFORM it]>
<"there", NP[PRO,NFORM there]>

;lexical rules to discharge PFORM
<"of", PO[PFORM of]>
<"to", PO[PFORM to]>
<"with", PO[PFORM with]>
<"about", PO[PFORM about]>
<"by", PO[PFORM by]>
<"for", PO[PFORM for]>
```

```
<"what", NP[+Q]>
<"which", NP[+Q]>
<"which", NP[+R]>
<"which", Det[+Q]>
<"which", Det[+R]>
<"whose", Det[+POSS,+Q]>
<"whose", Det[+POSS,+R]>

<"so", Deg>
<"too", Deg>
<"very", Deg>
```

References

Aho, A., and J. Ullman, 1972. *The Theory of Parsing, Translation, and Compiling*, Vol. 1. Englewood-Cliffs, NJ: Prentice-Hall.

Aho, A., J. Hopcroft, and J. Ullman, 1974. *The Design and Analysis of Efficient Computer Algorithms*. Reading, MA: Addison-Wesley.

Aho, A., and J. Ullman, 1977. *Principles of Compiler Design*. Reading, MA: Addison-Wesley.

Aho, A., R. Sethi, and J. Ullman, 1986. *Compilers: Principles, Techniques, and Tools*. Reading, MA: Addison-Wesley.

Barss, A. and H. Lasnik, 1986. A note on anaphora and double objects. *Linguistic Inquiry* 17(2):347-354.

Barton, E., 1984. Toward a principle-based parser. A.I. Memo No. 788, Cambridge, MA: M.I.T. Artificial Intelligence Laboratory.

Bates, M., 1978. The theory and practice of augmented transition network grammars. In *Natural Language Communication with Computers*, L. Bolc, ed. Lecture Notes in Computer Science 63. New York: Springer-Verlag, pp. 191–254.

Berwick, R., 1982. Computational complexity and lexical-functional grammar. *American Journal of Computational Linguistics* 8(3–4):97–109.

Berwick, R., 1984. Strong generative capacity, weak generative capacity, and modern linguistic theories. *Computational Linguistics* 10:189–202.

Berwick, R., 1985. *The Acquisition of Syntactic Knowledge*. Cambridge, MA: MIT Press.

Berwick, R., and A. Weinberg, 1982. Parsing efficiency, computational complexity, and the evaluation of grammatical theories. *Linguistic Inquiry* 13(2):165–191.

Berwick, R., and A. Weinberg, 1984. *The Grammatical Basis of Linguistic Performance*. Cambridge, MA: MIT Press.

Berwick, R., and A. Weinberg, 1985. Deterministic parsing and linguistic explanation. *Language and Cognitive Processes* 1(2):109–134.

Berwick, R. and K. Wexler, 1982. Parsing efficiency and c-command. *Proceedings of the First West Coast Conference on Formal Linguistics*. Los Angeles, CA: University of California at Los Angeles, pp. 29–34.

Blum, M., 1967. A machine-independent theory of the complexity of recursive functions. *Journal of the Association for Computing Machinery* 14:2, 322–326.

Bresnan, J., ed., 1982. *The Mental Representation of Grammatical Relations*. Cambridge, MA: MIT Press.

Chandra, A. and L. Stockmeyer, 1976. Alternation. *Proceedings of the 17th Annual Symposium on Foundations of Computer Science*. Houston, TX: Association for Computing Machinery, pp. 98–108.

Chomsky, N., 1956. Three models for the description of language. *I.R.E. Transactions on Information Theory* IT-2:113–124.

Chomsky, N., 1965. *Aspects of the Theory of Syntax*. Cambridge, MA: MIT Press.

Chomsky, N., 1980. *Rules and Representations*. New York: Columbia University Press.

Chomsky, N., 1981. *Lectures on Government and Binding*. Dordrecht, Holland: Foris Publications.

Chomsky, N., 1986. *Knowledge of Language: Its Origins, Nature, and Use*. New York: Praeger Publishers.

Chomsky, N., and Miller, G., 1963. Introduction to the formal analysis of natural languages. In *Handbook of Mathematical Psychology*, vol. II, R.D. Luce, R.R. Bush, and E. Galanter, eds. New York: John Wiley and Sons, pp. 269–322.

Clements, G., and E. Sezer, 1982. Vowel and consonant disharmony in Turkish. In *The Structure of Phonological Representations, Part II*, H. Van der Hulst and N. Smith, eds. Dordrecht, Holland: Foris Publications, pp. 213–256.

Cook, S.A., 1971. The complexity of theorem-proving procedures. *Proceedings of the Third Annual ACM Symposium on the Theory of Computing*. New York: Association for Computing Machinery, pp. 151–158.

Cook, S.A., 1980. Towards a complexity theory of synchronous parallel computation. University of Toronto Department of Computer Science Report No. 141/80.

Cook, S.A., 1981. Towards a complexity theory of synchronous parallel computation. *L'Enseignement Mathématique* 27:99–124.

Cook, S.A., 1983. An overview of computational complexity. *Communications of the Association for Computing Machinery* 26(6):400-408.

Earley, J., 1968. An efficient context-free parsing algorithm. Ph.D. dissertation, Department of Computer Science, Carnegie-Mellon University, Pittsburgh, PA.

Earley, J., 1970. An efficient context-free parsing algorithm. *Communications of the Association for Computing Machinery* 13(2):94–102.

Evans, R., 1985. ProGram—a development tool for GPSG grammars. *Linguistics* 23(2):213–243.

Fodor, J., T. Bever, and M. Garrett, 1974. *The Psychology of Language: An Introduction to Psycholinguistics and Generative Grammar*. New York: McGraw-Hill.

Freuder, E., 1978. Synthesizing Constraint Expressions. *Communications of the Association for Computing Machinery* 21(11):958–966.

Gajek, O., H. Beck, D. Elder, and G. Whittemore, 1983. LISP implementation [of the KIMMO system]. *Texas Linguistic Forum* 22:187–202.

Garey, M, and D. Johnson, 1979. *Computers and Intractability*. San Francisco: W.H. Freeman and Co.

Gazdar, G., 1981. Unbounded dependencies and coordinate structure. *Linguistic Inquiry* 12(2):155–184.

Gazdar, G., 1982. Phrase structure grammar. In *The Nature of Syntactic Representation*, P. Jacobson and G. Pullum, eds. Dordrecht, Holland: Reidel.

Gazdar, G., and G. Pullum, 1982. *Generalized Phrase Structure Grammar: A Theoretical Synopsis*. Bloomington, IN: Indiana University Linguistics Club.

Gazdar, G., E. Klein, G. Pullum, and I. Sag, 1985. *Generalized Phrase Structure Grammar*. Oxford, England: Basil Blackwell.

Goldschlager, L., 1978. A unified approach to models of synchronous parallel machines. *Proceedings of the 10th Annual ACM Symposium on Theory of Computing.* San Diego, CA: Association for Computing Machinery, pp. 88–94.

Guerssel, M., K. Hale, M. Laughren, B. Levin, and J. White Eagle, 1985. A cross-linguistic study of transitivity alternations. *Parasession on Causatives and Agentivity at the Twenty-First Regional Meeting of the Chicago Linguistic Society,* Chicago, IL: April 1985, pp. 48–63.

Hale, K., 1981. On the position of Walbiri in a typology of the base. Bloomington, IN: Indiana University Linguistics Club.

Hale, K., 1982. Some essential features of Warlpiri verbal clauses. In *Papers in Warlpiri Grammar in Memory of Lothar Jagst,* S. Swartz, ed. Berrimah, N.T.: Summer Institute of Linguistics, Work-Papers of SIL-AAB, Series A, Volume 6, pp. 217–315.

Halle, M., 1985. Speculations about the representation of words in memory. In *Phonetic Linguistics: Essays in Honor of Peter Ladefoged,* V. Fromkin, ed. New York: Academic Press, pp. 101–114.

Hobbs, J., 1974. A metalanguage for expressing grammatical restrictions in nodal spans parsing of natural language. Courant Computer Science Report No. 2. New York: New York University and the Courant Institute.

Hopcroft, J., and J. Ullman, 1979. *Introduction to Automata Theory, Languages, and Computation.* Reading, MA: Addison-Wesley.

Hopfield, J., and D. Tank, 1986. Computing with neural circuits: a model. *Science* 233:625–633.

Johnson, S., 1986. The $\mathcal{N}P$-completeness column: an ongoing guide. *Journal of Algorithms* 7:289–305.

Jones, N., and W. Laaser, 1976. Complete problems for deterministic polynomial time. *Theoretical Computer Science* 3(1):105–117.

Joshi, A., 1985. Tree adjoining grammars. In *Natural Language Parsing,* D. Dowty, L. Karttunen, and A. Zwicky, eds. Cambridge: Cambridge University Press, pp. 206–250.

Kaplan, R., and J. Bresnan, 1982. Lexical-functional grammar: a formal system for grammatical representation. In *The Mental Representation of Grammatical Relations,* J. Bresnan, ed. Cambridge, MA: MIT Press, pp. 173–281.

Karttunen, L., 1983. KIMMO: A two-level morphological analyzer. *Texas Linguistic Forum* 22:165–186.

Karttunen, L., and K. Wittenburg, 1983. A two-level morphological analysis of English. *Texas Linguistic Forum* 22:217–228.

Kasif, S., 1986. On the parallel complexity of some constraint satisfaction problems. *Proceedings of the American Association for Artificial Intelligence*, vol. 1, Philadelphia, PA: The American Association for Artificial Intelligence, pp. 349–353.

Kasif, S., J. Reif, and D. Sherlekar, 1986. Formula dissection: a divide and conquer algorithm for satisfiability. Unpublished ms., Department of Electrical Engineering and Computer Science, The Johns Hopkins University, Baltimore, MD.

Kay, M., and R. Kaplan, 1982. Word recognition. Unpublished draft ms. dated May 1982, Xerox Palo Alto Research Center, Palo Alto, California.

Kayne, R., 1981. Unambiguous paths. In *Levels of Syntactic Representation*, R. May and J. Koster, eds. Dordrecht: Foris Publications, pp. 143–183.

Kenstowicz, M., and C. Kisseberth, 1979. *Generative Phonology: Description and Theory*. New York: Academic Press.

Kirousis, L. and C. Papadimitriou, 1985. The complexity of recognizing polyhedral scenes. *Proceedings of the 26th Annual IEEE Symposium on the Foundations of Computer Science*, Boston, MA: IEEE Society, pp. 175–185.

Knuth, D., 1965. On the translation of languages from left to right. *Information and Control* 8:607–639.

Kolmogorov, A., 1965. Three approaches to the quantitative definition of information. *Problems of Information Transmission* 1:1–7.

Kosaraju, R., 1975. Speed of recognition of context-free languages by array automata. *SIAM Journal of Computing* 4(3):331–340.

Koskenniemi, K., 1983. Two-level morphology: a general computational model for word-form recognition and production. Helsinki, Finland: University of Helsinki Department of General Linguistics, Publication No. 11.

Kosaraju, R., 1975. Speed of recognition of context-free languages by array automata. *SIAM Journal of Computing* 4(3):331–340.

Kozen, D., 1977. Lower bounds for natural proof systems. *Proceedings of the 18th Annual Symposium on Foundations of Computer Science*. Long Beach, CA: IEEE Society, pp. 254–266.

Kroch, A, S., and A. K. Joshi, 1985. The linguistic relevance of tree adjoining grammars. Philadelphia, PA: Department of Computer and Information

Science, Moore School, University of Pennsylvania, Technical Report No. MS-CIS-85-16.

Levin, B., and M. Rappaport, 1985. The formation of adjectival passives. Cambridge, MA: M.I.T. Center for Cognitive Science, Lexicon Project Working Papers #2.

Lewis, H., and C. Papadimitriou, 1981. *Elements of the Theory of Computation.* Englewood-Cliffs, N.J.: Prentice-Hall.

Lieber, R., 1980. On the organization of the lexicon. Ph.D. dissertation, MIT Department of Linguistics and Philosophy, Cambridge, MA.

Lindstedt, J., 1984. A two-level description of Old Church Slavonic morphology. *Scando-Slavica* 30:165–189.

Lipton, R. and R. Tarjan, 1979. A separator theorem for planar graphs. *SIAM Journal of Applied Mathematics* 36:177–189.

Lipton, R. and R. Tarjan, 1980. Applications of a planar separator theorem. *SIAM Journal of Computing* 9:615–627.

Mackworth, A., 1977. Consistency in networks of relations. *Artificial Intelligence* 8:99–118.

Mackworth, A., and E. Freuder, 1985. The complexity of some polynomial network consistency algorithms for constraint satisfaction problems. *Artificial Intelligence* 25:65–74.

Marcus, M., 1980. *A Theory of Syntactic Recognition for Natural Language.* Cambridge, MA: MIT Press.

Marr, D., 1980. *Vision.* San Francisco, CA: W.H. Freeman and Company.

McCarthy, J., 1982. Prosodic templates, morphemic templates, and morphemic tiers. In *The Structure of Phonological Representations, Part I,* H. Van der Hulst, H. and N. Smith, eds. Dordrecht, Holland: Foris Publications, pp. 191–223.

Miller, G. A., and N. Chomsky, 1963. Finitary models of language users. In *Handbook of Mathematical Psychology,* vol. II, R.D. Luce, R.R. Bush, and E. Galanter, eds. New York: John Wiley and Sons, pp. 419–492.

Nash, D., 1980. Topics in Warlpiri grammar. Ph.D. dissertation, MIT Department of Linguistics and Philosophy, Cambridge, MA.

Perrault, R., 1984. On the mathematical properties of linguistic theories. *Computational Linguistics* 10:165–176.

Pesetsky, D., 1982. Paths and categories. Ph.D. dissertation, MIT Department of Linguistics and Philosophy, Cambridge, MA.

Peters, S., and Ritchie, R., 1973. On the generative power of transformational grammars. *Information Science* 6:49–83.

Peterson, I., 1985. Exceptions to the rule. *Science News* 128:314–315.

Phillips, J., and H. Thompson, 1985. GPSGP—a parser for generalized phrase structure grammars. *Linguistics* 23(2):245–261.

Pinker, S., 1984. *Language Learnability and Language Development*. Cambridge, MA: Harvard University Press.

Pippenger, N., 1979. On simultaneous resource bounds. *Proceedings of the 20th IEEE Symposium on the Foundations of Computer Science*. Los Angeles: IEEE Computer Society, pp. 307–311.

Pollard, C., 1984. Generalized phrase structure grammar, head grammars, and natural language. Ph.D. dissertation, Stanford University Department of Linguistics, Stanford, CA.

Poser, W., 1982. Phonological representation and action-at-a-distance. In *The Structure of Phonological Representations, Part II*, H. Van der Hulst, H. and N. Smith, eds. Dordrecht, Holland: Foris Publications, pp. 121–158.

Pratt, V., and L. Stockmeyer, 1976. A characterization of the power of vector machines. *Journal of Computing and System Sciences* 12:198–221.

Pullum, G., 1985. The computational tractability of GPSG. *Abstracts of the 60th Annual Meeting of the Linguistics Society of America*. Seattle, WA: Linguistic Society of America, p. 36.

Ristad, E.S., 1985. GPSG-recognition is NP-hard. A.I. Memo No. 837, Cambridge, MA: M.I.T. Artificial Intelligence Laboratory.

Ristad, E.S., 1986. Complexity of linguistic models: a computational analysis and reconstruction of generalized phrase structure grammar. S.M. Thesis, MIT Department of Electrical Engineering and Computer Science, Cambridge, MA.

Ross, J., 1967. Constraints on variables in syntax. Ph.D. dissertation, MIT Department of Linguistics, Cambridge, MA.

Rounds, W., 1975. A grammatical characterization of the exponential time languages. *Proceedings of the 16th Annual Symposium on Switching Theory and Automata*. New York: IEEE Computer Society, pp. 135–143.

Rounds, W., A. Manaster-Ramer, and J. Friedman, 1986. Finding natural languages a home in formal language theory. In *Mathematics of Language*, A. Manaster-Ramer, ed. New York: John Benjamins, in press.

Ruzzo, W., 1981. On uniform circuit complexity. *Journal of Computer and System Sciences* 22:365–383.

Sells, P., 1986. *Contemporary Syntactic Theories*. Stanford, CA: Center for the Study of Language and Information.

Shannon, C., 1949. Communication in the presence of noise. *Proceedings of the IRE* 37:10–21.

Shieber, S.M., 1983. Direct parsing of ID/LP grammars. *Linguistics and Philosophy* 7(2):135–154.

Shieber, S., 1985. Using restriction to extend parsing algorithms for complex feature–based formalisms. *Proceedings of the 23rd Annual Meeting of the Association for Computational Linguistics*. Chicago, IL: Association for Computational Linguistics, pp. 145–152.

Underhill, R., 1976. *Turkish Grammar*. Cambridge, MA: MIT Press.

van der Hulst, H., and N. Smith, eds., 1982a. *The Structure of Phonological Representations, Part I*. Dordrecht, Holland: Foris Publications.

van der Hulst, H., and N. Smith, eds., 1982b. *The Structure of Phonological Representations, Part II*. Dordrecht, Holland: Foris Publications.

Waltz, D., 1975. Understanding line drawings of scenes with shadows. In *The Psychology of Computer Vision*, P. Winston ed. New York: McGraw-Hill, pp. 19–92.

Williams, E. 1984. Grammatical relations. *Linguistic Inquiry* 15:639–673.

Winston, P., 1984. *Artificial Intelligence*. Reading, MA: Addison-Wesley.

Woods, W., 1970. Transition network grammars for natural language analysis. *Communications of the Association for Computing Machinery* 13:591–606.

Yngve, V., 1960. A model and an hypothesis for language structure. *Proceedings of the American Philosophical Society* 104(5):444–466.

Index